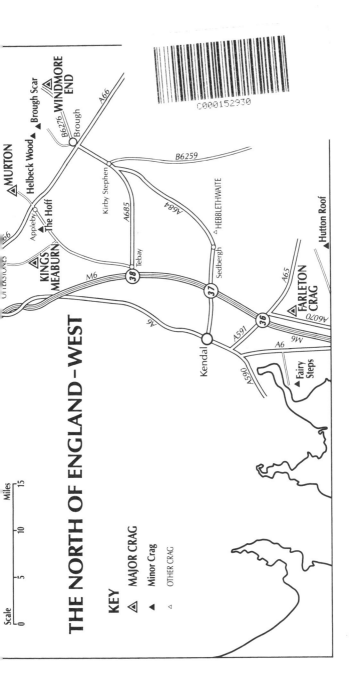

THE NORTH OF ENGLAND–WEST

KEY

⬠ **MAJOR CRAG**

▲ **Minor Crag**

△ OTHER CRAG

Scale

Miles

0 5 10 15

MURTON

Helbeck Wood ▲ ▲ Brough Scar

⬠ WINDMORE END

B6276

Brough

A66

A66

KINGS MEABURN

The Hoff

Appleby

A66

B6259

Kirby Stephen

A685

A684

△ HEBBLETHWAITE

M6

38

Tebay

A6

37

Sedbergh

Kendal

A591

36

A65

⬠ FARLETON CRAG

▲ Hutton Roof

A6070

M6

A6

Fairy Steps ▲

A590

C000152930

North of England Rock Climbs

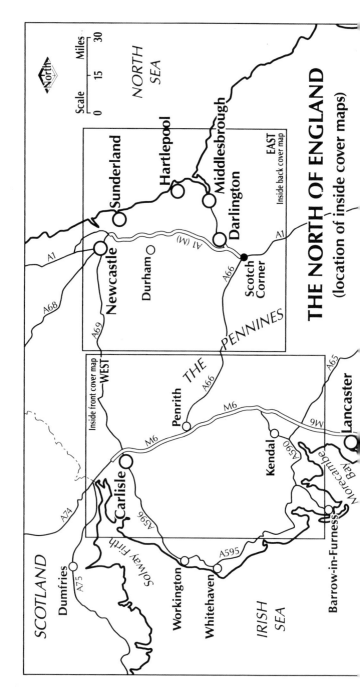

THE NORTH OF ENGLAND
(location of inside cover maps)

NORTH OF ENGLAND ROCK CLIMBS

By Stewart Wilson

Published by CORDEE Leicester

Copyright © Stewart Wilson 1992

ISBN 1 871890 41 1

British Library Cataloguing in Publication Data
A catalogue record for this book is available from the British Library

All trade enquiries to:
Cordee, 3a De Montfort Street, Leicester LE1 7HD

This guide book is available from specialist equipment shops and major booksellers within the area. It can along with most books and maps for climbing and outdoor recreation, be obtained direct from the publishers. Please write for a copy of our comprehensive stocklist.

CORDEE
3a De Montfort Street, Leicester LE1 7HD

CONTENTS

7   DURHAM DENES:

8   TEESDALE:

9   CLEVELAND HILLS

10   SWALEDALE:

11 COLSTERDALE:

CRAG PLANS

LOCATION MAPS

CRAG DRAWINGS & PHOTO-DIAGRAMS

PHOTOGRAPHS

INTRODUCTION

It has taken eleven years to produce the Second edition of The North Of England Guide. The First Edition for those who don't remember it, was a relatively slim, inexpensively produced affair which very quickly sold out. Ron Kenyon and I first conceived the book as an attempt to link all the isolated and spread out crags in the vast area of The North that were surrounded by other Guidebook Areas. The crags were duly sought out, climbed upon and recorded. The resultant small volume quickly excited an interest in the region and much new development resulted. The crags are very varied and whilst some are not of the highest quality, there are gems which bear comparison with climbing on outcrops in any area. Writing the guide has not been easy, the area is large and some crags are isolated. It is perhaps fitting that this wild and sometimes beautiful area has had to be struggled for. It is a bit like trying to establish legitimacy when all around, the powerful "reivers" of the established guides and more recently the selective guides,snap off a crag here and there to add to their already bulging volumes. The First Edition of the guide included the Swaledale and Colsterdale crags. These were North Yorkshire crags but through the geography of usage firmly aligned to the area of the North Of England Guide. Once the secret was out, the "big boys" wanted in, expecting us to give up our claim to Slipstones whilst not wanting the other "Yorkshire" crags in our area. The reasons are obvious.This kind of "heavy-handedness" can potentially jeopardize climbing in the region because if The North Of England Guide is to stand up for itself, it must not be deprived of its best crags, resulting in the remaining crags being undocumented. The only ones to benefit being landowners who would much rather see only sheep. Losing access to any recreational resource no matter how seemingly insignificant, in the present climate, could mean it was lost for good!

The present edition has set out to rationalise its boundaries and to this end we have included some Limestone Crags in South Cumbria which were mainly undocumented. In the Tyne and Wear area, we have received Causey Quarry and Hownsgill from the Northumberland M.C. aiding them in rationalising their own guide and bringing some good climbing to Tyne and Wearsiders which would otherwise be lost. Since the First Edition, there have been suggestions of combining the North Of England Guide with North York Moors Guide and to this end we have included with the help of Cleveland activists an up to date and more accurate account of climbing on three popular crags. This will certainly encourage a greater respect for an area where H.S. can mean anything up to E3!

So there it is, a bigger, better guide and one that everyone in the North and further afield have been crying out for. The guide has been written specifically to get you to the crags easily and to present the information in a readable form, rather than as a series of terse commands. The variety of style and standard of climbing throughout the area is tremendous and it can truly be said to be a guide for everyone. Climbing is essentially about enjoyment, physical and mental challenge and adventure. There is still room for discoveries here, at all grades. Its up to you.

TECHNICAL INFORMATION

This guide makes use of the English System of grading which attempts to describe climbs in an overall way by means of:

The Adjectival Grade as follows:

Moderate (M), Difficult (D), Very Difficult (VD), Severe (S), Very Severe (VS), and Extremely Severe (E1, E2, E3 on upwards). The prefix Hard is used in front of the Adjectives: Difficult (HD), Very Difficult (HVD), Severe (HS) and Very Severe (HVS), because some of them are! In other words these have now acquired full grade status.

The Adjectival Grade is about many things including steepness, quality of rock, possibilities for protection, individual wealth of the climber, remoteness of crag, length of pitch and how sustained the difficulties are, technical difficulty and the differing psychological thresholds of the individual climbers. So you see, it cannot possibly work and thats why climbing is so adventurous.

The Technical Grade:

This in theory starts at 1 and is subdivided into a,b and c. In practice it starts at about 4a and in this guide includes climbs and problems up to 6c or harder. The technical grade is related to the hardest single move on a climb. Again this system depends upon consensus and that's a funny-shaped person. In addition its very hard to grade a move at the top of a long, sustained pitch as it may "feel" harder.

In order to get the grades right in this guide we have enlisted the help of the smallest and the tallest climbers we know and pulled them into position via block and tackle to the crux moves of climbs. This means that fatigue and fear do not always enter into the equation and so "sport" grades have evolved. This is a new development and seems to be attracting a lot of interest in this country.

Putting two such unlikely bed-fellows together as the Adjectival grade and the Technical grade is fraught with hazards, but what we have attempted to do is to grade the routes from the point of view of a stranger arriving at the crag and making an 'On Sight' lead. If a route has been climbed in any other style, then this has been mentioned in the text at some point.

Stars have been used to denote quality and because all of the routes are O.K. unless otherwise stated, this exercise is largely a waste of time. A dagger symbol(†) is used to show that you shouldn't believe all that is in print and should feature more frequently in the graded lists of some Northern Guides.

THE USE OF BOLTS

The area covered by this Guide is unfortunately represented by two B.M.C. Area Committees, both of whom have a different policy on bolts. In Cumbria, bolts are O.K. on Limestone and in Quarries whilst in the North-East they are not allowed! This seems an odd situation as there are more bolts in one quarry in Tyne and Wear than in all the rest of the crags in the guide! Whilst bolting on natural Sandstone crags should be condemned there will be moves to bolt on Limestone and in quarries and if this is so then careful consideration needs to be given to the problem of which quarry or Limestone crag and then whether or not to equip all routes.

NEW ROUTES

Descriptions of all new routes can be recorded in the new routes books at the climbing shop at Eden Valley Centre, Ainstable or at Needle Sport in Keswick. In addition details should also be sent to Stew Wilson, Eden Valley Centre, Ainstable, Carlisle. CA4 9QA.

ACCESS AND CONSERVATION

RIGHTS OF ACCESS
THE MENTION OF A CRAG OR QUARRY IN THIS GUIDE DOES NOT AUTOMATICALLY CONFER THE RIGHT TO CLIMB. DESCRIP-TION OF CLIMBS ON MAN-MADE STRUCTURES IS A RECORD OF CLIMBERS' ACTIVITIES AND NOT THE AUTHOR'S INVITATION TO COMMIT TRESPASS OR OTHERWISE DAMAGE A STRUCTURE. CLIMBING IS A DANGEROUS ACTIVITY AND EVERYONE IS ACCOUNTABLE FOR THEIR 'OWN ACTIONS.

Many of the crags in this guide are on private land and access agreements have been arrived at as a result on-going dialogue with the owners. This has even involved placatory gestures and a lot of letter writing. One fine outcrop was almost lost when climbers insisted on doing "Handbrake Turns" in the sileage field upon whose edge the farmer allows climbers to park. The message is: Do not be a pillock.

Read the access section for each crag and always ask permission to climb if it is required.

Read and follow The Country Code. Do not try to be "clever" with farmers, foresters, gamekeepers or quarryowners, only you will suffer along with the rest of us.

Most landowners are reasonable and will not impede the enjoy-ment of others providing it does not interfere with their own interests. A tiny minority of landowners are a real "pain in the neck" and make a point of depriving everyone of not only pri-veleges, but rights. It is up to you to familiarise yourself with local situations; remember, its no use getting stroppy with some game-keeper if he tells you that the Public Right Of Way you are on is not. Remember, this guy has to produce results for his boss or else he is out of a job. Be firm, state your intentions in a civil manner and inform the Local Authority of the encounter. Do not take your dog to the crag as he is likely to immediately draw attention to your presence as well as to be a menace to other forms of life, including climbers whose butties could be snaffled when he gets bored with hanging around waiting for you. Large groups on crags are a real pain, Who wants loads of unwilling trainees "sport-abseiling" down your favourite, fragile wall? If you must take groups to the crags: Avoid popular crags. Visit the crag first and get clued up on the potential your group has for damaging fine climbs. Insist that only soft trainers are worn. Learn how to rig climbs to minimise wear on trees and rock.

Gardening new routes should be kept to a minimum and wire brushing is to be avoided as much as possible. Chipping holds (and this includes heavy wire-brushing) is totally out of order and all climbers should take to task anyone doing this. If you must top-rope, remember to use long slings thereby protecting the top of the crag and any trees used for anchors.

ACKNOWLEDGEMENTS

I would like to thank the numerous people who given information, advice and encouragement, particularly Fred Stevenson, Tom Ramsey, Stephen Fleming, Jordan Tinniswood, Alan Moist, Phil Rigby, Tony Marr, Dave Stainthorpe, Tim Moore, Mick Gardiner, Andy Moss, Bob Bennett, Alan Greig, Ray Parker, Mark Hetherington, Mark Tomlinson, Seb Grieve, Paul Stewart, Ian Dunn, Paul Ingham, Richard Kirby, Phil Woodyer, Jon Ginesi, Dave Wilson, Rod Anderson and Mark Turner.

Climbers who concentrated on specific crags must be particularly thanked: Gavin Ellis, John Boyle, Robin Curley, Pete Whillance, Pete Botterill, Chris Craggs, Colin Binks, Malcolm Lowerson, Stu Ferguson, Ian Cummins, Sue Ferguson, Dave Douglas and Dave Foster.

Going out on the crags in all weathers was a particularly uninspiring job particularly when it was for the Nth time. I was lucky enough to have mates who were willing enough to go out. Thanks to Stu Butler, Dave Bowen, Dave Bone, Phil Hope, Kelvin Neal, Stephen and Andy Williamson, Ian Walker, Dave Hetherington, Martin Holdroyd, Cath Davies, Leigh Blanks and Mick Johnstone.

To Roy May for re-drawing the Hag Wood diagrams when all around him was hassle and chaos- Thanks Roy. In addition the fine drawings of Goldsborough and Kepier by Karen Robson and Brough Scar by Sharon Murphy are much appreciated.

I would like to thank the Yorkshire M.C for the 'consolation prize' of a courtesy copy of their new Gritstone guide and for the incentive it gave Ian Cummins and myself to produce a better Slipstones section.

Paul Carling, Karl Lunt and Ronnie Kenyon are the climbers and friends to whom I am most indebted. They have all given unselfishly of their time and have been instrumental in getting the guidebook into its present form. All know more about the area than anyone else, are well-travelled and enthusiastic climbers and the fact that they can still enthuse about the area after so much involvement in the "spadework" says a lot for the variety and interest of the climbing.

I would like to thank my wife Maggie for sharing the "joys" of the work and the rest of the family for keeping the job going during my retreat, for moral support, buying the beers, as well as dragging me

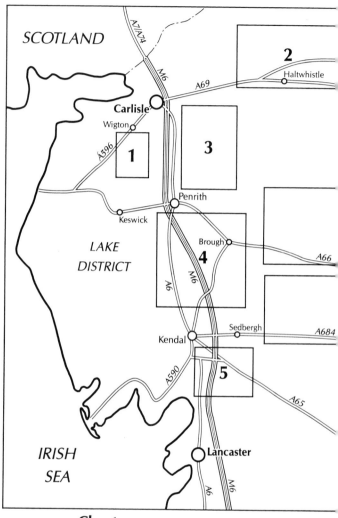

Chapters:

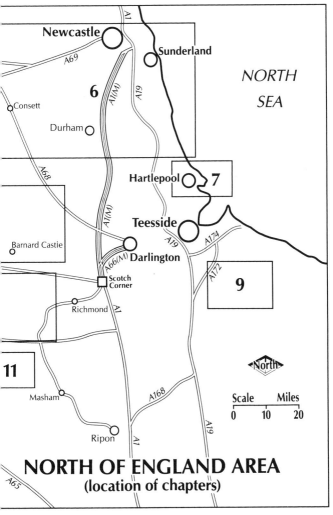

NORTH OF ENGLAND AREA
(location of chapters)

6 Tyne and Wear
7 Durham Denes
8 Teesdale
9 Cleveland Hills
10 Swaledale
11 Colsterdale

up the routes that were too hard. Thanks to John, Matthew, Greta, Laura and Joe.

Finally, thanks are due to all the climbers who have waited for so long for the guide, for their letters of support, encouragement and appreciation for what this unique area has to offer. I hope that the guide is what they deserve.

1 NORTH CUMBRIAN LIMESTONE

This area of small limestone outcrops lies around the Northern and Eastern fringes of the Lake District's Northern Fells. Most of the climbing occurs in disused quarries, but there are some small, natural outcrops on the Eastern fringe, between the Fells and the M6. The crags with the exception of Caldbeck Moor Quarry are very pleasant locations, some with outstanding views across the lovely North Cumbrian landscape. It must be emphasised that none of the crags provide outstanding climbing and those who visit them should certainly not expect too much.Headend is a good choice for groups and families, whilst Parkhead Quarry can offer the soloist a good 'workout.'

HEAD END QUARRY   O.S. SHEET 85   G.R. NY 249408

SITUATION AND CHARACTER

Whilst the quarry itself does not have much of an outlook, the top of the climbs command extensive views across the Solway Firth in one direction and in the other, a fine aspect of Skiddaw and the Northern Fells. The Quarry is a pleasant spot, favoured by picknickers, kite fliers and groups under instruction for whom it is emminently suited being mainly low-grade climbing.

Facing South and catching all available sunshine (and wind), these faces of Carboniferous Limestone dry very quickly and provide a good winter venue.

The quarry is about 40 metres long, 10 metres high and has good landings.The rock is generally sound, but care should be taken with a rather flaky stratum at the top. The popularity of the crag, particularly with beginners has meant that holds are rather polished. The climbs tend to be on steep slabs and walls and holds are generally positive. Stakes provide anchorage at the top.

APPROACHES AND ACCESS

The quarry is near the summit of Catlands Hill, Spot Height 304 m. It is two miles NNE of Ireby and six miles S of Wigton. Follow the B5299 from Caldbeck towards Boltongate. About one and a half miles before Boltongate turn right for Sandale. Beyond Sandale on an ascending road, the quarry entrance will be seen on the right just before the road bends sharply to drop down the other side of the hill.

There appear to be no access problems, but it is suggested that vehicles are driven into the quarry to avoid congestion on the narrow lane.

HISTORICAL

The quarry has a long history of useage by groups and individuals and it is strange that it is not more widely known. It was first documented in a small guide produced by the Border Bothies Association and then in the 1981 edition of the Rock Climbers Guide to the North Of England. The majority of the later routes were the work of Ron Kenyon or Stew Wilson.

THE CLIMBS
These are described from left to right, section by section and are easily located.

WEST END WALL
Identified by three steps in its left-hand arete and a chockstone corner crack at its junction with Suicide Wall.

1   Novices' Route   8m   M
Start just right of the arete.Climb an easy crack, moving left to the first step or, more difficult, climb direct to the top.

2   Catlands Wall   8m   HS
Climb the wall to the right of Novices' Route.

3   West End Groove   8m   HD   ★
A good route and popular. Start at the shallow cracked groove. Climb the crack and groove on good holds until a step right can be made on smaller polished holds to gain the top.

4   West End Direct   8m   VD   ★
Start immediately right of the last climb. Climb the steep face on small, worn holds.

5   Dodgy Neck   8m   S
Interesting rock and moves. Start 2 m right of West End Direct at a small corner. Climb onto a pedestal ledge on the left then climb the face direct to finish on some unusual calcite holds.

6   Diogenes   8m   S
A good companion to the last climb. Start as for Dodgy Neck. Climb directly up the vertical cracks to finish up the middle of the fluted, top block.

7   Controlled Gurning   8m   VS   5a
A pleasant and thought-provoking climb. Start immediately left of Headend Chimney below a steep wall. Climb the wall up to and over a bulge.

8   Headend Chimney   8m   HD
More a crack than a chimney and nicely insecure. Start at the crack at the junction of West End and Suicide Walls. Climb the crack awkwardly, but with good jams.

SUICIDE WALL
A steep wall of excellent rock bounded on its right by an arete of protruding blocks; Birds Nest Direct.

9   Kamikaze   8m   VS   4c   ★
A fingery exercise. Start immediately right of Headend Chimney. Climb the wall direct.

10   Nippo Crack   8m   HS   4a   ★
Start below a crack and groove, 1 metre right of the last climb. Climb this left-slanting break with a definite crux. Finish near Kamikaze Wall.

11   Letter-Box Direct   8m   S   *
Start as for Nippo Groove. Follow cracks diagonally rightwards to finish directly up the wall above the Letter-Box.

12   Letter-Box   8m   MS   **
Start a metre left of the arete. Climb onto a slot-like ledge; the Letter-Box. Follow good holds to finish up two, very thin cracks.

13   Bird's Nest Direct   7m   D   *
Follow the blocky, right-hand arete of Suicide Wall on good holds to below a steep crack. Climb this or move right to an awkward mantelshelf finish.

SUMMIT FACE
The most impressive face, consisting of a steep, narrow pillar with a bulging finish. Further right the face has a footledge at half-height and is less steep at the top.

14   Bilberry   10m   S
Climb the grassy crack just right of Bird's Nest Direct. Awkward.

15   Bloodhound   10m   HVS   5b
Start directly below the crack which cuts through the left-hand side of the top bulge of the pillar.Climb directly to the crack with ease and ascend the crack with considerably less.

16   Crusthound   10m   E1   5b   *
The hardest climb in the quarry and only just warranting its grade.
Start below the prominent crack in the centre of the bulge. Climb up to the crack with difficulty and climb it with greater lack of ease to the top.

17   Soap Gut   10m   S
Start in a slight corner just right of the bulging pillar which provides the two previous climbs. Climb the corner and crack above.

18   Snail Wall   10m   S
Start below the obvious white wall at a corner. Climb the corner and white wall to gain a good ledge. Finish up the finger wide flake crack above. Care with rock!

19   Devil's Kneecap   10m   VD   *
Steep and quite hard for the grade initially. Start about 2 metres right of Snail Wall. Climb the steep wall by means of widely-spaced but good holds to the obvious ledge. Finish up the pleasant wall above.

CRYSTAL WALL
This is the attractive steep slab, characterised by excellent rock, with, in places, a veneer of calcite which gives the wall some good but fragile holds and its name.

20   Blah   8m   S
Start below the twin cracks which run up to a bulge at the left end of the wall. Climb the cracks until a jam and a long reach leads to an awkward finish.

21   Crystal Cruise   8m   HS   4b   *
Start midway between Blah and the fine thin central crack. Gain and climb the slab direct.

22   Crystal Wall Direct   8m   MS   ★★
Perhaps the best climb on the crag. Start below the fine thin crack in the centre of the slab. Follow the crack on good holds to a long reach for the top break. Pull over the top with care.

23   Dids   8m   HS   4b   ★
Ascend the wall just right of the Direct.

24   W.A.C.   8m   MVS   4b   ★
A sustained climb with a difficult start. Start about 1m left of the bounding arete of crystal Wall. Climb the overlap on small holds. Delicate climbing follows up a shallow scoop. Move right onto the prow and finish with care.

25   The Butcher's Dog   8m   MVS   4c   ★★
Climb the arete direct to the top.

TERRACE WALL

The final section. This wall of good rock is unfortunately split by a grassy ledge at half-height.

26   Nut Smasher Crack   8m   VD
The name is awful, the climb worse! Climb directly up the crack which forms the angle between Crystal and Terrace Wall. Swing your nuts behind you.

27   Terrace Stairway   8m   M   ★
A good little climb with a fair degree of interest. Start below a crack just right of the last climb. Climb the crack to the terrace, then follow the interesting left-slanting staircase to the top.

28   Piggy Malone   8m   D
Start at the centre of Terrace Wall between two, slanting cracks. Climb the steep face and mantelshelf onto the terrace. The left-slanting scoop, awkward to start, is followed to the top.

29   Bobtail   8m   D
This route for Rabbits follows the easiest line up the wall right of Piggy.

30   Heads Or Tails?
An amusing traverse of the crag from left to right, starting at Novices' Route and finishing up W.A.C. Suicide Wall and Crystal Wall are the most interesting and difficult sections.

CALDBECK MOOR QUARRY   O.S. SHEET 85   G.R. 287 402

SITUATION AND CHARACTER

A disused quarry, set on the fells about three miles West-North-West of Caldbeck.It faces East and has an open aspect. The climbing is contained on the one hundred and fifty metre long, back wall and has a maximum height of ten metres. The rock is limestone, of variable quality, requiring some care on finishes. Belays are absent on top and stakes could be useful.

The wall has few distinguishing features and the established climbs are on the more obviously stable sections. More climbs could be available for the determined trundler.

NORTH CUMBRIAN LIMESTONE

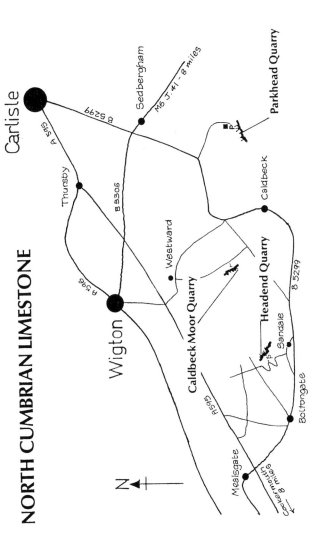

APPROACHES AND ACCESS

The best approach from Penrith and the M6 (Junction 41), is to follow the B5305 (Wigton road) through Sebergham to the cross-roads at Goose Green (String Of Horses Public House) and turn right on the B5299 for Caldbeck. Follow this road, uphill and over Warnell Fell, passing the turn off for Park Head Quarry on the left at the sharp right-hand corner. Continue to the next crossroads a distance of just over one mile and go directly across onto the unfenced fell road. This is followed for two and a half miles to another crossroads where a signpost points right to Wigton and Westward. Turn right and after another mile, the quarry will be seen on the left-hand side of the road by a disused building. It is possible to drive into the quarry. The quarry belongs to the local council and access is not a problem.

HISTORICAL

All of the routes are the work of Ron Kenyon and date back to the 1970's. They were all climbed solo as nobody would go there with him. Recently the quarry has been re-visited by Paul Ross and Chris Bonington who have cleaned and climbed another batch of routes.

THE CLIMBS

These are described from left to right. The descent is via a grassy ramp towards the left end of the wall and all the routes are to the right of this.

1   Faulds   6m   S
Start below a wide crack 17m right of the descent ramp. Climb the wide crack and the loose, V- groove above.

2   Lynedraw   7m   S
Climb the obvious corner to the right. Pretty awful.

3   Dunbeath   8m   HS   4c
Start just right of the corner of Dunbeath below a square-cut arete. Gain the arete from the wall to the right and follow it to the top. Six metres right of Dunbeath is a left-facing groove and a further five metres beyond this are two thin cracks which form a V.

4   Aughertree   8m   S
Climb the wall left of the V to reach the left-hand crack at mid-height. Follow this to the top.

5   Snittlegarth   8m   HS   4b
Climb the crescent-shaped crack 5m right of Aughertree.
A more broken area extends rightwards then the rock improves again to form the steep, smooth Main Wall.

MAIN WALL

6   Rash Raiser   9m   VS   4b   *
Climb the arete which forms the left edge of Main Wall.

7   Whelpo Way   9m   HS   4a   *
Start 5m right of the arete of Rash Raiser below a thin, crooked crack. Climb this. Moving right, beyond a left-facing corner groove, is another steep wall which is off-set from the line of The Main Wall.

8 Thistlebottom 10m VS 4b
Start by an overlap at the left side of the wall. Follow a right-slanting crack to its end then move left to a slab and finish up this.

9 Biggards 9m HVS 5a
Climb the curving right-hand crack which runs the full height of the wall.

PARK HEAD QUARRY   O.S. SHEET 85   G.R. 336 405

"Chris Bonington is the only person to climb the length of the crag backwards and forwards six times without falling off . . ."

"Who told you that . . .?"

"Chris Bonington did . . ."

SITUATION AND CHARACTER

This South facing outcrop of quarried limestone is in a truly delightful setting, perched on the side of a hill overlooking the valley of the River Caldew, with fine views towards the Caldbeck Fells.

The rock rises out of a meadow, whose soft grass provides perfect landings. It is a warm friendly place, ideal for an odd hours quiet bouldering. The rock is generally perfect, although the top of the crag is loose. Climbers not hell-bent on tearing tendons on the steep walls and traverses will need to take care when finishing the pleasant, middle-grade, micro-routes.

APPROACHES AND ACCESS

The crag is easily reached from either Carlisle or Penrith. From Carlisle, follow the B 5299 passing through the villages of Dalston and Welton. One mile South-West of Welton is a cross roads by the String of Horses Inn at Goose Green. Cross the B 5305 and continue past the inn and up the steep hill of Warnell Brow for about three-quarters of a mile. At a sharp right-hand bend in the main road, a signposted minor road on the left, leads in three-quarters of a mile, to Parkhead. From Junction 41 on the M6, just North of Penrith, follow the B 5305 passing through the village of Sebergham. About a mile and a half beyond Sebergham is the Goose Green crossroads. Turn left onto the B 5299 at this junction and follow the route described.

There are no access problems. The landowner, Mr Hird, is happy for climbers to use the crag providing that they call at the farmhouse, the last house at the end of the road on the right, to present themselves. This is a most amicable situation and it is hoped that ALL climbers will observe this simple courtesy. Cars can be parked in the large yard beyond the house, adjacent to the gate which leads into the meadow and the crag.

HISTORICAL

Everyone has climbed at Parkhead. The traverses are legendary.

Botterill, Whillance and Lamb climbed anything that looked worth doing, way back in the Eighties

Ron Kenyon, Stew Wilson and disciples added Gnorman whilst Stew unearthed Tutu whilst preparing this guide. A Shoulder To Cry On was the work of the inimitable Karl Lunt.

THE CLIMBS
The crag is approached from its right-hand end. A lime-kiln marks the right-hand end of the obvious:

LONG WALL
The short wall 15 metres left of the Long Wall is called SHORT WALL.

Left again are five walls separated by two aretes and two corners. This is FIVE WALLS AREA.

Because the quarry is so small in extent it has been decided to start describing the climbs from the left hand end, from left to right, a logical trend, sometimes followed in modern guidebooks.

FIVE WALLS AREA
These are found about 100 metres left of the limekiln and consist of five walls, set at right-angles to one another and separated by two aretes and two corners.

FIRST WALL
The extreme left-hand wall, about 20 metres long. A low, striated erratic boulder forms a convenient seat and marker.

1   Ash Groove   4a
Starts below a very shallow groove, 2m left of the boulder. Climb the groove past an Ash sapling to finish at a stout hawthorn. Lower off or down climb or get prickled.

2   The Rib   4c
Start 1m left of the boulder at the foot of a vague rib. Climb the rib to the top and reverse or make a dirty, precarious 5a mantelshelf to finish.

3   The Graduate   5b   ★
Start at the same point as The Rib. Climb the fine, steep wall 1m right of the rib. Good.

4   Tutu   5a   ★
Start 2m right of The Rib just right of the large Hawthorn at the top of the crag. Climb the wall just left of a very thin, vertical crack. Pass the horizontal break and move slightly right then finish direct.

SECOND WALL
This is the steep wall at right-angles to the First Wall. A large Ash grows above it. It ends at a fine arete on the right

5   Parson's Wall   5b/c   ★
Steep and awkward. Start below the large Ash. Climb the wall with the crux near the top.

6   Boyle's Law   5c   ★
Excellent, sustained climbing. Start just left of the arete and climb the wall without using the arete.

7   Sod's Law   5b   ★
Traverse Second Wall from left to right or right to left about one metre from the ground. There's always a "soft" landing.

8   Park Head Arete   4b   ★
Climb the extremely pleasant arete. The finish is a wee bit loose!

THIRD WALL

The clean, steep wall right of the arete.

9   Gnorman   5b   ★
Start two metres right of the arete. Climb the concave wall via a vague scoop.

10   A Shoulder To Cry On   5b
Start two metres right of Gnorman at a very slight rib. Climb the slight rib and ensuing wall to a loose finish.

FOURTH WALL

Scruffy and at right angles to Third Wall which ends at a stepped arete on the right.

FIFTH WALL

This is the wall that extends right from the stepped arete.

11   Twinkle   4a
Start a metre right of the stepped arete. climb the wall on small holds to a ledge and a loose finish.

12   Rippler   3c
Start at some stalactite-type incrustations. Climb the steep wall using these. Step left and finish up a loose groove.

13   Chunker   4c
Start 3m left of the large Ash growing at the top. Climb the wall direct.

14   Howler   3b
Climb the wall via a jammed block to finish at the large Ash.

15   The Girdle   3c
Traverse the Fifth Wall from left to right finishing at the large Ash.

THE SHORT WALL

This is about forty metres to the right of Fifth Wall. It consists of a long, low wall of very compact rock about 4m high. It provides numerous short problems from 4c-6a and a very good traverse 5c-6a depending on the level.

THE LONG WALL

This is fifteen metres right of the Short Wall. It consists of a very steep, left-hand buttress split by a fine crack. To the right the face is in the form of a long, fairly steep wall terminating at an old lime-kiln. This long stretch of rock is most useful as a stamina-training traverse. All of the vertical lines have been climbed but those in the middle section and right-hand end fail to produce sound finishes and so are not described.

16   Nook Crack   5a
Start more or less in the centre of the left-hand buttress below a fine, finger crack. Climb this.

Six metres right of Nook Crack, three cracks finish at a grass ledge.

17   Sceugh Crack   4b
Climb the left-hand, widest crack.

18   Night Hawk   4b
Climb the twin cracks above a stump, just right of Sceugh Crack.

19   Rowan Crack   3c
Climb the wide, briar choked off-width crack just right of Night Hawk.

20   Cracker Packer Wall   4b
Climb the steep, clean wall just right of the briar-choked crack.

21   Right Wall Girdle   5a/b
Fifty metres of strenuous climbing. Start at the foot of the left-hand buttress of the Long Wall left of Nook Crack. Crossing this left wall is the technical crux. Finish at the lime kiln.

Rating for continuous traverses without stepping off:

Quantity:	Rating:
1x	A poor effort, you should consider packing in climbing
2x	Standard for average club beginners meet.
3x	Practice more in secret and learn to lie.
4-6x	A bit more like it. Keep practising.
6-10x	A reasonable effort. Try using a Walkman or employ the local "drone" to talk you through the boredom.
10+	A quality performance, but your nose must get in the way.

CRAG GATE   O.S. SHEET 90   G.R. 402 346

SITUATION AND CHARACTER
A small intermittent edge of good quality limestone which extends for over 100 metres and faces Westwards into a gloomy wood. It is sheltered from the elements by a mature conifer wood, but this gives attendant problems: condensation and midges. When the trees are eventually felled and this could be soon, the crag and its Southern continuation will be a very fine little venue. The routes are short and the climbing is very pleasant and can provide entertainment for the solo climber. The landings could be better in some cases. The top of the crag is open and sunny and tree belays abound.

APPROACHES AND ACCESS
The nearest village to the crag is Lamonby which lies to the west of the B5305 Penrith to Wigton road. This road is picked up at Junction 41 on the M6 North of Penrith. Follow the B5305 past Hutton in the Forest and continue past the masts of the BBC transmitter on your right. About a mile and a half from here is a junction, signposted to Lamonby. The same junction is reached by following the B5299 from Carlisle, via Dalston and Welton until one can turn left at the Goose

NORTH CUMBRIAN LIMESTONE

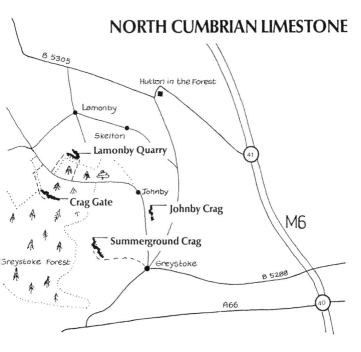

Green crossroads on the B5305. The junction to Lamonby is the fourth on the right about three miles beyond Sebergham.Follow the road into Lamonby and turn right at the crossroads in the centre of the village. Continue out of the village and at the next crossroads, turn left and follow the road with felled woodland on the right. A small layby will soon be seen on the right and leading from this is a muddy track through mature conifers. (If you reach a large layby and a forest road on the right, you have gone too far!). Park at the entrance to the small layby taking care not to block the entrance to the wood.

To reach the crag only takes five minutes. Follow the rutted track until a gate is reached at the far side of the wood. Go through the gate and follow the edge of the small fenced enclosure on the left. Continue under small crags with a fine outlook until a fence can be crossed. The crag extends from here, parallel to the wood. THE CRAG IS IN A FIRE RISK AREA so take great care. PLEASE DO NOT TAKE DOGS TO THE CRAG.

HISTORICAL
Crag Gate was discovered and developed by Stew Wilson and friends in 1986.

THE CLIMBS
The climbing on the crag is located on four sections: The Prow, Left , Central and Right Sections. The climbs are described section by section from left to right. Individual route heights are omitted as the crag nowhere exceeds 8 metres.

THE PROW
This is the prominent, small prow of rock first encountered as one crosses the fence by the wood.

1   Destination Zululand   HVS   5b   *
Climb the overhanging rib direct on wonderful rock.

2   Oohwallawallawalla   VS   5a
Climb the wall on the right, direct.
   20 metres right is:

LEFT SECTION
A prominent feature of this section is a steep corner above a large block. Further right are pleasant little walls and aretes.

3   Me Jane   D
Start at the foot of the easy-angled arete which bounds the left wall of the corner. Climb the arete on good holds.

4   Edgar   MS   *
Start below the steep, wrinkled wall left of the corner. Climb the wall. Easier than it looks.

5   You Tarzan   HD
Climb the obvious, steep corner which contains a tree stump.

6   Umbongo   S   4c
Climb the right wall of the corner via a groove. The start is strenuous.

7 Wanki HS 5a ★
Start on the front of the arete right of the last climb. Climb the overhang and slim groove.

8 Ovambo VD
Climb the wall below and right of the large Rowan, which grows at the top of the crag.

9 Griptight VS 5a ★
Climb the steep wall via a double edged flake. Care with rock!

10 Grumble and Grunt D
Climb the steep chimney crack.

11 Tarzan Goes To Johnby D
Climb the short, easy and least interesting arete before the rocks diminish entirely.

Sixteen metres further right, a large, spreading Rowan marks the start of the next section.

CENTRAL SECTION
This has two steep buttresses separated by vegetated rock. The right-hand buttress is very undercut and is split vertically by a crack which deteriorates into an easy chimney above.

12 Voie Grenouille HVS 5b ★
Climb the left arete of the left-hand buttress. Steep and good.

13 Crawfish Pie VS 4c
Start below the central crack of right-hand buttress. Jam the central crack through the overhang and swing up and left to an easier finish on the left arete.

14 Trouble In The Fields HVS 5b ★
Start below the centre of the face to the right of the central crack. Climb the overhang by a hard pull on sharp holds. The face above is pleasant.

To the right, a scruffy face peters out in a steep slope covered in low thorn and capped by a broken down drystone wall. The slope provides an easy descent. Further right is:

RIGHT-HAND SECTION
Beginning with two short, bulging faces: The Barrels.

THE BARRELS
These provide interesting problems:

15 The wall left of the central crack. (4c).

16 The central crack. (4b).

17 The extreme right-hand arete. Climbed on the front face. (5c).

18 The wall on the right. (5b).

SMOOTH WALL
This face is bounded on its left-hand side by a large block overhang of dubious stability. Further right, a large rowan grows from the crag just below the top.

19 Serengeti HS 4a
Climb the wall directly below the right-hand end of the block overhang. Pass this with care and finish direct.

20 Bundu Boys HS 4b   ★
A great little climb, its a pity its so short. Start below the Rowan tree growing out of the crag near the top. Climb the centre of the fine, smooth wall via a short crack then good slots to the tree. Finish easily through the top bulge.

21 Desmond VS 4c   ★
A steep and interesting climb. Start 2m right of Bundu Boys. A hard move for the short on small pockets enables a good hold to be reached. Swarm up the left curving line of bulges and finish direct.

OVERLAPPING WALL
Smooth Wall merges into this scruffy vegetated wall.

22 The Bickeridge Twins S
Start just right of Desmond. Climb the small corner and scruffy crack to vegetation.

23 Wack and Jill MS
Start a few metres further right at another small corner. Climb this and the wall above, to finish up a thin runnel in the top bulge.

24 Og MS
Start one metre further right. Climb the steep wall and slim, protruding pillar.

The crag improves again:

GREY BUTTRESS
An undercut buttress of good rock. A large block on the ground, marks the start of the next route.

25 Gagool VS 5b   ★
A hard start, but good nut placements. Climb the very thin crack above the large block to steep but easier climbing on good holds. Enjoyable.

NORTH CUMBRIAN LIMESTONE – MINOR CRAGS AND BOULDERING VENUES

LAMONBY QUARRY   O.S. SHEET 90   G.R. 409346
This very limited but pleasant Limestone quarry can be combined with a visit to Crag Gate as they are only ten minutes walk apart. The quarry consists of two walls at right angles to one another. the left wall is a steep, smooth slab about 7m high whilst the right wall is steeper. The rock is good and provides problems and short climbs but no quantity of great difficulty to sustain a visit for its own sake. A Public Right Of Way leads to the quarry, following the North-Western edge of a plantation on the opposite side of the road and fifty metres in the direction of Johnby from the Parking place for Crag Gate.

The routes are described from right to left starting with the wall to the right of the corner.

Frontispiece: Armathwaite, climber on The Exorcist F4 5c

RIGHT WALL

1   Split Shift   8m   VD   ★
Climb the steep crack to a ledge. Climb slighty left and up to finish on good holds. Excellent rock.

2   The Tube   8m   VD
Climb the obvious runnel in the middle of the face. Traverse left to finish up the crack of Big Ears.

3   Cheers! Big Ears   8m   HS
Climb the steep wall and the crack above.

4   Uncle Bulgearea   8m   HVS   5b   ★
Climb the steepest part of the overhanging buttress on the left end of the Right Wall. The final move is awkward.

LEFT WALL

The wall to the left of the corner.

5   Slape   7m   VS   4c
Climb the steep wall to the left of centre. Reverse off.

To the left of this wall are some scrappy faces until a small pronounced arete is obvious.

6   The Arete   6m   VD
Climb the arete.

7   The Flombel   7m   4b
Climb the wall via the slight, central bulge.

SUMMERGROUND CRAGS   O.S. SHEET 90   G.R. 419318

This idyllic, little Limestone outcrop lies just below spot height 361 and faces South-West with truly magnificent views across the valley of the Glenderamackin to Blencathra.

The outcrop is in the form of a continuous edge, nowhere more than 8 metres high. The rock is very good although the lower stratum can be loose, but this does not pose a problem.

The crag is on private land owned by Mr. N. Howard of Greystone Castle, Nr Penrith, Cumbria CA11 0TG. Telephone 07684 83221. Mr Howard will not grant access "as of right" but if persons ring or write he will agree to access if circumstances permit. Approaches are many and this needs to be agreed when asking for access. This is a fortunate situation and climbers are asked to do everything to make things work.

Summerground should appeal to climbers who want to do short,steep, limestone problems. The scope and variety is great and the situation magnificent. No groups or dogs please.

Rear of Frontispiece: Colin Binks on Technical Ecstasy,
E4 6a, Lazonby
Photo: Ron Kenyon

2 BORDER

The Border area is wild and lonely bounded to the South by the busy A69 road between Brampton and Haydon Bridge. To the North is the Roman Wall, and beyond, moorlands and huge man-made forests. The landscape is harsh and exposed with small, knuckle-hard outcrops of Fell Sandstone; a wonderful rock for climbing. Many of the outcrops face North and whilst providing superb, short climbs are not to be recommended in Winter or after damp weather. Lodges Quarry is a bit esoteric, but then its handy for locals, who can, to some extent overlook its drawbacks. Queens and Padda are however, superb, and on a fine day will provide as good bouldering as anywhere in the North. Spadeadam Crag is a bit limited and perhaps intimidating for the average boulderer, but the situation is great. Vindolanda Quarry is well-worth a visit. For those seeking accessible, easy climbing, The Tipalt is recommended. The Border area has much to interest the visitor and the "Roman" theme is well -catered for at Carvoran Museum and at Vindolanda. Both have good cafes.

LODGES QUARRY   O.S. SHEET 86
Haltwhistle, Bewcastle and Alston   G.R. 591 632

SITUATION AND CHARACTER
This old sandstone quarry faces North-West across the valley of the River Irthing near Low Row, on the A69 road, 5 miles East of Brampton.

The quarry is about 100 metres long and 12 metres high along its central section. Despite much gardening by the first ascentionists, the rock still tends to be dirty and loose due to little traffic in the event of information being unobtainable until now.It is hoped that increased traffic will improve the situation as it could provide useful entertainment for local climbers.The climbing itself is quite reasonable and the situation on fine evenings is far from un-pleasant.

Protection is often sparse, but an abundance of tree stumps along the top, can with care, provide ideal anchors for belaying/top-roping.

APPROACHES AND ACCESS
Five miles East of Brampton on the A69, just beyond the Low Row junction is a Filling Station.The quarry which faces North-West is set below a clump of trees,across the field behind and to the right of the Filling Station.To reach the quarry, drive past the Filling Station and park on the wide grass verge on the left just before a small,white building which is an Electricity sub-station.From the car, walk back towards the filling station until a gate leads into the field. Cross the field towards a solitary Hawthorn tree then turn right and follow the side of the wall until it turns a corner and goes

downhill. At the bottom of the hill is a gate on the left, which enters the quarry at its left-hand end. ON NO ACCOUNT SHOULD ANY WALLS BE CLIMBED.

HISTORICAL

Climbers have pottered around here for many years as evidenced by a few old pitons and well-chipped holds on one or two of the easier climbs. Most of the climbs were done during the Winter of '81/'82 by members of the Carlisle M.C., notably Dave Armstrong and Pete Whillance. All the routes were gardened by abseil and then soloed, apart from Irthing Ranger which has only been top-roped.

THE CLIMBS

The rocks at the point of arrival at the left-hand end of the crag are short and in the form of an obvious bay.Beyond The Bay to the right is the Long Wall which ends in a prominent corner leading up to a scoop under a roof.Immediately right of this corner is a fine, slabby arete.

Aretes Wall comes next and extends from the slabby arete to the obvious curving arete just beyond a big corner; Big Corner. To the right of this last arete and at an angle to it, is The Slab; a large dirty slab. To the right of The Slab are shorter walls but the routes have not been recorded.

The climbs are described left to right and because of the uniform height of 12 metres in the main part of the quarry, heights are not given, however in the Bay the climbs are much shorter.

THE BAY

The Bay is a deeply-recessed area at the left-hand end of the quarry.It is at the usual point of arrival.The Bay has at its left end some dirty corners with intervening ribs and walls.The Bay ends at an arete which has a prominent sentry-box.

1   Parsley   S   4a
Climb the short arete at the extreme left end. Scrappy.

2   Sage   S   4b
Climb the short wall immediately right, via thin cracks, to finish past a spreading, birch sapling.

3   Rosemary   VS   5a   ★
Start below a narrow rib between two dirty corners. Climb the rib direct.

4   Thyme   S   4a
Start below the second, steeper, dirty corner.Climb this passing an old peg in the left wall.

5   Oregano   HVS   5b   ★
Start below the centre of the slabby, right wall of the corner. Climb directly up the middle of the wall.Variations are possible.

6   Bay Gum (It were 'ard!)   HVS   5c   ★
Start below the prominent arete on the right. Climb the arete direct,to finish at a sheaf of thin saplings. The start is difficult.

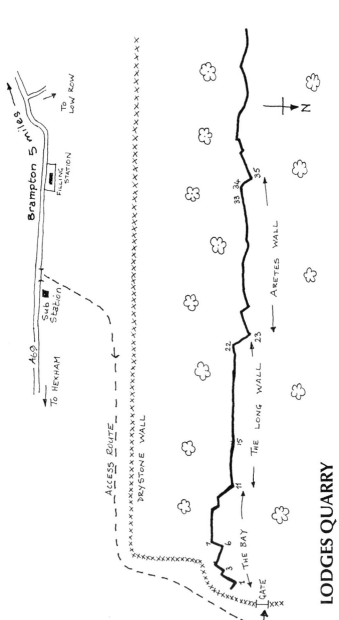

LODGES QUARRY

7   Rum Do   S   4b
Climb the vegetated corner to the right of the arete.

To the right of the grassy, loose wall at the back of the Bay is another rib with a corner on its right.

8   Dill Do   VD   3c
Climb the corner, moving left onto the rib to finish.

9   And Chive   VS   4c
Start below the centre of the wall on the right side of the Bay, at a faint, groove and rib.Climb the groove and rib to finish up the wall above.

10   Rock 'n' Roll Years   HVS   5b
Start just right of the faint groove. Climb flakes on the wall direct to the top. (Care with rock!)

11   Bay Bop   VS   5a
Start below the short rib with the sentry-box, which bounds the right side of the Bay. Climb directly out of the sentry-box to the top.

THE LONG WALL
The unbroken wall of steep rock which extends from the final arete of the Bay to the prominent,green corner in the middle of the quarry,right of which is a fine, slabby arete.

12   Stretch   VS   5a
Climb directly up the wall, 1 metre right of Bay Bop to finish at a small, beech tree.

13   Strain   VS   5a
Start 1.5 metres further right at a shallow, left-facing corner.Climb the wall to an obvious square hold and thereafter the top. The wall to the right has a band of small overhangs near the top.

14   Rubber Band   VS   4c
Start in the centre of the wall,2 metres right of the last climb at a steep slab. Climb diagonally right to join a crack at the right-hand end of the band of small overhangs.

15   Plastic Ono   HS   4b   ⋆
Start at a line of weakness in the convex face below the right-hand end of the band of overhangs, to finish as for the last climb.

16   One Man   VS   4b
Start 3 metres right of the line of weakness in the convex face, at a shallow, left-trending groove in the slab.Follow this. (Chipped holds!)

17   Willy the Dish   VS   5a
Start 1 metre right of the previous route,below the centre of a small band of overhangs at 2 metres.Move up to the right-hand end of the overhang.Climb flakes above and trend left to the top.

18   Mr. Wonderful   VS   5a
The next obvious line, a metre or so further right. Climb a slim groove which widens higher up.Finish at a large stump.

19   Dog Breath   VS   4c
Start at a thin crack 2 metres right of the previous climb.Climb the thin crack to finish at the tree stumps at the top of Mr.Wonderful.

20   Custard Gut   HVS   5b
Start 2 metres right again at the foot of a short rib. Climb the rib into a very shallow rectangular recess. Climb out of this onto a smoother, slabbier upper face and finish direct.

21   Irthing Ranger   NL   6a   ★
Start 2 metres right of the last climb below a 3 metre, flake crack directly below two, large stumps at the top.Climb the crack to overhangs and pull over to an awkward mantelshelf.Climb the slab above to finish at tree stumps.

22   Green Corner   HVS   5c
Climb the obvious green corner direct to a horizontal break below the overhangs.Finish as for route 21 or 23.

ARETES WALL

Aretes wall is the impressive face extending from the fine, slabby arete in the centre of the quarry, rightwards to an easy arete bounded on the right by a dirty slab. Four, large trees have escaped the chainsaws and continue to grow at the top of the crag.

23   Slabaretes Can Damage Your Health   VS   5a   ★
Start at the foot of the fine slabby arete.Climb this and the short corners above and right, to gain the left-hand end of a large, bramble ledge.Climb the short wall above to the top.

24   Tabend   HVS   5c   ★
Start just right of the arete.Climb the very thin crack up to the roof.Pull over direct and move up left, via a vertical edge to join the last climb just below the bramble ledge.

25   Breathless   HVS   5c
Start to the right of the thin crack below a green corner to the left of a bird-limed rib.Climb the corner and rib to gain a horizontal crack.Hand traverse right to a scoop.Step right and up a short wall to reach the right-hand end of the large bramble ledge.

26   Hush   VS   5b
Start just right of the bird-limed rib at a lesser rib. Climb the rib to an awkward pull into a scoop.Step up right and up a short wall to reach the right-hand end of the large bramble ledge.

27   Night Session   HVS   5b
Start from a large ledge on the wall, two metres up and to the right of the rib of Hush. From the left-hand side of the ledge, climb the wall direct to the top horizontal break. Traverse right one metre to finish up a broken crack in the wall, just left of a three-stemmed birch at the top.

28   Varne   HVS   5a
Start at a thin, ragged crackline two metres right of The previous climb. Climb a short, left-slanting groove to a small overhang. Climb the same broken crack in the top wall as for the previous route.

29   The Splits   VS   5a
Start 2 metres right of Varne.Climb a slight groove in the blunt rib to a band of small overhangs.The open groove above is followed to finish near small saplings at the top.

30   Home Brew   S   4b
Climb the obvious corner/groove one metre right of The Splits.

31   Fingal's Cave   HVS   5b
Start below the large cave in the upper wall. Climb the clean, scooped-wall, right of the corner direct, via x-shaped cracks to the cave.Exit leftwards.

32   Sula   S   4c
Start below the obvious, flat rib directly below a stump at the top which has a long branch growing out of it. Climb the rib until level with a good ledge on the left.Traverse right and upwards on large, hollow flakes to finish easily at the left-hand end of some overhangs.

33   Castanet   HVS   5c
An eliminate.
Start in the centre of the wall on the right behind a young Scots Pine.Climb the centre of the wall to gain the hollow flakes. Rattle up easily to the top.

34   Big Corner   S   4b
Start below the big corner which is capped by a roof. Climb the corner until moves can be made out left on large, hollow flakes. Finish easily at the left-hand end of the overhangs.

35   Curved Arete   VD   3b   *
Climb the obvious curving arete to the right of the big corner.Finish at a tall Scots Pine.

The last recorded routes are on The Slab.

36   The Slab   VS   4c
Climb directly up the centre of the slab to below a band of small overhangs.Move left onto the arete to finish.

37   Lone Tree Groove   S   4a
Climb the groove at the right-hand end of the slab to a Scots Pine.Finish up and rightwards.

38   Dirty Corner   S   4a
Climb the short, dirty corner to the right.The finish is awkward.

Numerous short routes and problems have been done on the walls to the right, but up to now they have not been recorded.

The Low Level Girdle   6a+
This has been made of the entire quarry.The best part from route 19 to 26 has been done at two levels, both of these are 6a+.

SPADEADAM CRAG   O.S. Sheet 86   NY 642 697

SITUATION AND CHARACTER.
This pleasant, South facing sandstone outcrop is in a delightfully remote, but easily accessible position in the Irthing Gorge, about 4 miles from Greenhead on the main A69 Newcastle to Carlisle road.

The crag consists of two buttresses of good quality Fell Sandstone.The outlook over the Irthing gorge is fine. Facing South, the crag dries very quickly and catches all the available sun.Climbs tend to be steep and belays at the top can be arranged on angle irons which have been placed.There are dozens of other crags

Padda Crag

Churnsike Lodge

Butterburn

Spadeadam Crag

High Old Shields

The Tipalt

Greenhead

B6318

Gilsland

A69

←Brampton 11miles

BORDER AREA   Not to scale

upstream and downstream some of which have provided, as yet, too few routes to make recording them worthwhile.

APPROACHES AND ACCESS.

The crag is on land owned my the Ministry Of Defence who let it out to farming and forestry. Access is open providing no damage is done and that dogs are left at home.

From the A69 leave the dual carriageway which now by-passes Greenhead and go into the village.Follow signs to Gilsland and from there to Spadeadam and Butterburn.At the top of the hill leading out of Gilsland are M.O.D. signs and a restricted entry road. Our road turns sharp right.Follow it for less than a mile to just past the only mature stand of conifers on the right-hand side of the road.After crossing a small bridge a large, muddy layby on the right provides ample parking. A sign will be seen pointing to the "Irthing Gorge" on the right. Follow this via a marshy track which takes a diagonal line away from the road heading down to the river. After 4 minutes a fence corner is reached and the crag can be seen on our side of the river, just beyond a stone building with a flat, concrete roof. Strike down to this building and descend rough steps to another building by the side of the river.The crag is now reached by ascending a grassy slope on the far side of the small, side valley that guards direct access to the rocks. Just downstream of here is a fine waterfall; Crammel Linn which is well-worth a visit.

HISTORICAL.

The crag was "discovered" and climbed on by Phil Hope, Stew Wilson and friends in the late 1970's. Most of the routes in the 1981 guide were by this team. No further activity was seen here until a visit by Karl Lunt and Andy Williamson in April 1988 resulted in the number of routes being doubled and some fine, hard problems resulting.

THE CLIMBS.

The climbs are described from left to right starting with those on Left-Hand Buttress and then those on Right-Hand Buttress 40m further right.

LEFT-HAND BUTTRESS.

1 Snakelet 7m VS 5a
The extreme left of the buttress has a cracked overlap at the top. Climb the bulging wall and finish direct over the overlap.

2 Back And Biting 8m HVS 5b ★★
Start just right of Snakelet below a steep, scooped slab. Make a hard move to gain the slab (chockstone on right).Finish direct or step left at the top (easier).

3 Viper 8m HS
Climb the corner 3 metres right of the left end of the buttress. Surmounting a block at mid-height provides the crux.

4 Serpent 8m HS
Start just right of Viper.Climb to a large flake. Ascend this and continue to the top.

5   The Mamba   8m   S
In the centre of the buttress is a broken section of rock. Start to the left of this below a curving corner. Climb the corner passing a tree at mid-height.

6   Snake Charmer   8m   HS
Start at the foot of an easy-looking rib. Climb the easy-looking rib, right of the corner of Mamba, to finish at a tree.

7   Wiley Sike   8m   MS
Start just right of the easy-looking rib below a pedestal ledge which gives access to a face broken by three cracks. Gain the pedestal and either finish staight up the left-hand crack or better, move out right to the right hand crack and finish on the fine arete.

The right side of Left-Hand Buttress has overlaps at mid-height.

8   Anaconda   8m   VS   4c
Climb the obvious wide crack just right of a jutting arete.

9   Venom   10m   E3   5c   ★★
A strenuous but pleasing line. Start 3m right of Anaconda below an obvious flake under the roof. Climb direct to the flake. Jam round its left-hand side and pull onto the wall above. Climb the wall direct.

10   Hissing Sid Vicious   10m   E1   5b   ★
Immediately right of Venom the wall is split by parallel twin cracks. Climb these to the roof, pull through onto the wall above and left to finish at some jutting blocks.

11   Krait   9m   MVS   4b
Starts at the right-hand end of the overhanging wall. Gain a sloping ledge and climb up to an overhang which is passed on the left. Move back right and after a heathery struggle, gain the top.

12   Black Adder   9m   E1   5c   ★
Climb the clean rib immediately right of the crack of Krait. The start is undercut and difficult.

13   Slow Worm   9m   HS   4c/5a
Start below a tree at the right-hand end of this buttress. Either climb a short, slanting corner on the right to reach the tree or harder, climb a steep, cracked corner on the left to reach the same ledge. Follow a groove above to the top.

RIGHT-HAND BUTTRESS

This is 50 metres right of Left-Hand Buttress and has a conspicuous overhanging arete.

14   Backstreet Crawler   10m   E3   5c   ★★★
The overhanging arete. Start just left of the arete. Climb the short groove then hand-traverse right onto the edge. Continue direct on large, well-spaced holds. A selection of Friends are useful.

15   Cobra   9m   HS
Climb the crack and V-groove just right of the overhanging arete. Care with blocks at the top of the groove.

PADDA CRAG   O.S. Sheet 86   NY 650 788

SITUATION AND CHARACTER

Padda Crag, properly called Paddaburn Crags, is the most important of a cluster of sandstone crags on Paddaburn Moor, six miles
North of Gilsland.

The crag is very remote and involves a tortuous drive followed by a
forty minute walk on good forest roads.

The situation of the crag near the top of the moor is very fine. The
surrounding countryside is coniferous forest, but fortunately the
forest does not encroach upon the crag whose aspect is sunny and
open.

Padda Crag is composed of excellent quality Fell Sandstone and
facing South it catches all the available sunshine. On the debit side,
lichen growth is luxuriant and very beautiful. In dry weather this is
not a problem but in damp weather, it is a place to be avoided.

The climbing is mainly on rounded holds on steep walls and the
potential for bouldering is enormous. The base of the crag is most
comfortable and on the top of the crag and a few metres back, the
forest provides plentiful anchors. The crag has a maximum height
of 10 metres.

APPROACHES AND ACCESS

The crag is approached from Gilsland a small Cumbrian village one
and a half miles from Greenhead on the A69(T) some 17 miles East
of Carlisle. Greenhead is now by-passed and it is reached by
following the signs from the A69.

After crossing the bridge in Gilsland take the first turn on the right
and follow this, the only road North. Ignore signs to Gilsland Spa
unless you fancy visiting the 'Popping Stone' where Walter Scott
'Popped the Question' and continue on for a further half a mile to
where the road turns sharp right. Bear right here and follow this as
the way straight ahead leads to Spadeadam Range which is a restricted area. A good but narrow road is followed past the parking spot
for Spadeadam Crag and on across open moorland and a ford at
Butterburn after six miles. A further one and a quarter miles leads
to a wooden bridge crossing the R. Irthing just short of Churnsike
Lodge. Cars need to be parked here for although the crag is on
Forestry Commission land access past Churnsike Lodge can only be
made on foot on a Public Bridleway.

Cross the wooden bridge and follow the road passing through the
Forestry Commision gate near the lodge. Turn left and follow the
well-maintained (ie, driveable) road for a couple of hundred metres
passing a ruin on the left and some well-grown young trees on the
right. Another 500 metres sees this track fork. Take the right-hand
fork and follow it diagonally uphill. Continue along this track
ignoring all junctions until after three-quarters of a mile or thera-
bouts the crag can be seen above and to the right. The best
approach from the Forest road is to follow the course of the small
beck for a short distance before open land can be followed to the
left-hand end of the crag.

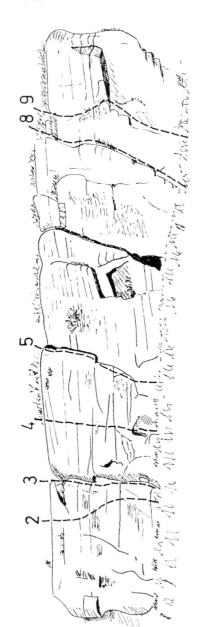

First Wall   Second Wall   Main Wall

PADDA CRAG – Left Hand Side

HISTORICAL

The crag was discovered in 1973 by Earl, Hutchinson and Edmondson who climbed a handful of routes including Padda Wall and Churnside Crack.

Following on from this the crag was visited quite frequently by Stewart Wilson,Dave Bowen which resulteed in the climbing and recording of all the routes in the 1980 North Of England Guide. Kelvin Neal and Wilson continued to develop the crag and between them were responsible in 1981/82 for the remaining routes, the best being Neal's, Vital Signs and Wilson's, Red Cloud and Four Horns.

THE CLIMBS

The climbs are described from left to right as one faces the crag.

Descents at various points along the crag are all easy.

FIRST WALL

At the left-hand end of the crag this rather featureless but attractive wall ends in a fine arete and just right of this, a chimney with jumbled blocks.

1   Piute   6m   S

Start 2m right if the left end of the wall below a shallow scoop. Climb into the scoop and move left to climb the wall just right of an overlap.

2   Padda Wall   7m   HS   *

A pleasant open route on good rock.Harder variations exist further left.

Start at thin, parallel twin cracks just left of the arete.Climb straight up then move leftwards at the top to a fine finish.

3   Oregon Trail   7m   MS   *

A good climb on good holds.Start at the foot of the fine arete just left of the chimney.Climb the arete direct with the crux at mid-height.

SECOND WALL

Extends for 13 metres right of the chimney to end at a deep cave-like recess.

4   Whoops   6m   VS

Start at the flake which leans against the foot of the crag just right of the chimney.Climb the initial bulge with difficulty then follow the wall direct on small holds.

5   Sioux Hare   7m   HVD

A good line but a poor climb.Start below the only wide crack on the wall.Climb it.

MAIN WALL

This interesting smooth wall extends from the cave-like recess rightwards for 10 metres.Main wall end at an easy-angled ridge below which on the path is a big boulder.

6   Creak   7m   HD

To the right of the cave is a rightward slanting crack. Climb the crack via wedged block.

PADDA CRAG – Right Hand Side

Main Wall Third Wall Fourth Wall Padda Tower

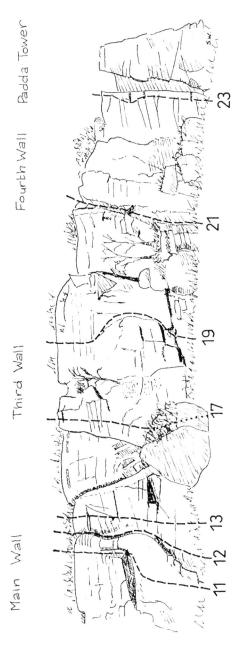

11 12 13 17 19 21 23

7 Four Horns 8m E1 5b ★
Climb the steep wall to the right of the cave on small holds.

8 The Funnel 8m VS 5a ★★
Good moves and gear. Climb the steep groove to pull out left at the top.Good holds to finish.

9 Sike Wall 9m HVS 5a
Start 1 metres right of the Funnel below the left end of the obvious overlap.Climb up to the overlap and climb it via a crescent-shaped flake.

10 Red Cloud 9m HVS 5b ★
Start 2 metres right of Sike Wall.Climb the smooth wall direct to a break in the widest part of overlap. Finish through this.

11 Lone Ranger 9m HVS 5b ★
Follow Red Cloud to finish up a short groove at the right end of the overlap.

12 Churnside Crack 9m S ★
A steep climb of character.Climb the attractive bulging crack which splits the wall right of the overlap.

13 Witch Hunt 8m HVS 5b ★
Climb the steep wall on small holds 1 metre right of Churnside Crack.

14 Arete Direct 9m HS 4a
Start at the foot of the arete at the right-hand end of Main Wall just in front of the huge boulder. Climb the arete, the start is undercut and awkward.

BOULDER SLAB
This is the easy slab to the right of, and at a right-angle to Main Wall.It lies between the arete and the easy cleft which has flakes jammed in its upper part.

15 Chisholm Trail 9m D
A good easy climb.Climb the centre of the slab to a steeper finish.

THIRD WALL
Third Wall extends from Boulder Slab to an overhanging nose above a ledge upon which grow two thin birch trees.A thin birch grows out of the face at half-height towards the right end of the wall.

16 Leaning Crack 8m S
Start 1 metre right of the easy corner separating Boulder Slab from Third Wall.Climb the right-trending diagonal crackline to the top.

17 The Niggler 8m MVS 4b
This pleasant climb starts at the foot of a steep clean wall 2 metres right of Leaning Crack.Climb the wall on lovely wrinkled rock between the lichenous drainage streaks.Gaining a small ledge at half-height is the crux.

18 Vital Signs 9m VS 5b ★★
A good wall climb. Start 1 metre right of the thin birch growing on the face. Climb a very thin crack with difficulty to a good jug. The steep wall above is an excellent finish.

19 Pipe Of Peace 10m MVS 4c ★★
Classic!
Start as for Vital Signs. Instead of climbing the thin crack, follow the overlap rightwards until some fingery moves lead to better holds. Swing across the wall on the left to gain the jug of Vital Signs and finish as for that route

20 Padda Stairs 8m D
Start below the final overhanging nose of the wall at the left end of the big ledge with two thin birches on it.Step left off the ledge and climb the wall until a step right can be made above the nose.Finish up the short open corner.

FOURTH WALL

Fourth Wall is about 10 metres long and extends rightwards from steep corner-chimney above the boulder-ledge upon which grow the two thin birches to an isolated pinnacle; Padda Tower.

21 Forked Tongue 8m VD ★
Steep and interesting and with good holds and protection. Start at the foot of a fine crack and groove a couple of metres right of the two birches.Climb the fine cracks and either finish up a steep crack or step right and finish up a shallow groove.

22 Tomahawk 8m HS
A tricky wall climb on indifferent holds. Start 2 metres right of the cracked corner of Forked Tongue below a very shallow line of resistance. Climb this direct.

23 Hiding To Nothing 8m HVS 4c ★
Climb the fine arete which bounds the right-hand end of Fourth Wall. The finish is intimidating.

PADDA TOWER

This fine broad-based pinnacle is bounded on its left by a gully. It has a shorter face where it abuts against the fellside.

24 Tower Crack 7m M
Start from the gully on the left-hand side of the Tower.Climb the wide,easy-angled crack to a platform.A pull lands one on the summit.

25 Teton 7m VD
Start just inside the gully. Climb the wall and arete on the East side of the Tower.

26 Ojibwa 7m MS
Start at the foot of the West arete of the Tower.Climb the wall on the right using the arete as required.

27 The Tower Ordinary 5m Easy
Start below a short crack on the West side of the Tower where it abuts against the fellside.Climb a short crack onto a pedestal, a pull up gains the summit.

Behind the Tower is a useful descent path from climbs on this part of the crag.

THE PLAYGROUND

This is the name given to the 50 metre stretch of small outcrops and

Andy and Caroline Fanshawe on Marik, VS 4c, Kings Meaburn

boulders between Padda Tower and the next continuous rock; Fifth Wall. One minor route is described;

28 Nasty Knobbles 5m S
Starts between a prominent flake and a vegetated crack on the steep wall 10 metres right of the Tower. Climb directly up the steep wall on small holds to finish at a pointed block.

FIFTH WALL

The steep wall to the right of the Playground has in its centre a huge detached block in a dark corner.The wall to the left of this corner has an overhang at chest height whilst the wall to the right of this corner has a prominent jutting neb low down.

29 One-Eyed Jack 8m VS 4c   ★
A very pleasant climb with no protection. Starts at the left-hand end of the wall below a steep shallow scoop. Climb over a small overlap and finish up the steep, shallow scoop.

30 Muleskinner 8m D
Start at the right-hand crack of the huge detached block in the corner.Climb the crack and exit on the right.

31 The Nebbish 7m MVS 5b
Starts below the Neb. Pull up on good holds and make a hard move to stand on them. Climb up to and out of a sentry-box.

SIXTH WALL

This is a further 12 metres to the right of Fifth Wall.It consists of a line of walls and buttresses ranging in height from 5-7 metres.Sixth Wall is divided into two halves by a gully.To the left of the gully is a smooth left-slanting groove and beyond this to the left a barrier of overhangs at head height guard the wall.To the right of the gully is a false wall leaning against the foot of the crag.The wall then ends in a jutting tooth-like arete on the right.

32 Little Groove 5m 4c
Climb the left-slanting, smooth groove.

33 Tusk 7m MVS 4c
Climb the jutting tooth-like arete.

SEVENTH WALL

This is the very steep wall of bubbly rock immediately right of the tooth-like arete.Seventh Wall terminates in a very deep recessed corner which has a fist-wide crack in the angle.

34 Hiawatha 7m VS 4c   ★★
A meaty little climb with good holds and protection. A reach near the top will not pose any problems for long fellows. Start at the foot of the obvious,steep flake crack immediately left of the prominent overhanging arete which forms the left edge of the deep recessed corner. Climb the flake and continue through the steep break with a long reach.

35 Papoose 7m MS
Start in the deep corner at the right end of Seventh Wall. Do not climb the corner,instead ascend the wall on the right to gain a good flake which is followed leftwards to the top.

THE TIPALT (COLLAR HEUGH CRAG)   O.S. SHEET 86   NY 672 670

SITUATION AND CHARACTER

This crag of excellent quality Fell Sandstone faces North, North-West across Thirlwall Common and could easily be combined with climbing at Spadeadam Crag or Lodges Quarry.It is remote but easily accessible with transport, being only a few metres from the road. Permission to climb must be sought (see Approaches and Access).

The Tipalt with its big, unclimbed roofs has a sombre appearance which belies the mainly medium grade routes on excellent rock with no shortage of good holds. Care is needed with belays at the top particularly if fence posts are used as anchorage. The crag does not seep and so winter climbing is quite pleasant.

APPROACHES AND ACCESS

Leave the A69 where it becomes dual-carriageway by-passing Greenhead (as for Padda and Spadeadam crags). Go through the village of Greenhead passing a petrol station and the Greenhead Hotel and turn immediately left onto the B6318 Military Road-.Follow this steeply uphill until a signposted left turn leads to Carvoran Roman Army Museum. Go past the museum and con-tinue on for about 1 mile until High Old Shield Farm is reached on the left.The crag is visible on the right.

IMPORTANT

The crag is on the property of Mr Batey of High Old Shield, the farm just below the crag. Unlike many landowners he is sym-pathetic to climbers and asks that they see him at the farm before climbing. THIS SMALL COURTESY IS ESSENTIAL IF CLIMBING IS TO CONTINUE. Cars can be left on the roadside below the crag providing they don't interfere with farming needs.The crag is only a few minutes easy walk away.

HISTORICAL

Discovered by the inimitable Alan Stark of Causey Quarry fame and developed by members of the Eden Valley M.C. in early 1976.

THE CLIMBS

Seen from below the crag consists of three sections:Left-Hand Buttress, Main Face and Right-Hand Buttress. Steep grassy gullies separate each section. The best descent is to the right of Right-Hand Buttress at the West end of the crag. The climbs are des-cribed from left to right as one faces the crag.

LEFT-HAND BUTTRESS

A barrel-shaped buttress with three faces. The front face is undercut.

1   Hopesike Wall   7m   VD

Not an outstanding climb. Start 4 metres up the slope from the front of the buttress at the foot of a broken groove.Climb the groove past a small jutting nose and after 3 metres step right and finish up rightwards on ledges.

2 Green Fingers 7m HVS 5b
Start just left of the front face at an obvious V-groove. Climb the V-groove to good holds in a break above the overhang.Pull over strenuously using a thin crack. Finish direct.

3 This 8m VS 4b ★

A good little climb, steep and interesting. Start at the foot of the front face at a square hole-like recess. Climb to the prominent overhang and ascend the thin crack splitting its right-hand side. Climb the wall direct on good holds.

4 That 6m S
A worthwhile steep wall climb. Start below the centre of the steep,right-hand wall.Climb the wall on good holds.

MAIN FACE
This is about 20 metres long and has a ledge system at half-height.The upper left-hand side is dominated by huge,jutting,unclimbed roofs.

The right-hand part has an obvious green drainage line which ends as a deep chimney/crack and is the line of Walk Like A Dog.The Main Face ends at an arete identified by an arrowhead-shaped overhang at 5 metres.

5 Snipe 8m HVD
Start at the foot of a dirty groove at the left side of the Main Face at a point to the right of which the roofs start to develop. Climb the dirty groove until pleasant moves on good holds lead rightwards above the overhangs.A wide cleft is then followed to the top.

6 Here 9m MVS 4b
Start on the first patch of level ground on the left side of Main Face, just left of the prominent undercut rib of the Snout. Climb the shallow corner to a large flat ledge. From the left-hand end of the ledge pull over the overhang on good holds and traverse diagonally right to finish.

7 The Snout 5m MVS 4b ★
Good value. Start below the jutting prow.Climb the undercut arete.'Thank-God' holds appear when most needed. Finish on the ledge above.

8 There 11m VS 5a ★★
The most impressive natural line on the crag and at its grade a hard-won though absorbing effort. Start 5 metres right of the Snout below the impressive V-groove which cleaves the top overhangs. Climb the initial undercut wall via a thin crack to gain a ledge.Pull under the roof and gain the upper groove. Follow this to the top moving out left to finish.

The base of the crag now forms a small bay or amphitheatre with a jutting roof at 2 metres.

9 Everywhere 11m MVS 4b
Start at the foot of the overhanging arete at the right-hand end of the amphitheatre.Climb the arete by the shallow groove on its left to a good ledge. Move just over a metre to the right and climb the wall above using a thin crack which soon peters out.

9a   Variation Finish   VS   4c
From the ledge, surmount the bulge directly above the arete and move left to finish at some prominent knobs of rock.

10   Walk Like A Dog   11m   S
Better than it looks with a steep finish. Start 2 metres right of the amphitheatre at the foot of the obvious green runnel. Race up the runnel to a ledge then struggle up the strenuous chimney above.

11   Crab Fair   16m   D   ★★
A fine combination of wall traverse and slab; a beginner's dream. Start just right of the obvious green runnel. Climb the steep wall rightwards on memorable holds to a good ledge. Traverse right easily and swarm onto a higher ledge. Just around the corner on the right is a groove. Climb this until it can be quitted for excellent jugs and slab finish on the left.

12   Goose Fair   11m   HS
A good steep climb but rather awkward. Start at the foot of the arete with the arrowhead-shaped overhang at the right end of Main Face. Climb the arete passing the overhang to gain the good ledge of Crab Fair. Finish as for Crab Fair by climbing the groove on the right until jugs on the left lead to a slab finish.

12a   Variation Finish   VS   4c
From the point of arrival on the ledge, climb directly up and over bulges to gain the top slab of Crab Fair.

RIGHT-HAND BUTTRESS
This is a smaller, scruffy and broken buttress at the right end of the crag. Short scrambles but nothing of any interest.

QUEEN'S CRAG   O.S. SHEET 86   NY 794 706

SITUATION AND CHARACTER
Queen's Crag is situated in the wild and remote-feeling country North of the Roman Wall at Housesteads. It faces North towards the Wark Forest and a landscape of moss and cotton grass. A lonely place, but in good weather a fine place to climb. The escarpment is nowhere higher than 8 metres and because 6m is more or less constant, heights are omitted. The rock is good, sound Fell Sandstone of the Northumbrian variety but it can be a little dirty, a fact which only detracts from the high-quality of the climbing in wet weather. The climbs tend to be steep and some may seem harshly graded when compared with routes on the Eastern Northumbrian outcrops. Many of the climbs although short, are of excellent quality but because few people have climbed there as a result of lack of information, star ratings have been used sparingly until such time as a concensus is reached.

APPROACHES AND ACCESS
The B 6318 Military Road is followed from Greenhead (as for the Tipalt), but instead of turning off at Carvoran continue for several miles to Housesteads. From here continue for a further 2 miles until immediately in front of a small cottage on the left side of the road,

an unmetalled road strikes off left.Follow this to the cluster of farm buildings known as Sewing Shields. IMPORTANT: Mr Murray the farmer is happy for climbers to use Queens Crag which is on his land but asks that ALL CLIMBERS ASK HIS PERMISSION. The farmhouse is to the left of the buildings and his door is in the corner of a small paved yard.

After stopping at the farm continue along the unmade road which turns sharply left over a ridge and descends below the vegetated crags of the Whin Sill. Once the track begins to cross an open area, the escarpment can be seen on the left across rough pastures about a mile away. Cars must be parked carefully on the verge of the track just before it turns sharp right to continue to more remote places. From the car walk along the top of the grassy ridge to reach the left-hand end of the crag.The climbing is described from right to left and so it is better to continue to the far end of the crag where a wall runs up to meet it and where a prominent cave forms a useful base for operations and should it rain(!!), shelter.

HISTORICAL

The routes recorded here are all the work of Pete Whillance,Pete Botterill and Dave Armstrong who in 1982, 'blitzed' the crag and recorded their efforts.However this is not the full story as Whillance states: "Some of the very easy lines must have been climbed before, but there was no evidence of this at all.The state of most of the routes, leads me to think that probably nothing at VS or above had been previously climbed----." and, "Geoff Oliver admits to having pegged Rabbitstone Crack many years ago!"

THE CLIMBS

The routes are described from right to left. A drystone wall runs uphill to meet the right-hand end of the main crag at a prominent cave(usual base of operations).From here and leftwards the Main Crag extends to a region of short easy slabs and cracks located by the presence of a large boulder on the slope below.This is BOULDER 2; the largest boulder on the crag.The section left of this more broken region is known as The Prows on account of the three jutting prows towards its left-hand end.

To the right of the cave and across the drystone wall short faces continue for about 100 metres to a prominent pinnacle - The Rabbit Stone.

MAIN CRAG

1   Boudicca   HVS   6a
Start in the cave just right of where an obvious thin crack cuts the roof.Pull over the roof on small holds to reach a horizontal crack.Hand-traverse right and climb the arete to the top.

2   Cleopatra   HVS   5c
Start below the thin crack through the left side of the cave. Climb the crack and the slim corner crack above.

3   Salote   VD
Climb the easy crack just left of the cave, identified by a large block and several chockstones. Dirty.

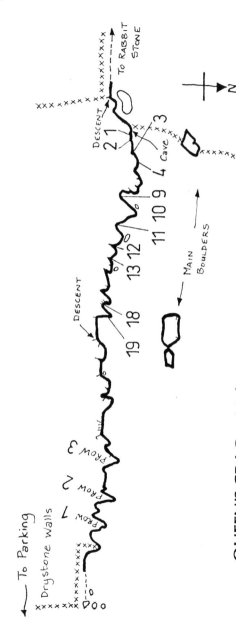

QUEEN'S CRAG – Main Section

4 Hera HVS 5b
Climb the arete direct, immediately left of the crack, to a sloping shelf. Finish above via an awkward mantleshelf.

5 Layback HS
Start 2 metres left of the arete below a wide crack with an overhang at half-height.Climb the crack by any appropriate method.

The next prominent buttress is identified by three good cracks on its front face.

6 Bicycle Race VS 5a
Climb the right-hand crack which has an undercut base and awkward jamming higher up.

7 Fat-Bottomed Girls HS
Climb the central crack direct.

8 Jazz VS 5a ⋆
A good route. Start in a groove set back from the other two cracks.Climb the thin crack in the groove by laybacking.

9 Grumble and Grunt S
Deep in the corner on the left is a crack formed by two huge flakes sat one upon the other. Climb the dirty crack.

The next prominent buttress has two very fine climbs and between them an unclimbed thin, snaking crack.

10 Gloriana E2 5b ⋆⋆
Start just left of a pedestal below the prominent arete. Climb the arete direct just left of a pedestal, then follow hollow flakes on the right side to gain an awkward sloping ledge just below the top. Bold!

11 Marie Celeste HVS 5b ⋆⋆⋆
Climb the striking corner to the left of the unclimbed wall. Superb!

The next feature is a hanging rib above a nasty-looking block.It is unclimbed!

The buttress to the left has a wide crack on each side.

12 Juno VS 4c
Start below the right-hand crack. Climb the crack which curves steeply up to a ledge on the left.Easier than it looks.

13 A Dream Of Wet Corgis S
An annoying thrutch. Climb the left-hand chimney/crack.

The next buttress has a very thin crack in its front face.

14 Security Risk HVS 5c ⋆
Start from a glacis and climb the thin crack in a slim groove on finger slots.

15 O.H.M.S. VD
Start round the corner on the left below a dirty, open groove. Climb the groove which has jammed flakes protruding from it.

About 3 metres further left of the dirty groove with the protruding flakes is a bulge with a thin crack running through it.

16 Queen of Hearts HVS 6a
Start below the cracked bulge. Climb the bulge using the crack and the wall on the right. Move right to finish. The scooped wall direct is so far unclimbed.

17   Etoile Vert   VS   5b
Start at a green, flared chimney just left of the cracked bulge. Climb the chimney to a large, wedged block. The finish is dirty and the climb is harder than it looks.

To the left of the green, flared chimney is an inset, square groove/ recess containing a number of sandwiched flakes and cracks.

18   Stell Green Groove   VS   4c
Climb the groove/recess via a pull on a jammed block and back and foot to exit on the right at the top. (Harder variations and eliminates are possible depending on what you choose to ignore - aren't there always?)

The final feature of the Main Crag is an overhanging rib.

19   Retch For The Stars   HVS   5b
Start on the left side of the rib.Pull on a faint, flake crack on the left side of the rib to reach a horizontal break. A flake on the wall above is then used to finish by a mantleshelf. Alternatively, hand-traverse right onto the hanging rib and pull up to a good finishing jug.

Left is a section of short, easy slabs and cracks providing quick ways up and down.Ten metres left is a thin, curved crack in a scooped wall which will give a short, desperate problem.

20   Starstruck   VS   5a
Climb the arete direct, just right of the curving crack.

There is also another, short, easier crack before the rocks gain more height.

THE PROWS

This is the name given to the section of crag to the left of the area of easy slabs and cracks.The three prows of rock after which the section is named are in the latter half of the described climbs, i.e. at the left-hand end.

The first climbs here are found on the first buttress to the left of the lower rocks described.This buttress is identified by a short crack on its front which ends in a sloping shelf.To the right of the crack is a curving rib.

21   The Furry Quean   HVS   5b
Climb the curving rib to gain the sloping shelf. The arete above has an awkward move.

22   Queen Bee   VS   5b
Climb the short crack on the front of the buttress to gain the sloping shelf.Climb the wall above to the top.

23   Bumble   D
Climb the obvious blocky chimney just left of Queen Bee.

24   The Sting   HVS   5b
Start immediately left of the chimney (and unfortunately within reach of it) below a short, sharp arete. Climb the arete direct to good finishing holds.

A bubbly wall (unclimbed!) on the left of the arete is followed by shorter rocks, then a series of tightly packed, loose-looking, flakes and cracks which provide the next two climbs.

25 The Haggler HS 4c
Start at the short, thin rightmost crack which is solid. Climb the
crack to an overhang and then follow twin cracks to the top.

26 Left-Hand Crack VS 4c
Climb the left-hand crack of the group via an overhanging start to
gain a ledge on the left.Finish easily.

The left-hand end of the crag has three distinctive prows.

27 Prow 3 VS 5a
Start on the right-hand side of the prow. Pull up to a sentry-box and
climb the groove above. Just left of Prow 3 is a short, green groove
(VS 5a), then easy slabs and a tiny prow before Prow 2.

28 Prow 2 HVS 5b
Start directly below the sharp arete.Climb the arete direct to
start,then on its scooped right side to the top.(Stepping off the
large block on the left to start lowers the grade to VS 5a).
Short rocks and problems lead to Prow 1.

29 Prow 1 VS 5b
Only a short problem.
Start on the right side of the prow.Use a pocket to reach up left to a
ledge above the undercut base (or jump!).Use the rib to gain a
standing position and reach the top.

*The left side of Prow 1 is much easier and a few more problems
exist.There are several large boulders about 100 metres further left,
but better boulders are to be found down the slope below the Main
Crag. Many problems are possible. Particularly worthy of note are:*

Boulder 1
*The large boulder directly below the cave at the right end of the
crag.It actually forms part of the drystone wall.The West face has
two short routes of interest.*

31 The Flutings VS 5a
Climb flutings in the centre of the wall to a break.Continue directly
up the wall on pockets.

32 Stewpot HVS 5b
Climb the wall to the right of the flutings to an obvious large
pocket.Straight up to finish.

Boulder 2
The largest of the boulders, lying below the centre of the Main
Crag.The North side presents a slabby face guarded by a bulging
wall.The best three routes are recorded:

33 Sigg Arete HVS 5c ★
Start at the curving arete on the right side of the bulging wall.
Climb the overhanging right side of arete and pull over onto the
left side to finish.

34 Botterill's Shelf HVS 6a ★
Start at the foot of the curving arete.Make a hard pull up left onto a
very sloping shelf.Climb the slab diagonally leftwards to the top.

35 Brighton Rock HVS 5b
Start at the left-hand side of the bulging wall.Climb a rightward-
slanting crack for a few feet.Pull over the overlap and continue
delicately to the top.

To the right of the Main Crag short faces continue for almost 100 metres to a prominent pinnacle – The Rabbit Stone.

THE RABBIT STONE

36   Rabbitstone Crack   HVS   5b   ★★
Start below the thin crack on the South side. Climb the thin crack in a slight corner by layback to big, spanking jugs at the top. Classic.

37   You Asked Ferret   S
Start at the foot of the North-West arete.Follow the edga all the way or climb the wide, left- slanting crack in the West face to meet the arete at half-height.

38   Lapine It Up   HVS   5b
Start at the lowest point at the foot of the N.E. arete. Move up the arete, then go right (crux) and up to finish up the middle of the slabby North face.

39   The Snare   VS   4c
Climb the East face steeply at first, on a series of flakes.A slabby face is climbed above these to reach the top.

40   The Magician's Hat   HVS   5b   ★
Start from a pocket just left of Rabbitstone Crack. Pull around the arete to small holds on the West face. Climb straight up using the edge to a large flake and the top.

The crag facing the Rabbit Stone offers several hard possibilities. Short routes and problems have been done on the buttresses left of the prominent overhang.

LONGSTONE QUARRY (VINDOLANDA QUARRY)
O.S. SHEET 86   G.R. 775 661

SITUATION AND CHARACTER

The quarry is in a commanding position on a ridge of high land overlooking Vindolanda Roman Fort. It faces West and has the sun in the afternoon and evening.

Longstone Quarry is named after the small, standing stone visible on the top of the hill as one approaches from the B6318.

A Sandstone quarry about 80 metres long and up to 13 metres high.The rock is slightly softer than normal Fell Sandstone. The climbing is mainly on steep walls with sparse protection in many cases.The base of the quarry is luxurious;soft turf and springy heather. Anchors at the top are non-existent and use of the tottering drystone wall above the quarry could be dangerous,if not to ascending climbers, then definitely to landowner/climber relations. Fixed pegs or ring-bolts on the firm,platform of rock at the top of the quarry may be the answer as stakes could not possibly be driven in. There is definitely much scope for new routes.

APPROACHES AND ACCESS

Approaching from the West, leave the A69 at Greenhead and follow the B6318 for 6 miles to Twice Brewed. A further one and a half miles past Twice Brewed a large farm complex visible on the left side of the road heralds the need for attention so as not to overshoot the unsigned, right turn a further 500 metres on. Turn right onto a road, "Unsuitable For Coaches" and follow this for 1 mile to a T-junction. Turn right for Bardon Mill and follow the road below a ridge, the Longstone being visible on the left. Just beyond a sharp, left-hand bend is a green, wooden seat on the left side of the road and a parking place for a couple of cars on the opposite side of the road. From the car, follow the road to a metal gate just before a house. A pleasant path leads via a slanting route across pastures and through a wall to the quarry which is out of sight. Time from car 3 minutes.

HISTORICAL

The quarry has been used in the past for pegging and scars and rotten stubs are visible, particularly along horizontal breaks. There was however no evidence of free climbing. The routes recorded are the work of P. Whillance and D. Armstrong who soloed them after pre-cleaning by abseil. This was in the early part of 1982. Visits to the crag in 1991 by Pete Botterill resulted in some worthwhile additions notably the Concave Wall routes, Teflon Effect, False Start, Chariot Of Fire and Mosaic.

THE CLIMBS

Seen from below the quarry consists of four main sections from left to right: Concave Wall, Short Wall, Main Wall Left, Main Wall Right.

Between Main Wall Left and Main Wall Right are easy slabs and a grassy corner which can provide a descent route, although descents at either end of the quarry are safer. The climbs are described from left to right according to section.

CONCAVE WALL

The impressive wall at the extreme left-hand end of the quarry. It is about 9 metres high and is split by a long, thin crack. Concave Wall ends at two, short parallel cracks, about 1 metre apart.

1 Pullover 6m S
Start at the extreme left end of the wall below a pronouced right-slanting overlap. Climb up to the overlap and reach over to holds. Hand traverse right until standing on the chipped hold of Jumper. Now pullover!

2 Jumper 6m E1 5b
Start just right of the overlap below a thin crack. Reach the thin crack with the aid of a triangular hold on the left and reach an ancient chipped hold. A long move gains the top.

3 Sweater 8m E2 5c
Climb the thin central crack direct with the crux at the top.

4 Flanker 9m HVS 5a   *
A pleasant, open climb of contrasts. Start 1 metre right of the thin, central crack. Climb to a ledge at 2 metres. Step right and climb the wall via a blunt-edged flake.

5 Parallel Crack 1

6 Parallel Crack 2

BORDER AREA

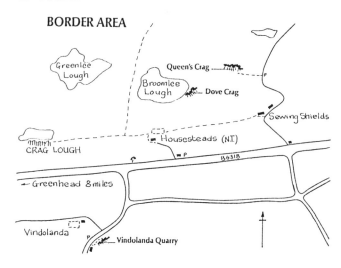

SHORT WALL

This extends from the parallel cracks for about 10 metres to a grassy, pedestal ledge just right of a prominent undercut at 1 metre.
The climbs are short, about 5-6 metres and the rock here tends to be dirty, with awkward finishes.

MAIN WALL LEFT

A fine, attractive face about 10 metres high which extends from the pedestal rightwards. A band of overhangs guards the upper left-hand end and a prominent, green groove leads up to these. To the right, the wall is more featureless but the central portion has an overlap near the top. The right-hand end of the wall 'Problem Wall' is shorter and climbs on this part terminate on a big heather ledge. The section ends at the shelved slab which can be used as a descent route.

7   The Teflon Effect   10m   VS   5a
Start to the left of the green groove at a blunt rib with EGI inscribed in the rock. Climb straight up to good holds under the roof. Pull over and reach the top.

8   Tusk   10m   E1   5b   ★★
An impressive route. Start just right of the green groove at a short, vertical crack. Climb the wall to the horizontal break and continue up the obvious line of flakes to the top.

9   False Start   10m   E2   6a
Start just right of Tusk. Unusual climbing leads to a poor flake and then a good hold under the overlap. Move left and finish up Tusk.

10   Vindolanda   10m   HVS   5a   ★
Start 8 metres right of the previous climb, below a pointed, flake-ledge at full reach. Climb the wall to a good ledge. Step right and climb steeply to a short groove up which the climb finishes.

11   Gaul   9m   HVS   5a   ★
Start 2 metres right of Vindolanda at a left-slanting ledge. Climb the steep wall to the horizontal break. Follow the vague,rightward slanting flake to the top.

12   'Cos Its There!   9m   VS   4b
Start 2 metres right of Gaul at a blunt arete. Climb up and rightwards over a large block to a big,heather ledge.Climb easily to the top.

13   Problem Wall Left   5m   5c   ★
Start just right of the previous route. Climb the steep wall to a small overlap.Pull up and leftwards to reach the large block on 'Cos Its There!

14   Problem Wall Centre   5m   5c   ★
Climb the centre of Problem Wall to a horizontal break.Make a long reach to holds above and move onto the big ledge.

15   Problem Wall Right   5m   6a   ★
Start at the right-hand side.The break is reached via hard moves on sloping holds.Finish easily on ledges.

16   Main Wall Left Girdle   5c   ★
The whole of the Main Wall Left can be Girdle Traversed via the obvious horizontal break.

MAIN WALL RIGHT

The most impressive face in the quarry.It starts just right of the easy, stepped slab and presents a uniformly steep face of about 14 metres high.The climbing is on steep walls and is bold, in addition the high quality of the routes is somewhat marred by the presence of lichen and grass on ledges as a result of underuse.The situation should soon change as the quarry gains in popularity.

17   Curving Crack   12m   S   ★
Start below the prominent crack at the left-end of the face. Climb the crack direct.

18   All Along The Watchtower   14m   E1   5a
Start as for Curving Crack.Climb the crack for a metre until it is possible to move rightwards up the wall to a horizontal break. Step right and follow the right-hand side of the wall to the top.

19   Mosaic   12m   E3   6b
Start to the right of Curving Crack at a small overlap in the steep wall which has a lichenous streak running its full height. Climb straight up to the right-hand end of the easy Hand traverse and make hard moves up and right to a hold beneath a ledge which marks the end of the difficulties. Step left and climb straight up to twin finishing cracks and nut/Friend belays just below the top.

20   Wild Thing   12m   E1   5c
Ten metres right of the left end of the wall is a stepped corner. Start 3 metres left of this from the top of a grassy mound. Climb up and right to an obvious pocket, then move diagonally leftwards to a ledge in the middle of the wall.Climb more easily up rightwards to the top.

21   Giant's Steps   13m   HVS   5a
Climb the obvious, stepped corner to a small overhang. Continue up the slabby wall above.

22   Steppin' Out   14m   HVS   5b
Start as for Giant's Steps below the stepped corner. Climb the
stepped corner onto the first ledge.Climb the wall to a thin, horizontal crack and move right and up to a sandy ledge. Climb the
short wall above to the top.

23   Bananarama   12m   E1   5c
Start 8m right of Giant's Steps at a tapering, right-facing groove.
Climb the groove and pull up to a good ledge in a scoop. Move up
the grassy break and up the short wall above to the top.

24   Chariot Of Fire   12m   E2   5c
Start below the steep rib to the right of the groove of Bananarama.
Climb the rib direct. No protection, poor landing.

25   Did Those Feet   12m   HVS   5b
Start below the thin,flake crackline 5 metres right of Bananarama.
Climb up over a grass ledge and follow a faint, green groove to an
overhang. Climb the flake crack to a large, heather ledge and
continue in the same line up a thin, flake crack in the wall.

26   Starkey's Crack   11m   HVS   5a   ★
Start 4 metres left of the grassy corner which bounds the Main Wall
Right. Climb the short groove which leads to the steep crack. Climb
the crack direct.

BORDER – MINOR CRAGS AND BOULDERING VENUES

CHRISTIANBURY CRAGS   O.S. SHEET 80   G.R. 578821
Remote and splendid, these small tors of hard Sandstone sit on top
of the fell bearing the same name. The crags are only a few miles
South of the Scottish Border and are best reached by following
minor roads North from Brampton via Lanercost, Askerton Castle
and Bewcastle. The only road North from Bewcastle leads to a
remote cul-de-sac and a dwelling; The Flatt, on the edge of the
forest. The crags are about three miles North-East of here on the
summit and this involves a rough walk until Forest roads near the
upper part of the fell can be utilised. The climbing on Christianbury
Crags is more extensive than at first meets the eye. Many routes
have been climbed over the years but nothing has been recorded.
The crags can also be approached more easily from the North,
particularly if one has a key to the forest gates.

BLACK STANTLING   O.S. SHEET 86   G.R. 594799
This is a small crag of absolutely superb, Fell Sandstone with a
maximum height of 10 metres. If it were not for its remoteness, it
would be a popular bouldering venue on account of the potential
for hard problems. Black Stantling faces South West, overlooking
the upper valley of the White Lyne on the same edge as Christianbury Crags, clearly visible to the North West. Only one route has
been recorded: The Nose Right-Hand (S). This climbs the obvious
crack to the right of the jutting nose of the Main Buttress and was
climbed by Mick Johnson. This is definitely a crag for Mountain
Biking climbers as good forest roads lead from The Flatt via The
Loan gently uphill until just after the line of low outcrops known as

Slaty Crag, at a slight bend in the road, a little valley strikes off to the East. This and the ensuing wall and fences lead to the hollow where the crag lies.

COMB CRAG   O.S. SHEET 86   G.R. 591649

This tiny outcrop of good quality Sandstone faces West on the spur of a meander on the River Irthing. It is reached by following the Lanercost road from Brampton to Banks. From Banks, turn right on the narrow road parallel to the Roman Wall and follow this for one mile to Wall Bowers. A Public Right Of Way descends from here in a Southerly direction to the Irthing Gorge. There is a prominent spur with crags on both sides. Comb Crag is on the right hand side as one faces the river. About six climbs were made here in the early 80's (4c-5c).

LEAP QUARRY   O.S. SHEET 86   G.R. 594650

This South-West facing Sandstone quarry is quite impressive and may be worth a look. It is about half a mile upstream of Comb Crag on the same bank.

WALLTOWN CRAGS   O.S. SHEET 86   G.R. 677666

North facing crags of the Whin Sill. These extensive crags are similar to Peel Crags but in a relatively undeveloped state. Several climbs have been made here, but these have been a "Labour Of Love" for those involved as they require a lot of cleaning and trundling.

CAWFIELDS CRAG   O.S. SHEET 86   G.R. 716667

These extensive Whinstone crags have received quite a lot of attention and continue to yield climbs of a similar genre to Peel Crags. There are about fifteen routes up to HVS and all are the work of Mick Johnson

BISHOP HILL QUARRY   O.S. SHEET 86   G.R. 613588

A Limestone quarry consisting of a West facing steep, slabby wall and at the right-hand end, a taller overhanging buttress. This is best reached from the A689 two miles East of Hallbankgate, by turning off this road into the village of Tindale. A track across some waste land leads to a parking place by some cottages. A Public Right Of Way leads Westwards to the quarry, a distance of 300 metres. This quarry has always attracted attention but promises to return in good weather have always gone adrift. A bit of effort and some fixed gear might result in some just O.K routes.

LAMBLEY VIADUCT QUARRIES   O.S. SHEET 86   G.R. 675584

Situated directly under Lambley Viaduct (worth a visit in its own right!) are two quarries, one on the upstream side and a bigger one on the downstream side. The rock is Whinstone and the lines are stunning. The rock however leaves much to be desired. Some climbs have been made here and no doubt climbers will keep returning just to satisfy themselves that another visit will definitely not be justifiable.

SWALLOW CRAGS   O.S. SHEET 86   G.R. 742690

Along line of North facing and lichenous Sandstone Crags about a
mile West-North-West of Crag Lough. The crag is best reached by
turning off the B6318 at Twice Brewed and following the road past
Steel Rigg car park until after a further half a mile a farm road on the
right leads to Gibbs Hill Farm. Permission to park here and to visit
the crags is usually freely given, providing one asks! The crags are a
few hundred metres due West of Gibbs Hill. Jim Fotheringham,
Mick Johnson and friends have cleaned and climbed a number of
good routes here, but nothing has been recorded.

DOVE CRAG   O.S. SHEET 86   G.R. 795697

A steep Sandstone crag facing North-West across Broomlee Lough.
Dove Crag is quite impressive but the rock is fairly soft and friable
in places. It is best visited in combination with Queens Crag by
walking due South from Queens for about half a mile to Broomlee
Lough. Alternatively it can be reached from the B6318 at Moss
Kennels via the Roman Wall. The crag was developed by Carlisle
based climbers when Queens was developed and two decent
routes have been made:
Route 1 (HVS 5a)
Climb the overhanging wall right of the big roof.
Route 2 (HVS 5b)
Climb the wide crack to the left of the roof.

3   EDEN VALLEY NORTH

To the West of the M6 between Carlisle and Penrith lies a truly delectable and yet relatively unknown area where the mighty Eden flowing uniquely Northwards has cut a tremendous gorge through the beautiful, wooded, sandstone hills. The scenery is further enhanced by the looming proximity of the beautiful Geltsdale Fells whose flanks provide small outcrops of compact limestone. The crags at Armathwaite and Lazonby are the most famous in the area, each providing contrasting, excellent climbing on good sandstone. The setting is unique, and to walk along the footpaths by this beautiful river is almost as good as the climbing itself. Nearer to Penrith and easily accessible are Scratchmere Scar and Cowrake Quarry. The former provides short, varied climbs on good rock in a fine position whilst the latter whilst useful for the locals is best regarded as somewhere to "work-out" rather than a serious venue for visiting climbers.In Armathwaite, the Dukes Head provides good meals and a climbing shop and new routes book can be found at Eden Valley Centre in Ainstable, the next village.

ARMATHWAITE   O.S. SHEET 86   NY.505 452

"The steepness of the crag,the in-situ sand pit and the hungry midges make this an idyllic spot."
D.Jones.Rock Climbing in Britain 1984

SITUATION AND CHARACTER
This outcrop of excellent quality sandstone is properly called Coombs Crag. It is situated on the East bank of the River Eden five hundred metres upstream of the bridge at Armathwaite. Its situation in beautiful woodland on the banks of the Eden is outstanding, a factor adding charm to the the excellent climbing of all grades to be found here.It has long been recognised as a wet weather alternative to the Lakes and even in the depths of winter, can provide sheltered climbing. It faces West and so gets its fair share of sunshine (always assuming Cumbria gets its fair share!) The climbing ranges from longer, two pitch climbs to fierce bouldering. The situations are fine and thanks to a caring population of local climbers, litter and other squalid mess are unknown.

We all hope it will stay that way.

The crag is composed of Penrith Sandstone, a red, desert sandstone of Permian Age and because of its wind borne origin, cross-bedding is everywhere evident. Differential weathering of these beds and the ubiquitous "Armathwaite Pockets" are responsible for the best of the harder routes.The pleasing thing about climbing here is however, the changing character, as one moves from section to section of the crag.

The obvious Overhanging Wall which rises out of the sandy river beach at the left end of the main crag was at one time quarried as

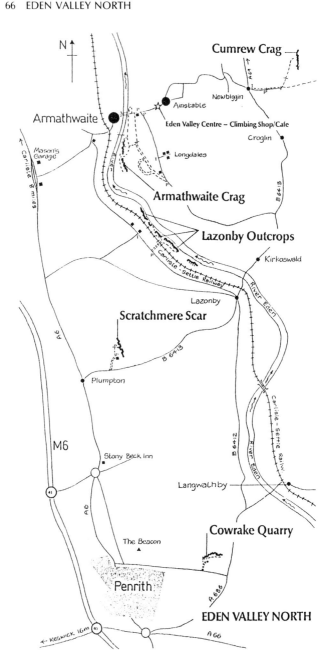

was the rock in the alcove of Hetherington's Bay some 30 metres to the right.This has produced more square-cut holds, where a thuggish approach helps.In contrast, the Central Buttress extending rightwards from Hetherington's Bay has rock more akin to that found on the E. Northumberland crags and produces "Classic" easy and middle-grade climbs on good weathered holds.

Further right again,the Red Buttress and Final Section climbs are on softer rock using the tendon-searing omnipresent pockets and wrinkles.

On all the climbs the friction is good although not as solidly abrasive as Northumberland Sandstone or as secure. A soft rag is useful for dusting holds.

A problem that the softness of the rock and its popularity has thrown up is erosion. Bouldering out moves at the base of the crag and traversing has led to heavy wear and a return to top-roping could certainly help.

Top-roping however brings attendant problems such as grooving in the top of the crag.To avoid this long slings and careful rigging are essential. **It is also recommended that groups under instruction find an alternative venue – there are plenty nearby. If Group usage is unavoidable then leaders must "do their homework" and get to know the crag thus avoiding the kind of situations where leaders blithely allow their charges to abseil down the line of splendidly delicate routes,kicking off crucial holds and smearing mud. Finally, will leaders ensure that soft shoes are worn rather than vibrams,tricounis or crampons.**

On a more serious note, **the greatest damage to the crag has been done by a small minority of climbers who seem to think that seemingly blank faces can be wire-brushed into submission.** Such egocentric quests can only hinder the pursuit of difficulty in the succeeding generations.In any case we should set a better example to the many talented youngsters who frequent the crag and who as yet malleable may wish to ape their elders.

Finally with regard to the hardest leads at the crag:
The style of the first ascent in most cases involved abseil inspection and top-rope practice prior to the lead.This should be borne in mind by anyone attempting an 'on sight' lead.In addition the **protection on the majority of hard routes is often absent or illusory.**

APPROACHES AND ACCESS
Read fully and carefully
The crag is best approached from the village of Armathwaite which is reached by following the signs from the A6 at Mason's Garage(this is on the only section of dual-carriageway between Carlisle and Penrith.Both of these towns are some 10 miles from this point.)The bridge crossing the Eden in Armathwaite is the focal point of the village and a few cars can be parked on the side nearest the Fox and Pheasant Inn. A squeeze stile in the parapet of the downstream side of the bridge nearest the Fox and Pheasant and a short flight of steps leads to a path which via a stile gets one under the bridge and along a good path going in a upstream direction.

The situation with regard to this path is at present somewhat strained as the owner of the land over which the path passes has over-zealously erected ugly notices to the effect that the path is not a Right of Way and that LOCALS can apply for permission to use it. Even more recently Mr Stapleton has erected a padlocked gate barring access. Many people rightly or wrongly gained the path after the erection of the gate, by climbing over the parapet of the bridge on the upstream side. The landowner then took the law into his own hands and instructed a local craftsman to construct a double row of eight inch, sharpened, metal spikes. These were installed into the wall below the parapet, hidden from view. The consequences of a hapless child, climber or animal vaulting over the wall onto this "trap" are unthinkable. This act was reported and the landowner had to instruct his fellow to remove it. This situation has irritated locals as they and their predecessors have walked this path for decades past without let or hinderance.To ask for permission to walk it would set a dangerous precedent tantamount to an admission that no rights have ever existed. **Climbers remember that access has been negotiated, be firm but civil. Exercise your rights.It is a simple matter to climb around the end of the padlocked gate.** This path forks when one is above an impressive rapid; a natural weir where the Eden crosses the Armathwaite Dyke, a spectacular intrusion of Quartz-Dolerite.

At this point one can descend rightwards to the river and continue upstream to reach the FACES. Alternatively if the MAIN CLIFF is your destination,continue along the left fork which goes above the crags of the Faces for a short distance before descending sharply via rocky steps to river level. As one faces the river, the Overhanging wall is on your right whilst the Main Cliff is on your left, upstream. A good path follows the bank of the river upstream and from it, it is possible to view all parts of the crag.

It must be pointed out that the crag can be reached by following the footpath which leads through the yard of the Fox and Pheasant Inn. This path is followed until a stile gives access to the forest road.A track on the right leads to the top of the 'Faces Section'.To the right is the weir whilst to the left are the descent steps between Stinkhorn Buttress and the Overhanging Wall.

Coombs Crag is on Forestry Commission land but the previous owner retained the Sporting Rights and so the situation here is somewhat different to that on F.C. land. Access agreements are constantly under review and the result of much hard work and negotiation with other parties involved. It is essential that climbers observe the usual courtesies with regard to other landusers, particularly fishermen and shooters. Shooting takes place about three or four times in the season in Coombs Wood, usually on a Friday or Saturday so it is safer to stay near the crag when shoots are in progress. **DOGS MUST NOT BE BROUGHT TO THE CRAG.**

HISTORICAL

The crags were discovered in the Summer of 1973 by Alistair Yarrow and Stewart Wilson.During this summer,the partnership made ascents of many fine climbs in the easier grades following natural lines. A Big Hand was the first, soon to be followed by Glenwillie Grooves, Bullgine Run and the excellent Flasherman.They were joined by Roy May and Ron Kenyon and produced Barnacle Bill and

Codpiece but had to resort to pegs for aid on these climbs. At this time it was usual to ascend routes of this standard from bottom to top without prior cleaning or inspection.The end of this phase of development saw ascents of the bold Monkeyhanger and the steep Time and Motion Man. By the end of 1973 the secret was out and a group of talented young local lads inspired by the forceful approach of Jeff Lamb brought new ideas of what was possible and new approaches.This period saw a change of approach to new routes in that they were inspected, cleaned and top-roped prior to being led.

In this period, Jeff Lamb put up three important climbs; Cally Crack named after the Caledonian Inn in Carlisle which was the meeting place of the Carlisle lads at this time, the incredible Dome Slab which is anything but a slab and the ferocious Exorcist.Some suggested that The Exorcist be named Joiners Arms as that was Jeff's occupation.The protection peg placed on the first ascent is still there now and sees good service even though a youthful Ron Fawcett climbed it without.Lamb's contribution to the development of fine hard climbing on the crag also included the beautiful line of Paper Moon and a lead of what he called New Moon Direct, which is now described as New Moon, a desperate route! Jeff's contribution can only be approached by Pete Whillance whom it is rumoured used to climb the steep rocks, alone on Winter nights by the light of a headtorch in the pre-climbing wall era. Whillance in his way contributed climbs of a more subtle nature up the bold slabs and walls that abound on the crag.These routes although inspected and top-roped prior to being led, typify his boldness and technical mastery and at the time would rank with the best outcrop leads anywhere in the country. The intricate Free and Easy led finally to the commitment to lead the precarious Wafer Thin. It is doubtful whether these last two climbs have received an "on sight" lead or even a second ascent by any approach! In this period Whillance produced The High Girdle which girdles the crag's Final Section, an outrageously bold undertaking. The Dome was also breached by others and Talking To Trees was climbed by Pete Botterill to provide a fine companion route to Dome Slab. In 1977 the Overhanging Wall was breached in two more places by Phil Rigby: Blast Off and The Orbit represented a move towards extremely steep and serious climbing on rock whose stability left a lot to be desired. On the first ascent of The Orbit a number of capable seconds declined to follow Phil's lead on account of a healthy fear of the potential for a bone-crunching pendulum. Throughout this period test pieces were top-roped such as Blue Lugs named after the landlord of a local pub and Lamb soon led this. Another ascent of this period worthy of mention is Andy's Slab by Andy Hunter.It has kept many climbers occupied for a lot of time and even with sticky rubber doesn't seem any easier,in fact its alternative name; Once In A Blue Moon, sums it all up. The 1980's saw the addition of various useful climbs but nothing of particular note apart from the ascent in 1986 of The Viennese Oyster by Geoff Brown and Hughie Loughran which breaks out right of Erection and climbs the wall above in a fine position. Geoff went on to solo the incredible wall left of Free and Easy after inspection and cleaning,

ARMATHWAITE CRAGS

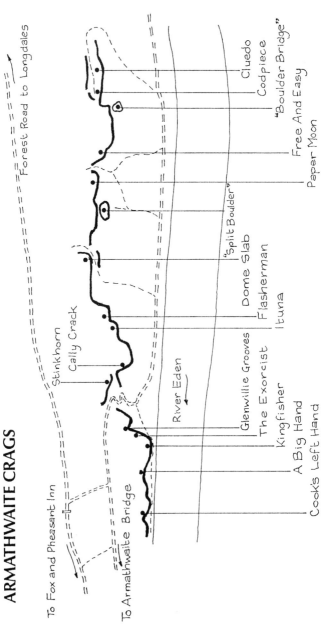

to give One Hand Clapping.The winter of 86/87 was the culmination of the quest to wring from the crag every last secret.In this last phase of development Alan Greig and Ray Parker; erstwhile partner of Pete Whillance inspired all and sundry to push the limits, top-roping many of the last problems with no small success. Unfortunately in a few cases hitherto futuristic creases and crannies in the rock's defences have been wire brushed to produce in the soft rock, holds that can be climbed at today's standards; a worthless act in that it denies future climbers the opportunity for technical satisfaction.Will they then brush out the brushed holds to create even harder problems as standards continue to rise?

THE CLIMBS

These are described section by section and from left to right as one faces the crag.The Faces section is most easily reached from the weir and because of its relative independence from the rest of the crag,it will be described first.

THE FACES SECTION

Easily approached from the weir,in all but high-water conditions,by following the edge of the river upstream.An idyllic situation,some good easy climbs and some poor rock has ensured its lack of popularity.The main features of this section are two indentations or bays,the first,nearest the weir is Botany Bay whilst the second Faces Bay is remarkable for the strange and rare carvings on its walls.The carvings are of faces and a salmon,whilst high up is a beautifully executed inscription, a mis-quotation from Isaac Walton's "Compleat Angler": "O the fisher's Gentle life etc . . ." Also nearby at the start of A Big Hand is an inscription of much greater antiquity, possibly Roman in origin.The carvings and the later inscriptions are almost certainly the work of William Mounsey, scholar,traveller and local gentleman of the last century. Other examples of his work can be seen at the Caves of St.Constantine at Wetheral and on the long lost Jew Stone at the source of the Eden in Mallerstang.

1   F.B.S.J.   10m   V.D.
Start at the foot of the left arete of Botany Bay behind a tree.Climb the face behind the tree leaving this with some reluctance on a voyage of discovery up the rock above on good holds.

2   Boomerang   12m   VS   4b
Start at the foot of a shallow right-slanting groove directly below the obvious deep chimney of Aborigine.Climb the groove and then Hand-Traverse left onto the arete.Climb this to the top.

A more direct start to this arete is provided by:'

3   Blank's Expression   4m   VS   5a
Start at some roots just right of F.B.S.J.Climb the difficult left-curving groove to join Boomerang at the arete

4   Aborigine   12m   HVS   4c
Starts right of Boomerang at a slightly overhanging scoop a few metres below a small cave.Climb to the cave then move left into the chimney. Follow this until moves right lead into the groove and the top.

The prominent twin cracks which converge some distance up the right wall of the bay are:

5   Cook's Left Hand   12m   VS   4b
Climb the right-slanting crack to a hard move into a deep groove.Follow this to the top.A good climb.

6   Cook's Crack   12m   VS   4b
Climb the steep crack to the right of the last climb.Move left into the groove of Cook's Left Hand with difficulty and finish as for that climb

7   Cook's Apron   5m   VS   4c
Climb the centre of the face between the cracks.Worthwhile.

8   Cook's Tour   12m   NL   5b
Climb the centre of the impressive wall to the right of Cook's Right Hand.

The next few climbs are a few metres right of Botany Bay in the smaller Faces Bay.The first route starts below a corner just left of a carved salmon:

9   Blockbuster   12m   HS   4a
Climb the steep corner past a large dubious block.Move right and into another groove.From a ledge below a roof either move right and to the top on unstable rock or safer, go to the left of the roof and climb to the top on better rock. Not an outstanding route!

A poor route called The Scroll climbs the face to the left of the fine inscription but as it uses the inscribed area it is suggested that climbers' avoid it.

10   A Big Hand   12m   S
A very pleasant but dirty slab,very low in its grade but serious on account of a lack of protection.

Starts at the back corner of Faces Bay.Layback up the corner passing a small 'neb' to a ledge.Climb up a short way until an obvious traverse line is followed to the right for a couple of metres.A delicate step up on poor handholds leads one to the trailing branches of a large oak.Thankfully these lead one to a leafy bower and security.

This route marks the end of any worthwhile climbing on the Faces Section.It is possible to reach the Overhanging Wall and the Main Cliff by traversing at river level upstream.This is exciting and introduces unexpected elements like deep water and lurking Chub.It seems to hold a fatal attraction for well-dressed, water-loving picnickers! Be warned!

THE OVERHANGING WALL

This popular area, which is really the southern or upstream end of the Faces Section is best reached by returning to the weir and striking up onto the good path which runs above the Faces Section.Follow the good path in an upstream direction for perhaps 100 metres until after passing a narrow exposed section with an excellent view upriver,the path descends via some rough steps to arrive again at the riverside.The right fork of the path as one faces the river, leads in a few metres, past some easy slabs to a fine sandy beach below the Overhanging Wall.The left fork of the path goes under the Main Cliff. The Overhanging Wall section consists of an overhanging wall of rock to the left of the prominent corner;

Glenwillie Grooves.To the right of this corner is a wall bounded on its right by a nice arete.The section peters out around the corner from the arete with some pleasant slabs.

11   Kingfisher   16m   VD   *
Steep and satisfying and with big holds.It has provided several leaders who don't know left from right with an unexpected swim! Starts to the left of the tree which is left of the sawn-off stump below the left arete of the Overhanging wall..Climb up to the LEFT of the tree which guards access to the open groove.An easy corner is followed by a steeper corner and the top.Tree belay.

12   Kaleidoscope Eyes   15m   E1   5b
Start from the top of the sawn stump at the left-hand end of Overhanging Wall. Move up and leftwards to a step below the steep arete.Climb the arete direct to finish on the ledge of Time and Motion Man.

13   Grey Duster   15m   E1   6a   **
An entertaining climb with a steep start. Start 2 metres right of the sawn stump which is just right of the arete.Climb the centre of the bulging wall on finger-caressing edges and layaways into a very shallow groove.A good hold on the left enables the final crack to be viewed and climbed.Finish up the groove above a good ledge as for Time and Motion Man.

14   The Arete   15m   E1   6c   **
Another little gem which should guarantee hours of fun! Starts 1m right of Grey Duster below an overhung rib.
Levitate up to the conspicuous little blackened pocket at 3 metres,rejoice and continue on better holds to finish directly up the upper continuation of the arete to the ledge below the finish of Time and Motion Man.Finish as for Time and Motion Man

15   Time and Motion Man   16m   E1   5b   **
The crag's infamous, "Nasty VS". A strenuous,awkward and thought-provoking climb for all would-be "VS Flashers". Start in the damp alcove just right of the undercut rib of The Arete.Move up and leftwards with great difficulty and some contortions onto a very narrow wall under some small square-cut overhangs.Better holds lead to jugs below a little bulge guarding a fine groove.Enter the groove with some relief and exit almost immediately on its left wall to gain a good ledge. (Friend protection here).Move left and climb a slight groove to an awkward finish.It is possible to finish straight up about 1 metre right of the ordinary finish at another slim corner.

There are many good problems in this area, notably traverses. A particularly good traverse is to start at Kingfisher and move right to Time and Motion man. This involves some technical fingerwork. To reverse the same is desperate. The traverse in both directions from Time And Motion Man to Glenwillie Grooves is pumpy and good for the soul. Many more sequences are left for the individual to discover.

16   The Orbit   25m   E4   5c/6a
A committing and serious route which girdles Overhanging Wall from bottom left to top right. Start as for Time and Motion Man.Climb into the prominent groove at 5 metres. (Runners can be arranged on the ledge of Time and Motion Man above left). Move

out across the right wall of the groove onto ever steepening rock until one can make an ascending traverse to the good ledge which crosses the face at two-thirds height.(Junction with The Exorcist.)From this ledge,traverse right,moving down slightly (to protect these moves it is possible to flick a sling over a flat-topped spike above and to the right) until a hand-traverse leads down into the fine corner of Glenwillie Grooves.Finish up this.

17 Blue Lugs 18m E5 5c   *
Starts below the painted initials WT.Climb the bulge strenuously on good holds to reach and follow the obvious line of a hairline fault.At the top overhangs move out left with difficulty and make a strenuous exit.

18 The Exorcist 18m E4 5c   ***
This route put the "arm" in Armathwaite. An excellent line, steep and compelling on good clean rock. Starts where the Overhanging Wall abuts on the right to form the steep corner which marks the direct start of Glenwillie Grooves.A hard pull onto a ledge leads up to a peg at 5 metres. Move out with trepidation to a pocket on the right.A sequence of strenuous and technical moves lead back left then straight up.Rising doubts as to the peg's solidity urge one upwards to a good ledge.From the sanctuary of the ledge a bulge is climbed into the top groove.It is best to exit on the left.

19 Blast Off 20m E4 6a   *
Steep situations, indifferent protection and funny rock make this climb a very serious undertaking.The line is not as fine as that of the Exorcist. Starts immediately right of The Exorcist where the Overhanging Wall meets the slab at a corner.Ascend the pleasant corner of the Direct start to Glenwillie Grooves for about 3 metres until the impending crack on the left wall can be climbed.From the top of the crack traverse left into a shallow niche.The bulging rock above leads to the ledge common with The Exorcist.Move up and right to a roof conspicuous by an eroded hole on its underside. Climb out steeply using this hole and continue steeply to better holds.Finish via a jutting prow on the left. Warning:The rock above the ledge should be treated with suspicion.

20 Glenwillie Grooves 18m HS 4b   **
A very good climb indeed and popular.The crux is short, sharp and very safe in a fine position right at the top. Start from a tar-spattered ledge 3m right of the corner of Blast Off. Climb the wall just right of a thin crack until a good ledge is gained on the left.The slab above and right of the ledge leads delicately to a foothold next to a sheaf of saplings.Climb the wall to the left of the saplings and finish with a steep pull onto a stance below the final corner.Place a very large nut, don't forget to clip in, then spread your legs, layback and enjoy it. Caution:The slope leading up to the tree belay needs care!

21 Glenwillie Grooves Direct 16m MVS 4b
Hardly an improvement on the normal route.Rock needs care.
Start at the foot of the steep corner as for Blast Off.Climb directly up to the small ledge and finish up the crux of Glenwillie Grooves.

To the right of Glenwillie Grooves the rock is less attractive,nevertheless one or two useful climbs exist.

22 Harry's Arete 16m E2 5b
Starts just right of the tar-spattered ledge of Glenwillie Grooves at
the foot of a narrow groove. Climb this groove and from large
footholds,swing awkwardly left onto the arete.A move around the
arete leads onto an easier angled slab.Finish as for Harry's Groove.

23 Harry's Groove 16m HS 4b
Start 4m right of the narrow groove of Harry's Arete at a shallow
groove just left of a prominent,undercut beak of rock. Climb the
groove towards a loose break in a bulge.Move over this into a
heathery recess and follow this up right to a ledge.Move left along
the ledge and layback the stepped corner.

*The crag to the right of Harry's groove is a pleasant wall capped by a
small roof.The blunt arete which bounds this wall on the right
marks the start of the next climb:*

24 Smiling Faces 16m VS 4b   *
Climb the blunt arete on small but good holds until a hard move
enables one to step up onto a slab.Follow the slab to a ledge below
a wide, bottomless crack.Follow this to the top.Strenuous.

*The crag now turns a corner and loses height.The slabby rocks can
be climbed almost everywhere, but a good easy line exists:*

25 The Thirty-Nine Steps 13m VD   *
Starts 2 metres right of the arete behind a birch tree. Climb the easy
wall on good holds until a short groove leads onto a triangular
ledge.Mantleshelf onto a higher bigger ledge in a fine position.The
short slab to the right is ascended until steep moves up the wall
above lead to a pull out at a solid tree. Satisfying. Variation:From
the triangular ledge it is possible to climb the rib on the right to
finish at the same place.Only slightly harder.

The descent steps now divide the crag.

THE MAIN CLIFF

*This is the main escarpment of the crags.It extends for about 200m
above the riverside path and is divided into six separate sec-
tions.The first section is Stinkhorn Buttress which is the first buttress of rock across the descent steps from Overhanging Wall. The
six sections described from left to right are:*

STINKHORN BUTTRESS
HETHERINGTON'S BAY
CENTRAL BUTTRESS
DOME SLAB
RED BUTTRESS
THE FINAL SECTION.

STINKHORN BUTTRESS

*A few metres upstream of Overhanging wall and a short scramble
up an easy rake leads to a grassy ledge below the obvious wide
crack at the right-hand end of this steep and generally featureless
face.*

*All of the climbs start below this crack which is the line of the
original climb; Stinkhorn.*

26   Herbie   10m   VS   4c
Climb the bulge just left of the crack of Stinkhorn until a comforting flake can be followed leftwards to a gap.The continuation is steeper and eventually it is easier to move right to finish at a tree.

27   Meat Is Murder   10m   NL   5c
A steep climb which avoids the real issue of the prominent arete. Climb the steep crack of Stinkhorn until holds on the left wall can be used.Pull onto the arete to a sharp flake.Climb the rippled bulge above the flake and move up and left around the corner and gain a ledge

28   Astral Wall   10m   NL   5c
This steep climb follows the line of very fine cracks up the face to the right of the arete. Climb the crack as for Stinkhorn,then embark onto the steep wall and climb it about 1-1.5 m right of the arete.

29   Stinkhorn   10m   S
Phalls short of its initial promise! Climb the obvious bulging crack to a good ledge.The continuation is disappointing.

HETHERINGTON'S BAY

This popular little hollow lies at the foot of the crag just above the riverside path.It is really the left hand side of the large and complex Central Buttress.The back of the Bay has a steep corner with an undercut left-slanting slab above. The right-hand wall is vertical and high above is the thin overhanging Cally Crack which finishes on a spacious ledge known as Heugh Chare.

Hetherington's Bay is a popular bouldering area with reasonable landings.

There are particularly good strenuous traverses across the lower walls of the Bay whilst interesting problems find their way through the slim grooves to the left of the corner.The steep wall right of the corner has been climbed but is hardly a boulder problem,whilst the right-slanting arete on the extreme right is good but with an awkward finish.

30   Petit Mal   10m   VD
Starts at the left-hand end of the Bay about 1m left of the flat rock ledge bearing shot holes.

Climb the groove by the line of least resistance to gain a flake.Follow this to gain a good ledge.Tree belay.

31   Nosescratcher   16m   HS
A serious climb on doubtful rock.Care needed to protect the second. Start at a low ledge bearing shot hole opposite a Birch tree. Climb onto this ledge and step up and right onto the slab.Climb up and right across the slab to a blunt arete.Follow this on poor rock to a ledge.Belay up and left at a crack.Friends adviseable or move further left to trees.Scramble off down to the left below Stinkhorn.

32   Joe Soap's Corner   16m   VS   4b
A good line but not a brilliant climb on account of poor rock.
Starts in the corner of the Bay.Climb straight up the corner which is pleasant.The left-slanting line above is followed with care to reach the ledge and belays as for Nosescratcher.

33   Cally Crack   12m   E3   5b/c   *
A very steep climb,intimidating and bold.Start in the corner of the Bay. Climb Joe Soap's until moves can be made out right to the foot of the crack.Climb the wall just right of the crack or the crack itself.

33a   Indians Revenge   NL   6b
This very steep and strenuous climb provides an alternative finish to the upper part of Cally Crack. Climb the latter until the wall on the left of the crack can be climbed.

34   Jeff's Wall   8m   E3   6a/b   *
Climb the centre of the steep wall right of the corner.A variety of finishes exist.

CENTRAL BUTTRESS

This is the complex buttress nearest the riverside path.It is about 27 metres high and is bounded on the left by the overhanging arete which forms the right edge of Hetherington's Bay.The right-hand boundary of Central Buttress is a steep grassy gully guarded by a short wall just right of the very impressive overhanging arete; Erection Arete.

Central Buttress has a long grassy ledge at 13m with a big Oak on the right.Above the Oak is the big,juggy slab of Bullgine Run. Above the left-hand end of the long ledge and 5m higher is another comfortable ledge;Heugh Chare,again having good tree belays and the start of The Schnuck.Further right,Central Buttress becomes shorter but three well-defined grooves provide some excellent climbs including the classic; Flasherman.Central Buttress provides some excellent climbing in the lower and middle grades and it is hoped that more use will see these revert to their former pristine condition.

DESCENTS: The climbs on Central Buttress end at a narrow path, slippery when wet.This path can be followed above Stinkhorn Buttress and then down a steep grassy slope to meet the main path above the descent steps leading to the Overhanging Wall.Alternatively follow the narrow path in an upstream direction until the steep earthy gully to the south of Domed Slab can be descended.

35   Princess Anne's New Ring   26m   S
Quite a good climb. The first pitch is the crux. Start at the foot of the little slab below the overhanging arete of Hetherington's Bay.

1.13m
Climb the 3 metre slab then move diagonally leftwards above the overhanging arete on shelving rock to a point below the Oak tree on Heugh Chare ledge above.From here,bear right until the wall on the left can be climbed to the Oak.Belay.

2.13m
Climb the corner at the back of the ledge to a deep groove. Swing out left to a good ledge. The corner above leads to the finish.

36   The Monkeyhanger   35m   HVS   **
An excellent climb, particularly serious on the top pitch which is in a fine position. The finish can be dirty! Starts as for Princess Anne's at the foot of the little slab below the problem arete on the right edge of Hetherington's Bay.

1.16m   4a
Climb the slab rightwards for 3 metres,then move right onto a wall

of good rock by a small beech.Climb past this to the left end of the long,grassy ledge.Climb the steep wide crack on fantastic holds to a tree belay on the Heugh Chare ledge.

2.19m   4c
Climb the short overhanging wall at the back of the ledge to gain a shelf.Traverse right for about 4 metres and step up to another ledge.Some indifferent protection can be arranged before stepping up and right in a very exposed position onto the front of the upper wall.The slab above is awkward to finish.Lichen can be a problem in damp conditions!

37   The Schnuck   14m   VS   4c
This provides a good steep alternative last pitch to either Princess Anne's or The Monkeyhanger. Start on Heugh Chare and climb the steep wall to gain the flat shelf as for The Monkeyhanger. The steep wall is now climbed on flat holds.The ensuing narrow groove leads to a small ledge on the left and a tree belay above.

38   The Bullgine Run   30m   VD   ★★
A superb and serious top pitch with a definite crux makes this a classic of its grade.It uses the big rightward-slanting slab in the upper half of Central Buttress. Start at the toe of the Central Buttress below a couple of mossy breaks leading onto some right-slanting ledges below a big Oak.

1.10m
Climb either break to the ledges.Follow these rightwards to just below the big Oak on the long ledge above. Ascend boldly up a series of small flakes just left of the tree or alternatively creep rightwards and then sidle left to an undignified grapple with the tree. Belay.

2.20m
The obvious juggy slab behind the tree is now followed easily up rightwards to a steepening.Climb this on awkwardly-placed holds to a detached horizontal block. "Walk the Plank" along this block to the right. Keep moving right until an easy gully leads left to a tree.Belay.
WARNING: Beware of loose blocks when scrambling up the gully.

2a   The Crack Finish   S
Climb the crack above and right of the "Plank".A direct but illogical variation.

39   Victory   V   18m   E2   5b
An unpopular variation finish to The Bullgine Run in an impressive position. Starting from the big Oak on the long ledge 13m up the face climb the steep wall to the left of the slab of The Bullgine Run. A ledge is reached at 9 metres. Climb the V-groove above and finish just to the right of The Monkeyhanger.
Variation Finish: E2   5b
Climb the overhanging crack to the right of the V-groove.

40   Zephyr   22m   VD
Another variation top pitch to The Bullgine Run. A much better climb than it appears although little of it is apparent from below! Start at the big Oak at the right-hand end of the long ledge. Step right from the Oak along the long ledge until a scruffy corner just left of a smooth slab can be reached.Step into and out of the corner

in favour of the slab on the right.Climb this diagonally rightwards until it abuts against a break in the steep wall above. Climb the wall delicately to a ledge on the right.Broken rock above leads to a final steep wall which provides a pleasant but avoidable finish.

41 Ituna 30m S   *

A much better climb than appearances would suggest as not much is apparent from below. It follows a fine gangway slab to the left of and parallel with Flasherman and provides mild, friction climbing in an exhilarating position. Seven metres right of Bullgine Run, right of and above a small cave/recess at ground level is a block embedded in the ground below a shallow corner with a smooth right wall. This marks the start. Bridge the corner and follow a traverse right to a ledge on the arete. Continue up, climbing the clean right-hand corner to an awkward finish on a good ledge. The fine slabby gangway is followed to the top to finish at the same point as Flasherman by a downward pointing small Oak.

42 Douber 25m HS 4a

Not a very popular climb but it certainly has its attractions if you can be bothered to seek tham out. Certainly worthwhile.
Start at the foot of the blunt and dirty rib four metres right of the corner of Ituna. Climb the short rib to an awkward finish at the junction with Ituna. The cracked groove above and left leads up the buttress, always with interest, to the top.

Up to the right and around a corner one arrives at a very open and interesting face which is remarkable for its fine rock architecture a fine towering arete on the right and a gigantic block overhang to the left of the arete, whose appearance has nothing whatsoever to do with the choice of route names in this area. An Open Book corner marks the line of the superb Flasherman.

43 Flasherman 26m VS 4b   ***

A classic! One of the best sandstone climbs anywhere. Low technicality but a runout crux, ensures an adventurous experience for middle-grade climbers. Start in a cave below an overhang below the big Open-Book corner. Climb diagonally right up the slabby right wall of the cave and pull over the bulge to a block on big holds. Step left and enter the corner and follow it to the large flake at the top. Step right on the flake (runners) and climb boldly up the shallow groove to good holds. Move left to finish at the downward pointing Oak as for Ituna.

43a The Direct Finish HVS 5a

From the top of the big corner instead of moving right, climb the very steep continuation corner direct on small holds.

44 Erection 26m HVS 5a   ***

Yet another fantastic experience, heightened further by a lack of protection at the top. Start a few metres right of Flasherman at a steep wall directly in line with the prominent block overhangs. Climb the wall and then more easily move up the overhangs on the right. Jam the obvious right hand crack of the biggest one and via a contortion attain the top of the flake. The shallow scoop in the steep wall to the right is climbed with trepidation in a wonderful position.

45   Viennese Oyster   27m   E3   5c   ⋆
An intimidating line which offers varied climbing in superb situations.
Start as for Erection. Climb the steep wall and slab to below the block overhangs. (It is recommended to climb up to fix a high runner in the crack to the right of the 'phallus'). From the level of the lower block overhangs traverse right to an obvious jug on the bulge. Pull over the bulge (strenuous) then step left and move over a small, triangular roof. (PR in situ on right). Reach high and right for good holds. Traverse steeply right and pull round the arete. A few more feet brings one to the top.

  The fine, overhanging arete to the right of Erection is an obvious feature. Separating this from the next section; Dome Slab, is a steep broken wall which runs into a deep open, gully.

46   Erection Arete   Original   22m   NL   5c   ⋆
Start beneath the steep broken wall, just right of the arete and below the gully. Climb the centre of the wall and move up a crack on the left until a left-slanting undercling crack can be followed towards the arete. A hard move up gains a right-slanting break where moves left up the wall gain the top of the arete.

47   Soft Touch   22m   NL   5c   ⋆
Start as for Erection Arete Original. From the top of the broken wall move out left two metres lower down than the undercling crack to gain a flake and pocket. Follow the steep arete to the top.

48   Nurts Way   22m   HVS   5a
Start at the foot of the steep wall below the gully. Climb the wall as for the two previous routes and scramble up the gully to below the steep right-slanting crack on the left wall. Climb this to finish at an Oak tree.

DOME SLAB

This is the clean buttress of pale yellow rock separated from Erection Arete by a steep, dirty wall and ensuing gully. Dome Slab consists of slabs and walls sandwiched between attractive roofs and overhangs and hosts a bevy of quite fearsome climbs. The best descent is via a gentle gully on the upstream end of the buttress. From the foot of the gully an easy ledge slants under the front of the face.

49   Close Encounters   10m   E1   5b/c   ⋆
A very good short route which proves to be harder than it looks.
Start at the left side of the buttress below the right-hand end of the first barrier of overhangs. Climb easily up rightwards to the weakest point in the overhang and reach through to gain a horizontal line of very small holds. Traverse left on these with difficulty until they lead to an easing and jugs. A hard move up leads to a fine flake hold and the final step to the tree.

50   Mellow   14m   NL   5c
Another pleasant route. Start as for Close Encounters and move easily rightwards beyond where this route move up through the bulge. The second tier of overhangs is breached by a left-slanting break. Follow this to attain with difficulty a standing position above the traverse of Close Encounters. Move diagonally leftwards up the slab to finish at the tree.

51   Talking To Trees   14m   E3   5c
An interesting route with an awkward crux right at the top. Start at
the same point as Close Encounters, but continue moving easily
rightwards until the second tier of overhangs can be breached via a
vertical, fluted runnel to reach a large triangular block below the
top overhang. (Runners can be arranged in the crack on top of the
block.) Pull over the bulge awkwardly and struggle up past a small
sapling using a thin flake crack to gain the top.

52   Beyond The Thunder Dome   14m   NL   6a/b
One very hard move. Start below a a rock scar on the lower slab
four metres right of Close Encounters. Climb past the scar and
move up diagonally rightwards to the next break through the
second overhangs, to the right of the vertical runnel of Talking To
Trees. Surmount the overhang and climb direct to the top overhang which is surmounted via desperate moves right up a shallow
slanting flange.

53   Dome Slab   14m   E5   6a   ★★★
Hard, serious and intimidating. Retreat from the crux could prove
to be a nasty experience although the crux itself calls on reserves of
strength and determination not usually brought into play. A 'real'
climb. Protection must be carefully arranged in the block below the
finish of Talking To Trees. Start directly below the widest point of
the top roof at the right side of the buttress. Ascend pleasantly up
the gradually steepening line of shelves and shallow corners to just
below the roof. An extended move up brings a thin crack to hand
which is used to reach out left to the prominent right-trending
flange on the lip. Use this and good but low-placed holds to make
the depressingly difficult crank onto the slab above and reaffirm
your faith in Divine Providence.

DESCENTS

An easy descent gully exists on the upstream side of Dome Slab.
RED BUTTRESS
A few metres right of Dome Slab is the Red Buttress. This consists
of a left-hand very steep wall of soft rock below which is the famous
'Split Boulder'. Further right is a slab seamed with wrinkles and
overlaps. This slab provides some excellent climbs, amongst the
best at the crag. Red Buttress peters out at the descent route on the
right between it and the Final Section.

54   Red Spider   16m   E2   5b
A horrible route and best avoided. Start on the good ledge above
the 'Split Boulder'. Climb out of a little corner and move up and
right on reasonable rock to a ledge below the prominent V-shaped
recess of Red Monkey. Follow the best and soundest line up and
leftwards to reach a tree overhanging the face. It may be preferable
to enter the recess of Red Monkey to fix the good nut runner
located there.

55   Red Monkey   16m   E1   5b   ★
A good climb which deserves greater popularity. The crucial moves
right can be well-protected by a nut in the back of the recess. Start
level with the top of 'Split Boulder' a couple of metres right of Red
Spider below a good short flake in the steep wall. Pull over the

small bulge on excellent holds and climb the fine little wall to an easing below the recess. Enter the recess (runner) and exit via hard moves on the right wall to gain the obvious prow. This finish is somewhat heathery now.

56   Red Lion   11m   HVS   5a
Named after the pub in Armathwaite. A hidden gem. Start as for Red Monkey. Climb up towards the recess but before getting there move rightwards up a lower, parallel diagonal break to finish at the top of the heathery crack.

57   Coombs Crack   8m   HVS   5a
An esoteric experience, at least until a bit more traffic has rid this tremendous classic of its vegetation. It used to be worthwhile.

The buttress now changes character and becomes a steep slab of excellent rock.

58   Wafer Thin   12m   E5   6a/b   ★★
One of the most exacting leads in the area. The crux involves some excrutiating footwork and body placements that would do justice to the Royal Ballet. Start just right of Coombs Crack below a steep, blunt rib with a slab above it. Climb the blunt rib on undercuts until the small flakes on the left can be trodden to gain access to the slab. A series of moves up and slightly leftwards enable one to reach up right to the top break. Finish through a gap in the heather above.

Direct Finish: Climb directly up the slab from the top of the blunt rib. Slightly harder than the original but not as fine.

59   Bad Moon Rising   13m   NL   6b
Start as for Paper Moon about a metre right of Wafer Thin below the left end of the dominating right-curving line. Gain the overlap and make a couple of moves up this before moving left to climb the slab above by a series of hard moves.

60   Paper Moon   13m   E3   5b   ★★★
A magnificent climb. This scary lead is one of the major climbs of the crag and provides continuous interest and difficulty on good rock with a finely-placed crux right at the end. Start below the left end of the dominating curving overlap. Climb up and slightly leftwards to gain the start of the overlap. This is followed rightwards to an intriguing finish which makes good use of a vertical crack to the right whilst gaining a ledge above the overlap.

61   Devil Moon   13m   NL   6b/c
Start as for Paper Moon. Climb up for three metres and where Paper Moon moves left to gain the main feature, move right to an arch and use this to move right to gain a right-facing flake edge. Finish up the final obvious vertical crack of Paper Moon.

62   New Moon   10m   E5   6b   ★
A desperately hard problem, though not as fine as the others hereabouts. Good footwork is again as important an asset as steel-reiforced tendons, but thats obvious isn't it? Start about four metres right of Paper Moon, just left of the thin right-curving crack which is the line of the start of Moondance. Climb out of the recess using a set of undercuts, transfer to the next undercuts above and aim to gain a rounded, knob on the slab above. Finish up Moondance.

63 Moondance 13m HVS 5a
A route which utilises a popular boulder problem for its start. Start at the foot of the short, thin, right curving break. Climb the break until the slab above can be gained. Without recourse to the right, climb the centre of the slab and gain and climb the wide right-facing groove/crack to an awkward finish.

To the right, a shallow gully with tree roots provides an easy way to the top of Red Buttress and climbs on the left end of the Final Section.

THE FINAL SECTION
One of the most popular sections at Armathwaite, this long section commences with the steep wall of Free And Easy, identifiable by its short, thin curving crack near the top. Further right, a large boulder abuts against the face to form a low arch beyond which is the fine arete of Swing Off Sister. The deep corner on the right of this is Barnacle Bill. Attractive slabs steepen into pocketed walls containing Pickpocket and the crag whilst not diminishing in height, becomes less attractive, but nonetheless provides some good pitches before petering out at a small roof just left of the descent route. In the main the rock is excellent and care should be taken to avoid uneccessary wear at the top of climbs.

64 The Mantleshelf 4m 5b
A good little problem. Start at the left end of the buttress in the shadow below a big tree growing from the short wall a few metres up. Hard moves up the small ledges lead to a hard mantleshelf finish just right of the tree. Dirty.

65 Moving Pictures 9m NL 6a/b
Avoids the real issue of the wall but provides a logical enough line. Start at a short corner below and one metre left of the thin crack high on the wall which is the finish to Free And Easy. Climb up this corner and pull onto the slab above. Traverse the sloping ledge leftwards for about three metres until a mantleshelf move brings one below a very shallow scoop. Climb the scoop via a long reach for a poor hold.

66 One Hand Clapping 12m E4 6a   *
A bold climb taking on the challenge of this very "classy" wall. One of the better recent developments. Start as for Moving Pictures. Follow this route to the mantleshelf. Step right until it is possible to climb straight up to a very hard finishing move.

67 Free And Easy 12m E5 6a   ***
An outstanding, absorbing and serious climb requiring technical competence and a cool approach. One of the best routes on the crag. Start below and one metre right of the upper crack. Climb the short wall onto a little ledge and reach good holds in the first break. A hard pull on the next break leads to a rest.Move slightly right onto the sloping holds in the break (wires) and ease up leftwards to use the best of a cluster of pockets to establish oneself on sloping footholds below the top crack. Climb the top crack with rising hopes that are soon shattered as the top is gained. Now finish.

68 Plain Sailing 12m NL 6b   *
A fine pitch of some character and much difficulty. Start 3m right of Free And Easy at a left-facing corner. Climb up the short corner to a

ledge. The vague arete above is climbed first slightly left, then slightly right to two prominent small pockets. Move up and slightly right to finish.

69   Sailing Shoes   12m   NL   6a
Start as for Plain Sailing at the short, left-facing corner. Climb this to a ledge, then ascend the wall above bearing right to an obvious, horizontal overlap. Undercling this and make a desperate move right onto a sloping ledge. Finish up the slab and corner above as for The Crescent.

To the right of this climb is a huge boulder which form a narrow passage between itself and the crag. At the top of the passage a jammed block bridges the gap and forms a tunnel.

70   Mr Bundy's Best Friend   15m NL   6b
Start below the steep wall at the foot of the huge boulder. Climb the wall direct for 3m to gain the centre of the curving shelf of the initial traverse of The Crescent. Climb the wall above just right of the obvious jug which marks the crux of Crescent and gain a line of pockets above and right. Move right from these to a very strenuous finish.

71   The Crescent   13m   E2   5b   ★
A good climb with an intimidating and unprotected crux. Much easier for the tall. Start just left of the tunnel. Climb onto the obvious curving shelf and follow it leftwards for 4m to where the shelf curves up. Sharp but small edges on the wall above provide the means of gaining a good jug. Once gained, pull up and stand up. The slab and corner above are easier.

72   Jelly Terror   9m   E1   5b
A good climb, strenuous but protectable. Start on top of the jammed block below the obvious crack. Climb the slim crack and pass a strenuous bulge. The wider cracks above are easier, but still strenuous. Five metres right of the tunnel the crag bends into a prominent, deep corner capped by a triangular overhang.

73   Swing Out Sister   10m   NL   6a
Start just left of the prominent corner below a well-brushed narrow wall. Climb the centre of the widening wall and using the left arete, gain a cluster of finger pockets. Use these to pull up and swing over the edge of the arete to gain a standing position. Climb the yellow, friable wall above by the line of least resistance.

74   Y-Front   11m   E2   5b   ★
A bold climb on generally positive holds. Start at the foot of the prominent corner. Layback the corner until stopped by the triangular roof. Pull out left to gain side holds and step onto the rib below the hanging cleft. Climb the cleft using holds on the right in horizontal breaks. Near the top, transfer onto the wall left of the cleft and finish at the top of the arete.

75   Barnacle Bill   13m   E1   5b   ★★
A superb classic corner with a delicate and fairly bold crux. Climb the layback corner to the roof. A very fine sequence of moves right under the roof gains the continuation crack which is thin though protectable.

76   Limpet Lil   11m   NL   5c
A minor variant on Barnacle Bill. Climb Barnacle Bill to the roof. Pull

over this to the next horizontal break. Move slightly right and up, to gain a good right-handhold. A long reach now gains the top.

77 Andy's Slab 13m E3 6a   ★
A much tried test-piece. Remarkable for its time, before 'sticky rubber' Start 6m right of Barnacle Bill at the first vertical break in the lower, smooth slab. Climb the break and stand on a very sloping ledge. The next moves require good footwork and follow a tenuous series of scrapes, diagonally right to gain a slight right-trending gangway. Gain the gangway (crux) and swing right onto a left-trending ramp. Follow this to the top.

78 Smear Or Die 12m NL 6b
Start as for Andy's Slab. Follow this until instead of moving right from the sloping ledge, move up and slightly left to a layaway for the right hand at the left-hand end of the obvious curving feature in the centre of the slab. Use this hold to gain a shallow left-facing scoop just right of Barnacle Bill. Finish up Barnacle Bill.

79 Codpiece 12m E3 6a   ★★
Climbed direct this offers a desperately hard climb on poor jams and layaways with difficult to arrange protection from small wires. Start 5m right of Andy's Slab below a prominent flaring crackline which has a slim ramp leading off left at four metres height.Climb the crack direct to a gruntingly strenuous section above the ramp. The finish is difficult and insecure.
Bridging onto the ramp on the left reduces the grade to 5c

80 Codpiece Left-Hand 12m E1 5b   ★
A good climb at the lower end of the grade. Popular. Start as for Codpiece. Climb the crack and enter the ramp by a difficult step up (crux). The ramp above leads to easier climbing up ledges to the top.

81 Pickpocket 10m E3 5c   ★★
A very fine climb of sustained difficulty and interest. Start as for Codpiece. Climb the vertical crack until a line of foot pockets can be traversed right assisted by a difficult handchange and a long reach right. Better holds in more pockets and continuing moves right lead to a handledge in a horizontal slot. Use this to gain the wall above and climb this via a prominent protruberance.

82 Pickpocket Superdirect 9m E3 6a   ★
Four metres right of Codpiece crack and three metres up the face is a left-facing layaway hold. Start below and just right of this. Gain the layaway by a very hard move on low finger pockets. Finish as for Pickpocket.

83 The Black Russian 9m NL 6b
A very hard problem which can be use as a finish to the Superdirect or the ordinary route. From the layaway hold on Pickpocket Super-direct, use pockets on the right to gain a series of horizontal creases which enables the upper wall to be climbed direct a couple of metres left of the normal finish.

84 Pickpocket Direct 9m E2 5b   ★
Start just right of Pickpocket Superdirect where a ledge at waist height runs rightwards into a bulge-capped, small recess. Traverse right along the ledge into the recess. Move onto the slab above below a steep wall and move left to gain the horizontal slot. Use

this to gain the wall above and finish via the obvious pro-truberance.

85   Solitaire   13m   E2   5b
Start as for Pickpocket Direct. This generally unpopular route finds a way rightwards up the steep slab capped by the red bulge. Traverse the ledge as for pickpocket direct and move out of the bulge-capped, small recess rightwards. Traverse diagonally right to finish at the obvious Silver Birch at the top.

86   Pocket Solitaire   10m   NL   5c
Start below and 1m left of the Silver Birch. Climb the wall direct into a small recess at 5m. Step left and gain the ledge above on 'slopers'. Finish up the short wall to the Birch.

87   Cluedo   11m   E2   5b
Start at the foot of the buttress at the lowest point directly beneath a huge Pine tree. Climb to a ledge with help from a small Beech on the right. The flakes above, lead up to a very dirty finish which should be inspected. Finish at the Pine.

88   John's and Frog's Route   9m   E2   5b
Start 2m right of Cluedo below a right-facing small flake just right of the small Beech. Climb the wall to the flake. The face above is climbed to finish at a Silver Birch.

89   Gwalchmai   8m   NL   5c
Start 4m right of John's And Frog's below a left-slanting ramp at 5m. Climb the bulging wall via poor layaway holds to gain the ramp. Move leftwards up this to the top.

Six metres further right is a short, clean wall with a Birch growing at the top, right on the edge.

90   Tramlines   6m   E2   5b   ★
Start below the Birch. Climb the wall using the thin line of intrusions running up the wall.

At the far right end of this wall are two small roofs with a tree growing below and close to the rock.

91   The Green Knight   6m   HVS   5a
A pleasant climb when its clean! Start 2m left of the tree. Surmount the first bulge to reach the ledge. Step 1m left and using poor handholds on the slab above, step onto the slab over the overlap and continue to the top direct.

92   The High Girdle   60m   E6   6a/b   ★★★
A fantastic expedition which crosses the most imposing part of The Final Section at a high-level. Start at the left-hand end of the Final Section just right of The Mantelshelf. Gain the obvious sloping ledge and foot traverse this rightwards passing below the thin final crack of Free And Easy. Continue rightwards with great difficulty round the blunt arete to gain the break across the wall above The Crescent. Follow this to Jelly Terror and continue rightwards on suspicious rock to gain Barnacle Bill by descending slightly. Finish up the final corner of Barnacle Bill.

THE LAZONBY OUTCROPS   O.S. SHEET 86   GRID REF: 527427

SITUATION AND CHARACTER

These important crags form the main feature of the Eden Gorge, lying on the west bank of the River Eden between the villages of Lazonby and Armathwaite. They consist of a line of separate walls and buttresses strung out along a length of two miles of river bank. There are 3 main groupings of outcrops with the central, largest group holding the best climbing and perhaps the single, most impressive sandstone crag in England.

The crags face east, away from the prevailing weather and this combined with their sheltered position in the Eden Gorge means that climbing is possible throughout the year. The rock dries quickly after rain.

The rock varies from a soft red type to a form which is almost gritstone-like in hardness.Sometimes all variations can be experienced in the course of just one climb. A peculiar feature of these crags are the presence of veins of harder rock which due to differential weathering, stand out as small ribs or sometimes as large protruding fins.Several climbs make use of these.A warning must be sounded with regard to protection on these climbs. As with all sandstone, great care must be exercised when placing runners. Trusting runners for long falls is to be avoided. In addition, damp rock tends to break much more readily than dry rock.

Lazonby has a unique and powerful atmosphere which can easily intimidate the first-time visitor. For the competent and experienced climber, coming to terms with the climbing here will give a taste of the best that the Eden Valley has to offer.

APPROACHES AND ACCESS

The land on which the outcrops lie is part of the Lazonby Estate. There is a Public Right of Way along the foot of all the outcrops. This footpath is the Eden Gorge footpath on the West bank of the Eden between Lazonby and Armathwaite. Access to the crags was first negotiated with the Lazonby Estate in the late '70's, for 'bona fide' climbers, and has not been a problem since, although this situation could change if the new landowner's "track record" with regard to other footpaths (see Armathwaite) is anything to go by. If the situation becomes difficult with regard to approaching the crags from above, then climbers will have to resort to approaching from either end along the riverside Public Right Of Way between Lazonby Bridge and the mill above the weir at Armathwaite.

The best access point is from the road running above the Eden Gorge between Lazonby and Armathwaite. This is via a gated track marked on a sign as: "Lazonby Estate Route 3".

Leave Armathwaite and head south from the village, passing under the railway. Turn left at the next junction and then left again very shortly at Coombe Eden. Follow this road for two miles to a junction near Baronwood Farm and a Telephone Box. Continue straight on over a cattle grid and after a further half a mile, park on the wide verge on the opposite side of the road to the gated track of "Lazonby Estate Route 3".

The track which leads downhill brings one to another gate. Pass through this and cross the Carlisle-Settle railway line. Turn right and follow a track past a circular stand of conifers on the right.This track leads to the top of Cave Buttress, easily identifiable by the many magnificent Scots Pines growing there. A gate in a recently constructed wooden fence is passed and the wide track curves steeply down below Cave buttress to meet the riverside Right Of Way.

As one faces the river immediately below Cave Buttress, the Far Upstream Buttresses are reached by turning right and following the muddy path alongside the river in an upstream direction. Wirewalk Buttress is immediately on one's left and the rest of the crags are downstream of this.

HISTORICAL

The Lazonby Outcrops have long been commented on by climbers as they are blatantly obvious to all who pass along the Public Footpath of The Eden Gorge Walk between Lazonby and Armathwaite, one of the finest walks of the type anywhere in the U.K. The first climber to consider the rocks for climbing was John Simpson in 1969. He returned to the Wirewalk Buttress in 1970 and along with John Workman, Alan Beatty and Dennis Hodgson, all from Penrith, climbed Gadzowt (because it goes out!) and Merry Monk Variations. John Workman in turn, lured a young and impressionable Ronnie Kenyon to the crag one evening in 1970 and after repeating Merry Monk Variations, Ronnie was so "smitten" that he returned with John Aldridge and Barrie Dixon in December and climbed Merry Monk with a deviation at mid-height. Kenyon and Beatty returned in Christmas week of 1970 to produce Cream Cracker Wall, The Old Girdle and Cave Route. Early in 1971 Barrie Dixon and Alan Beattie added two very impressive climbs which showed up the potential of the crag. These were Silicosis and Pneumoconiosis. The impending right-hand side of the River face had to wait until September of 1971 before it was breached by The Swinger.

The Winter of 1971/72 saw an interest in the other buttresses downstream of Wirewalk Buttress and One Of The World's Many Problems climbed at the optimistic grade of Severe by Al Beatty the original "Beast-Master" was one of the best. Phil Rigby began to make his mark on these crags about this time and was always in on the action. It was he along with Beatty and Kenyon who "opened-up" the Isolated Buttress by climbing Catastrophe Corner in January 1972. This was an ascent of epic proportions involving a near catastrophe with a large loose block near the top of the chimney. Gumbo Variations was another Rigby route dating back to February 1972. Isolated Buttress and Gumbo Buttress have been left alone since the publication of the last guide due to the area being deemed to be "Out Of Bounds". It may now yield more secrets?

Tim Dale another young Penrith climber entered the fray and along with Alan Beatty and Phil Rigby made up what was probably the most formidable team in the Eden Valley at this time. Hernia on the Wirewalk was their work and at the end of 1972, Tim and Phil forced the exciting finale of Microman. Another of their climbs was

Cobweb Wall which like Microman used aid from pegs. In March 1973, Bill Lounds and Stew Wilson straightened up Merry Monk to produce what is now one of the "Classics" of the North of England. On the same day Phil, Tim, Stew and Bill top-roped The Horror. In 1974, Phil Rigby and Stew Wilson climbed Inside A Cosmic Orgasm. This was not an outstanding climb but it certainly pointed the way forward in terms of the more technical climbing to be had on the crag. At about this time, the secret was leaked to the Carlisle climbers and the talents of Jeff Lamb and Pete Botterill were brought to bear on this hitherto insular situation. Pete padded up Tigerfeet and Jeff made a typically fine ascent of Red Chipper eradicating the blatantly chipped hold in the process. In 1975 Phil Rigby produced the superb Fingers an exciting excursion onto the fine exposed headwall of the Upstream Face of Wirewalk. The route which marked the end of the early development is perhaps Ace Of Wands. This was climbed by a very strong team consisting of Phil Rigby, Ron Kenyon and Dave "Dids" Bowen. This was in 1978. Since the publication of the 1980 guide, the number of climbs on the Lazonby Outcrops has almost doubled. Karl Lunt a Lancastrian "exiled" in Carlisle in the mid to late 1980's was the undoubted local expert at Lazonby. He systematically blitzed the crag, dispensing with aid points, leading top-roped problems and creating superb and commiting new routes. Karl got things off to a fine start with Technical Ecstasy which he climbed in April 1986. It was by far the hardest climb on the crag at the time and several recent ascents have confirmed its quality. On his first attempt Karl took a fall from the top of the pitch and hit the ground on the rope stretch. Luckily, his second, Chris Crowder was belayed to a 'Friend' or the outcome may have been more serious. In October 1987 Lunt and Andy Kay produced The Fearful Void which finds a way through the big roofs above the cave on Cave Buttress. On the same day they found Eye In The Sky, a good day's work. The leaning wall of Microman attracted Karl's attention and in 1988 this was climbed without pegs and completely free to give the exciting Machoman. At this time Seb Grieve was poking about at Lazonby and with the aid of a reluctant and ageing second produced Neptune. Not to be outdone, Lunt made a bid for The Horror and succeeded in leading this old top-rope problem in the company of Andy "Lurch" Williamson in May 1989.Seb Grieve retorted in July 1989 with the hardest route at Lazonby: Why Flymo When You Can Napalm. It still awaits a second ascent.

THE CLIMBS
THE FAR UPSTREAM BUTTRESSES

The easiest approach is to stay close to the river bank when walking upstream from Cave Buttress area. The first rocks are met just before a large Oak tree. Some lines have been climbed here but the rock is composed of large detached blocks and cannot be regarded as safe. Some fifty metres further upstream the crags gain height and are very vegetated and broken to begin with. The first climbs are located just beyond an Elder tree growing from the foot of the crag. A huge, rectangular recess splits the upper part of the buttress. The climbs are described from RIGHT to LEFT moving

THE LAZONBY OUTCROPS

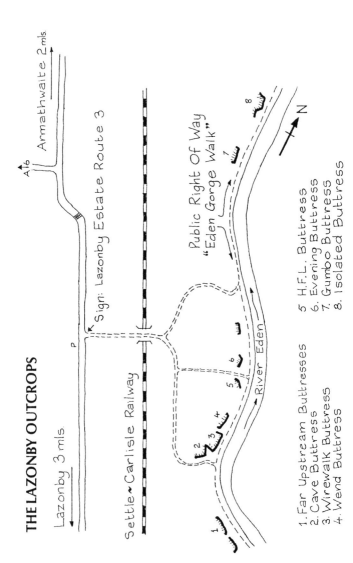

Lazonby 3 mls.

Armathwaite 2 mls.

A16

Sign: Lazonby Estate Route 3

Settle~Carlisle Railway

Public Right Of Way
"Eden Gorge Walk"

River Eden

N

1. Far Upstream Buttresses
2. Cave Buttress
3. Wirewalk Buttress
4. Wend Buttress
5. H.F.L. Buttress
6. Evening Buttress
7. Gumbo Buttress
8. Isolated Buttress

upstream, in contrast to the climbs on the other buttresses ie. Cave Buttress and downstream of it which are described from Left to Right.

CARE NEEDS TO BE TAKEN WITH THE ROCK ON THE NEXT SIX CLIMBS AS THEY HAVE HAD VERY FEW ASCENTS.

1 Stained Class 15m VS 4c ★
Follows the rib right of the rectangular recess.
Climb a short groove to below a large roof. Move left to bypass this, then climb the crack and rib above, to finish at a tree.

2 Gothic Horror 15m VS 4b
Start below and left of the rectangular recess. Climb the gardened wall, to gain the base of the recess. Follow the crack system up the left retaining wall. Move left, near the top to an exposed finish.

Moving upstream, the rock retreats once more beneath a cloak of vegetation. About twenty metres beyond Gothic Horror is:

3 Nemesis Towers 25m HS 4c
Start to the right of a shallow gully below a large roof. Climb a groove to the roof then traverse left into the gully. A tricky move above here, gains easier ground which leads to the final overhang. Avoid this by finishing to the left.

The remaining routes are located on another buttress further left which is set up the bank at a higher level facing somewhat upstream.

4 Far Above The Splat Mat 13m E1 5b ★
Start near the right edge of the buttress at a shallow, square niche. Climb the wall directly above the niche. Pull onto the undercut upper slab to finish awkwardly at a small Pine tree.

5 Herbal Abuse 12m VS 5a
Further left, the wall is pierced by a prominent cave. Gain this from below and slightly left. Finish up the interesting jamming crack above.

6 Snowball 12m VS 4c
Start 3m left of a vegetated groove, left of Herbal Abuse. Climb the wall direct to a prominent, projecting block. Finish by moving right towards a tree.

CAVE BUTTRESS

This should properly be called Samson's Cave Buttress as it is named after its one-time occupant; a fugitive Irish navvy employed on the building of the Carlisle-Settle line, who was eventually hunted down by the police for his part in the murder of another navvy during a drunken brawl at Armathwaite.The event is documented possibly somewhat inaccurately in a novel by the Lakeland writer; Graham Sutton.

The cave can be reached quite easily from the foot of the left-hand side of the buttress and below an obvious, big, left-facing corner. A short scramble and a couple of tunnels lead to the comfortable cave.

The rock on this buttress can be rather soft in places, so care must be taken.

The first climb is located on a small, roofed buttress to the left of the scramble to the cave.

7   I Can't Breakdance!   8m   E1   5c   ★

Start below the roof. Climb into a niche, then undercling the crack which splits the roof. A gymnastic pull round this leads to an earthy scramble off.

8   Demolition Dancing   12m   HVS   5b

Start just left of the scramble to the cave. Climb the short corner above and move right to a ledge. From here follow the hanging rib to a landing on steep soil.

The next four routes are gained by scrambling up to the ledge below the big corner, as for the cave.

9   The Crack   12m   S

The crack on the left wall of the Open-Book corner is climbed to a good ledge. Move right to an earthy finish.

10   The Corner   12m   MVS   4b

Climb the obvious steep corner.

11   Technical Ecstasy   12m   E4   6a   ★★★

A brilliant, sustained route – protection is good. The wall to the right of the Corner is split by a thin crack which runs the full height of the face. Climb the crack to finish over a small roof.

To find the next route it is necessary to crawl through the tunnel into Samson's Cave.

12   The Fearful Void   12m   E3   5c   ★★★

An intimidating pitch with a wild finish! Start in the mouth of the cave and belay here (Big thread). Climb the pillar on the right of the entrance (facing into the cave) for a few metres. Step left above the cave and traverse below the overhang to gain a crouching on the jutting neb of rock. Finish directly above here at a small tree.

The remainder of the routes on Cave Buttress are described moving right from the scramble to the cave. The ground slopes down and a number of small trees just in front of the crag are useful for locating climbs.

13   Dirty Old Pillar   9m   S

Just right of the scramble to the cave is a crack which widens to a chimney. Follow this past a thin birch tree to belay on the ledge above.

14   Sahara Crossing   20m   HVS   5a

Start 2m left of the first, small tree at a winding, flake crack.
Follow this until it peters out (thread out to the left), then move up and left over a bulge. Climb up a few metres then traverse right over soft rock to reach the cave.

15   Cave Route   30m   S

Start immediately right of the first tree.

1.15m

Climb up to and ascend the steep, difficult chimney to the cave.

2.15m

Traverse right and ascend the loose chute, trending left to a tree belay.

16 Neanderthal Man 15m VS 5a

Start midway between the second and third trees. Climb the wall to a ledge then ascend another wall to a ledge on the right. Enter the V groove and follow this moving leftwards to the cave.

17 Pneumoconiosis 30m E3 5b ★

A commiting and serious route. Start at a shallow groove in the centre of the buttress behind the sixth tree. Climb the the lower wall with ease. The overhang above is awkward and a pull-out left onto a wall can be made.Climb the wall trending left until better rock can be followed rightwards to a chimney up which the climb finishes.

18 Phred 30m VS (Aid) 4c

Right of Pneumoconiosis is a large, arch-shaped recess. Directly above this is a V groove high up. Start right of this in another, bramble-choked, recess. Move leftwards below the corner-groove of Barney, but continue to traverse horizontally leftwards to reach the V groove (2 pegs for aid). Follow the groove, then move right to a tree at the top.

19 Barney 25m VS 4b

Start in the bramble-choked, recess as for Phred.Move leftwards to the corner-groove and climb it. To finish, either move out leftwards or head right for a tree and climb a vegetated groove to the top.

20 Mandrax 18m S

Not a very pleasant experience! Start further up the slope where a large bulge has a short groove its left. Climb the loose groove.

21 Rattle and Hum 12m HS 4b

Start directly below the large bulge. Climb up to this and pull out right to a ledge above. Ascend the front of the pillar above, direct.

The easy gully on the right, divides Cave Buttress from Wirewalk Buttress. This gully provides a useful means of descent.

WIREWALK BUTTRESS

Known locally as Chain Rock, this is the biggest of the Lazonby Outcrops.Wirewalk Buttress is possibly the most impressive piece of rock, covered by the North Of England guide.The majority of routes are steep, hard and most have a very serious feel to them – this is certainly no place for the faint of heart!

In general, the rock is better on the upper sections than those near the river. However some climbs have good rock throughout, but then we are talking about sandstone!

For purposes of description, Wirewalk Buttress can be regarded as having Three sections: Upstream Face, River Face and Downstream Face.

The Upstream Face has a tree-lined ledge at half-height and is in full view from the approach path below Cave Buttress. The River Face rises directly out of the river and thus cannot be easily viewed, although in dry summer conditions a pleasant "plodge" will allow a cursory inspection of lines on the right side of the face. It is possible to traverse the foot of the face via a ledge and iron stanchions in all but flood levels. The Downstream Face is dank and uninspiring and thankfully only has one route.

THE UPSTREAM FACE

22   Red Barchetta   12m   HVS   5c
Across the gully, opposite Rattle and Hum, is a short rib. Start on the wall right of this and below a tiny overhang. Move up and left to a jug on top of the rib. Go up this to a ledge then climb the awkward chimney just left.

23   Fear Is The Key   12m   HVS   5a   *
Start between the rib and the prominent corner at a shallow, left-facing groove. Climb this past an overlap to a ledge, then finish up the short wall above.

24   Adam   12m   S
Climb the obvious corner to the right. Exit up a short chimney on the left.

25   Virtually Part One   12m   S
Start in the corner of Adam but climb the wall just right of it and finish up a short groove.

26   Mystery Achievement   15m   E1   6a   ★★
A bewildering crux which can be well protected using runners on the tree. Start at the foot of the arete next to a tree. Gain the top of the detached block, then make tricky moves up and left, round the arete. Easier climbing follows, moving right near the top for maximum exposure.

27   Pavane   13m   E2   5b
A bold route! Start below the obvious gully right of the arete. Scaramble up, to reach the Dog-leg crack on the left wall (good runners). From the top of this, launch up and left over a slight nose to finish straight up.

28   Eve   12m   VD
Climb the loose gully in its entirety.

Moving right from Eve, the ground drops away and a ledge holding two small birch trees can be gained. The nearer of the two trees provides a useful belay for the next three routes whilst the further one overhangs the void.

29   Footfall   9m   E2   5c   *
Start below the wide groove next to the birch tree belay. Climb the groove past an awkward bulging section to finish on good jugs.

30   Fingers   26m   E1   ★★
A steep and fascinating climb, in turn, both bold and exposed. Start below the birch tree ledge 3 metres right of a burned stump.

1.13m   5a
Climb the wall direct on small holds to reach the birch tree ledge and belay. A bit short on protection!

2.12m   5a
Climb the impressive wall above the right-hand tree past a horizontal break to reach a crescent-shaped overlap. Step right from here to finish. A superb pitch!

31   Eye In The Sky   12m   HVS   5b   ★★
Enjoyable climbing in a stunning position. Start at the birch tree belay used by the previous routes. A gently rising traverse leads rightwards onto the exposed, blunt rib. Excellent protection can be

arranged here, which makes the awkward moves up the rib more palatable. Finish on good jugs.

32   The Toe   6m   VS   5b
The isolated pinnacle on the slope below Fingers. Climb the arete facing the river. Hard to start.

THE RIVER FACE

An impressive piece of rock whose true proportions can only be fully appreciated from further upstream or from across the river.The left-hand side is merely vertical, whilst to the right of the incredible central groove of Merry Monk, the rock gently overhangs.

33   Silicosis   30m   E1   *
A fine climb, marred slightly by the worrying nature of the first pitch. Start on a large, sloping shelf in a recess at the left-hand side of the face.

1.15m   5b
Climb the awkward, shallow groove then crack to a ledge on the left. Care with rock!

2.15m   4c
Traverse right and ascend the gangway and corner to the top. A fine pitch.

34   Perilous Journey   30m   E3   **
A tremendous route which saves its hardest moves until the end. A large Friend might help those in peril on the crux! Start to the right of the recess of Silicosis where a steep vein, slants up the left-hand side of the red wall.

1.15m   5b
Climb the vein, then move left to a creaky flake (runners). From the top of the flake, move left onto another flake. Enter a shallow scoop above this then move up and right to a belay on a large ledge. Serious!

N.B. The flakes on the first pitch have fallen (1990) and the pitch has not been climbed in its present state. However, Pitch 2 is superb on its own.

2.15m   5c
Climb the groove directly behind the belay, to reach a large, jammed block. Pull throught the overlap just left of this, then sprint up the leaning headwall, passing, amongst other things, some horizontal breaks. (Friends!)

35   Inside A Cosmic Orgasm   15m   E2   5b
Contrived and hard to protect. On the first ascent a peg runner was used to protect the moves on and beyond the traverse. Start at the vein in the red wall. Climb the vein for a short distance until a finger traverse leads rightwards across the steep wall. Move onto the rounded arete and beyond. Climb the wall until one can move back left into a narrow but prominent groove. Climb this to a ledge and belay. Finish as for Gadzowt.

36   Machoman   15m   E4   6a   *
The free version of the old aided route Microman. A sensationally positioned pitch. Protection is good, only where it is most needed.

Start from the belay ledge shared by the previous two routes. Alternative starts are provided by the first pitches of Gadzowt. Climb a short rib on the right, as for Gadzowt, to arrive at the impending headwall below two parallel cracks. Climb the left-hand crack with increasing difficulty to the top.

37   Gadzowt   33m   HVS
One of the easier climbs on the river face, but nevertheless an exposed climb which can prove thought-provoking. Start to the right of Perilous Journey below a short but very steep crack which opens out into a big, recessed bowl, at 6m.

1.15m   5a
Climb the awkward crack then ascend the open groove to the overhang above (good runners – at last!). Traverse left under the overhang to a good ledge.

2.18m   4c
Climb the rib on the right to a ledge then move right and follow a short, awkward crack to the top.

38   Tigerfeet   30m   E2   5a
A serious route up an impressive wall. Unfortunately its finish which it shares with Red Chipper is a bit of a disappointment. Start below the wall to the right of Gadzowt. Climb the wall via a crack and continue up to a ledge below an overhang. Move right, to enter a short groove which leads up to the middle ledges. Climb the grooves above as for Red Chipper.

39   Red Chipper   30m   E3   5c   ★
A good, steep and technical initial section gives way to very ordinary climbing above. Start 4m right of the cracked corner of Gadzowt, below the fine, wide rounded crack which terminates tantalizingly out of reach. Gain the foot of the crack passing the eradicated chipped hold which gave the climb its name. The crack is not easy, but better jams soon lead to good handholds. Continue up the steep wall to the area of ledges. The grooves directly above lead logically, but disappointingly to the top.

40   Ace Of Wands   40m   E3   ★★
A very fine and impressive climb with a technical and bold first pitch and an exciting finale. Start below the steep wall right of Red Chipper, just right of the H. Simmons inscription.

1.20m   5c
Climb the steep wall to a flat hold and peg runner below the overhang. Climb the overhang and move right to gain a ledge below a square, roofed corner as for Hernia.

2.12m   4c
Climb past the overhang as for Hernia and continue up the steep groove above until a long step can be made rightwards to a good foothold on the arete. Pull around to the right to a good ledge, below and to the left of the final pitch of Merry Monk.

3.8m   5b
Climb the impending crack above to a resting place in a corner. Surmount the overhang above to finish.

41   Hernia   30m   E2   5b   *

Strenuous and bold on the lower section. Start to the right of the H. Simmons inscription below a steep crackline. Climb the wall then follow the crack to a ledge beneath the overhang. Move left into an overhanging corner where the overhang can be tackled strenuously on large, dubious flakes. Easier climbing now leads to a ledge (possible belay) followed by an open corner to the top finishing at two conifers.

42   Merry Monk Variations   33m   VS   *

The original climb on the crag, offering the easiest way up the River face. Start as for Merry monk below the huge corner groove.

1.18m   4a

Climb the corner on good holds for about 12m then move up and left across the wall to belay beneath a prominent overhang.

2.15m   4c

Move up to the overhang and pass this awkwardly, to gain the corner above. This leads to the top passing a number of unstable blocks.

43   Merry Monk   33m   HVS   ***

One of the finest natural lines in the North of England, offering continuous interest and exposure. Start below the obvious huge corner which dominates the centre of the buttress.

1.15m   4a

Climb the fine corner on large holds to a small stance by a crack which sometimes 'squeaks'.

2.12m   5a

Climb up the groove above to its top, moving right to gain a good ledge below a short, steep wall. 3. 6m 4c

The wall is awkward. Trend right to a tree.

44   Neptune   30m   E4   6a

An exciting climb with a steep and strenuous start. Start as for Cobweb. Climb the overhanging wall as for Cobweb, but swing left at five metres on flat holds. Continue up the steep face above with poor runners until a grassy ledge is reached (junction with Cobweb). Climb the green, flaky face above till a red section is reached. Climb leftwards across this to a shallow groove and follow this to a small Pine at the top.

45   Cobweb Wall   34m   E3   **

This climb was made famous by the 'photoclimb' of Tom Proctor making the first ascent in the Crags magazine. Powerful climbing at the start has resulted in many attempts and fewer successes. Start 5m right of Merry monk below an optimistic break; a right-facing groove, out of reach and breaching the grossly overhanging wall.

1.16m   5c

Climb the wall to gain the right-facing groove. Exit rightwards to gain the crack which is followed on good jams. Climb past a loose block to a good ledge. Peg belay (not in situ).

2.18m   5a

Pull onto the wall above and move rightwards to gain and climb a short, but awkward chimney- groove. Exit on the right.

46 Why Flymo When You Can Napalm? 30m E5 6b †
A steep and exhilarating route with a wild finale. Start four metres right of Cobweb Wall at an iron stanchion. Pull up to a peg runner at three metres then swing left and climb straight through the roof (crux) past peg runners onto a short wall. Move up into a right-facing corner capped by an overhang (peg runner) and pull straight over this and up to a grassy ledge. Step left four metres and climb the wall above trending slightly leftwards until below the final overhang. Climb this past two peg runners using brittle holds and finish via a large protruding spike.

An aided route Symbad Wall ascended the overhanging wall between Cobweb Wall and The Swinger. Two pegs were used to gain the ledges and cracks were followed rightwards to the tree belay on The Swinger.

47 Variations On A Swinger 35m E3 ★
A good climb, once the indifferent rock on the crux has been negotiated. A Friend 3.5 could prevent a splash landing!! Start at the third iron stanchion of the old wirewalk (counting from the downstream end).

1.26m 5c
Climb strenuously up a bulging crack into a niche. (Friend 3.5 above). Traverse left with difficulty on soft rock to reach a small, sloping ledge. Pull onto the ledge and reach a doubtful block. Climb the small overhang and crack above, on better rock. From the top, move right and belay at a tree below a chimney.

2.9m 5a
Climb the chimney to the overhang then gain the slab on the left. Ascend this moving right to the finish.

48 King Of The Swingers 9m HVS 5b ★
Provides a more direct finish to Variations On A Swinger. Start from the belay ledge of that route. Climb the chimney to the overhang and continue bridging and jamming up the crack to good finishing jugs.

49 The Swinger 30m HVS
An interesting route with good situations. Start at the tree at the right-hand end of the River Face.

1.21m 5a
Climb the tree to a point some 5m up and level with a ledge above the river. Gain this by a swing on good handholds. Traverse the ledge and climb the wall above, moving left slightly, to a tree below the wide chimney.

2.9m 4c
Finish as for Pitch 2 of Variations On A Swinger.

50 Suspended Animation 30m E2 ★★
A fine route with an impressive finale. Start just up the slope from the large tree at the downstream end of the River Face.

1.18m 5b
Climb up and left to reach the base of a wide crack on the arete of the buttress. Climb the crack almost to its top then step left onto the face. Climb straight up to belay on a ledge.

2.12m   5c
Move up and left to reach a short, thin crack leading with difficulty to a jammed block below the overhang. Traverse left to a large pocket below the widest part of the roof. Pull over this moving rightwards on excellent holds to the top.

51   The Mole   25m   HS   4b
Start below the broken crack several metres up the slope from the large tree of Swinger. Climb the wall to a sloping ledge. Crawl through a chimney and ascend the groove and crack to a tree belay at the top.

Moving downstream from here for about 100 metres one comes to a steep face with a barrier of overhangs at head-height. This is WEND BUTTRESS. Above and left of Wend Buttress is a fairly scrappy wall, OVERGROWN BUTTRESS.

OVERGROWN BUTTRESS

A scrappy wall with two unremarkable climbs.

52   Bucket And Spade Job   12m   VD
Climb the groove system at the left-hand side of the buttress. Move right to finish.

53   Compost Wall   12m   S
Start below a corner at the right-hand side of the buttress. Climb directly up to meet the corner then follow this past a tree at mid-height to finish by a tree at the top.

WEND BUTTRESS

This buttress can be reached by following the riverside Public Right Of Way downstream for 100m beyond Wirewalk Buttress. This face is fairly attractive and is recognisable by a barrier of overhangs at head-height on the left-hand side and by a large chimney at the other end.

54   The Horror   15m   E3   5c   ★
A couple of brutish bulges provide all the fun. Reasonable protection can be arranged with a selection of camming devices. Start below the prominent bulges at the left-hand end of the buttress. Climb the wall to a ledge below and left of the lower bulge. Launch out rightwards over this and finally tackle the overhanging wall above.

55   Savage Rib   15m   HVS   5b   ★
Enjoyable gymnastics without the ferocity of The Horror. Start just right of The horror under the lowest bulge. Climb up to and straight over this bulge. Move right to gain the rib and follow this to a tree belay at the top.

56   One Of The World's Many Problems   15m   HVS   5b   ★
An enjoyable pitch whose main problem lies in getting off the ground!
Start below and right of the corner crack at 5m. A hard pull over the bulge gains the corner which is followed to a tree belay at the top.

57   Cream Cracker Wall   20m   HVS   5a
A worrying climb which weaves its way up the wall to the right. Start 3m right of One Of The World's Many Problems at the next

jagged, protruding vein of rock. Use the vein to gain a slab above, then move left and climb the steep wall on flaky holds. A rightwards traverse on suspect rock gains a long ledge. Climb the steepening wall above to a heathery landing just left of the twin-stemmed Birch tree.

58   Trundle Wall   18m   VS   4c
Climb the wide crack immediately left of a steep mossy slab to reach a sloping ledge. The steep upper wall leads to an awkward heathery landing between the two trees at the top of the buttress.

59   Pseudonym   13m   S
Starts at a wide groove at the right end of a smooth, mossy wall. Climb the wide groove, then make a rising traverse right above bulges. Finish up the wall above. Pleasant.

60   Swing Off   12m   E3   5c
A bold and commiting lead. Start below and right of the obvious large bulges. Climb the short cracks then cut loose up and left over the bulge to gain easier territory above.

61   Al's Chimney   10m   HS   4b
Climb the obvious, dirty chimney at the right-hand end of the buttress.

Some 200m downstream of Wend Buttress, a steep path drops down the hillside to meet the riverside Public Right Of Way. This path comes down from the approach path leading to Cave Buttress and Wirewalk Buttress in the vicinity of a copse of conifers and provides the quickest approach to the next two buttresses H.F.L Buttress and Evening Buttress which are located on either side of this path at its junction with the Public Right Of Way running along the West bank of the Eden between Lazonby and Armathwaite.

H.F.L. BUTTRESS

Located on the upstream side of the junction of the paths, this presents a small compact buttress whose main feature is a prominent, right-facing corner. A vegetated ledge extends along the lower part of the crag some 3m above ground level.

62   Scorpion   9m   HVS   5b
Start at the left end of the vegetated ledge at a short, wide crack. Climb the crack to a shelf and pull right onto the face. Follow the left edge of the face to an awkward, bulging finish.

63   Mij   9m   S
Start on the ledge below a groove which contains a tree low down. Climb the groove.

64   Electric Avenue   15m   HVS   5b   ★★
A sustained and well-protected outing. Start on the ledge below the impending front face of the buttress. Climb straight up past a square- cut nick and over several overlaps.

65   Cellnet   15m   E1   5b
Start below the big, right-facing corner of Teragram. Climb the corner until it is possible to move left onto the hanging rib. Follow this with a hard move to reach the Birch tree at the top.

66   Teragram   15m   S
Gain and follow the big, right-facing corner to a loose finish.

67   Lip Service   15m   VS   4c   ★
Start below the right edge of the slab which extends out rightwards
from Teragram. Climb the edge of the slab then a short flake crack
gaining the left end of an overlap. Traverse right on the lip to a
sapling and finish straight up.

68   The Neighbourhood Bully   12m   E1   5b   ★
A gymnastic little pitch. Start directly below the sapling on the
traverse of Lip Service. Climb easily to the big roof and pull over
this. Good holds lead to the sapling. Finish direct.

EVENING BUTTRESS

A small overgrown buttress on the downstream side of the junction
of the paths.

69   Jamboree   6m   S
Climb the jam crack on the left side of the buttress.

70   Moonlight Sonata   7m   HS
Climb the groove right of Jamboree to a niche and a vegetated
finish.

71   Sunflower   6m   VS   4c
Climb the clean rib to the right of Moonlight Sonata to a tricky
finish.

AVIATOR'S BUTTRESS

This small buttress lies a short distance downstream from Evening
Buttress and is set well back from the path. In appearance it consists of a flat, vertical wall, split by several horizontal breaks.
Towards the left-hand side of the buttress is a vertical vein of rock
which runs the full height of the crag.

72   The Right Stuff   8m   E1   5b
Start 2m right of a large detached block at the left-hand side of the
buttress. Climb a flake crack to a bulge. Pass this using the tree
above to finish.

73   The Cockpit   8m   VS   4c
Climb the prominent crack, 5m right of the detached block.

74   Red Square Dare   11m   E1   5a
Start below a crack in the overhang, further right. Climb the crack
in the overhang to gain a niche. From here step left onto a bulge,
then climb the wall above direct.

GUMBO BUTTRESS

This is the next buttress encountered downstream in about 5-10
minutes walk from Aviators Buttress.The Buttress is reached by a
short steep scramble up the hillside. The main feature is an unclimbed right-slanting corner bounded on the right by a steep and
attractive slab. A superb, dry cave is located under the crag to the
left of the corner.

75   Look To The Future; Its Only Just Begun   24m   HVS   5a   †
This climb finds a way up the steep, but relatively broken wall 6m
left of the obvious corner. Start below a small tree. Climb the rib
and move right to the tree. The wall above is climbed and a
mantelshelf onto a ledge provides the crux. Move rightwards up

ledges to a short wall and circumnavigate it by devious moves left then right along ledges. climb a short groove above to finish at a tree.

76   Gumbo Variations   18m   HVS   5a   †
Start at the foot of the obvious corner. Climb the corner until it is possible to hand-traverse leftwards across the left wall and onto the front of the buttress. Traverse left and climb up to a tree belay. Climb the corner above to finish.

77   Sisyphus   21m   VS   4c   †
Start to the right of the obvious corner and beyond the smooth slabs, below a cleaned corner. Climb the wall to a ledge. Move right to pass a tree and move back left to stand on a jammed block. Gain the ledge above and move right to another ledge. A ramp on the left is gained with difficulty. Follow this to escape on the right. Tree belay.

ISOLATED BUTTRESS
This is a tall, impressive buttress which rises directly above the good riverside footpath less than 100 metres downstream of Gumbo Buttress. The routes have possible only had one ascent as the area was placed out of bounds in the last guide.The climbs have not been re-checked and so caution should be exercised on account of possible undergrading. The rock is very soft Millet Grain Sandstone which does improve the higher one climbs. However the blocky nature of the upper face is also potentially hazardous. The main feature of the buttress is a long, corner crack which is the line of Catastrophe Corner.

78   J.J.   18m   VS   4b   †
Climb the corner to the left of Catastrophe Corner.

79   Catastrophe Corner   24m   HVS   4c   †
Scramble up to the foot of the buttress below the corner crack. Climb loose rock to a ledge below the steep crack. Climb the crack to a sloping ledge and continue up a narrow chimney which leads to a small ledge on the right. Move right to the top.

80   Rat Salad   30m   HVS   †
The upper face is seamed by a central groove which has two branches. This climb gains the right- hand groove from the left. Start 6m left of a small cave.

1.15m   4c
Climb up and right to a large ledge. Traverse right (peg runner advised) and mantelshelf onto a ledge. Climb the wall above to another ledge and move right to a belay.

2.15m   4c
The groove above is quit in favour of the loose, right-slanting wall. Variation Start: Climb the wall above the cave using bolts for aid to join the normal route at the mantelshelf.

81   Insanity Groove   24m   VS   4c   †
Start below the corner at the right-hand side of the buttress. Climb an awkward wall to gain the foot of the corner. Climb the corner with care, negotiating a small overhang to reach a ledge. Continue up the loose corner to the top.

THE WALLS

These are a series of small faces extending downstream of Isolated Buttress as far as the big meander in the river which is dominated by the huge face of Red Rock on the opposite bank.

Below the face just before the meander is a low cave which has metal boot-mooring ring embedded in the rock nearby.

82   Gone   12m   S

Start to the right of a V-groove which cuts through the roof above the cave. Climb directly towards a large Oak at 6m but before reaching the tree traverse horizontally left and make a hard move over an overlap. Move up past a small Larch tree and scramble off.

Two other climbs were made hereabouts: Mr Woo (S) and The Gripe (VS). but a recent earthslip has obliterated them.

Going downstream from here, the large face of Red Rock on the far bank is most impressive and has been ascended in one place but no records exist. Further downstream the West bank beyond an open meadow, is Cat Clint, a tall pillar of rock. Some routes have been climbed but not recorded.

CUMREW CRAG   O.S. SHEET 86   G.R. 562 502

SITUATION AND CHARACTER

A small,part-quarried,part natural outcrop of generally compact limestone.It is situated in a fine position on the West side of Cumrew Fell above the village of Newbiggin.The outlook is superb and it is an excellent place for a spot of bouldering or as a place to take the family.

Cumrew Crag faces West at a height of over 350 metres O.D.The rock is quick to dry even in winter.In common with most limestone the climbs tend to be steep, but untypically, big holds are lacking on many of the climbs. Whilst there are some natural lines,some of the harder climbs are a bit crowded. However this can be con-strued as a source of inspiration for the unimaginative and a chalice of delight for the pedant. Some angle irons are in place above the Main Wall and Amphitheatre otherwise anchors are absent.

APPROACHES AND ACCESS

The crag is best approached from the Bluebell Inn at New-biggin.This can be easily reached from Brampton by following the B6413, or by following the same road in the opposite direction from Lazonby/Kirkoswald. Newbiggin is only 15 minutes drive from Armathwaite via Ainstable turning left at the crossroads here and eventually picking up signs for Newbiggin. Just North of the Blue-bell Inn is a crossroads. Follow the minor road into the village and towards the Fell. After passing the last bungalow on the left a track can be seen climbing the steep fellside alongside a wood. Park on a small grassed area by a bridge and follow the track which is gated at the top and bottom.After passing through the top gate and emerg-ing onto open fell,follow the left fork of the track above a drystone wall until another gate is reached. The continuing track is grassy but well-defined and passes under small outcrops. Cumrew Crag is directly behind the first ruined limekiln above the path. Time from car 15 minutes.

HISTORICAL

The crag has been climbed on by local climbers for about 20 years. All the routes, in the main, are the work of Tim Dale, Ron Kenyon and Stew Wilson, with Alan Hewison contributing the bold duet of Starsky and Hutch. The harder, more recent routes were added by Karl Lunt.

THE CLIMBS:

The crag lies behind the limekiln and is divided into 2 areas:

AMPHITHEATRE WALL and MAIN WALL

A steep chockstone chimney separates the two areas.
Several metres left of the crag is another small bouldering area.
Descents are at either end of the crag.

AMPHITHEATRE WALL

To the left, above a low grass-covered ridge of spoil is a series of walls with low-definition ribs.

1   Cryptic Crack   7m   HS
Climb the steep crack at the left-hand end of the crag.

2   Starsky   9m   VS   4c
A bold little climb.
Starts just right of Cryptic Crack,below and left of a white-streaked overlap.Climb a short,awkward wall to a good ledge below the overlap.Pull over this to the right and continue direct to the top.

3   Kojak   15m   E2   5b
Climb Hutch to the bulge then make a delicate,rising traverse to reach a white ledge. Continue left to finish at the top of Cryptic Crack.

4   Hutch   9m   VS   4c
A good climb. Starts to the right of 2. below a shallow,left-facing little groove which is left of an area of more broken rock.Climb this little groove direct.Step onto the arete at the top of this groove and finish straight up.

To the right is a more broken area,then a steep rib with a very smooth wall on its right.This smooth wall is short and finishes at a good ledge halfway up the crag.

5   The Wand   4m   5b
Climb the steep rib left of the smooth, 'White Magic' wall.

6   Stoney Butts   9m   S   4a
Starts immediately right of the steep rib.Climb the break in the steep wall to gain the ledge by a delicate step left.Climb the broken groove to the top.

7   White Magic   4m   6a   ★
An excellent fingery problem with a good landing. Climb the centre of the steep smooth wall gaining holds above a slight slab. Finish up and left.

8   Creepshow   9m   VS   5a
Climb the corner groove just right of White Magic.This leads steeply to a good ledge.Climb the short wall above to the right of a prominent groove.

9   Black Magic   9m   MS
Starts at the foot of the wall just right of the initial corner groove of Creepshow.Climb the wall on good holds to a jammed block.Pull up steeply to a good ledge and move left under the final wall of Creepshow to finish up the steep,prominent groove.

10   Cauldron Wall   9m   MS   ⋆
Start below the right-hand end of the mid-height ledge.Climb the wall leftwards on good holds to a fine horizontal break.Pull out left onto the right-hand end of the middle ledge.Climb the tall detached block and the easy upper groove.

11   Grey Malkin   9m   E1   5b
Starts as for Cauldron Wall but instead of moving up and left as for that climb,climb direct to the horizontal break and pass between two saplings.Climb the bare upper wall.

12   Toil and Trouble   9m   E2   6a   ⋆
Starts below the steep calcited wall at the foot of the chimney. Climb the steep wall passing the break(crux).Trend slightly right-wards up the wall above.

13   The Cauldron   9m   VD
Climb the chimney over chockstones to the top.

MAIN WALL
The Main Wall is split by several obvious thin cracklines.

14   Grey Yaud   9m   D   ⋆
Interesting and pleasant. Start at the left-hand end of Main Wall at the foot of a short slabby wall.Climb this wall on sloping holds to a ledge.The curving flake crack is followed to the top.

15   Tabby   9m   VD
Start at the foot of the thin right-trending crack just right of Grey Yaud. Climb this crack and move left at the top to follow the small corner parallel to and right of the finish of Grey Yaud.

16   Black Cat   9m   E1   5b   ⋆
Starts at the foot of a thin crack with a 'pothole' at head height. Climb the crack past the pothole (Beware of the Owl) to the over-lap. Finish with difficulty up the steep wall just left of the thin crack.

17   White Spirits   9m   E2   5b
Climb the wall between Black Cat and The Croglin Vampire via the white streak. Gain good footholds above the overlap and finish direct up the wall on small holds.

18   The Croglin Vampire   9m   VS   4c   ⋆⋆
The classic of the crag, steep and fingery with adequate protection. Start at the foot of the thin crack a metre or so to the right of the pothole.Climb the crack on poor holds to a horizontal break. Power the overlap on excellent holds and luxuriate in the positive nuances of the steep upper wall.

19   Phantom   9m   E1   5b/5c   ⋆
So close to the Vampire you may incur the wraith of anyone on that

route! Start just right of the Croglin Vampire.Climb the wall to the overlap (runners). Follow the small V-groove then climb the wall direct.

20   The Renwick Bat   9m   VS   4c   ★
Harder than the Vampire and more serious. Starts at the right-hand end of the Main Wall at the foot of the obvious corner.Climb the corner to the horizontal break.The overlap above has a crack going left and up.So must you. Finish as for Phantom.

21   The Fenny Thing   9m   S
Climb the rib to the right of the corner to a ledge.Move right and finish up the short wall.

The slab a few metres right and the walls right again provide bouldering on good rock. To the left of the Main Crag are several bouldering areas the one nearest Main Crag being best. The small natural edge further left has some immense loose blocks and routes have been climbed here.

SCRATCHMERE SCAR   O.S. SHEET 90   G.R. 516379

SITUATION AND CHARACTER
Located on the side of Lazonby Fell just a couple of miles East of the A6 at Plumpton midway between Carlisle and Penrith.The Southerly aspect of this small crag of Immaculate Penrith Sandstone and its a fine position above a wooded slope looking across the surrounding countryside to the Lake District Fells means it is a delectable but never crowded venue. The climbing is on a number of buttresses never more than eleven metres high and often quite a bit less. The climbing is always steep but good holds tend to be plentiful in the form of pockets and flakes of a harder intrusion. The climbing at Scratchmere is also more varied than is usual on Penrith Sandstone and most major features apart from slabs are encountered. This is a crag for the easy to middle grades, but one or two harder test-pieces and some good bouldering would make it a good choice for the competent soloist. The crag can often be a good choice on fine days in Winter as it is very quick to dry. The numerous trees above the crag provide good anchors.

APPROACHES AND ACCESS
Best approached from the A6 at Plumpton about seven miles North of Penrith (leave M6 at Junction 41 and follow A6 Northwards). From Plumpton, follow the B6413 road towards Lazonby and after a mile of uphill road, the crag will be seen across to the left above Scratchmere Scar Farm. Turn off the road at the Scratchmere Scar sign and follow the private concrete road down the hill into the farmyard. It is essential not to block any access required by the farmer and it is essential to ask at the farm for permission to park. Mr Brendan Atkinson farms Scratchmere and he allows climbers access over his land as well as parking. The crag itself is on land belonging to the Economic Forestry Group and access has been negotiated by the author with this body. It is essential that dogs are not taken to the crag and that fire precautions are stringently observed. When the access agreement was made, posts directed climbers up to the crag. It is essential that this route is followed

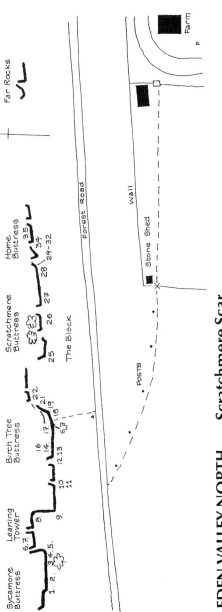

EDEN VALLEY NORTH   Scratchmere Scar

although some of the marker posts may be missing. To reach the crag, gain the field under the wooded hillside via a gate beside the concrete and wood sileage shed and follow the boundary wall of the farm underneath the crag until a barrier is crossed to the left of a small stone shed. The path on the other side is followed for about ten metres until a branch slants up to the right. The path then slants diagonally leftwards through trees passing yellow-topped marker posts to meet the forest road. Turn right along the road and after thirty five metres a cairn on the left side of the road marks the path up to the crag. A steep ascent leads to the foot of Birch Tree Buttress.

HISTORICAL

The first people to climb here were Ronnie Kenyon, Tim Dale and Stew Wilson who in the early Seventies were responsible for most of the original climbs on the crag including Stormy Petteril, Greta's Climb, John's Climb and Blondie. Following on from the first guide Stew Wilson climbed Herne in 1982. Pete Botterill scouted out several very hard short climbs on either side of Milligram including Scratch, the hardest climb on the crag which in all liklihood has not had a second ascent. Robin Curley in 1983 and Karl Lunt in 1985 both contested the steep face to the right of Extraction to produce two good climbs Peanuts and Into The Light. The obvious finish over the roof however was not led. This was top-roped by by Andrew MacKay and called Upright Pavement. The fine little bouldering area at the far right-hand end of the crag was Stew Wilson's secret climbing gym in the early 1980s and some very worthwhile problems were produced which should become popular. There are still some hard eliminates to do in this area. Karl Lunt with typical thoroughness found No Comebacks and Get Close in 1988, both very good climbs. Some "last problems" exist, notably the wall to the left of Blondie and the left arete of The Block. These could soon be history.

THE CLIMBS

These are described from left to right and buttress by buttress. Descents at either end of the crag.

SYCAMORE BUTTRESS

This is at the extreme left-hand end of the crag. It has a large Sycamore tree growing close to the centre of the buttress.

1   Skeet   9m   VD

Start at the foot of a tall, cave-like recess 2m left of a protruding block at head height. Climb up the cave until the sloping shelf on the right can be followed. Climb the corner on the right (Pheasant Groove) until a swing left on a ledge leads into the upper gully. Finish up the cracked arete on the right. Care with potentially loose blocks.

2   Pheasant Groove   8m   D   ★

A very enjoyable climb for the grade! Start below a finger crack immediately left of the protruding block. Climb the finger crack and corner above to a good ledge. Climb the corner above on good holds.

3 Over And Under 8m VD
Start immediately behind the big Sycamore. Climb steeply up cracks to a chimney recess (harder than it looks!) and gain a ledge on the left. Step right and climb the short, rectangular chimney to the top.

4 Side By Side 8m HD
Climb the steep, wide crack which is easier than it looks and finish up the short, rectangular chimney of Over And Under.

5 The Arete 8m S   ★★
Excellent. This delicate climb starts just right of the arete, right of the steep crack of Side By Side. Climb the right side of the arete using this for the left hand throughout.

The recessed bay right of the arete has an easy chimney in the left-hand side and a recessed groove in the right-hand side. A steep rib separates the two breaks.

6 Sidelock 8m D   ★
Start at the foot of the easy chimney which has a chockstone near the top. Climb the chimney until a horizontal crack is reached on the left wall. Swing left on this and pull up to good holds on the next horizontal break. Climb the cracked wall above to the overhang and move left to finish as for The Arete.

7 Choke 8m M
Climb the chockstone chimney throughout

8 Boxlock 8m D
Start below the right-hand break of the bay, to the right of the central overhanging rib. Climb the recessed groove to a ledge and finish to the right of a protruding block.

The steep, smooth right-hand wall of the bay is part of the next buttress:

THE LEANING TOWER
This monolithic block has a fine off-width crack splitting its front face. The upper part of the face is cut across by a wide ledge below the capping overhangs.

9 Herne 9m HVS 5a   ★
A really good climb worth hunting out. Friends could be useful. Start below the left arete of the Leaning Tower. Climb this mainly on its left side to the ledge, then finish straight up to good holds.

10 Blondie 10m HVS-E2 5b   ★★
A versatile grading, which as usual, is a function of one's thickness! Climb the fierce off-width crack with speed and determination passing a possible technicality in the upper half. Pull directly over the overhang above the ledge to finish.

11 Leyline 14m VD   ★
A very good climb in the "Traditional Classic" idiom, following a totally illogical series of weaknesses up a steep bit of rock. Start at the foot of the off-width crack of Blondie. Move rightwards up a glacis and ascend a short corner to a Sycamore tree. Step left, delicate at first, until the good shelf is gained. Traverse left along the shelf to the left-hand end of the overhangs. Excellent holds enable the bulge to be overcome by a swing right to finish.

BIRCH TREE BUTTRESS

This is the most impressive of all the buttresses at Scratchmere Scar, has the best rock, the best and longest climbs and is the point of arrival at the crag. The buttress projects out of the hillside and presents a short face towards The Leaning Tower. The front face is longest and has a large Birch growing out of the face just above head height. To the right of the Birch is a very steep wall with roof at mid-height providing short, hard problems finishing on a good ledge above, whilst the right-hand wall has a fine flake crack providing one of the best routes here: Greta's Climb.

12   Extraction   10m   HVS   5a   ★
A good climb at the lower limit of the grade. Care needs to be taken in the placing of protection. Start from an embedded flake just left of the left-hand arete of the front face. Climb the arete on flat holds to a recess below an overhang. Continue up the rib above via a square hole.

13   Out Of The Dark   14m   VD   ★
A good climb with a steep start and a sympathetic conclusion. Recommended. Start at the left arete. Pull up steeply and struggle onto the top of the flake. Traverse right for about 4m to a corner by the Birch. Climb the corner which is easy and move onto a ledge on the right. (stance and possible belay on nuts). The shallow corner on the left is the easiest escape.

14   Into The Light   11m   E1   5b
Another good climb whose main interest lies in the smooth wall below the final roof. Unfortunately it moves left to finish. Start 1m right of the left arete. Climb onto the top of the flake and gain a small ledge above. The middle of the steep wall is climbed on small holds to the horizontal break beneath the roof. Traverse left under the roof to finish up the last few metres of Extraction.

15   Upright Pavement   11m   NL   5c
The direct finish to Into The Light, straight over the roof.

16   Peanuts   12m   E1   5b
This climb accepts the challenge of the attractive left-facing, shallow corner below the roof, but disappointingly, exits right. Start 1m right of the left arete as for Into The Light. Climb onto the flake and move easily right to gain the top of a block below the shallow, left-facing corner. Climb the corner which is technical and fine and move out right below a small overlap to gain the obvious left-slanting crack (Stormy Petteril) to finish.

17   Stormy Petteril   12m   HVS   5a   ★★
At the lower end of the grade, but a fine climb with a slippery-feel to the rock in the higher section. Start directly below the big Birch tree on the face. Climb the vertical, fist-wide crack to gain the Birch. Easy rock above leads to a slim crack trending left to the top of a pedestal block. Swing left on smooth holds to gain and finish up the fine, left-slanting crack above.

To the right of the Birch is a smooth wall split by a central groove. The wall is capped by a small roof. This section provides four short but technical climbs on impeccable rock:

18   Overdose   6m   NL   6c   ★
Start just left of the central groove and below a "stoneground"

smooth wall. Climb the wall to the roof. The wall above the roof is green-streaked and provides a desperate sequence involving long reaches and some pretty "nifty" footwork.

19   The Black Streak   6m   E2   6a   ★★
A much sought-after and attractive problem. Start at the central groove. Climb the groove to the roof and surmount this to finish up the shallow, dimpled, black-streaked scoop.

20   Milligram   6m   E1   5b   ★★★
Magic! The original and best climb on the short wall. Start 1m right of the central groove directly below the slim, hanging flake crack. Climb direct to the roof. Gain the flake and proceed carefully to the top.

To the right of Milligram, the wall bends round to the right and gain height.

21   Scratch   7m   E4   6b   ★★
Sustained and devoid of runners. The landing could be better. Start 2m right of Milligram and just right of the blunt arete of the lower wall. Climb the right-hand side of the arete to a horizontal pod at half-height. From the pod move up the steep wall above, but slightly right to benefit from presence of the odd edge here and there.

To the right of Scratch, the ground at the foot of the crag steps up via a pedestal of rock.

22   Greta's Climb   11m   HS   4b   ★★
One of the original climbs and still one of the best. Strenuous and a bit bold. The finish is superb. Start from the top of the pedestal block to the right of Scratch. From the top of the block, layback boldly up the flake crack to gain a good ledge. From the point of arrival on this ledge, it is possible (and necessary) to reach a good horizontal break in the smooth wall above (runners). Swing right along this (exciting) to reach a groove and good finishing holds.

23   Don't Worry   9m   VS   4c
Start 1m right of Greta's Climb below a groove and a cave recess. Climb the groove to the cave. Finish direct on good holds or right at a similar grade.

24   Be Happy   9m   HVS   5b
Rather contrived but still worthwhile. Start to the left of the obvious Birch tree 2m right of Don't Worry. Climb the wall behind the tree using a thin crack and the right-hand edge of the cave. The crag to the right of Be happy is broken and of no interest for ten metres. A large Oak tree above the face is a landmark hereabouts.

THE BLOCK
This fine isolated pillar-like block about six metres high, lies below and just left of the massive Oak.

25   Spiral Stairs   7m   S   ★
Easy for the tall! Start at an embedded block at the foot of the pillar. Step up and rightwards on ledges to gain the steep right arete. Finish up this arete.

SCRATCHMERE BUTTRESS

This is a fairly extensive buttress which is hard to view as a whole. The major part of the buttress is to the right of an open gully and is identified by a barrier of overhangs at the bottom and another at the top of the crag. To the left of the gully is a rib which fades into a steep, upper wall immediately left of the big Oak tree.

26   Hesitation   7m   VS   5a
Start below the rib to the left of the open gully. Climb the rib until a tricky move on the wall above leads to a swing left and good finishing holds.

27   John's Climb   8m   HS   4a   ★★
An intriguing, rather bold climb with an exciting finale on good handholds. Start to the right of the open gully from a flat rock ledge below the bottom overhang. Make a stiff pull over the overhang and move left onto a slab. Climb directly up to a ledge. The rib above has a shallow, cracked groove on its right. climb this by a bold entry and finish on better holds.

28   Fitch   8m   HD
A very good and strenuous pitch on fine holds. Start 1m right of the bottom barrier of overhangs, at a Sycamore tree. Climb rightwards and up block corner to a good, big ledge. Pull out right onto the front of the rib and gain good footholds. Pleasant climbing on good holds leads to the top.

29   No Comebacks   8m   HVS   5b   ★
Accepts the challenge of the fine, finger crack in the upper, front wall of Scratchmere Buttress. Start from a pedestal at chest height below the smooth "problem wall" leading to the good ledge on Fitch. Climb the wall to the good ledge. Bridge up the corner above and left to the roof and pull left into the finger crack which is followed to the top.

30   Get Close   7m   VS   5a   ★
Climb No Comebacks to the roof and pull round to the right and finish up a short jamming crack.

31   Jam Today   7m   HS   4c
Start 3m right of the Sycamore below a wide crack leading up to a curving bulge. Climb the wide crack and move left over the bulge to finish up Fitch.

32   Hob   6m   D
Climb the steep gully just right of Jam Today taking care with potentially dangerous blocks.

HOME BUTTRESS

The wall and arete immediately right of the corner of Hob and its more broken continuation rightwards.

33   Home, Sweet Home   6m   HVS   5b
Climb the steep wall to the right of Hob and just left of the arete. This leads to an awkward, sloping finish.

34   Bobbery   6m   VS   4c   ★
Start directly below the arete to the right of Hob. Climb the arete easily until it steepens. A short, sharp section on small finger holds leads to an easier finish.

35   The Cheesepress   7m   D   *

Start to the right of the overhanging arete of Bobbery, below a steep, flake crack. Climb easily up to the crack and follow this more enjoyably to the top.

THE FAR ROCKS

These are reached by traversing the wooded slopes to the right of Home Buttress for a few minutes. They consist of three buttresses up to six metres high. The Middle Buttress is the biggest and is located by the presence of a huge Scots Pine above it.

The Left Buttress has a number of easy climbs.

The Middle and Right Buttresses have several good problems up to 5c.

This is an excellent bouldering area with fine rock and good landings. It is dirty because until now it was infrequently used.

COWRAKE QUARRY   O.S. SHEET 90   G.R. 541309

SITUATION AND CHARACTER

This old quarry of Penrith Sandstone is on the Eastern spur of Beacon Hill, the obvious, wooded hill above the town of Penrith. The quarry is nowhere more than seven metres high and is quite extensive. The West end of the quarry gives the best climbing and bouldering whilst the Eastern end tends to be more overgrown and less popular. The quarry faces South and is a sunny spot, much frequented by the proud burghers of Penrith and their offspring. Set amidst sandy banks, grassy knolls and towering Scots Pines, the rocks are a very pleasant place to spend an odd hour. The views are superb. The climbing whilst pleasant and even problematic is not superb. The rock tends to be snappy, especially in the cracks and care needs to be taken. The area to the right of Jughandle and the Broom Wall are perhaps the best sections for soloing.

Belays can be a bit of a problem and there are stakes above the Main Wall. The place is ideal for organised groups.

APPROACHES AND ACCESS

From the A66/A6 roundabout just South of Penrith, follow the A686 Alston road through the village of Carleton. About one mile beyond a big left-hand bend a road joins the A686 from the left, signposted to the Golf Course. Turn into this with the steep wooded slope of Gibbet Hill on the right. Four hundred metres along this road a couple of buildings will be seen on the left-hand side of the road. Just beyond these on the right is a little, gated lane entered by a stile which leads up the hill to the quarry which is hidden from sight beyond the large Scots Pines. Parking for a couple of cars is available beside the stile.

To reach the quarry follow the lonnen until it bends right then strike up the left one of three paths which goes steeply uphill and parallel to the walled field on the left. This brings one in five minutes to a level area at the left-hand end of the quarry. A path to the right meets a network of paths beneath the quarry walls. The first rocks visible on the left from this path and through the trees is the California Area.

The quarry is council property and no access problems exist.

HISTORICAL

Cowrake has been an adventure area for the youngsters of Penrith for decades. Into this rich tradition of War and more occasionally Love-Games, the climber has blended. The quarry has served an important function as a training ground for the Penrith Mountain Rescue Team and members of this organisation were probably responsible for all of the climbs here. Local climbers however have added less-likely problems and variations on countless, sociable evening training stints.

THE CLIMBS

These are described section by section from left to right.

CALIFORNIA AREA

This steep and rather featureless wall has an overlap just above head height. There used to be a climb here called Yosemite Wall. This has fallen down and a loose groove remains. Not quite up to its more famous namesake.

Ten metres right of California is:

PROBLEM WALL

This is a rectangular wall about three metres high which provides some amusing problems.

1   Gratir Pissage   4b

A not very pleasant experience. Climb the left end of the wall using a thin crack for the left hand to pass a pink scar.

2   White Snake   5b

Climb the centre of the wall above the biggest overlap.

3   Problem Wall   5a

Climb the wall in the line of a downward pointing flake. Big layaways to finish.

4   Pis En Lit   4b

Climb the wall on a vertical sequence of layaways to finish just left of a small Scots Pine. A number of traverses have been made and they represent the hardest problems on the wall. All 5b+.

Fifteen metres right of Problem Wall is:

MAIN WALL AND ARETES AREA

This is the most impressive part of the quarry. It is fairly open and dries quickly. The Main Wall is steep and seamed by a fine thin crack at its left end and some vaguer lines further right. A steep shallow corner marks the division of Main Wall from the Aretes Area. The Aretes Area consists of four corners with intervening walls and aretes. The second corner has a large Pine Tree on a ledge at mid-height, above and to the left of it. The rock on Main Wall is snappy and requires care, but it improves in the Aretes Area.

5 Udder Crack 3m 5a
Climb the thin cracks 2m from the left end of the wall, past a niche and up to a heathery finish.

6 Sacred Cow 6m VS 4c ★
Climb the continuous thin, vertical crack 1m right of Udder Crack.

7 Holy Cow 6m HVS 4c
Start 2m right of the continuous, finger crack. Climb the scruffy right-slanting groove. Climb the groove and move left up a slanting overlap to a ledge. The wall above is climbed direct, via twin cracks. Very loose.

8 What's Coming Up? 7m HVS 4c
Should be called What's Coming Off? Start 1m right of Holy Cow. Climb directly up a flaky, cracked wall until it is possible to step right onto a small ledge. Move right and climb the thin crack which deepen into a groove.

9 Cows Pie 6m VS 4c
Climb the undercut, shallow corner at the right end of Main Wall.

The crag to the right of Main Wall is a series of corners and aretes:

10 The Arete 5m VS 4c
Start at the foot of the arete, 2m right of the corner of Cow Pie. Climb the arete on good holds to an overhang. Above the overhang a slim groove on the right side of the arete is followed to the top.

11 Deadend Groove 6m VS 4b
Climb the loose groove 1m right of The Arete.

12 Jughandle 7m VS 4c ★
Only one hard move and then only for dwarfs, but its near the top. Starts at a very thin crack in the middle of the fine wall right of The Arete. Climb direct on good holds with an interesting move to reach a jug on the left at the top. Nasty landing!

A large Scots Pine grows on a ledge at mid-height and impinges on the next two routes.

13 Aunt Aggie 6m HS 4c
Climb the groove below and left of the big Scots Pine. Move left at the tree and climb the cracked wall on the left.

14 Scots Pine 6m MS 4a
Climb the next big groove to the Pine. Finish up easy rock above.

15 Pine Wall 5m VS 5b ★
Climb the right wall of the groove rather precariously to gain a high, finger crack. Finish up this.

16 Dirty Dave 5m VS 5c ★
Climb the fine arete to the right of Pine Wall. The start involves a leap or a technical layaway move. From the good hold finish up the arete above.

17 Desperate Dan 5m S 4b
Start at the foot of the steep groove just right of Dirty Dave. Climb the steep corner and ledges on the left and finish up a loose groove in the left-hand wall.

18 Tom Thumb 6m HVS 5b ★
A good problem. Start as for Desperate Dan. Make a move up the groove and quit it almost immediately to move up and rightwards

via a break on the right wall. Move round the rib to the right and follow the line of a thin crack to a good hold on the arete. Finish direct from the good hold. Start as for Desperate Dan.

19   Prunesquallor   5a/b-6a   ★
This Low-Level Girdle of the Main Wall and Aretes Area provides an interesting excursion. The move around the arete of Dirty Dave is the crux.

A path now leads rightwards through a tangle of Gorse and Bramble passing under some ribs of poor quality rock with the odd problem. The path soon descends to a fine, flat grassy "landing pad" below a steep wall of good rock. This is:

POD AREA
This is probably the most popular area with excellent though limited bouldering on the best rock in the quarry. A horizontal break- The Pod is a central feature of the upper part of the face.

20   Heather   3m   5a
Start 2m right of the extreme left end of the face and climb the blunt arete direct or alternatively left into a niche reaching the top via a good hold on the left.

21   Gorse   3m   4c   ★
Start 1m right of Heather. Climb the discontinuous, thin vertical crack and finish to the left of The Pod.

22   Broom   4m   5b   ★★
Start below the left-hand crack formed by a large jammed block to the right of The Pod. Climb the left-hand crack to The Pod. Move slightly left and finish up the fine, little crack above, on improving holds.

23   Bedknobs   5m   6a   ★★
Climb the first crack of Broom then climb the wall above to the top, moving rightwards.

24   Brambles   4m   4c
A route for connoisseurs! Climb the crack to the right of the jammed block and move up the groove above and slightly right.

25   Bramble Arete   4m   4a
Climb the arete right of Brambles.

26   Prickles   4b-6a   ★
A very popular Low-Level traverse from the left side of the wall to the wedged block on the right. Many variations are possible. Good for training when done back and forth with a sack of rocks.

From The Pod Area it is possible, if you are stupid to make a bee-line for the next area on the right and could involve encounters with: Trees, bracken, brambles, para-military survivalists, decomposing army rations, spent condoms, local activists (delete as necessary).

It is far easier to pick up the main track a short distance from and parallel to the rock face. Follow this rightwards until a tree-filled bay is reached. This bay contains quite a bit of rock, but it is very overgrown and soft. To the immediate right of the bay is the next area:

TWIN CRACKS AREA

This is located to the right of the big tree-filled bay. A very big Birch Tree grows above a corner. The rock to the left of the Birch is loose and unattractive, but to the right of the corner is a short, slabby wall with at right-angles to it, a longer, steeper wall with a barrier of overhangs low down (almost at ground level on the left). The front of this longer steeper wall has two, slim, parallel cracks running up the middle of it.

27   Ordinary Route   3m   5c
Climb the crack to the left of the corner with the Birch above it.

28   Cracked Slab   5m   3b
Start at the arete right of the corner and just left of the roof-barrier. Climb the arete via a good slanting crack on the left to a ledge. Finish up the slab on the left moving towards the big Birch.

29   Fine Tuned   3m   5b
Climb the thin crack 2m right of the arete. Only use the crack.

30   Pot Black   3m   5c
Start 3m right of the arete. Climb the left-hand of the twin cracks.

31   Twin Cracks   4m   4b
Climb the twin cracks. Surmounting the lip of the low roof being the crux.

32   The Vixen   4m   5a
Very close to the right-hand Twin Crack. Climb the left-facing layback crack avoiding the use of a convenient ledge on the right, below the roof.

33   The Ferret   4m   5a
Start 1m right of The Vixen. Pull out right onto a good sidepull and surmount the overlap to gain a protruding hold at the top of the wall.

34   The Polecat   3m   4b
Climb the faint break direct to the Larch Tree at the top of the wall.

35   The Fox   5m   5a
Climb the obvious layback crack, 4m right of Twin Cracks.

36   Upstairs   4c
Traverse from Cracked Slab to The Fox with hands above the roof.

37   Downstairs   6a
The same as Upstairs but this time with hands below the roof.

To the right of the Twin Cracks Wall are three more short climbs on the ribs of rock emerging (just) from the tangle of vegetation. They are described by their perpetrators as "Mountaineering routes, destined to become minor classics". These are:

38   Slabs 2   3m   3c
Climb the left edge of the slabs 5m right of The Fox.

39   Slabs 1   3m   4c
The slab on the right.

Just to the right of The Slabs is:

40   Blackberries   5m   4a
Climb the crack just right of the Slabs.

From Twin Cracks Area regain the path and continue Eastwards to reach in about fifty metres another shallow pit containing an extensive wall:

MEDUSA TREE AREA

This is at the extreme right-hand end of the quarry. It consists of a continuous wall of rock up to seven metres high. The extreme left wall is split by a steep sharp-edged crack finishing at the Medusa Tree. Right of this wall is a prow of rock which points leftwards and forms a chimney recess between itself and the actual rock face. To the right, the face is guarded by a barrier of overhangs at approximately head-height, the most obvious feature hereabouts being a left-facing, bottomless layback crack; Red Cherry. The rock in this area leaves a lot to be desired and on this account, the climbing is serious, particularly for the inexperienced who should really give it a miss.

41   Stoneface   6m   HS   4b
Start 2m right of the extreme left-hand side of the wall. Climb over the overlap and follow the lines of cracks to an overgrown finish.

42. Permian Face   6m   E2   5c   Climb the wall midway between Stoneface and Medusa.

43   Medusa   7m   HS   4b
The one of the better climbs hereabouts. Climb the left-facing flake crack which runs up the face to the right of the line of overlaps. Finish at the Medusa Tree.

44   The Gorgon   6m   HS   4b
Climb the crack to the right of Medusa. An Elder adds to the complications.

45   Keaton Wall   6m   VS   5a
Start 1m right of The Gorgon. Climb direct to the bulge and ascend the wall above, to the left of the yellow veneer. The holds are good but need careful handling.

46   The Mirror   5m   VS   4c
Start 2m right of Keaton Wall below a slim crack leading up to the overlap which is cracked at this point. Climb up to the overlap and ascend the cracked, shallow groove above to a loose finish.

47   Climb At Your Peril   6m   VS   4b
Start at the foot of the corner leading into the cave between the prow of rock and the actual rock face. Climb into the cave and exit to the left. Take great care with rock.

48   Who Dares Might Win   6m   HVS   4c
Start at the foot of the arete of the prow of rock. Mount good, but loose layaways to reach and climb the middle of the front of the prow on loose holds.

49   Pegleg   6m   HVS   4c
Deserves a Black Spot. Start 1m right of the arete. Climb the lower groove and then the horrendous-looking upper groove to finish at a tree.

50   Virgin   6m   HVS   5b
Start at the foot of a thin crack 4m right of Pegleg, just left of where the barrier roof commences at head-height. Climb the crack exiting right, to finish below a huge Scots Pine.

51   Red Cherry   6m   VS   5a
Start 3m right of The Virgin below the prominent, bottomless, flake crack. Climb the crack to a recess above which is a loose but easier finish.

52   The End   5m   S   4a
Start 1m left of the right-hand end of the overlap. Reach up for a good hold and keep moving right on good holds to finish on a heathery ledge below a bent Pine tree.

53   In Search Of The Chinaman   6a
A continuously interesting (?) Low-Level traverse. Start at Medusa and keep moving right to finish, strangely enough, at The End.

EDEN VALLEY NORTH
MINOR CRAGS AND BOULDERING VENUES

THE GELT BOULDER   O.S. SHEET 86   G.R. 563555
A fine little boulder enjoying something of an international reputation on account of its somewhat erronious inclusion in a guidebook to European climbing.

The Geltstone is situated on the side of the River Gelt about seven miles South-East of Brampton in Cumbria. The boulder is about six metres high and is composed of a fine-grained Quartzite. The climbing is steep, sometimes slightly overhanging and the holds are small, so strong fingers are essential to make the best of it. Even if you can't get up the routes its worth a visit as just downstream is an excellent swimming pool for all the family in the clean water of the Gelt.

Another reason for trying to visit is the perfection of the landing pad. Give it a whirl, but remember, Midges can be a problem on still evenings and of course the visiting hordes of Euroclimbers looking for this 'super-boulder' could lead to some overcrowding.

From Brampton on the A69 Carlisle to Newcastle road, follow signs for Castle Carrock.The B6413 leads after about six miles to Castle Carrock and signs lead past the two pubs and uphill to Geltsdale. Park cars on the obvious right-hand bend at Jockey Shield cottages. A track leads downhill and crosses the river at Hynam bridge. Turn right and walk under small crags beside the river until the derelict cottage of High Hynam is reached and the main path goes uphill. Continue on a small path by the river and after a couple of minutes a fine little swimming pool with a waterfall is passed. Continue upstream for a couple of hundred metres and the boulder will be found abutting against the path. No access problems exist and the place is popular with walkers and picnickers even though the land is privately owned. Please respect this privilege and observe the usual courtesies. Dogs must be left at home or access problems will occur.

The boulder was first climbed on by Stew Wilson in the 1970's and the main problems date back to this time.

There are three faces: The River Face, The Upstream Face and The Main Face.

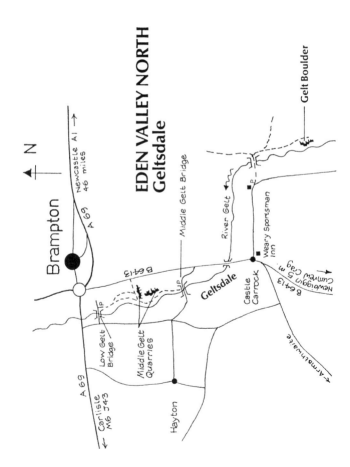

EDEN VALLEY NORTH
Geltsdale

THE RIVER FACE
A couple of longer routes on loose rock of VD standard.
THE UPSTREAM FACE
This narrow face can be climbed anywhere at up to 5c.
The best problem is just left of the arete.

THE MAIN FACE
The arete is very fine 5b/c.
The wall just right of the arete 5b/c and superb.
The section between the wall right of the arete and the crack has problems from 5a-5b whilst the crack and the wall to the right are 4c.
Several traverses can be made and by eliminating holds some desperate problems can be worked out.

MIDDLE GELT QUARRIES   O.S. SHEET 86   527586
Gelt Woods is a famous beauty spot accessed from the A69 just West of Brampton. The valley between Low Gelt Bridge and Middle Gelt Bridge is an excellent and spectacular walk. Huge faces of Sandstone up to thirty metres high dominate the scene. The quarries are numerous, but the best lie where paths coming from Unity farm and Capon Tree to the North of the valley, meet the main valley path. Many climbs have been made on these faces of compact but soft rock, but these have depended entirely on aid from pegs and bolts. Lines of rotting ironmongery can still be seen on the vertical and overhanging faces. A wall of constantly overhanging rock about 15m high lies just off the main path to the right of the path leading to Unity Farm. This has provided steep, bouldering up to now. The rock is soft and dirty, but with a little work it may be a useful bouldering venue.

ST. CONTANTINE'S CELLS CRAG   O.S. SHEET 86   G.R. 467534
Situated in the popular Wetheral Woods these crags lie to the right of and below these hewn-out cells-three in number, which are thought to date back to the days of the Border Reivers or even earlier. They are sometimes called the Wetheral Safeguards. The crags are reached by parking in Wetheral village and descending the steep hill past the church to the river bank. A good footpath follows the river bank in an upstream direction for about half a mile to reach the Caves. The crag just downstream of the cells has two climbs:
A Chimney/corner on the right (VS 4c) and Lammas Tide (HVS 5a) the deepening grooveline on the left. The rock is soft and the climbs are serious.
The buttress below and upstream of the cells has a number of Top-rope problems- all difficult, on soft but compact rock. The crag has probably reverted back to nature. There are many ancient inscriptions hereabouts including one of Roman origin: "Maximus scripsit." On the walls leading down to the cells are some fine inscriptions made by William Mounsey, one in Bardic Welsh and another which is his name spelt backwards except that he uses the Latinised form of William.
Mounsey was a scholar and traveller and was also responsible for similar inscriptions on the Faces Section at Armathwaite.

GREAT CORBY QUARRY   O.S. SHEET 86   G.R. 477545

A scruffy little Sandstone quarry located on Great Corby Common and reached in less than a minute by going through the school playground in Great Corby. Limited bouldering on soft rock.

CAIRN BRIDGE   O.S. SHEET 86   G.R. 503543

Pleasant bouldering on the stone pillars below this road bridge over the Cairn Beck, half a mile South-East of Heads Nook.

LOW HOLM GILL   O.S. SHEET 86   G.R. 510499

Sandstone crags on a spur of land dividing the valley of Chapelwell Beck just North of Low Holm. The crag is reached via a track from the village of Hornsby. Several easier routes have been done on the slabs to the right of the main crag whilst a steep crack in an isolated buttress across the stream has been climbed (VS).

THE SANDS CENTRE CLIMBING WALL, CARLISLE

This D.R. Wall is situated at The Sands Centre at Hardwick Circus in Carlisle. It is open most days until 10.30 pm, but it is worth ringing up to see if it is available (0228-25222).

The wall provides reasonable climbing on vertical walls with a narrow overhanging wall at one end.

4   EDEN VALLEY SOUTH

This area is the open Vale of Eden South of Penrith. It is an area of contrasts ranging from the flanks of the High Pennines, East of the A66 below Cross Fell to the wonderful pastoral landscapes of the lush, limestone valleys of the Lyvennet and Leath to the West of the A66. The upland crags on the flanks of the Pennines at Murton Scar and Brough Scar offer some very hard climbing on good limestone, very reminiscent in some ways of Attemire Scar (without the Yorkshiremen). Helbeck Wood Crag is pleasantly sheltered and with more traffic, should turn out to be pretty good, that is if climbers are discreet in their use of the place. Windmore End is an old quarry which gets all the sun and wind and dries quickly. The shorter routes provide very good bouldering with lots of choice and interest. The climbing is all relatively new and any loose material should soon disappear.

The climbing at King's Meaburn in the Lyvennet valley is much better than it looks and is often a good Winter venue. If you have never climbed on conglomerate, then visit The Hoff, only one minute from the car and close to the fleshpots of the "fun city" of Cumbria, Appleby-in-Westmorland which has some good pubs, cafes and a climbing shop.

THE OTTERSTONES   O.S. SHEET 90   G.R. 553238

SITUATION AND CHARACTER

Situated on the South side of the River Leith five miles South of Penrith. This small Limestone crag faces North in a sheltered valley. It is never likely to be very popular, but the situation and some good low-grade routes on reasonable rock make it worth an evening visit. The Otterstones are just upstream of the crag and consist of a jumble of immense blocks of rock. This was a favourite beauty spot at the turn of the century. The crags consist of s series of walls and corners up to nine metres high. When the climbs were first made, the crag was given a good clean-up but in the intervening years, grass has recolonised the place, particularly the finishes. Vegetation however is not too great a problem and regular use should see the climbs become considerably cleaner. There remains much scope for development.

APPROACHES AND ACCESS

Follow the A6 South from Penrith for about four miles. Immediately before the A6 crosses the M6, turn left and follow the minor road via a sweeping bend towards Melkinthorpe. The road passes under the railway and within a few hundred metres, a right turn is taken leading to Great Strickland. After about half a mile a bridge crosses the River Leith and cars can be parked just beyond in an overgrown gateway on the right To reach the crag, return to the bridge and enter the wood on the South side of the downstream parapet.

Follow the wooded slopes above the river until a mossy, vegetated jumble of huge blocks – The Otterstones – are reached on the opposite bank. To view the Otterstones, it is necessary to cross to the North Bank. Continue downstream until the escarpment on the South bank is reached in a further five minutes. This is identified by a fine wall behind a pile of large blocks: Main Wall. Time from the bridge is about ten minutes as the valley sides are strewn with the debris of timber extracting operations. The woods are private but there are no problems with access, provided the route of approach described is followed and group size is limited. On no account should a shorter route be taken route through the field to the South. Do not take dogs to the crag as ground nesting birds will be disturbed.

HISTORICAL

The crags were discovered by Stew Wilson in the early 1980's. Stew, Ron Kenyon and Paul Carling visited the crags several times resulting in the present routes.

THE CLIMBS

These are described from left to right and section by section.

BUTTRESS 1

The extreme left-hand buttress. Steep or overhanging rock terminating on the right at a big corner with a cave-recess in it.

1   Bad Manners   6m   HS   4b
Start 5m left of the corner with the cave at half-height. Climb onto the pedestal and follow the face to the left of a dirty crackline. Move left to finish at some Ash saplings.

BUTTRESS 2

This is bigger than buttress 1. It extends rightwards from the corner with the cave at half-height and finishes on the right some metres beyond an obvious stepped arete at a point where a huge block fills the bottom-half of what would be a big corner.

2   Bad Mouth   7m   HVS   5a
Start 2m right of the corner with the cave at half-height at a slight overlap left of the undercut arete. Climb up to the right of the small overlap to a broken area of rock above, near a hole.The face face above is climbed via a shallow line of overlaps leading left to a horizontal break. Move left and finish at a notch at the top.

3   The Gob   7m   VS   4c
Start at the foot of the undercut arete right of the corner with the cave at half-height. Climb the undercut arete to a good ledge; the step. Follow the arete above on its left-hand side.

4   Lutra   7m   VS   4c   ★
A good climb which is being masked by an Ivy mass. Start 3m right of the arete at a small left-facing corner/groove. Climb the corner until a prominent, little hole is reached. Move right onto the Ivy-masked ledge then climb the wall above bearing left to finish

To the right of the corner with the huge block filling its bottom half is:

THE MAIN WALL
This takes the form of two steep walls on either side of the main corner of the crag. The right-hand wall has a pile of large blocks in front of it.

5 Summer Bird 9m HS 4a *
Steep climbing on excellent rock. Start from behind an Ash tree, 2m left of the main corner. Climb the wall to the right-end of a long, narrow ledge. The steep upper wall has good holds and this provides a pleasant finish.

6 Matty's Corner 8m D
Climb the corner on the outside. Much better than it looks.

7 In Through The Out Door 9m HVS 5b **
An excellent steep, wall climb with good protection. Start 2m right of Matty's Corner below a very thin crack. Climb the line of the very thin crack and finish up the steepest part of the face directly above, passing a horizontal break.

8 Fool In The Rain 9m HVD
Start at a steep crack below and right of an Elm tree growing on a ledge on the face. Climb the cracked wall passing the tree to gain and climb the wider crack above. An interesting route.

9 Crayfish 9m S
Start 2m left of the right hand arete of the wall and just left of the undercut base. Climb the wall direct to reach the left-hand end of a ledge. Steep climbing up and leftwards leads to better holds and the top.

10 Amber 9m S
Start just right of the right-hand arete of the Main Wall. Move leftwards onto the arete and gain a small ledge. Continue to a bigger ledge. The arete above is climb mainly on the left to a good tree at the top.
    To the right of the arete, the base of the crag consists of a complex of large blocks forming at half-height a good ledge below a square-cut chimney and some ribs to the right. To the right of this is the final section:

PLONGEUR SECTION
This consists of a steep corner crack with a slabby left wall and a much steeper, undercut right-hand wall which is split by a hand crack above a small Sycamore growing out of the face.

11 Gelert 9m S *
Better rock than appearances suggest. A very pleasant climb – when clean! Start below the centre of the left-hand wall. Climb steeply on good holds until the angle eases. The wall is climbed moving slightly leftwards to finish at a break, just right of a dead tree.

12 The Plongeur 9m MVS 4b *
Steep climbing on good holds with good protection. Start 4m right of the corner in the middle of the right-hand wall at a right-facing corner. Climb the short, right-facing corner to a ledge just left of a sapling Sycamore. Follow the twisting, vertical crack to finish.

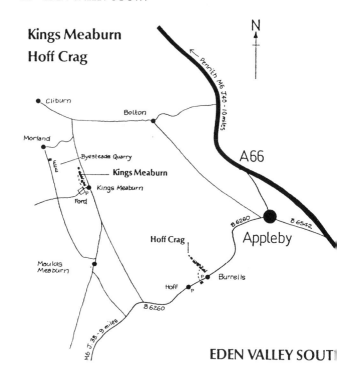

Kings Meaburn
Hoff Crag

N

Cliburn

Bolton

Penrith M6 J40 - 10 miles

Morland

A66

Byesteads Quarry

Kings Meaburn

Kings Meaburn

Ford

B 6260

Appleby

B 6542

Hoff Crag

Moulds Meaburn

Burrells

Hoff

B 6260

M6 J 38 - 9 miles

EDEN VALLEY SOUT

KINGS MEABURN – JACKDAW SCAR
O.S. SHEET 91   G.R. 618213

SITUATION AND CHARACTER

An outcrop of variable quality Carboniferous limestone rising above the River Lyvennet just West of the village of Kings Meaburn. The crag, better known locally as Jackdaw Scar, faces West and has an idyllic location in an area largely unknown to the tourist or for that matter, the climber. The area, part of an extensive rolling upland of limestone, hosts a scattering of very attractive villages along with several excellent inns to revive the weary climber.

The crag takes the form of a continuous wall of limestone, divided into a number of bays and has the unusual feature of being perched atop a base of soft sandstone. In general, the limestone overlaps the sandstone and many of the climbs sport overhanging, gymnastic starts. The crag is sheltered and in a sunny position and so can provide good climbing in winter. Some sections of the crag are however, lichenous and can make life unpleasant in damp weather. The rock in general is good, but as with all limestone, care should be taken with brittle edges. Descents should be made by abseil from the many trees on the top or by walking along the top of the crag and descending at the extreme left-hand end via some rocky shelves beyond the First Bay.

APPROACHES AND ACCESS

The crag is best approached from Penrith. Follow the A6 south towards Shap, but after crossing Eamont Bridge (traffic lights), a minor road, the second on the left, just beyond a layby, is followed to Cliburn. Beyond Cliburn, the road crosses a small river and one and a half miles beyond, a junction on the right near a telephone box, is signposted to Kings Meaburn. In the village, go past the White Horse Inn and turn immediately right down a steep and narrow lane to park on land in front of a ford across the River Lyvennet.The crag is clearly visible above and left of the cottages.

Kings Meaburn can also be reached from the A66 West of Appleby by taking the first left turn beyond the Appleby bypass heading for Penrith. This leads through the village of Bolton and beyond, to the junction with the telephone box, signposted to Kings Meaburn.

The crag is easily reached by following the well-marked path in front of the cottages, then strike up to the crag to arrive in the Fifth bay near a massive beech tree. **There are no access problems but climbers must not climb beyond the drystone wall, above the cottages.**

HISTORICAL

Details of climbing are vey sketchy until about 1973, but prior to this J. Simpson, J. Workman and D. Hodgson climbed Marik, using aid.

A couple of visits by R. Kenyon, T. Dale, A. Beatty and P. Rigby renewed interest and in this period many of the climbs were recorded. Ron Kenyon was instrumental in the first free ascent of Marik, a fine plum to pick.

The Gebbeth was ascended on a top-rope by Alan Beatty. Beatty soon led this route which was something of a 'Horror Show' at the time on account of the loose rock. This phase of development soon led onto the blanker walls, when Phil Rigby contributed Phall and Pete Whillance showed up to claim Maid Marian Way.

The two fine lines of Gont and Windkey were popular top rope problems. Gont was first led by Stew Wilson and Chris King, unbeknown to one another around the same period, not so Windkey.

Paul Carling was towed along to the crag by Stew Wilson and pointed at Windeye which he did in good style only to have mud thrown in his eye by certain locals who made the second ascent and placed a peg which Paul promptly removed.

Development in the latter part of the Eighties was entirely in the hands of Karl Lunt and friends. In June 1987, he solved a long-standing problem by leading the difficult Windkey in the company of John and Stewart Wilson.

One year later, Lunt led the Headmaster Ritual and in November 1988 several easier climbs were done after abseil cleaning, the best being Small Assassin. Three days before the end of the year, Lunt

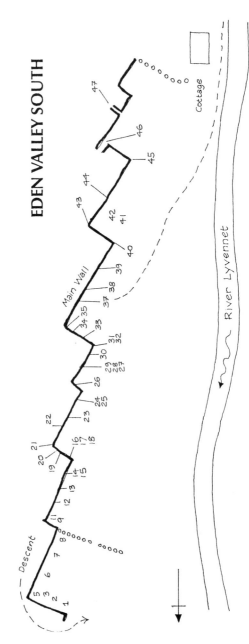

EDEN VALLEY SOUTH

Kings Meaburn – Jackdaw Scar

climbed The Ring of Confidence with Tom Phillips. In May 1989, Lunt accompanied by Andy Williamson led the old top rope problem, Trilogy but had to resort to side runners.

THE CLIMBS

These are described from left to right, beginning in the First Bay at the Northern or downstream end of the scar. To reach this point, walk a short distance in a downstream direction at the foot of the crag, passing through an old gateway in a stone wall.

FIRST BAY

The First Bay consists of two walls at right-angles to one another. A large tree has fallen from the base of the right hand wall.

1   Tree Chimney   6m   D
Climb the chimney, behind the tree on the left wall.

2   First Wall Eliminate   6m   HVS   5c   ∗
Start to the right of the chimney, below a narrow pillar. Climb the centre of this, without recourse to the holds in Owl Crack.

3   Owl Crack   6m   MS
Start just right of the pillar and climb the obvious wide crack which bounds it on the right.

4   Twist and Shout   6m   MVS   4b
Start immediately left of the corner of the bay. Climb the thin crack, which slants up the left wall.

5   TD Corner   8m   MS
The corner of the bay is climbed on good holds. Beware of loose rock at the top.

6   Phall   8m   E1   5b
A delicate wall climb, with no protection.
Start below the right wall, where a large tree root emerges from the foot of the crag. Climb gymnastically up the short, steep wall to a small ledge. Move up and rightwards to finish just right of the tree at the top.

7   Ivy Crack   8m   HVS   5a   ∗∗
Start of a clear scar where a large dead Elm has fallen. Hard moves at the start lead to a crack. Finish up this.

8   Maid Marian Way   8m   E2   5b   ∗
Another bold wall climb. Start to the right of the clean scar and climb the wall direct, passing just left of a patch of rippled calcite. Better holds arrive near the top. Protectionless.

SECOND BAY

To the right of the drystone wall is the second recess. A huge, three-stemmed sycamore grows out of a ledge 2 metres up the right wall.

9   Trilogy   9m   E3   5c   ∗
A sustained climb, which can be protected with side runners in the crack of Liang Shan Po. Start just right of where the drystone wall meets the crag. Climb bulging rock, to reach a rightward slanting crack. Pull onto the wall immediately left of this, then climb directly

to an overlap. Move left with difficulty into a short corner just right of the arete and finish up this.

10   Liang Shan Po   9m   HVS   5b
Start as for Trilogy. Follow the rightward slanting crack without straying onto Slipway. The overhang at the top constitutes the crux.

11   Slipway   9m   HS   ★
Quite a classy line with pleasant positions and good holds.
Start at the gnarled boss of roots below a fine, steep corner. Climb up the sandstone band and follow the corner moving right at the top to finish up a short wall.

12   Bay Rum   9m   VD   ★
A good climb with some nice positions. Start on the ledge behind the three-stemmed sycamore. Climb the easy- angled corner to a steep finish.

13   Nightride   9m   VS   4c
Start behind the three-stemmed sycamore. Climb the wall to the right of the crack of Bay Rum. Move right to a small tree in the centre of the wall. A leftward ascending line of doubtful flakes is followed to the top.

14   Ged   9m   MVS   4c   ★
Steep, with good holds and protection. Start 3m right of the right-hand stem of the sycamore tree. Climb the sandstone band and ascend the steep, cracked wall to the top.

15   Double Jeopardy   9m   HVS   5a
Start at the foot of Ged, but climb up and right over two, big jammed blocks (care!). Ascend the wall above, direct.

THIRD BAY

Below the crag is a huge Yew tree. The Third Bay lies behind this. Two thorn bushes grow on a ledge which runs along the base of the left wall at a height of 2 metres. Scramble onto this ledge to gain the starts of the next routes.

16   Steph   9m   MVS   4b   ★
A one move crux, but nevertheless a good climb.Start on the ledge, 2 metres right of the left-hand arete. A short, undercut groove provides a difficult start. Move up more easily and follow the interesting crack in the arete.

17   Crabstack   9m   VS   4b
Start as for Steph by climbing the crucial groove then move right up the steep crack above to the top. Care with loose rock!

18   Tove Wall   9m   MVS   4b
Start on the ledge by the large thorn bush to the right of the previous routes. Climb the steep crack to the right of the thorn (ouch!) passing a small ledge.

19   Rune Wall   9m   HS   4a
A small thorn bush grows out of the base of a wide crack. Climb past the bush and up the crack via a wedged block and a tree. Finish up a short gully.

20   Headmaster Ritual   9m   E3   6a   ★
A bold, fingery climb. Small wires are useful. Between Rune Wall and the corner of the bay is a tapering pillar. Climb the centre of

this, using a very thin crack to start. Better holds are reached near the top.

21   Percy Throwup   9m   VD   ★★
Good solid jug-pulling. Start below the corner of the bay. Climb the steep, twin, corner cracks to a ledge. Finish either right or left.

22   The Ring of Confidence   9m   E1   5b
Six metres right of the corner of the bay, the sandstone base is undercut. Start just to the left of this point and move rightwards above the overlap on jugs to gain the edge of the wall. Climb up past a thread trending slightly leftwards to finish up the wall above.

23   Fast and Hideous   9m   VS   5a
Six metres right of the corner of the bay is a prominent, steep groove, in which grows a tree at 4 metres. Climb the crack past the tree to the bulge and pull round this awkwardly to the right.

24   Fickle Flake   9m   HVS   4c
This is a steep and serious climb on spooky rock. Start 1.5 metres left of the right-hand arete of the bay. Climb the sandstone band and surmount a bulge to gain the thin flake. Awkward laybacking on doubtful holds leads to the top.

25   The Bulge   9m   E1   4c
A dangerous undertaking with suspect rock requiring "Full Throb" useage. Protection is poor. Not recommended! Start as for Fickle Flake, but move right below the bulge, onto the arete. Ascend this on good holds to finish up broken ledges.

FOURTH BAY
A small recess. It is most easily identified by the large, right-slanting flake crack: "the Flake" on its right wall.

26   The Small Assassin   9m   VS   5b
The left-hand wall of the bay contains a prominent, straight crack with a tree at three-quarters height. Climb the sandstone band with difficulty to gain the crack. Pass the tree on its left and climb the broken, continuation crack.

27   Bulging Crack   9m   HS   4b
Start at the foot of the corner crack to the left of "the Flake". Climb the crack, finishing up past trees on the left or alternatively up the wall on the right.

28   The Flange   9m   HS   4b
A bit artificial in that it climbs the crux of Bulging Crack, but the last few metres are worthwhile. Start as for Bulging Crack. From the first bulge of that route, pull out right and climb the right edge of the large flake to the top.

29   The Flake   11m   HS   4b   ★★
A fine climb which requires a determined approach.
Start at the foot of the corner, as for Bulging Crack. Gain the bottom of the flake and move up the flake crack rightwards until the groove above can be climbed to an easier finish.

30   Scarlet Lyvennet   11m   MVS   4a
Start to the right of "the Flake" at an Elder bush. Climb the wall above the bush to pass an arch-shaped overlap. Climb the wrinkled

wall above to a ledge then move up and right to finish at the top of the arete. The top is quite runout.

31   Babel Towers   12m   HS   4c
Start at the foot of the right-hand arete. Climb this gymnastically to a groove, then follow this to a ledge. Move left to finish as for The Flake.

FIFTH BAY

This is the arrival point at the crag using the described approach. The right-hand wall (Main Wall) is the largest, most continuous stretch of rock on the crag and holds the greatest concentration of hard climbs at Kings Meaburn.

32   Bogey Arete   12m   VS   4c
Start as for Babel Towers but instead of moving left, climb the arete directly to the top.

33   Kirsten Wall   12m   HS   4a   ★
An intimidating-looking wall which proves to be quite pleasant. Start 2 metres right of the left arete of the bay. Climb the overhanging corner to a ledge above the sandstone band. From here, climb the centre of the cracked wall above, trending right, to finish at a tree.

34   Trundle Crack   11m   HS   4a
Start in the corner of the bay. Gain the ledge above the sandstone band. Climb the crack to the left of the actual corner crack.

35   Leaning Crack   11m   HS   4a
Follow the previous climb to the ledge, then climb the corner crack.

36   Havnor   11m   VS   5a
A good route, eclipsed by Marik. It is steep but has good holds and protection. Start from the ledge as for the previous two routes. Climb the wall behind the tree.

37   Marik   14m   VS   4c   ★★
A fabulous climb, steep and interesting and at the top end of the grade. Start at the left-hand side of the Main Wall below a thin crack which is a prominent feature hereabouts. Climb awkwardly up the sandstone band until the crack, with perfect protection, can be climbed through a bulge to a resting place. Finish direct or more easily, right then left just below the top.

38   The Windeye   17m   E3   5c   ★★★
A superb wall climb which can be surprisingly well-protected. High in the grade, especially so for the short. Start 3m right of Marik. Climb through the overhang at a slight groove to reach a good, horizontal break. Traverse right to an in-situ thread then pull onto the wall above with assistance from a thin crack above and to the right. Hard moves trend up and left into a very faint scoop. From here climb up diagonally rightwards on improving holds to the top. Small wires are useful.

39   Gont   14m   E2   5c   ★
A climb of contrasts: a brutish overhang, then a fine, thin wall. Start below the centre of the overhang where it is split by a hairline crack. Climb up to and overcome the overhang with difficulty to

reach better holds in the break above. Move right to a stump, then climb the cracked wall above. An easier alternative is to gain the stump starting from the corner at the right-hand end of the wall. (E1 5b).

40   Windkey   14m   E3   6a   *
Strenuous and technical on the crux, but protection could be excellent. Some insecure holds require care. Start at the foot of the right-hand arete of the Main Wall. Climb the sandstone band to a ledge. Move up and slightly left to reach a short, thin crack and follow this steeply (crux) until better holds turn up. Finish up the wall above.

SIXTH BAY

This bay can be identified by the large Beech tree growing on the path below it. The sandstone band, here forms a steep, mossy slab below the right-hand wall. The rock from here onwards is not above suspicion in places and caution must be exercised on some routes.

41   The Gebbeth   14m   E2   5b   *
A steep and sustained climb which just warrants its grade. Start just right of the right -hand arete of Main Wall in a cracked recess. Climb up to the roof and pull round this to a ledge. Climb the wall above via the thin, discontinuous cracks to the top.

42   Curvy Crack   14m VS   4b
Start at the foot of the curving crack to the left of the corner of the bay. Climb the crack.

43   Toolie Corner   14m   MVS   4b
Climb the corner of the bay.

44   Something to Remember   12m   VS   4c
Start in the middle of the right wall where the sandstone band is split by a thin crack holding a sapling. Climb the crack then move up rightwards to gain a crack in the wall above. Follow this to the top.

45   Titus Alone   12m   NL   5b
The stuff that legends are made of! A thoroughly dangerous place. Start at the foot of the right-hand arete and climb it. Overhanging scree!

SEVENTH BAY

This is the last section of the crag. The broken drystone wall defines the right-hand boundary. DO NOT CROSS THE DRYSTONE WALL TO REACH THE ROCK ABOVE THE COTTAGES.

46   Titus Groan   12m   E1   5a
The blatantly obvious cleft.This very intimidating prospect is not helped by the presence of several tons of 'Hanging Death' that has to be climbed under around and over to reach the sanctuary of the upper face. Start in the corner of the bay. Climb the cleft until moves on the vertical right wall enable the left wall to be bridged up to the overhang. Pull around this and gain a groove which is followed to the top. Technically reasonable but adventurous!!!

47   Flic-Flac Crack   9m   VS   4c
Start at the foot of a wide crack, 6 metres right of Titus Groan and just right of an untidy boss of roots and branches. Climb the crack to tree belays.

48   Crippling Crack   9m   S
Start on a ledge, 3 mtres right of Flic-Flac Crack below a corner. Climb the corner on good holds.

THE HOFF   O.S. SHEET 91   G.R.675179

SITUATION AND CHARACTER

The crag in the meadow! The Hoff is a strange eruption of lovely vertical conglomerate rising abruptly out of a tranquil pasture above the Hoff Beck.

The situation could hardly be bettered, at least not for those operating in the lower grades. The rock, Brockram, is a conglomerate of lumps of sandstone and limestone in a very strong natural cement. The climbing tends to be steep, but the holds are usually good. The rock is clean and dries in minutes and so is good at all times of the year. In damp conditions however the finishes, on the level, turf top can be quite bold.

The topography is quite simple, a single long wall with a short wall at the left end hingeing around a right-angled corner.

Protection is possible, but not entirely trustworthy. The landings however must rate with the best anywhere and for this reason it is popular with solo climbers. If you must top-rope, please extend anchors over the edge of the crag to avoid the horrible grooving of the turf top. If you wish to lead climbs, then it might be a good idea to have an extended anchor to protect the dodgy moves over the top.

Descents can be made at either end of the crag, but the right-hand end can be very slippery in damp conditions.The crag has a uniform height of about 8 metres, so heights are omitted in the descriptions.

APPROACHES AND ACCESS

The crag is easily reached from either Appleby or from Junction 38 on the M6 at Tebay by following the B6260. Approaching from Appleby, follow this road through the village of Burrells and beyond, for about 300 metres. On the left-hand side of the road is a bungalow whilst on the right over the hedge the crag is clearly visible. There is room for one vehicle on the verge opposite the bungalow, but lack of vision makes this hazardous to all road users. It is better to continue a further 400 metres and park near the pub at Hoff. It is possible to combine a trip to this crag with a visit to Kings Meaburn: from Hoff follow the B6260 in the direction of the M6 for just over a mile to the first junction on the right. Turn right and follow this road to the village of Kings Meaburn.

The crag at Hoff is approached via a gate into the meadow.

The crag is on private land and access has been granted on the understanding that no litter is left or damage done to property, fences etc. There are no public rights of way below the crag or beside the beck. **Dogs must not be taken to the crag.**

PERHAPS THE MOST DISTRESSING VANDALISM AT THE CRAG IS PERPETRATED BY HORDES OF SO CALLED 'ACADEMICS' BENT ON KNOCKING HELL OUT OF THE CRAG IN THE NAME OF GEOLOGY. PLEASE REMONSTRATE IF YOU ARE UNLUCKY ENOUGH TO BE WITNESS TO THESE ACTS.

HISTORICAL

The crag has been climbed on by local climbers since the 1970's. The recorded routes are the work of Ron Kenyon, Tim Dale, Phil Rigby, Dave Bowen and Stew Wilson.

THE CLIMBS

The climbs are described from left to right as one faces the crag.

AFTERTHOUGHT WALL

The steep wall some metres left of the main crag. It has a steep wall with a stepped arete on the right.

1   Afterthought   MS
Climb directly up the steep wall.

2   Little Wall   S
Climb the right-hand side of the wall to finish over a bulge at a break in the arete.

MAIN WALL

3   Afterlife   HVS   5b
Climb the prominent, jutting arete left of the corner, on its right-hand side. Serious.

4   The Corner   MS
Climb the obvious corner at the left-hand end of the Main Wall. Not very good.

5   Going Green   MS
Start at the foot of the wall, just right of The Corner. Climb the wall in the line of a small tree just below the top.

6   Rainbow   HS   4a
Start just right of Going Green at a rib, just left of a shallow corner. Climb the left side of the rib to the top.

7   Dig For Victory   MVS   4b
Start below the shallow corner, right of Rainbow. Climb the wall just right of the corner and move into the corner to finish.

8   The Shades   MVS   4b   *
Start 2m right of the shallow corner. Climb the smooth wall and pleasurably surmount the overlap at 3m, via a pocket. Climb the shallow runnel directly to the top.

9   The Devon   HS   4a
Start below the wall and overlap just left of the steep crack holding a tree. Climb the wall and overlap.

10   Mojo   MS
The first major crack on Main Wall. Climb the crack in its entirety, passing the tree either left or right.

11   Gromerzog   HVS   5b   ★

A horrible name but a fine little climb. No more chipping please!
Start 1.5 metres right of Mojo at the foot of a very steep, smooth
wall. Climb direct, eschewing **all** pockets on the left. The line
continues over the right-hand end of a tapering overlap at 5 metres.

12   Blonde Ella   VS   4b

The smooth wall of Gromerzog takes on a rougher texture 3 metres
right of the crack of Mojo. Climb up this textured wall trending
leftwards to finish left of the band of small overhangs at the top.

13   Slap Bang in the Middle   VS   4c

Start at the incipient crack, just right of Blonde Ella. Climb the steep
wall direct, through an area of very compact rock. Finish through
the centre of the overhang at a layaway flake.

14   Brant   S

Start at a set of left pointing flakes on the wall, 2 metres right of Slap
Bang In The Middle. Climb the flakes and the very faint rib above,
to finish up a shallow scoop.

15   Barwise   HS   ★★

Super holds! Start immediately below a small stump, at head height
just right of Brant. Climb past the stump and continue up an
obvious runnel. Finish directly up the steep wall.

16   Slosh Wall   S   ★

Start 1 metre right of Barwise. Follow the wall just left of the
second, obvious crack on Main Wall, passing a 'hole' near the top.

17   Havers Crack   S

Start below the obvious crack with a large, mangled stump at 3
metres. Climb the crack.

18   Spare Rib   HS   4a

Climb the rib above and to the right of the large, mangled stump in
Havers Crack.

19   Pig Meat   HS   4a   ★

Start 1 metre right of the mangled stump. Climb the shallow
groove, just right of Spare Rib.

20   Wormrigg Wall   HS   4a   ★

Start 2 metres right of Pig Meat. Follow the steep wall, slightly
rightwards on a series of sharp flakes. Finish left of a small sapling.

21   Saxon   S

Climb the wall directly below the small sapling.

22   Burrells   S   ★

Start directly below the small tree, sprouting just below the top of
the crag. Climb direct to the tree via cracks. The wall above the tree
is steep.

23   The Arete   VD

Ascend the right-hand arete of Main Wall.

Girdle Traverses

There are numerous possibilities for traverses at all levels.

MURTON SCAR O.S. SHEET 91 G.R. 733 226

SITUATION AND CHARACTER

Perched high on the Southern slopes of Murton Pike, this lime-stone crag occupies a prominent position overlooking the Upper Eden Valley. The crag takes the form of a single, steep wall banded by overhangs and offering few easy options. Although there are some worthwhile lower-grade climbs, Murton will appeal more to the lover of technical limestone. Facing South, the crag is exposed to the prevailing winds but also catches the sun and dries quickly after rain. The rock is sound and compact on the lower part of the crag but caution is necessary higher up where the rock is more broken. Several of the harder climbs contain in-situ pegs and threads. The ground below the crag falls away steeply so belays are advisable.

APPROACHES AND ACCESS

Murton village is easily reached from the A66 near Appleby. Follow signs for Hilton and Murton. After passing Hilton the road enters Murton and crosses a bridge over the beck. Immediately beyond this, turn right and park on the grass near the cottage at the end of the lane. A gate allows access to the open fell and a recently constructed track can be followed first left and then right as it cuts across the flank of Murton Pike. A more pleasant, direct route is to follow the obvious tracks running through the brackento reach the made-up track below the crag. Steep grass leads to the foot of the buttress. Descents can be made at either end of the face.

HISTORICAL

The first records of climbing on Murton Scar, date back to November 1975 when Ron Kenyon and members of the Eden Valley club visited the crag. In this period the most notable ascent was Kenyon's Murton Moggy. The deep gully of the crag was climbed by Alan Stark and named Keach.

The crag was not very popular because the 'lines' were generally steep and intimidating and did not always provide natural protection. In addition the upper part of the face is composed of easier rock and the 'real meat' of the routes involves only twelve metres of climbing.

On 24th April 1976, Ronnie returned with Sally Dixon and Ray Parker and the trio had a very productive day, climbing Meal Ticket, Brown Dirt Cowboy and Felix. Ron then turned his attention to the fine central line of the Main Overhang Section and after a struggle, finished the line, calling it Sunshine Super Sal, but unfortunately had to resort to using aid from two nuts in the upper crack.

The next real phase of development involved Robin Curley, Chris Thwaites and Noel Stansfield, all from Appleby. In the Summer of 1983 they concentrated their efforts on Murton Scar producing a fine collection of difficult climbs. Robin Curley climbed Sunshine Super Sal completely free and then went on to produce Morgan's Lane. Chris Thwaites climbed the fine unclimbed groove to the left of Sushine Super Sal naming it Mind Over Matter. The fine left-

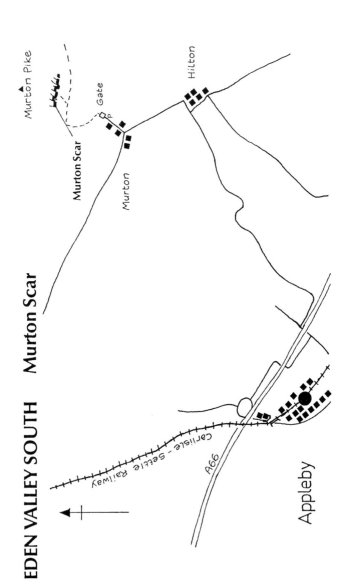

curving line on the Left Wall provided Thwaites with All Along The Watchtower; one of the best climbs on the crag. Curley inspected the blank wall to the left of this and after placing a peg and thread runner, led The Haunted Smear which involved some extremely hard climbing on superb rock. Noel Stansfield contributed his Bigus Dickus and joined Curley in Incontinentia Buttocks.

The clean, tall prow to the left of Murton Moggy could not escape the attention of Curley and eventually, this provided a hard and bold lead named Red Hot Spankers.

THE CLIMBS

These are described section by section and from left to right.

The crag can be conveniently divided into three distinct sections:

Left Wall; Main Overhang section and Right Wall.

LEFT WALL

This consists of a steep, smooth wall of excellent rock topped by a continuous band of small roofs, with more broken rock above. This wall terminates on the right where a steep, crack/groove abuts against the bulging buttress at the left-hand side of the Main Overhang area.

The left-hand end of Left Wall is split by two slim cracks. The second one curves leftwards to meet the roof.

1   Earl Street   15m   E3   6a   **★★**
Start below the second crack which curves leftwards. Climb the thin crack, passing an 'in situ' ring peg. Continue in this line to the roof. Traverse right for a couple of metres until a break in the overhang, containing a wedged block is reached. Surmount the roof and finish up easier grooves above.

2   Earl Street Direct   15m   E3   5c
Start below a thin crack just right of Earl Street. Climb this crack direct to the good foothold on All Along The Watch Tower. Climb direct to the roof and surmount it just to the right of the wedged block. Above the roof, step left and finish as for Earl Street.

3   All Along The Watch Tower   16m   E3   6a   **★★★**
A superb line with continuously interesting climbing. Start 3m right of Earl Street at the foot of the question mark-shaped curving flake. Climb the flake passing an 'in situ' thread runner at 5m. Step left to a good foothold. Make a difficult pull, up and right and pull through the roof 2m right of the break containing the block (Earl Street). Finish up a deep groove which contains a flake-edged block.

4   The Haunted Smear   15m   E3   6b   **★**
Start below the centre of the steep, smooth wall just right of the curving flake of All Along The Watch Tower. Climb the centre of the smooth wall, passing an 'in situ' peg runner and move slightly right to an 'in situ' thread, to a junction with Morgan's Lane which comes in from the right. Move left to enter a groove which leads up to a metre wide roof above. Climb this at its centre on excellent jugs and finish up easier rock.

Murton Scar

5   Morgan's Lane   16m   E3   5c   ***
Start below a 2m high, thin crack on the right of The Haunted Smear wall. Climb this short crack and step right into a little, grassy recess. Climb up and leftwards on underclings, passing a couple of 'in situ' threads to the junction with The Haunted Smear. Move left to enter a groove which leads more easily to a one metre roof above. Climb this at its centre to good jugs. Climb more easily to the top.

6   Mind Over Matter   15m   HVS   5a   **
The "steep, unclimbed groove" of the 1981 guide. Start below a faint crackline which opens into a square recessed groove to the left of the overhanging left buttress of Main Overhang Section. Climb the faint crackline just right of Morgan's Lane, passing a small thread runner at 4m. Continue via tricky moves to enter the niche which contains a sapling. Climb up and out of the niche, following the groove to exit right to easier rock and the top.

MAIN OVERHANG SECTION
This extends rightwards from the "unclimbed groove" of Mind Over Matter to a deep chimney/gully containing loose-looking blocks which provides the line of Keach. The Main Overhang is imposing and provides a difficult exit to routes in the centre of the section.

7   Sunshine Super Sal   15m   E1   5b   ***
One of the original routes, now a magnificent free climb. Start 2m right of Mind Over Matter at a short 1m high, blunt spike of rock below a thin crackline. Climb the thin crackline, taking care with the semi-detached finger of rock in the lower part. At a downward pointing spike, step right under the bulge to move up to a good ledge below the Main Roof. A good crack leads diagonally leftwards following a sensational traverse line through the roof. After a couple of metres climb directly up the vertical continuation crack in the headwall. Easy ledges lead to the top.

8   Body Rock   15m   E3   5c   *
This route accepts the challenge of the Main Overhang. Start 1m right of Sunshine Super Sal below a faint groove in the crozzly wall directly below the Main Overhang. Climb the slim groove and wall to below the major break in the overhang. Climb the break through the overhang into a slim groove above which has a protruding block in it. Pass an 'in-situ' thread runner on the left. Finish easily above.

9   Deadend Groove   17m   VS   4c
Start below a slim groove 1m right of Body Rock. Climb the obvious slim groove on reasonable holds until the roof is reached. Traverse right below the roof for about 4m to reach the continuation, steep, cracked corner above the block-filled chimney of Keach. Finish up this.

10   Keach   15m   VS   4c
Start at the foot of the open, block-filled chimney/gully at the right-hand end of the Main Overhang Section. Climb the steep gully to a ledge. Finish up the steep, cracked corner above. Care with rock and protection.

RIGHT WALL

The Right Wall is generally less-steep than the other two sections. It consists of two steep corners on the left-hand side with between them a, steep buttress, topped by a fine prow. Further right, the crag is more slabby and swings around and up the hillside to terminate in a short-steep buttress: The Egg.

11   Bitter Fingers   15m   VS   4c
Start 2m right of Keach at the foot of the next obvious, shallow corner. Climb the shallow corner to a grassy ledge above which is a patch of grey, smooth rock. Move directly up to another ledge and climb the twin, cracks above to the top.

12   Red Hot Spankers   16m   E3   5c   ★★
Start below the middle of a very steep, narrow, white wall just right of Bitter Fingers. This wall has an 'in situ' thread runner at mid-height. A bold climb! Climb the wall direct past the thread runner. Finish by pulling leftwards over the prow which is left of the finish of Murton Moggy.

13   Murton Moggy   16m   VS   4c   ★★
At the upper end of the VS grade. Start below the next obvious line where a white cone of rock, cracked on either side leads up to a pronounced groove. Climb the left side of the cone of rock into the groove above which is followed to a ledge below a bulge. The bulge is overcome by means of a left-trending crackline. Finish up easier ledges above.

Five metres right of Murton Moggy is a left-slanting crackline at the base of which is a downward pointing, small nose of rock. The next two climbs start at the foot of this crackline.

14   Catlike Tread   15m   MVS
Follow the left-slanting crackline to some small saplings. Exit above and rightwards on loose rock.

15   Meal Ticket   15m   VS   4b
Start below the downward pointing tongue of rock as for Catlike Tread.
Move up rightwards to ascend a fine, blunt rib leading to a prominent, narrow corner-groove. Ascend this with difficulty to ledges and the top.

The next feature of note is The Egg, a prominent short, steep buttress of excellent rock on the right end of the crag, commencing at half-height.

16   Brown Dirt Cowboy   12m   HS
Climb the corner to the left of The Egg either in the corner or via its left wall.

17   Felix   12m   MVS   4b   ★
A good cat whose bark would appear to be worse than its bite. Climb up to below the corner of Brown Dirt Cowboy then move right onto The Egg to follow a steep, crack to the top.

18   Bigus Dickus   12m   VS   4c
Start below the front face of The Egg, to the right of Felix. Climb the wall direct, passing an overhang at mid-height.

19   Incontinentia Buttocks   12m   E3   5c   ★
Start below the steep crack on the arete of The Egg. Climb the steep crack on the arete direct on excellent rock.

HELBECK WOOD CRAG   O.S. SHEET 91   G.R. 787 167

SITUATION AND CHARACTER

A limestone crag situated at the North end of Helbeck Wood about three quarters of a mile West of Brough Scar and accessed as for that crag.

Helbeck Wood Crag faces South-West and despite its altitude is a sheltered place to climb. The rock is sound and compact and does not run to large holds. The crag contains some excellent natural lines, amongst the best in the Eden Valley.

ACCESS AND APPROACHES

The crag is on private land and their are no Public Rights Of Way but the approach described has been used by climbers without hindrance for some years now. From Brough Scar take a rising line up and over the crest of the ridge to gain a wall. Follow this Westwards, crossing it where it bends sharp left. Continue along the flank of the ridge over the rise passing to the left of a small tarn. Descend past an area of tilted limestone pavement to meet another wall which can be crossed at a gap. Follow this wall down to the left where it joins the boundary of Helbeck Wood. The crag is over this wall extending away to the right. Time from Brough Scar is 25 minutes.

HISTORICAL

All of the routes are the work of Karl Lunt and Tom Phillips in the 1980s.

THE CLIMBS

These are described from left to right and it is best to walk along the base of the crag to the left end to locate the first routes. The major feature of the left end of the crag is a large roof with two parallel grooves leading up to it.

1   Sergeant Rock   12m   HVS   5a

Follow the right-hand groove. At the roof swing right onto a small ledge. Finish up blocks above.

To the right is a large, easy-angled corner. The next route is on the left wall.

2   Shoot To Kill   12m   E4   6a   ★★

Follow the parallel cracks finishing above the left-hand one. Desperate.

3   Fylingdale Flier   13m   HS

Climb the easy-angled corner.

Variation: VS   4c

At two-thirds height, break out onto the left wall and finish up this.

4   Judge For Yourself   12m   VS   5b

Start midway along the right wall and climb this direct. An easier start utilizes the undercut flake crack, just right.

Nearby, one stem of a large tree has split and rests against the rock. The next route starts just right of this:

5   Rabbit On The Windscreen   15m   HS   4b
Layback the crack and continue up the groove-line to a ledge.

The section of crag right from here contains several excellent routes all on sound rock. The first major feature is a right-slanting ramp line.

6   Crossfire   17m   VS   4c   ★★★
Follow the ramp to the overlap. Swing up and right on good holds then continue in the same line to finish.

7   Silkworm   15m   E2   5b   ★★
Start below a wide, open groove right of Crossfire. Climb boldly up the groove and at the overhang, pull up left to join Crossfire up which one can finish.

The groove of Silkworm is bounded by a blunt, undercut rib.

8   Stealth   15m   HVS   5a   ★★
Start from blocks below the rib. Reach up for a good hidden hold to gain the rib which is followed delicately. Finish up a tiny corner and short crack.

To the right, a groove line leads to a small roof.

9   The Hollow Karst   15m   VS   4c
Start below the groove. Climb up the groove and over the roof to finish at a large, prominent flake.

10   The Professionals   15m   E2   5b   ★★★
Start 4m right of The Hollow Karst below a corner capped by some large roofs. Climb the corner to the first roof. Pull into the short groove then move right below the second roof to finish up the hanging rib in a fine position.

11   Lethal Weapon   13m   E3   5c   ★★
Start below the rib to the right of The Professionals. Climb the rib which is difficult to start but which eases near the break. From here pull up into the hanging groove just right. Finish up this.

The crag is now vegetated and the next route is at the right side of a smooth wall some 25 metres right of Lethal weapon. A small tree grows out of a crack and there are some large fallen blocks.

12   Trench Warfare   15m   E2   5c   ★★
Start below a small dog-legged crack at 3 metres. Gain this crack and the break above which has good holds. Move right and pull onto the cleaned ledge. Climb the wall above to a tricky finish.

Four metres right is a large roof.

13   Rocket To Russia   15m   E1   5b   ★★
Start below the corner. Climb the corner then swing right to gain the top of a massive flake. Climb the blunt rib to the break then finish up the wall above.

The next two routes start in the small bay just to the right.

14   Fight Or Flight   15m   E2   5b   ★
Start at a crack formed by the massive flake. Jam the crack and make gymnastic moves to stand on the top of the flake. Climb the blunt rib to the break then finish up the wall above as for Rocket To Russia.

15   Deterrent   15m   E1   5b   ★
Start below the obvious crack at the back of the bay. Climb the

crack and at the overlap, move right to ascend a faint scoop passing another overlap.

N.B. A rockfall has removed the lower part of this climb.

Ten metres further right, a prominent corner is capped by overhangs.

16 Superpower   20m   HVS   5b

Start below the prominent corner. Climb the corner easily, then traverse awkwardly left to a niche in the arete. Difficult moves past a bulging rib gain good holds above to finish.

Near the right-hand end of the crag are some massive blocks which lie against the crag.

17   Privates On Parade   15m   S

Start at a chimney 4m left of the massive blocks. Climb the chimney then follow the right-hand layback crack to a large ledge. Finish easily.

18   Judgemental Jibe   15m   HS   4c

Start 2m right of Privates On Parade. Mantleshelf onto a ledge and take one of various possible finishes above.

BROUGH SCAR   O.S. G.R.   NY 799 163 and 792 164

SITUATION AND CHARACTER

Brough Scar is the name given to the area of limestone escarpments high up on Musgrave Fell to the north of the A66 near Brough. These escarpments look attractive and have often been remarked upon by climbers driving past on the way to the Lake District.

On closer inspection however, the crags although reasonably continuous, lack any height in all but a few places. These areas have been developed and provide enjoyable climbing on mainly excellent rock. As with most limestone, particularly when traffic has been light, care should be taken, especially on the finishes.

The crags all face South and dry very quickly. Considering the amount of use they have had, they are quite clean. Well worth a visit.

APPROACHES AND ACCESS

Brough Scar is approached from the village of Brough which is reached from either the A66 or if coming from the M6, then by the A685 from the Tebay Junction.

At the west end of Brough Main Street, a road is signposted to Helbeck Quarry. Follow this road uphill for about one mile until a large quarry is reached on the left. Park here. A Public Right of Way follows the continuation cart track past the quarry entrance and uphill, after passing through a gate. After about ten minutes a small quarry marks the junction of another track. Leave the main track and follow this left-hand track for another five minutes.The compact face of Main Buttress will be seen on the hillside above. A clump of five Hawthorns half way up the slope identify the buttress.

The crag has been climbed on since 1984 and access has not been a

Brough Scar

problem. Recently however shooting interests have appeared in the form of a duck flighting pond so perhaps climbers may not be tolerated so readily.A gamekeeper is employed by the estate and whilst he seems to be friendly, it is up to climbers to behave in a reasonable way. It is probably best to keep a low profile and if approached, point out that you are willing to do everything to makes his job easier, except, give up the right to climb.

HISTORICAL

Mentioned in the 1980 guide, no developments were forthcoming until 1984 when a small isolated band of very young, keen lads, inspired by Robin Curley paid a visit to the crag. Over the next twelve months they developed the crag. Local climbers ignored the development and most of the pioneers lost interest in climbing. The climbs were all re-ascended in 1990 by a strong team from the North-East who confirmed the quality and grades of the climbs. Its a pity the lads didn't get the encouragement they deserved at the time.

MAIN BUTTRESS

This offers the best climbing on the Scar. The buttress presents a very compact face guarded at its base by a belt of bulges and overhangs. The rock is good and in many places provides good, natural thread runners.

Although only short, it offers steep, fingery and often strenuous climbing. Route appearances are often deceptive, looking easier and shorter than they are. A stake above the crag provides an anchor for abseil and belaying. Routes are described from left to right as one faces the rock.

THE CLIMBS

The left-hand end of the buttress is scrappy above 5 or 6 metres, whilst below this it is uniformly overhanging. The main challenges here are represented by two, cracked, breaks.The first break has an undercut edge.

1   Boogey Down   12m   E1   6a
Start below the first break. Gain the undercuts and pull over the bulge via a thin verical crack.

2   Dynamo Hum   12m   E4   6b   ★★★
Start below an obvious thread, 3m right of Boogey Down, where the bulge eases.Extend up and right (Thread Runner) across the bulge to a good hold. Climb direct to the top.

3   Arty Farty   12m   E2   5c   ★
Start below the fine, slim, left-trending groove, one metre right of an embedded block.The groove is guarded by a bulge at head height.Climb the groove till it meets a bulging headwall. Move right artd up the corner.

4   Magic's Wand   12m   E3   6a   ★
Artificial in that it shares some holds with the previous route. To the right of Arty Farty is a thin wall, just left of the very obvious groove line of Necromancer. Start as for Necromancer by climbing into the groove. This is quit almost immediately in favour of a very

shallow left-trending gangway in the thin wall on the left. Finish leftwards, through bulges (excellent).

5   Necromancer   12m   E1   5b   ★★
Start below the most obvious groove line 2m right of Arty Farty. Climb the slim groove to a thread runner. Finish up the square-cut, hanging corner (good).

Three metres right of Necromancer, the face has a shallow, but large diamond-shaped feature at mid-height. The left-hand side of the feature is unclimbed but the right hand side provides:

6   Roxanne Shante   12m   E3   6a   ★★
Start at the obvious line 3m right of Necromancer. Climb the to the first thread, well-protected but thought-provoking. Continue past another thread runner and finish directly over a roof. (Care with holds!)

An alternative finish is possible:

Chicken Variation   E3   6a
Climb the normal line to the second thread and escape rightwards to the tiny Rowan tree.

To the right of the last climb, the bulges guarding the base of the crag become bigger.

7   Style of the Street   12m   E4   6b   ★★★
This very fine route requires strength in reserve once the initial bulge is overcome. Start at a white pillar just right of a little clean-cut corner. Climb up to and across the roof, past a thread to a good hold. Reach through for a jug and finish at the tiny Rowan tree.

8   Cuttin' Herbie   9m   E1   5b   ★★
Sensational roof climbing at a modest grade.Start just right of Style of the Street below an obvious slanting handrail which cuts through the roof from left to right. Gain a bracket-type hold (thread runner) and make a long reach for jugs above lip. "Rock-over" into a small groove to the left of the rib and finish left at a thread. Abseil off.

Other smaller buttresses have provided a number of short problems.

These buttresses are further Northwards on the West side of the small valley. An interesting conical hill in the valley has a steep face and may reward some exploration. The woods at the end of the valley near Fox's Tower contain the crags of Hellbeck Wood.

WINDMORE END   O.S. SHEET 91   GR 822169

SITUATION AND CHARACTER
Windmore End is a long escarpment of quarried limestone situated close to the Brough to Middleton in Teesdale road. Facing South-West at an altitude of 400 metres, the crag is exposed to the elements and is quite capable of living up to its name. However the rock is very quick drying and climbing may be possible at any time of the year.

Quarrying finished a long time ago and the rock has weathered sufficiently to provide a rough, almost natural surface. Grass has re-colonized the quarry floor and the turf offers a soft landing for the pumped-up boulderer. Loose rock can be a problem on some climbs – the finishes of some are definitely unstable – but this is usually obvious. In general, the rock is sounder towards the right-hand end.

There are good climbs in most grades, the bulk of routes featuring thin crack or technical wall climbing and a rack of small wires will be found most useful here. Belays at the top can be a problem and it might be a good idea to bring your own stake.

On still sunny days, when the outlook over the Eden Valley can be fully appreciated, the crag is a delectable place on which to climb or boulder.

APPROACHES AND ACCESS

From Brough follow the old A66 route and turn left onto the B6276 towards Middleton in Teesdale after three quarters of a mile. Going uphill, the long, smooth faces of Windmore End will be seen on the right-hand side of the road from time to time. After two miles a minor road branches off to the right. To reach the left-hand section of the crag continue past this and park beyond the next bend near a gate on the right. The crag can be reached by passing through this gate and walking up the field.

The easiest approach to the right-hand section (Far Wall) is to turn right on the afore-mentioned minor road. There is room for several vehicles in a small space beyond the cottage of Windmore Green. Further along the road a gate allows access to the field and the crag is quickly reached by slanting up the hill below an old lime kiln.

Drystone walls separate the crag sections and these have to be crossed with care. The left-hand section belongs to the parish council, the middle section to the owners of Windmore Green and the right-hand section to the farmer of Windmore End farm. Access is not a problem and should remain so as long as gates and walls are treated with respect.

HISTORICAL

People have climbed here for many years, including Peter Day and others from Kirkby Stephen, however it was not until the 1970's when climbers from Cleveland climbed extensively on the crag. This group was inspired by Kelvin Neal who produced a comprehensive guide to the crag forming the basis for the previous guidebook. Undoubtedly there have been occasional pioneers in the intervening years but nothing appears to have been recorded until Karl Lunt and Andy Kay paid a couple of visits in September 1987. They added a number of short climbs in the main Wall area the best being Andy's Arete and A Week Before The Beast. Two years later Lunt returned with Tom Phillips to realise the potential of the Far Wall with its long stretches of seemingly blank rock. Some excellent wall climbs were added, some of them solo, due to a scarcity of protection, good examples being Viva Garibaldi! and Rock And A Hard Place. The brilliant Rebel Without A Pause was ascended free of the aid mentioned in the previous guide. Leo Fallon was also involved in several of these ascents. A brief visit in

EDEN VALLEY SOUTH

Windmore End   Brough Scar   Helbeck Wood Crag

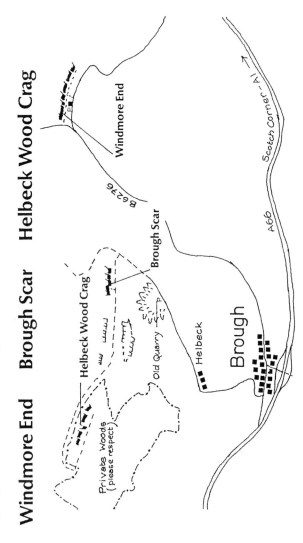

March, 1990 saw more additions to the Far Wall including the difficult Strangeways.

THE CLIMBS

These are described from left to right as one faces the crag.

RECESS AREA

Left of the stone wall at the left-hand end of the crag is a recess with a smooth back wall.

1   Twin Cracks   5m   HS   4b
Climb the twin cracks up the left-hand side of the right wall of the recess.

2   The Mantleshelf   5m   HS   4c
Climb the crack to the right of Twin cracks to gain a ledge (care!) and the top.

MAIN WALL LEFT

This is the expanse of rock stretching rightwards from the left-hand stone wall to end in a steep, square-cut arete. The face is set forwards some 5 metres right of the stone wall and here can be found:

3   Finger Tip   4m   VD
Climb the arete just left of Tabend.

4   Tabend   4m   S
Climb the centre of the wall via a thin crack.

Ten metres right of the stone wall is a large ledge with an undercut front. To the right of this the crag forms a long, flat wall whose main features are two, stepped overlaps: one near the left-hand end which slants left, and another near the centre of the wall which slants right.

5   The Hum   6m   HS   4b
Starts just right of where the undercut ledge ends. Climb the hand-width crack which ends in a grass-choked slot.

6   Agrippa   8m   MVS   4b   *
Immediately right of the left-slanting overlap is a finger crack. Climb this pleasantly to a ledge.

7   Romulus   8m   MVS   4b   *
Three metres right of the left-slanting overlap are two diverging cracks. The thinner, left-hand one is climbed. Sustained.

8   Remus   8m   S   *
Climb the right-hand crack which gives a good jamming exercise.

9   Longman   8m   S   *
Two metres right of Remus is a crackline with a tiny pod just below half-height. Climb it.

Further right is a right-slanting overlap.

10   H.T.Z.   8m   HS
Start one metre left of the overlap (two boreholes at the foot of the crag!). Climb the crack which leads interestingly to a ledge near the top.

11   Colin's Dilemma   8m   VS   4c   ★
Climb the wall direct immediately left of the overlap. A tricky move gains the ledge.

12   Fingers   8m   VS   5a   ★
Two metres right of the overlap is a thin crack. Climb this with difficulty to a ledge and tiny corner.

13   Kel Floff   8m   S
Seven metres left of the right-hand arete is a prominent, straight crack. Climb it.

14   Headstone   8m   HS
Climb the wall and crack left of the Tomb to a death-defying finish.

15   The Tomb   9m   VD   ★
Climb the V-crack three metres left of the right-hand arete then move right along ledges almost to the arete.

16   Snowflake   7m   S   ★
The thin crackline just left of the arete gives an interestingly delicate problem.

17   Andy's Arete   7m   HVS   5a   ★
Climb the right side of the arete, pulling onto the left side near the top.

18   Rain Stopped Play   7m   VS   5a
To the right of Andy's Arete is a corner. Climb the bulging, right wall by using a crack up to the right.

MAIN WALL AREA
This is a long section of crag which starts with an impressive flat wall. Descents are possible down the ledge complex to the left of this. The finishes to some of the next few routes should be treated with suspicion.

19   Bowline   13m   VS   4b
Near the left-hand side of the flat wall is a prominent, right-facing corner. Climb this to a bulge at four metres then gain a ledge and finish up the cracked wall above.

20   Plumbline   13m   HVS   4c
Three metres right of the corner of Bowline is a straight crack which widens near the top. Climb this.

The guidebook team refused to check the grades of the following two routes on account of loose rock. YOU HAVE BEEN WARNED!

21   Tached   13m   DEADLY
Climb the wall two metres right of Plumbline to reach a sloping ledge. Continue up the wall above with care.

22   Supremo   13m   DEADLY
Seven metres right of Plumbline , climb the very thin crack which goes straight up the wall past a ledge at six metres.

23   Serendipity   13m   VS   4b
Climb the prominent rightward-slanting crack just right of Supremo. This leads to a loose, square-shaped sentry-box at the top.

24   Hobbit   13m   VS   4c
Three metres right of Serendipity is a short, right-facing corner.

Climb this to a small ledge, step right and follow the thin, converging cracks to a ledge then the top.

25   Staircase   13m   HS   4c
Two metres right of Hobbit is a short, hand crack which leads to a comfortable ledge. A tricky move leads up to broken ledges and the top.

26   First Choice   11m   VD   *
Climb the obvious wide crack which contains a large jammed block at five metres.

The crag now continues as a series of corners. The first one has an overhang at three metres.

27   Pork Chop   11m   HVS   4c
Ascend the overhung corner to an overlap, then cross the wall diagonally rightwards to finish above a short, wide crack. Bold.

28   Second Best   11m   S
Three metres right of the overhung corner is an obvious wide crack slanting up to the right. Climb this to a ledge then to the top.

29   Mealybugs   10m   HVS   5a   *
Just right of Second Best is a slanting overlap. Climb direct to this via a thin crack. Pull over onto the wall above (avoid the loose block) trending slightly right to finish.

30   Purk   10m   VS   4c
Right again is a small grass ledge at one metre. Climb the crack system above this ledge to meet the end of the rightward trending overlap.

31   Little Pinkie   10m   VS   4b   *
Just right of a short corner there is a thin crackline which snakes up to the top. Climb this with a slight deviation to the left near the top.

32   Big Plonker   10m   VS   4c
Start 2 metres right of Little Pinkie. Climb the wall which has a hairline crack in it. (Small RP's useful.)

33   Brass Monkey Job   7m   HS   4b   *
The crag now cuts back. Climb the left side of the arete. Quite gymnastic!

34   Hughie's Route   9m   VD
Climb the corner where the crag cuts back then move up and left across a slab to the arete.

35   Most Sincerely   8m   HS   4b
Start three metres right of the corner of Hughie's Route. Climb direct up the wall using a thin crack.

36   Arty 8m   S
Start five metres right of Hughie's Route at a shallow, square-cut groove. Climb the thin, left-hand crack.

37   Andon   8m   VD
Climb the wide, right-hand crack.

38   Chocky   8m   VS   4c
To the right of Andon is a grassy corner. Climb the thin, jagged crackline three metres right of this to a steep, awkward finish.

39 Strangler 7m HVS 5a ★
The crag now cuts back to form a steep arete. Climb this boldly on its right side.

40 Confidence Trickster 7m VD
Climb the corner to the right of the arete of Strangler.

41 Moss Trooper 7m VS 5a
Climb the wall two metres right of Confidence Trickster. A hard start leads to a faint scoop.

42 A Week Before The Beast 7m HVS 5b ★
Climb the hairline crack in the bulging wall just right of Moss Trooper.

43 Short And Sweet 7m HS
Climb the slanting crackline on the right, to a loose finish.

44 Steppin' Out 8m VS 5a
Start two metres right of Short And Sweet at a right-facing groove. Climb this to a bulge then move left and ascend the wall direct.

MAIN WALL FAR RIGHT

This is the sector extending towards the next drystone wall some distance away. The rock gradually diminishes in height and quite a few individual problems can be worked out beyond what has been recorded.

An unusual chimney gully with a grassy cone at its foot provides the left-hand boundary of this area and is a useful means of descent.

45 Room 101 6m HS 4b
The crackline just left of Workout.

46 Workout 6m S ★
Climb the wide, weatherworn crack seven metres right of the descent gully.

47 Pump It Up 6m HS 4c ★
Climb the smooth wall just right of Workout and marked by hairline cracks.

48 Postman's Knock 6m HS
Three metres right of Workout is a thin crack. Climb this moving right to an insecure finish.

49 Second Time Around 6m HS
Climb the cracked face, one metre right of a short, right-facing corner to the right of Postman's Knock.

50 Teatime Special 6m S
Climb the wide crack three metres right of the corner.

A few minutes walk further right brings one to the drystone wall. Cross this with care to reach:

SECOND WALL

This sector lies between the two drystone walls directly behind the cottage of Windmore Green. The area can be construed as two sections divided by a wide, grassy bank which provides a useful means of descent.

The climbs on this sector are amongst the best at Windmore both in terms of length and quality. The easiest approach is probably through the gate from the unmade road between Windmore Green and Windmore End farm. The climbs are described from left to right.

SECOND WALL LEFT SIDE.
The face to the left of the grassy descent bank, has a low, grassy ridge a short distance in front of the crag. The main feature of this left-hand side of Second Wall is a straight corner; Fern Crack which runs the full-height of the face. To the left again is an area of short corners and ledges.

51 Dogleg 6m HVS 5b
Climb the smooth, bulging wall on the left, using a thin, disjointed crack. Strenuous.

52 H.T.J. 5m S
Climb the short, steep arete which forms the right-hand side of the smooth wall.

53 Consolation 6m S
Gain the large ledge just right of the arete then climb a short corner.

54 Zoot Route 10m VD
Gain the ledge of Consolation from the right and climb the wall to another ledge. Continue to the top past a small tree.

55 Fern Crack 10m VS 4c   ★
Climb the obvious, fern-bedecked corner which runs the full height of the crag. This is quite ustained.

The wall to the right of Fern Crack is smooth and featureless ending some eight metres away in a vague rib.

56 Sauron 6m S
Climb the vague rib on good holds to a large ledge.

57 Archtype 12m S   ★
Further right is a smooth slab, bounded on its left by a slanting corner. Climb the slab to gain a large ledge then follow the corner above past a tiny Hawthorn.

58 Epitaph 12m VS 4c   ★★
Climb the slab just right of Archtype direct to a short headwall. Ascend this to the top.

59 Scoop And Wall 12m E3 5c   ★
Start just right of the slab below an open, bulging scoop. Climb up the right side of this with difficulty to gain the arete above. Move left onto the slab (without using the triangular ledge on the arete!) then ascend the slab and headwall above. Very bold.

60 Androx 12m HVS 5a   ★
Start below a shallow, left-trending groove. Climb this to a triangular ledge then finish up the short corner above.

61 Yellow Peril 12m HVS 5a   ★
Climb the blunt rib just right of Androx. This leads steeply to a small ledge. Finish up the wall above.

The centre of the bay contains a large ledge on which grow several small trees.

62   Gulliver's Traverse   18m   HVS

This is a traverse of the left side of Second Wall Left (Got it?). Start at the left-hand end of the large, tree-bedecked ledge. Move left onto the ledge of Yellow Peril then continue leftwards onto the slab of Epitaph to finish up the corner of Archtype.

63   Nature Trail   18m   S

Well-named! Start below the right end of the tree-covered ledge. Jungle-bash up to this and fight a way through to the corner on the left. This provides a means of escape.

64   Simulator   12m   VS   4c   ★★

Start just to the right of the tree-covered ledge. Climb the groove-cum-crack which runs the full height of the crag.

65   The Helm   12m   NL   6b   ★★

Excellent technical climbing up the face between Simulator and Motivator. Start from a boulder left of Motivator and follow the thin crack to a break at half-height. Climb the wall above just left of the blunt arete.

66   The Motivator   12m   VS   4c   ★

Climb the large, left-facing corner with an overhang at the top. Beware of loose rock near the top.

67   Coffastroni   13m   E2   5b

The steep wall right of The Motivator terminates in a short corner. Start just left of this and climb up leftwards to a small ledge. Finish straight up the wall above. A serious route.

68   Trime   11m   VD

Climb the short corner which is loose to a fight with the large tree on the ledge above. Escape here or climb the wall behind the tree.

SECOND WALL RIGHT

This is the more open section of the crag to the right of the grassy descent bank.

69   Sneakthief   8m   HS

Start near the left-hand side of the wall below a small grass ledge at head height. Climb the short, left-facing corner and the continuation crack above.

70   Bloodbath   9m   HS

Start four metres right of the grass ledge of Sneakthief at a small, square-cut corner. Climb this to a series of ledges and finish up the wall above.

71   Centurion   9m   HS

Start three metres right of Bloodbath's square-cut corner. Climb a short, jagged crack to a ledge on the left. Finish up the wall above.

72   Legion   9m   HS

Climb the slab just right of Centurion to reach a shallow groove leading to a ledge. Climb the wall above to finish.

73   Palace Guard   9m   E1   5b

A difficult and sustained route. Start from a sentry-box left of the prominent crack which is just around the rib to the right of Legion. Climb from the sentry-box up a steep crack to the ledge of Legion. Finish up the right side of the wall above.

74 Zero Route 9m HS 4b   *
Start below the prominent corner to the left of the white-flecked wall. Climb the corner crack. Pleasant.

The white-flecked wall holds two hard climbs on excellent rock:

75 White Wall 8m E3 5c   **
Start directly below the square-cut bay at the top of the crag. Ascend the centre of the wall. Unprotected.

76 A Scent Of Orchids 8m E3 5c   **
Start below the right-hand side of the prominent block overhang overlooking the wall. Climb the faint crack up to the right of this. Unprotected and sustained.

This section of the crag is now interupted by a series of broken ledges.

77 Serutan 6m VD
Start part way up the broken ledges and climb the wall direct.

78 Rubstic 8m E2 5b   **
Start just right of the broken ledges at a slim, right-facing corner. Climb this then move right into a shallow groove which exits onto a ledge. Finish up the short wall above. A difficult and bold problem.

79 Rubstic Direct 8m E3 5c
Climb the corner as for Rubstic but move up and left onto the face and climb this to a steep finish. A seriously bold route.

To the right of Rubstic is a sweep of slab which has a curved overlap near its centre.

80 Jizzle 8m VD   *
Start at the left side of the slab and ascend diagonally rightwards to finish at a small grass ledge.

81 Suntrip 8m S   *
Climb the centre of the slab to the curved overlap and follow this leftwards onto the ledge of Rubstic. Climb the short wall to finish.

82 Cranch 7m VD
Climb the crack which bounds the slab on the right.

83 Ribble 7m HS 4b
Climb the steep and interesting rib to the right of Cranch.

84 Differential 7m VD
Start below the open corner just right. Climb the corner and the short prow above.

85 Parson's Nose 7m VD
Start at the arete to the right of the open corner. Climb the arete.

FAR WALL
This is the section of the crag to the right of the drystone wall beyond the cottage of Windmore Green. When approaching from the gate between Windmore Green and Windmore End Farm it is the first part of the crag to be reached. This is probably the best section of the crag with good compact rock, although there is some loose rock on the top few feet of some of the lines. It hosts a good selection of harder climbs and micro-nuts are "de rigeur".

86   Light Bulb   6m   VS   4b
Start one metre right of the drystone wall. Climb the face at a faint crackline.

87   Smoke Ring   6m   S
Start four metres right of the drystone wall. Climb to a sloping ledge, then trend right to the top.

88   Far Groove   6m   VD
Start at a groove just right of a blunt rib. Climb the groove.

89   Windy Nook   6m   D
Climb the more pronounced corner just right of Far Groove.

90   Flake Crack   6m   S
Climb the short layback crack right of Windy Nook. This leads to a ledge.

The crag now forms a long, steep wall, overhanging at its left-hand end and offering good climbing on the best rock at Windmore.

91   Anticlimbax   7m   VS   4c   ★★
Climb the overhanging crack left of the bulging wall into a short corner.

92   Rebel Without A Pause   7m   E3   5c   ★★★
Start below a thin crack to the right of the bulging wall. Climb this to the top. Superb.

93   Viva Garibaldi!   8m   E2   6a   ★★
Start three metres right of Rebel below a small, arched overlap at two metres. Climb straight through the overlap to good holds then move up and left across the wall to the finish of Rebel.

94   Alverton   9m   E2   5c   ★★
Start just right of the arched overlap at an indefinite groove line. Climb this for a few metres then pull out left onto the wall and head for the finish of Rebel. Largely made redundant by Rebel and Strangeways!

95   Strangeways   7m   E3   5c   ★★
Climb the indefinite groove as for Alverton but continue directly up the wall above.

The wall to the right is smooth with few identifying features.

96   Rock And A Hard Place   7m   E3   5c   ★★
Start three metres right of Alverton. A small "T" is scratched on the rock near ground level. Climb direct to a tiny arched overlap in the centre of the wall and continue up the steep wall above. Bold and unprotected.

97   Touching The Void   7m   E2   5b   ★★
Start four metres right of Alverton. climb the wall following a hairline crack to a steep finish. Another bold climb!

98   Chill Factor   7m   E3   5c   ★
Start three metres left of the thin crack of Becher's Brook below a very shallow groove. Climb this then the steep upper wall rightwards on fragile holds.

99   Becher's Brook   7m   HVS   5a   ★★
Start six metres left of the grassy corner (Grassy Crack) at an obvious thin crack. Climb this and either pull left through the overlap to finish or move right to a ledge.

100   Squeeze My Lemon   7m   VS   5a
Climb the wall two metres right of the crack of Bechers Brook.
Trend slightly right to a ledge near the top.

101   Lime Street   8m   S
Start two metres left of Grassy Crack and follow a left-trending
weakness to the top.

102   Wall Street   7m   VS   4b
Climb the slab immediately left of Grassy Crack.

103   Grassy Crack   7m   VD   ★
Climb the grassy corner. A pleasant climb.

104   Beanz Meanz ....   7m   E2   5b   ★
Start one metre right of Grassy Crack. Climb directly up the pillar
which is split by a hairline crack.

105   Wind Power   7m   HVS   5b   ★★
Start three metres right of Grassy Crack. Follow a thin, right-
trending crackline.

106   Windy Moss   7m   S
Start six metres right of Grassy Crack below a small ledge at head
height. Gain this ledge then climb the wall above.

107   Windy Miller   7m   HVS   5a
Start two metres right of the small ledge of Windy Moss. Climb the
wall direct.

108   Wind Breaker   7m   VS   4c
Start further right below the next more obvious feature; a thin
crack system. Climb this wall.

109   Wall Of Wind   7m   HVS   5b   ★
Start at the smooth wall right of the thin crack system. Climb this on
small incut holds.

110   Sue's Route   8m   VS   4c   ★★
Climb the crack which slants up right and which is the most prominent feature hereabouts. The loose block at the top needs care.

111   Hurricane Force   8m   E2   5b   ★
Start three metres right of Sue's Route at a tiny groove. Climb this
groove to a sloping ledge then enter a scoop below the roof. Step
left to finish.

112   C.90   8m   E1   5b   ★★
Climb the thin crack which runs straight up the wall five metres
right of Sue's Route.

113   Crozzly Wall   8m   E2   5b   ★
Start just right of C.90 at some small, stepped overhangs. Pull over
these and climb the wall direct on mosaic-work rock.

114   Tamalin   8m   E2   5b   ★★
Climb the wall two metres right of the stepped overhangs, using
thin, discontinuous cracks.

115   Speeding Like A Jet   8m   E3   5c   ★★
Start a further metre right where the wall is split by a vertical,
hairline crack. Climb this with some difficulty.

116   April Fool   7m   HS   4c
Start below a downward pointing flake two metres right of
Speeding Like A Jet. Climb the wall above the flake, moving right to

a tiny ledge. Finish direct. The crag continues further right. Several problems have been done but are unrecorded.

EDEN VALLEY SOUTH
MINOR CRAGS AND BOULDERING VENUES

MORLAND BYESTEADS OLD QUARRY   O.S. SHEET 91
G.R. 603216

A small Limestone quarry beside Byesteads farm just South of Morland village and visible on the left-hand side of the road to King's Meaburn. A handful of steep, difficult climbs with in-situ gear (pegs and tat) which may be unsafe. Developed by R.Curley and friends. Permission to climb must be sought at the farm.

DUFTON GILL OLD QUARRIES   O.S. SHEET 91   G.R. 688249

Located in Dufton Gill on the South edge of the village of Dufton about 4 miles North of Appleby, these impressive Sandstone quarries may provide some bouldering.

HIGH CUP NICK   O.S. SHEET 91   G.R. 745262

Impressive outcrops of Dolerite of The Great Whin Sill. Climbs have been made here but nothing has been recorded. A pinnacle on the North side has been ascended: Nick's Last (VD).

JUBILEE BRIDGE QUARRIES – APPLEBY   O.S. SHEET 91
G.R. 687201

Impressive walls of Sandstone on the North bank of the River Eden just downstream of Jubillee Bridge. Climbs have been top-roped here.

AUGILL BECK   O.S. SHEET 91   G.R. 818152

A delightful Limestone gorge, worth a visit even if not for the climbing. One route has been top-roped; Savage Arete, a 30 metre obvious white arete. The gorge is reached by following the B6276 Teesdale road out of Brough (as for Windmore End). After half a mile turn first right into a minor road and follow this foranother half mile to Mount Pleasant Farm. A Public Right Of Way leads from the farm East-North-East to Augill.

ARGILL BECK   O.S. SHEET 91   G.R. 858132

An impressive 20 metre crag of variable quality Limestone in an easily accessible gorge in the upper Argill Beck only two miles West of Stainmore Summit. Approaching on the A66 from Brough, leave the dual carriageway after a few hundred metres in favour of a minor road for Barras. After crossing Argill Beck, and going uphill, an unfenced road turns right to South Stainmore. Follow this for half a mile above and parallel to Argill. The presence of woods around the stream indicates the location of the crag. Descend a dry valley to the stream and crag.

The central grooveline has been climbed: Scraggy Cap (VS 4c). Start below the lower groove at a short wall. Climb to the first horizontal break and climb to the second break using a peg, then a nut to gain this. Ascend the groove above and move right to another groove. Climb this to an overhang. move right and ascend a short overhanging wall with the help of a tree root.

Mucky Pup (HS)Gain and climb the obvious crack in the steep wall to the right of Scraggy Cap to reach a ledge. Move slightly left to gain the central ledge with a tree on it. Move right and climb a short groove to a tree at the top. The climbs were done in 1976 by Ron Kenyon and friends.

AISGILL   O.S. SHEET 98   G.R. 771974

Located on the lower South-Eastern flank of Wild Boar Fell in Mallerstang; the upper valley of the River Eden. Aisgill is a most impressive ravine containing many crags, however the best lie relatively low down, only a couple of hundred metres West of Aisgill Farm, at which it is advisable to seek permission to climb. From the farm, ascend via slopes on the other side of the road to the gill, passing under a bridge carrying the famous Carlisle-Settle railway. The first and most impressive crags are on the North side of the gill, facing South.

The Main Face is obvious and up to twenty metres high. This has three routes. The cracked corner on the left is The Navvy (VS 4c), the central crackline is Raising Steam (HVS 5a) which has a potentially lethal block below a overlap and finally on the right flank of Main Face to the right of the right arete is On The Footplate (VS 4b) which ascends the more broken face.

To the right of Main Face is a fine sweep of clean rock about twelve metres high. Shark's Fin Soup (VS 4c) starts right of a prominent fin of rock and ascends to a ledge. The fin is followed up to the final wall. The final buttress is to the right and is less attractive. The steep chimney/crackline is followed by Colonel Biffo (VS 4a). Much remains to be discovered here. The development is the work of K.Lunt, R.Kenyon, S.Wilson and A.Kay between 1982 and 1987.

5   SOUTH CUMBRIAN LIMESTONE

This is a very small, compact area in the South of the county. The crags are to be found mainly to the South of Junction 36 of the M6 and to the East and West of the M6. Fairy Steps is to the West of the A6, just South of Milnethorpe and provides wonderfully varied bouldering and short climbs on sometimes perfect limestone. The woodland setting is most attractive whilst its proximity to the sea imbues the area with a quality of light that is almost magical. It is an ideal family venue and much remains to be discovered. In contrast, Farleton Crag and Hutton Roof Crags, to the East of the M6 are more airily located on the low, limestone fells which dominate the area, providing quality, short climbs on good limestone. The non-serious nature of the climbing, combined with the ambience of the limestone country; short turf, wild thyme and light, dappled woodland make these crags very attractive. Of course if such fare is felt to be lightweight, then many alternatives like Scout Scar, Chapel Head Scar and Trowbarrow are available nearby.

HEBBLETHWAITE HALL GILL   O.S. SHEET 98   G.R. 698 932

SITUATION AND CHARACTER

The crag, also known as Penny Farm Gill, is a small limestone gorge set on the edge of open moorland about one mile or so East of the town of Sedbergh.

The proximity of the Dent Fault has had a profound influence on the geology of the area: to the west, Silurian slates have formed the grassy, rounded Howgill Fells; to the east the younger Carboniferous sequences of limestones, shales and sandstones occur. The effect of the Dent Fault has been to tilt the limestone strata so that in some places they are vertical.This is especially noticeable on the northern wall of the gorge, where rock rises out of the beck in large, flat sheets.

Unfortunately, another effect of the Fault has been to ensure a degree of loose rock in places, this is not a major hazard on the established routes.

The gorge has a sheltered aspect and can be climbed in throughout the year. Routes on the north side of the gorge dry quickly after rain whilst those on the south side tend to remain damp longer, due to lichen.

Belays are scarce above some of the buttresses: a stake may prove useful.

APPROACHES AND ACCESS

Leave Sedbergh on the A 683 Kirkby Stephen road. Parking is possible in a loop layby on the right about 800 metres beyond the bridge over the River Rawthey. The bridleway to Hebblethwaite Hall lies a further 100 metres up the road and leads as a metalled lane to the Hall buildings. Beyond a gate, a grass track leads forward through more gates, to cross Nor Gill and then meets the ravine on a sharp bend near a cave. A low fence is crossed to enter the gorge proper.

HISTORICAL

Climbing seems to have taken place in Hebblethwaite Hall Gill for some years but no written records exist. Evidence of activity is scattered over the various buttresses in the form of old pegs and bolts, even some metal belay stakes. The first people to record their climbs were Karl Lunt and Geoff Dawson who in early 1987 produced a batch of routes on the South Wall, the best being "Like an Arrow". Three years later this pair developed the First Wall area.

THE CLIMBS

FIRST WALL

This is the first climbing to be met upon entering the gorge. It consists of a flat wall which rises out of the beck, the left-hand end being brown in colour. The climbs are described from left to right.

1 Mite 5m E1 5b
Climb the brown wall direct, starting just to the right of a curving crack. Bolt belays.

2 Midget 6m E1 5b
To the right, is an arch-shaped overlap. Climb the left-slanting crack rising from the extreme left edge of this. Bolt belays.

3 Morsel 7m E1 5b
Climb through the arch-shaped overlap via a prominent, hand-jam slot, then climb the wall direct to a small tree. Step left to finish. Bolt belays.

4 The Mighty Micro 10m E1 5b
Climb through the apex of the arch and continue directly up the wall passing two breaks. Stake belays back from edge.

About 20 metres beyond the First Wall, the stream cascades over a choke of boulders.

5 Strange Times 24m E1 5b
The groove in the prominent rib bounding the right-hand end of the flat walls. Start near the first big boulders in the stream. From the streambed, pull up to a right-trending break. Traverse right across the slab to a bulge (tape runner over this). Pull up, then climb to an overlap below the grooved rib. Ascend this, using a combination of the groove and the face on the right. Belay on a large holly. Scramble off rightwards.

The remaining routes are all to be found on the south side of the gorge (ie, north facing and slower to dry). A short distance upstream is an undercut buttress with a smooth slab on its right-hand side.

6 Respect Your Elders 14m VS 4c
Start to the left of a square-cut niche at the left side of the buttress. Move up a few metres, then step right onto the slab. From the end of this, pull into the small niche, containing a small tree, on the left. Finish direct.

PINNACLE FACE

Twenty metres further upstream is another buttress, the front of which has slipped to form a large, detached pinnacle separated by an easy rake from the main mass of the buttress. The first two routes use the face of the pinnacle and are described from Right to Left.

7   Out on a Limb   22m   E1

Start at the right-hand edge of the pinnacle.

Pitch 1   14m   5b

Make some hard moves to gain the obvious groove. Follow this more easily to a good, tree belay.

Pitch 2   8m   5b

From a split block, step onto a slab and follow the overlap leftwards onto the rib. Finish direct, by a small rowan.

8   Bitter Creek   21m   E2

Start midway along the front of the pinnacle at a slight alcove.

Pitch 1   15m   5c

Climb the bulging crack, up and right, into a slim groove. Ascend this, using the rib on the right, to reach the top of the pinnacle.

Pitch 2   6m   5b

From behind the pinnacle, gain a sloping shelf then use a short, overhanging crack and the rib to the right to finish at a tiny, rowan tree.

9   Like an Arrow   15m   E2   6a   ★

Start directly below the obvious, right-facing groove in the upper part of the wall. Climb directly to the groove. Ascend this past an ancient, peg runner to the top.

HUTTON ROOF CRAGS   O.S. SHEET 97

The Rakes: 565782 and Uberash Breast: 554781

SITUATION AND CHARACTER

A series of small, West facing crags up to eight metres high. The Rakes, the most popular has a secluded location with a limited but pleasant outlook whereas Uberash Breast has more extensive views but with less pleasant climbing. The rock is very good to excellent limestone and runs to holds. The climbing is enjoyable with the range of difficulty mainly in the lower to middle grades. Having said that, the dedicated boulderer can always slot in much harder moves. Seekers of difficulty may be disappointed here and if this is important perhaps it would be better to leave this pleasant spot and go to Fairy Steps or Farleton. There is more to discover than is described here and a bit of exploration may locate a "Northern Fontainbleau"

APPROACHES AND ACCESS

The crags can be approached either the West or the East side of the fell.

The Eastern approach from the village of Hutton Roof one and three quarter miles West of the A65 at Kirkby Lonsdale is the shortest and steepest approach and is the quickest way to the

To Kendal

N

Farleton

Farleton Fell

Farleton Crag

Newbiggin

Holme

Clawthorpe

M6

Plough Inn
(Lupton)

A65

To Kirkby
Lonsdale

Limestone Link L.D.P.

Hutton Roof Crags

Hutton Roof

**Farleton Crag
Hutton Roof Crags**

SOUTH CUMBRIAN LIMESTONE

Rakes. Leave the village via a narrow footpath lane opposite the road signposted to Kirkby Lonsdale. This track, the "Limestone Link" is followed past a cottage on the right and gives out onto a grassy track. Turn right and follow the good grassy track which swings under craglets on the left. The path continues beyond the trees until a straight grassy uphill climb levels out and a path on the left at right angles to the main track is reached. Turn left and follow this through a shallow valley in the ridge to emerge at the left hand end of the Rakes at Sector South America. The Western approach is from the village of Clawthorpe three miles South of Junction 36 of the M6 on the A6070. From Clawthorpe, follow the minor road leading North-East. This ascends to point 192 metres. Cars can be parked on the wide verge just South of the "Limestone Link" footpath.

Follow the Limestone link Eastwards passing above a house known as Kelker Well and continue through dwarf hazels until after the highest point the path drops into the sheltered small valley containing the best of the climbing on the Rakes. This crag is clean and quite long with two areas particularly attractive. To reach Uberash Breast it is necessary to strike rightwards at the start of the "Limestone Link" heading uphill in a Southerly direction. The top of the hill is marked by three cairns and the rocks are below these facing West.

HISTORICAL

The crags at Hutton Roof have been climbed on for at least twenty five years and considering that they provide climbing equal in quality and stature to Upper Warton, it is surprising that no one has bothered to record the routes. The folly in "writing off" a crag as something for "the connoisseur to discover at their leisure" only means that very few people ever bother to visit it and other places suffer as a result of overuse becoming polished and unpleasant with attendant problems of ground erosion and aggravated access. The following routes are the work of Karl Lunt, Matt Ellis, Maggie Wilson and Stew Wilson in 1991. They have all been climbed before but not recorded.

THE RAKES

The Rakes are several, small scarps which march westwards on the Hutton Roof side of the fell. The climbing area is obvious comprising an almost continuous edge up to eight metres high and having a fine wall; South America Wall at its left end and some mature Ash trees under the crag towards the right-hand end.

THE CLIMBS

These are described sector by sector and from left to right starting with South America Wall.

South America Wall

This is the best face on the crag. It is situated at the extreme left end of the crag and has a steep prow shaped like the continent of South America. To the right of this are two very steep grooves above a steep wall.

1   Straight Crack   D
Starts 4m left of the tip of South America. Gain the straight crack and climb it, and the face above on good holds.

2   West Coast   D   ★
Start at the tip of South America and climb the left edge of the continent to finish up an easy crack.

3   Sendero Luminoso   HS   4b   ★
Start as for West Coast. Climb into the niche on West Coast, then move up right to follow a thin crack in the centre of the face. A long reach gains a good break and good holds lead directly to the top.

4   Belize   VS   5a   ★
A great little climb both technical and strenuous. Start just left of the obvious vertical crack 3m right of the tip of South America. Climb the left trending crack to gain good footholds. Climb the overhanging flake on good holds.

5   Sandenista   HVS   5b/c   ★
Very sustained and fine in the lower half. Start at the foot of the very thin vertical crack just right of Belize. Climb this crack with

difficulty avoiding using the ledges on Belize. The steep corner above is easier than it looks.

A short, desperate problem exists up the the centre of the smooth wall between Sandenista and San Miguel. (6b+).

6   San Miguel HVS 5a *

Start 2m right of San Denista at the foot of another thin vertical crack. Climb this crack, moving left to a good flake on the underside of the bulge. Climb directly over the bulge and finish direct.

7   San Antonio VS 5a **

One metre right of San Miguel is a slight vertical crack leading up to the obvious V-corner above. Climb the crack to the horizontal break and finish up the very steep corner above.

8   Pablo S

A good route. Climb the steep corner to a jammed block. Pull over the bulge rightwards and finish on excellent sculpted holds.

The jumbled blocks to the right provide numerous pitches of moderate difficulty. The smooth slab which runs into a steep corner further right is pleasant.

CAVE SECTOR

Just right of the smooth slab is corner with overhangs above it. To the right, the crag extends as a long wall with a barrier of overhangs at two metres forming a cave-shelter at the left end.

9   Wrinkled Slab HVD   **

A bold little route! Start below the steep corner at the left end of the wall. Climb the corner until it is possible to step rightwards onto the wrinkled slab. Move right and up the edge of this.

10   The Flake S

One metre right is a jammed block below a flake. Climb up to and past the flake.

11   Pot Belly S 4b

Climb the rounded buttress one metre right via a bulge to a vegetated crack finish.

12   The Barrier Roof S

Start just left of the barrier roof. Climb a left-facing flake and the wall above just right of an Ash.

13–16   Roof Problems 5b-5c   Strenuous.

17   Sinister Crack MVS 5a

Start one metre right of the long roof. Climb the cracked wall to a small roof with a left-trending diagonal crack. Getting established in this is the crux.

18   Dexter Wall HS 4c

Start one metre left of the right end of the wall. Climb the cracked wall and make long reaches from one horizontal break to another to finish.

SECTOR SYCAMORE

To the right of Cave Sector is a taller bow-fronted buttress behind a large Sycamore tree. The left-hand end consists of a separate, easy-angled slab with the following pleasant route:

19   Imitation Verdon   M   ★
Start on a large block. Climb the easy rocks to the slab which is ascended rightwards on memorable rock.
Moving right 6 metres to the bow-fronted buttress.

20   Sylvie   S   4b
A pleasant climb. Start just right of corner at a steep arete. Climb the arete and the face above just right of an Ash.

21   Daphne   MS
Start one metre right at a right-trending flake below a five-stemmed Ash. Climb the flake and wall just left of the Ash.

22   Hebe   VD
Start above an embedded sharp-edged flake. Climb a groove and step right onto the slab which is followed to the top.

SUNNY WALL

Just right of Sector Sycamore, the crag is open and easy-angled. The left end of this face has a large block leaning up against it and above this is an Ivy mass. To the right moving over huge blocks is a slight descent into a bowl surrounded by trees. A large Ash grows up against the face.

22   Hedera Wall   D
Climb the wall just right of the Ivy mass.

24   Sunny Groove   D
Start one metre right of the Ivy and climb a shallow groove directly above large blocks.
Three metres further right is an upstanding sharp-topped flake.

25   T'Owd Man   VD   ★
Start by the sharp-topped flake. Climb the wall direct and to the right of some wind-blasted ash remnants on the face. A good steep route.

26   T'Owd Trout   VD
An attractive climb. Ascend the obvious shallow cracked groove two metres right of the sharp-topped flake.
The blocks are now descended into the hollow.

27   The Crooked Man   HVD   ★
Another good climb although little is apparent from below. Start at the foot of a steep layback crack. Climb this and move rightwards in the shade of a big Ash to a shallow groove in the steep wall above. Climb this on excellent rock.

ASH TREE WALL

A nondescript sector of wall and easy cracked slabs which extends rightwards from the Big Ash in the hollow to the fine crack of Wings on Sector Ronson Kirkby.

28   Ash Tree Slab   VD
Start immediately right of the Ash. Climb the slab and small corner up to the left.

29   The Chopping Block   VD
Start two metres right in front of the corner of a large block at the

foot of the face. Climb the slab and finish steeply between two little corners to a steep "mushroom" of rock.

30   Cracked Groove   MS
Start two metres right at a cracked groove. Climb this and the wall above to finish.

Six metres further right is a jumble of blocks below a steep wall.

31   Speedy Recovery   S   4c
Climb the steep wall to a bulge and follow the short ragged crack to the top.

32   The Ashes   D
Start one metre right below twin Ash saplings. Climb the wall and crack above the Ash saplings on good holds.

33   Ash Gully   M
Climb the gully containing the Ash tree.

34   Left Wall   VD
Start just right of the gully below a left-facing flake at head height. Climb onto a ledge and climb the flake and slab to the top.

35   The Rib   HS   4b   ★
Start at a faint rib just left of the obvious crack of Wings. Climb the rib via a nice step up using a runnel.

SECTOR RONSON KIRKBY

Towards the right end of the escarpment and beyond the cloak of Ash trees in front of the crag is a fine clean face having an obvious bulge at half height and a straight crack running the height of the face on the left of the bulge.

36   Wings   VD
A very pleasant climb. Climb the continuous crack to the left of the bulge. The move at the bulge is good.

37   Pegasus   VS   5a   ★
Start below a horizontal slot on the lip of the bulge. Climb up to some blocks below the bulge. Pull over on the horizontal slot and reach good holds to gain the upper wall.

38   Cyclops   HVS   6a   ★★
Start below the obvious "eye" pocket above the lip at the right end of the bulge. Climb the wall below and slightly right of the "eye" on poor holds to reach the horizontal break. Gain the eye and swarm up the easy face above.

39   Serpent   MS   ★
A fine easy finale. Start just right of the right end of the mid-height bulge below a little, waterworn crack. Climb the crack steeply and gain the sloping crack above the bulge. Foot-traverse left with ease and finish up the centre of the top wall.

40   Ronson Kirkby   VD
One metre right of Serpent is a good flake. Climb this to a good ledge. on the right. Climb direct to the next horizontal break and move left along this to the top.

41   Little Corner   HVD
Start two metres right of the good flake. Climb steeply to the good ledge. Climb the little corner above finishing up the wall on good holds.

42   Concave Wall   HVD
Start one metre left of the descent gully. Climb easy cracks to a diagonal crack slanting left. Follow this to the top horizontal break and move left to finish as for Little Corner.

SECTOR FOUR WALLS
Just right of the descent gully to the right of Sector Ronson Kirkby are four walls ending 15m further right by a mass of Hazel and Ivy.

43   First Wall Rib   MS
Climb the rounded rib of the First wall.

44   Cracking   D   ★
Excellent climbing on super holds. Climb the crack between First wall and Second Wall.

45   Smooth Rib   S   4b
Climb the smooth rib immediately right of Cracking.

46   Second Wall   S   4b   ★
Start at a square recess at the base of the face. Climb up the wall with a hard move into a short crack at the top.

47   Crazy Paving   D
Start one metre left at a crack-seamed slab. Climb the well-cracked slab and wall above.

48   Pedestal Crack   D
Climb the crack between wall 2 and 3 via a pedestal.

49   Third Wall Central   VD
Climb the centre of the wall via a single pocket.

Fourth Wall is to the right of a small Ash. The large block above the easy-angled slab is POTENTIALLY DANGEROUS – BE WARNED!

50   Spike Route   HD
Start just right of the large block at the top. Climb the easy slab and ascend a short crack via a blunt spike.

51   The Runnel   MS   ★
Start below and right of a brown water-stain. Climb the dark runnel above on excellent rock.

52   Curving   HD   ★★
Start one metre right of the Runnel. Climb the curving breaks on perfect rock. Super.

Twenty five metres further right is one of the best areas:

SECTOR GORILLA
This consists of a long undercut wall on the left which gains height and becomes a fine buttress of excellent rock. The upper wall is pure jug-pulling pleasure but to reach it, some hard-work on the bulge at chest-height is necessary.

53   Primate   HS   5a   ★
Start two metres right of the left end of the wall at a slim groove at head height. Reach up to good holds on a ledge and pull strenuously up the bulge to finish above on parallel, vertical cracks.

54   Swamp Fever   MVS   5b
Start below an obvious right hand flake hold at four metres. Climb direct to this and the wall above.

55 Malaria MVS 5b
Start one metre right below a vertical crack. Reach this with difficulty and continue more easily.

56 The Lemur's Tail HS 4c   *
A good route despite its proximity to the Hawthorn.
Starts at the foot of the slim continuous crack. Climb the crack, steeply at first and finish up the continuation just left of a Hawthorn.

57 Gibbon Take HS 5a
Start five metres right of The Lemur's Tail. Climb the left-hand of the two parallel cracks which are one metre apart.

58 No More Monkey Business HS 5a
Climb the right-hand crack.

59 Chimp HS 4c   *
Just right of The right hand crack is a slanting crack above the bulge. Pull over the bulge on good holds and finish up the face just right of the Ivy mass.

60 Gorilla Berengii HS 4c *
Just right and growing from the face is a slim tree. Start one metre left of the tree and pull over the bulge on an excellent flake hold. Easier climbing leads to the final crack.

61 Gorilla Gorilla MVS 4c   **
Start below the slim tree in the centre of the wall. Climb the bulge and pass the tree to reach the horizontal break. Climb directly up the front of the buttress just right of a curving nut- crack. More sustained and finer than its neighbours.

62 Pithocanthropus Erectus HS 4c
Start at the right-hand end of the overhang. Climb direct to the horizontal break and make along reach to a hand rail. Finish direct.

63 Damned Spot 6c   **
Traverse the sector at low-level, left or right using only the red-spotted handholds.

FARLETON CRAG   O.S. Sheet 97   539 794

SITUATION AND CHARACTER
Farleton Crag is on the flank of Farleton fell in Cumbria only a short distance from Junction 36 on the M6. It provides high quality short climbs on excellent limestone with a beautiful outlook (M6 apart!) over the wooded hilly country towards the Kent Estuary. The crag faces West and is a sunny, sheltered place despite its relative altitude (180m O.D.)

Popularity has given some of the climbs a high gloss and previous guides seem not to have taken this into account in terms of grading. As with all limestone individual loose holds should be used with care, but particular care should be taken with massive instability. This occurs at one or two places eg Primrose Way and the top block of Doodlebug. They will fall, sooner or later, be "switched on" or "switched off"!

A superb venue.

APPROACHES AND ACCESS

Approaching from Junction 36 on the M6 follow the A65 East direction Skipton for 200m to a small roundabout. Leave the A65 here and follow the A6070 South passing below the fine sweep of Farleton Fell. Less than a mile South of the turn off to Farleton Village is a farm on the left with a prominent silage tower. This is Holme Park Farm. Cars can be parked on the wide verge opposite, near a cul-de-sac leading to some houses. Do not park in the cul-de-sac.

From Holme Park Farm, follow the lane signposted: Public Bridleway: Clawthorpe Fell. The lane leads gently uphill until after about 800 metres the confines of the lane are quitted via a gate onto wooded fell land. Proceed past concrete mountings on the left and branch off left almost immediately onto an obvious grassy track which slants gently up the fellside. Do not break out right too soon but follow paths trending right over small tiers of limestone pavement until the crag can be seen above, lightly cloaked by small trees. The point at which to strike up to the crag is at a grove of trees containing a number of large boulders. A path goes up the screes and then bears up grass to the foot of the escarpment. Follow the escarpment leftwards to the first face of any height which presents at its highest point, a smooth wall to the right of an obvious corner groove. This is the wall of N'Yoka.

HISTORICAL

The climbing at Farleton was first discovered by Ian Dobson, Roger Gott and friends in the late '60's. This group climbed many of the easier lines including Doodlebug, Farleton Crack, Idleness and Appleton Crack.

Ian introduced Stew Wilson to the crag and his main contributions were Deb's Crack and the splendid Shriek Of Baghdad. Stew let Bill Lounds and Chris Eilbeck into the secret and inspired by Bill's forceful and energetic approach other lines quickly fell including N'Yoka and Agrippa whose handjam must rank as one of the most painful in the North of England. Bill and Stew also visited Farleton Quarry and Uhuru succumbed to Bill's powerful leading.

This story would not be complete without mentioning Ian "Sherpa" Roper who "spilled the beans" to the Yorkshiremen.

Sherpa ascended the fine Family Way and Allan Austin produced the excellent Roughneck and the mean Gent. Strong climbers including Tony Mitchell, Dave Bates and Tom Walkington latterly climbed some hard problems including The Coil. The story is far from complete and whilst many of the gaps have been climbed nothing has been recorded.

THE CLIMBS

These are described section by section from right to left starting with:

N'YOKA BUTTRESS

This is the first sizeable bit of rock approaching by the approach described. It is almost in line with the distinct line of a hedge boundary in the fields below. An easy descent down a stairway of huge blocks marks the right end of the section. A medium sized Ash grows near the foot of N'Yoka.

1 Lumumba 8m HS 4a
Starts at the right end of the face behind an almost prostrate hawthorn.
Climb the discontinuous, thin cracks to a horizontal break and swarm up the steep, hand-crack above.

2 N'Yoka 9m E1 5c   ★★
The snake and a sinuous move at that! Only VS 5a for anyone over six feet! Start one metre left of Lumumba by an Ash and a Hawthorn. Climb thin cracks to a slim corner. The horizontal break is used perplexingly to gain the slot way, way above. Its all over now and a quick heave on jugs completes the climb.

3 Eggyoka 8m VD
Not as oeuful as the name! Climb the open corner to the left of N'Yoka on good rock to gain and climb the pleasant cracked corner above.

4 Monkey Wrench 9m MS
A good climb. Start two metres left of the open corner below a bulging buttress split by a crack. Climb the front of the buttress to the horizontal break and finish up the wide crack above.

5 Rock Ivy Line 9m HVD
Start two metres further left below a slight, vegetated groove line. Climb this with a hard pull near the bottom and finish left of a stunted Ash.

6 Anaconda HS 4b
A 'star' quality route spoilt by the hollow, potentially leg-breaking flakes at mid height. Start two metres left of Rock Ivy Line below a slim, finger crack. Climb the crack and use the suspect flakes to the right and left at its top with great care and rejoice in the firmness of your intent and the upper wall.

To the left of Anaconda is a bleached, gnarled Yew stump at the top of the crag. A traverse called Primrose Path which starts at Lumumba and traverses from right to left at Severe standard crosses under this stump and across the wall on the left. AVOID THIS. The wall on the left is a huge detached flake on a tiny base, veritable "Hanging Death!" A far better finish to Primrose path would be to gain Anaconda and finish up this.

Fifty metres further left passing under small walls one comes to an easy slabby arete with an easy way down to its left and a few metres further left is a steep wall of superb rock with a long crack running up its left hand side. This is:

FAMILY WAY WALL

7 The Coil 6c
Climb the thin crack in the centre of the wall to the horizontal break.

8 The Pill 7m HVS 5b
Start below the slim crack which runs the full height of the left end of the wall as for the Family Way. Climb this to the break. Hand-

traverse right for a few metres and pull over at an area of fretted rocks to finish.

9   The Family Way   7m   HVS   5a   *
An excellent route, not high in the grade but steep and commiting. A high gloss finish provides a good reflection of one's technique. Start below the slim crack which runs the full height of the left end of the wall. Climb the crack to the horizontal break and do not layback the upper crack. Good protection.

10   Chastity   7m   HS   4c
Not a bad little route. Start just right of and below the conspicuous Ash growing from the face one metre left of Family Way. Climb the bulging wall via good but small holds to gain a good ledge. The V-groove above is still steep but holds are good.

CALIBAN WALLS

Further left are some smaller faces until after twelve metres the wall gains in stature and then gradually reduces in height but not steepness to end at the jutting, undercut prow whose left wall is ascended by Caliban. Where the wall is at its maximum height, a Thorn tree grows from the foot of the wall. The next route is found three metres left of this:

11   Green Machine   11m   HVS   5b
Climb the left edge of the wall via the flake cracks. At the break, move right and ascend the diagonal crack in the wall above.

12   Pudding Club   9m   S
Climb the obvious block-filled groove immediately left of Green Machine.

13   Dimple, Dimple   9m   HVS   5b
Gain and follow a line of dimples 1.5m left of Pudding Club. Pass the bulge and continue to the top.

14   Clayfire   6m   VS   5a
Start below a thin crack at head-height, 3m left of Pudding Club. Climb the crack.

To the left of Clayfire is a broken groove leading up to a small thicket of trees. The next route starts some 2m left of this.

15   Flaykier   7m   VS   4c
Climb up and left on knobbly, flake holds.

16   Cracker   5m   HVS   5b
Start below the small, undercut corner just right of the jutting prow. Climb this.

17   Prowler   5m   VS   5a
Climb the front of the jutting prow to gain easier ground.

18   Caliban   5m   VS   4c
Start below a curved crack on the left face of the jutting prow, facing G Squared. Climb the curved crack and finish on curiously eroded rock above.

About 4m to the left of Caliban, a large Ash tree grows out from the foot of the crag.

19   G Squared   11m   HVS   5a
Climb the crack immediately left of the Ash tree. Move left along

the break until a short, vertical crack permits an upward escape to be made.
To the left again is:

THE MAIN FACE
This is the highest section of the crag. The Main Face section is bounded on the right by a recessed face above which are over-hangs. To the left again is a steep face which has a big Ash growing at six metres. A white scar to the left marks a recent rockfall and the smooth cracked wall soon gives onto the fine buttress up which the Shriek Of Baghdad ascends via the stunningly obvious, polished layback crack. To the left is the fine, deep corner of Slime Gut and left again is a left trending crack in a steep wall which is Hazy Daze. Main Face ends at another big Ash which grows from the crag two metres up.

20   Pork Chop   9m   HVS   5a
Start at the foot of the blunt rib forming the right-hand side of the recessed face.
Pull onto the blunt, undercut rib using flaky holds. Continue directly up the wall above past the break.

21   Doodlebug   9m   VS   4a
A good climb, which would be exhilarating and fine if it were not for the dubious stability of the enormous block which constitutes the crux.The grade is for seriousness. Start below the shallow groove at the right -hand end of the recesses wall below the very obvious jammed block. Climb the groove and using the crack alongside the block exit steeply. Not a route to take the innocent or ignorant up!!

22   Instant Whip   9m   VS   4c
Ascend the shallow groove in the centre of the recess, passing a small roof at two-thirds height.

23   Idleness   10m   VS   4c   *
Climb the flake crack at the left of the recess which leads up to the big roof. Pass this by jamming the crack which splits it.
Five metres left of the recess is an Ash tree growing half-way up the crag.

24   Feet Of Clay   8m   HS   4b
Start just right of the Ash at a square-cut groove. Climb the groove and finish behind the Ash or Move right and exit with more dif-ficulty via a faint scoop.

25   Fat Good Crack   9m   VS   5a
Start below a flake crack below and left of the Ash. Climb the flake crack leading up and left to a ledge. Finish up the steep, eroded scoop above.

26   Doggo   9m   HS   4b
Interesting although the first wall is totteringly awkward. Start 2m left of Fat Good Crack below a steep cracked wall. Climb the cracks and pull rightwards onto the ledge. Move right and swing across the obvious scoop to good holds and a juggy finish, as for Fat Good Crack.

27   Earwig Two   11m   VS   4c
Start at the foot of the chimney formed by a huge, white flake. Climb the rattling rift to a jutting edge and traverse right on this to meet the upper chimney. Ascend this on the outside or if slim , a character-building squirm inside the rift may lead to the top.

28   Earwig One   10m   HVS   5a
Follow the chimney as for Earwig Two, but at the break, continue up the hanging groove above.

29   Agrippa   9m   E1   5c   ★
This provides a painful experience and is hard in the grade.
Start 4m left of the Earwig Chimney below a vague crack running up to meet the roof. Climb the vague crack and surmount the roof by means of a very painful jamming. Finish by a small tree and corner.

30   Herod   10m   HVS   5a   ★
At the lower limit of the grade but sustained. Start below a thin cracked groove which goes up to a stepped break in the overhang one metre left of the crack of Agrippa. Climb the groove on poor holds and gain the horizontal break (Crux). The move into the upper crack is awkward and tiring. Follow this past a stump.

31   The Shriek Of Baghdad   10m   HVS   5a   ★★
A polished three-star! This excellent climb sees many failures and requires a commited approach. Start at the foot of the obvious, polished layback crack. Climb the crack on improving holds until a move left at the top leads to an alarming move to gain the ledge above. Shake up the easier corner above.

Four metres left of The Shriek is a corner-groove; Slime Gut, with a small tree at its base.

32   Watching The Motorway Flow   10m   VS   5a
Climb the leaning crack in the right wall of Slime Gut passing a small tree near the top.

33   Slime Gut   9m   HS   4c
A better climb than the name suggests. Climb the obvious groove.

34   The Girdle Traverse   28m   HVS   5a   ★
Usually climbed in two pitches taking a tree belay on the ledge to the left of Idleness. Climb Idleness to the roof and follow the break leftwards. It is usually necessary to descend a little to cross the wall to Agrippa before following the vague crack of this route to regain the break. Continue traversing on this line to cross The Shriek and finish as for Slime Gut.

35   Appleton Crack   9m   VS   4b   ★
Interesting with a bold finish. Start below the V-groove 2m left of Slime Gut. Climb the groove to the overlap and move slightly right until the slab above can be gained and climbed.

36   Hazy Daze   8m   HS   4b
Climb the obvious slanting crackline on the wall to the right of The Easy Way.

37   The Easy Way   7m   D
Climb the shallow, stepped corner.
This is the last route on The Main Face. A large Ash growing at two metres marks the end of this section.

Causey Quarry, climber on Telstar Direct VS 4c

DEBS SECTOR

The large Ash growing at two metres below the steep Farleton Crack is a convenient feature from which to describe the following area and its climbs. Debs Sector basically consists of two upstanding buttresses with a fine wall in between. The left hand buttress is in fact a semi- detached prow behind which is an easy but polished descent chimney.

38 Farleton Crack 8m VD
Climb the wide fissure just left of the large Ash at 2m. There is a small tree near the top.

39 Deb's Wall 9m 6b
The wall between Farleton Crack and Deb's Crack bulges and ripples. So must you if you wish to ascend it.

40 Deb's Crack 9m VS 5a   ★★
Age has not been kind; a sweaty struggle with this well-worn harridan is a lecture in climbing polished cracks. Start below the slim groove and crack 4m left of Farleton Crack. Climb the crack.

41 Super Dick 9m HVS 5b   ★
Climb the narrow, left wall of the prow left of Deb's Crack. At the break, follow the arete above to the top.

42 Pleb's Chimney 8m HVD
Climb the wide, polished chimney left of the prow. Not as good as it looks.

Extending leftwards from Pleb's Chimney is a flat wall. The next route starts near the left edge of this.

43 Heatwave 9m HVS 5a   ★
Start just right of the vertical crack which runs up the left side of the wall. Climb up and rightwards to gain the break near an old stump (no touching!). Pull up past this with commitment and continue direct on good holds.

44 Shower Crack 8m VD   ★
Climb the groove/crackline up the left edge of the flat wall. A pleasant finish is to foot traverse the break containing the old stump and finish as for Heatwave.

45 Avalanche Route 7m HVD
Climb the wide fissure 1m left of Shower Crack. The left side of this is a huge detached prow behind which is the descent chimney.

46 Mon Cadastre 7m HVD   ★
Start at the foot of the prow just left of Avalanche Route. A hard move gains better holds. These are followed directly up the arete.

The detached prow conceals an easy way down.

Ten metres beyond the easy way down a pile of large, fallen blocks lie against the crag. The topmost block is crowned by a sloping "meadow". The flat wall of excellent rock just beyond the pile of blocks is Roughneck Wall.

ROUGHNECK WALL

On the far side of the pile of blocks the crag presents a steep face of impeccable rock this becomes a less ferocious proposition the further left one goes.It terminates in a short undercut rib.

47   Pleasant Wall   6m   S
Start just right of the pile of blocks. Climb the wall on rounded holds in horizontal breaks.

48   Scraper   7m   S
Start immediately left of the pile of blocks. Climb the obvious groove and crack line on the extreme right end of the flat wall.

49   The Gent   7m   E1   5c
Climb directly up the wall 1m left of Scraper.

50   Roughneck   7m   E1   5c   ⋆
Start 3m left of Scraper. Climb direct to a short vertical crack. Hard moves gain the horizontal break and a steep finish via a runnel. Fine.

51   Rough Crack   6m   S   ⋆
Climb the short, steep crack which forms the left boundary of the flat wall.

52   The Spoon   6m   VD   ⋆
Start 3m left of Rough Crack below a steep wall with an open, concave scoop at the top. Pull up the steep wall and enter the scoop direct and follow it moving leftwards to the top on satifying holds. The scoop can also be entered from the right. This is slightly easier.

The escarpment continues leftwards and many problems can be found. Forty metres left of The Spoon and just left of a large block lying below the path is a wide left-facing crack leading up to a pedestal.

53   Slip Stitch   7m   S   ⋆
Climb the wide crack to the horizontal break. The fluted front of the block above is followed to the top. Good.

THE UPPER CRAG
Something of a misnomer as whilst it is higher up the fell than The Main Crag, it is actually a continuation of the band of rocks which lie below The Main Crag. The rock on The Upper Crag is not as good as elsewhere and in certain places it is loose. Please take care.To reach The Upper Crag, walk about 600 metres North of The Main Crag to where a drystone wall is seen.

As it is easily seen from the roads below, and not screened by trees, this area is often taken to be The Main Crag by first-time visitors. Most of the routes on The Upper Crag are concentrated around a large, cracked roof at the top of the crag some 20 metres right of the drystone wall. The first route lies 25 metres further right again. A huge, triangular roof juts out over a Hawthorn bush and the routes are described moving leftwards from here.

54   Buckshot   10m   HS
Climb a short corner up to the triangular roof. Traverse left then move up and right below a bulge to finish up cracks.

55   Avoidance   15m   VS   4b   ⋆
Start directly below the large, cracked roof at a chimney. Climb the chimney to below the roof then traverse right and finish up a short corner and crack.

56   Rose Amongst Thorns   15m   VS   4c   ★
Climb Avoidance, but move left below the roof to the corner. Use the roof crack to move out left to an exposed finish.

57   California Dreaming   12m   E1   5b
Start 6m left of Avoidance below a slim groove in the broken wall. Climb the slim groove to the roof. Move right and ascend the crack which splits the bulge.

58   Blood On The Tracks   11m   NL   5b
Climb the area of rock left of California Dreaming and finish up the prominent, acute V-groove slashing through the upper bulges.

59   Silent Jim   10m   HS
Start 5m left of Avoidance. Climb up to a prominent, vertical fin and continue rightwards, past a tree to finish up a groove to the left of the upper bulges.

FARLETON QUARRY

This lies behind the village of Farleton on the fellside. It is a single wall of rock. The handful of climbs here are described from left to right.

60   Yoruba   9m   VD
Climb the crack at the left side of the wall. Tree at head-height can be used.

61   Hark To Bounty   9m   VS   4c
Climb the centre of the wall between Yoruba and the next crack along.

62   Ebo   10m   HS   4a
Climb the steep, loose central crack.

63   Uhuru   12m   E2   5c   ★
Start at a block at the foot of the steep wall. Climb the wall and thin crack to a bulge. The bulge is the crux and the wall above leads steeply to the top.

64   The Pit   6m   VD
Climb the short corner on the right. The wall has been traversed in two directions:

65   Mr. Universe   37m   HVS   5a/b
Start at a large ledge in the right-hand corner and traverse the wall leftwards to reach and follow the break running into Yoruba, up which the climb finishes.

66   The Pit And The Pendulum   37m   VS(A)   4c
A left to right girdle with a rope move to cross the steep wall to the right of Uhuru.

FAIRY STEPS   O.S. Sheet 97   G.R. 486 789

SITUATION AND CHARACTER

Fairy Steps is the name given to a narrow cleft at the Southern end of Underlaid Woods near Beetham in Cumbria. The Fairy Steps are reputed to possess magical properties, and if the old tales are correct, anyone passing through the cleft without touching the sides will be granted a wish. The climbing at Fairy Steps is located in two separate areas. The first is on the rocks on either side of the

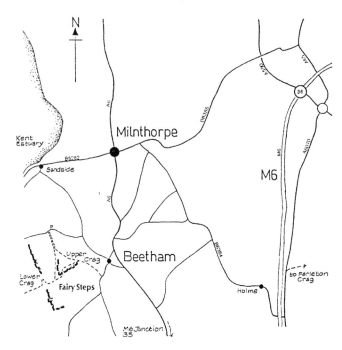

SOUTH CUMBRIAN LIMESTONE

Fairy Steps. The second and more important area is further down the track from Fairy Steps towards Hazelslack. This Lower Crag, particularly the section North of the track to Hazelslack demands a certain amount of perseverance as the paths are presently overgrown or else encumbered with branches.

Underlaid woods provide a lovely setting for climbing with views across the estuary although the climbing itself does not often share this outlook.

The climbing tends to be short and steep and the quality of the rock for the most part is excellent, some of the best limestone in the area in fact with waterworn pockets, Gouttes d'Eau, runnels and flutings.

This could be a "Boulderers Paradise", with a bit of a manicure below some of the blocks i.e. removal of foresters' brashings and ankle breaking rocks. Those who don't like soloing can easily lead the harder problems as protection is usually available. The Upper Crag also provides superb mini- routes for climbers of less ambitious needs as well as some quite hard problems.

It is inconceivable that this important area has been ignored and written off as a place to be used for pottering about at, as this has only resulted in paths becoming lost, lichen growth and an overuse of the documented crags. The crags face West and as a result of tree clearing many of the buttresses enjoy afternoon sunshine. This is an important little crag and as an amenity deserves greater recognition in its own right.

APPROACHES AND ACCESS

The crags are best approached from Beetham on the A6 South of Milnthorpe. Travelling South from Milnethorpe on the A6 just after crossing the bridge over the River Bela turn right into Beetham at a sign for the Heron Corn Mill and turn right again just before the Wheatsheaf Inn. Follow a narrow minor road to a junction and take the left fork signposted to Storth and Arnside eventually trending uphill until the brow of the hill is reached. There is a layby on the right and over the road a locked gate with a stile to its right gives access to the track leading to Fairy Steps. Follow the track for six hundred metres to a clearing and signpost at a fork. Follow the right fork and re-enter woodland. The escarpment of Whin Scar; the Upper crag, containing the Fairy Steps is soon visible through the trees on the left. Continue on the track with the rocks in view until at a T-junction, a well worn path turns sharp left to reach, in a few metres the cleft of Fairy Steps. To reach the Lower crag, turn right at the junction and continue downhill to a splendid viewpoint. Descend from this via another cleft and steps of more ample proportions than the Fairy Steps to the foot of the crag, which extends in both directions from this point.

The Lower crag can be reached by following a good path from Hazelslack Tower G.R. 477 787 this path arrives at the foot of the aforementioned wide cleft.

HISTORICAL

We all know who climbed here first in their natty green and yellow tights, but it was Bill Lounds and various mates from Lancaster who recorded the first routes. These routes, twenty nine in all, were published in the Lancashire Guide of 1975 by Dave Powell-Thompson and were popular.

Subsequent publications wrote the venue off for various reasons, most of which are of no interest to climbers. The net result was that existing routes soon became dirty and the paths overgrown.

Clearing of woodland, renewed interest and an available record of the climbs should soon change matters.The following additional climbs were climbed and recorded by Matt Ellis, Karl Lunt, Stew Wilson and Maggie Wilson in 1991. Some are first ascents many are not.

THE UPPER CRAG (FAIRY STEPS)

The climbs are described as one faces the crag, Sector by Sector from right to left working left of the "Steps", and left to right working right of the "Steps". Some of the easier routes next to the "Steps" have bolt anchors at the top. (NB Single bolt anchors should be backed up!)

THE CLIMBS LEFT OF THE "STEPS"
SECTOR CARTOON

This extends leftwards from the fine easy arete above the cleft to an overhanging buttress some metres further left which is smothered by a Holly.

1   Fantasia   8m   D   ★
Climb the super arete just left of the "Steps".

2   Mr T   8m   S   4c   ★
Climb the corner left of the arete and finish up the slab direct without using holds to the right.

3   Cruella   8m   S   4b
Climb the blunt rib left of the corner and finish up the slab on initially poor holds.

4   Silveste   7m   VD   4a
Climb the corner below the Yew. Step right of the tree to finish.

5   Felix   7m   MS   4a
Start to the left of the corner at a block below a steep wall. Climb the centre of the wall to good finishing holds.

6   Popeye   7m   MS   4a/b
Climb the thin flaky crack on the wall just right of the chimney.

7   Olive   7m   D
Climb the chimney.

8   Sweetpea   7m   M
Climb the arete left of the chimney.

The next five metres left consists of Ivy-covered rock. A big block marks the starts of the next climbs.

9   Tom   7m   VD   ★
Climb the shallow left facing corner starting from the top of the block.

10   Jerry   9m   MS   ★
Start as for the last climb, but leave the corner via a foot-traverse on the first horizontal break for two metres. Finish up a vertical break. A bad landing!

The continuation of this escarpment leftwards has some excellent faces which will repay some attention, particularly those at the extreme left-hand end.

THE CLIMBS – RIGHT OF THE "STEPS"
SECTOR FAIRY STEPS

The easy-looking wall of good quality rock about 8m high immediately right of the "Steps". This sector ends at a large block below an overhang above which a Yew sprouts out of the top of the face.

11   Imago   4m   4a
Start in the steps where it levels out. Climb the steep right wall on flakes.

12   Puck   8m   M
Start at the right of the foot of the steps at a big block. Surmount the block and follow the obvious crackline to the right of a small tree.

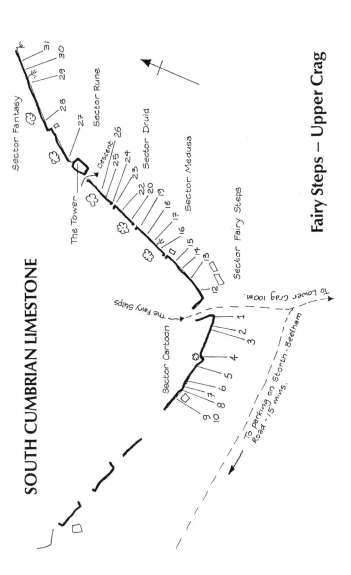

SOUTH CUMBRIAN LIMESTONE

Fairy Steps – Upper Crag

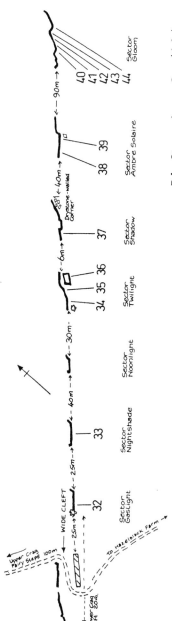

Fairy Steps – Lower Crag (right)

13 Robin 8m M
Start one metre right below a jammed block. Climb the right wall of the groove and climb the crack above and right (or finish direct from block).

14 Merryweather 8m D
Start on little protruding "doorstep" and climb the wall to the horizontal break. Climb the bulge above on good holds and continue straight up.

15 Sourmilk 8m D
Climb the wall above three parallel, short, vertical cracks and finish up the crack above.

SECTOR MEDUSA

The next sector right. It extends for twelve metres and ends at two large blocks below an open cleft at the top. A large Yew grows out of the face on Sector Medusa and is a point of reference.

16 Medusa D
Start at the bent tree just left of the big Yew. Climb the easy steps to a steeper finish at a little corner.

17 Stoneface S
Climb the steep face just right of the Yew.

18 The Sword S
Climb the steep crack to the right of Stoneface.

19 The Shield S
Start just right of The Sword. Climb onto the ledge on top of the block. Finish up the steep face above.

SECTOR DRUID

This consists of two fine steep faces separated by a steep crack which widens to become a chimney. Both faces have a more or less continuous bulge at mid-height. The climbing is both steep and interesting on surprising holds.Ten metres of more broken rocks further right ends in a cave recess formed by fallen blocks. (A useful descent route).

20 Cormach 8m HS 4b ∗
Start two metres left of the central crack from the block behind a slim tree. Climb leftwards and turn the overhang on the left continue up left to a short vertical runnel and the top.

21 Cernunnos 8m VS 5a ∗
An excellent steep climb on good holds. Start just right of the slim tree on a big block. Gain the flanges on the left of the bulge and move right on jugs. A long reach leads to a pocket and the top.

22 The Druid 8m HVS 5b ∗∗
Poor holds and a poor landing combined with a technical start make this a hard route. Start on top of the large block below a v-shaped vertical slot in the bulge. Climb up to the bulge on undercuts and gain poor holds in the first horizontal break. A hard pull reaches a good vertical edge high up on the right. Finish more easily.

23 Gofannon 8m MS 4a
Climb the crack/chimney separating the two steep walls.

24   Epona   8m   MS   4a   ⋆
Climb the rib one metre right of the chimney moving slightly right to finish. Surprise holds.

25   Mabon   8m   S   4b   ⋆⋆
A great climb on superbly sculpted rock. Just right of the crack is a sheaf of Hazels. Climb up to the bulge just right of the hazels, a pull over the bulge on twin, vertical runnels leads to fantastic holds and the top.

26   Taranis   8m   MS   4a   ⋆
A good route. Start from a block one metre right. Climb up to and through the next break in the bulge.

THE TOWER

Just right of the cave of blocks is a tower of excellent, steep rock. It presents two faces separated by a fine cracked arete.

SECTOR RUNE

This extends rightwards from a corner to the right of the tower. An inscription on the rock face just right of the corner identifies it. Other inscriptions of some antiquity are to be found hereabouts. The sector ends where a large block abuts against an arete, thirteen metres right of the corner.

27   Scrawl   6m   VD
Climb the wall just right of the corner between two trees.

SECTOR FANTASY

An important sector with superb steep rock and some fine lines. To the right of the block leant against the arete is a shallow cave. The very steep face extends rightwards and has a fine flake on it. Right of a small corner the face, still very steep continues to a large Yew. The continuation face to another large Yew provides easier climbs.

28   Taliesin   8m   VS   5a   ⋆⋆⋆
Great climbing with steep moves but a good landing.
Start one metre right of the large block in front of the recess at the left side of a finger-flake at chest-height. Pull strenuously onto the flake and climb the very steep wall direct on flat holds to finish at a good flake.

29   Celyddon   8m   VD   ⋆
Start immediately left of the first big Yew. Climb the flake edge and recess above.

30   The Dark Stair   8m   M
Climb the easy groove right of the big Yew. A useful descent.

31   Goddeu   8m   D
Start at a tall upstanding flake to the right of the first Yew. Climb the wall on good holds.

THE LOWER CRAG

The climbs are described from left to right, starting right of the steps in the wide cleft (as one faces the crag) first. Finally the climbs to the left of the wide cleft are described from right to left.

THE CLIMBS RIGHT OF THE WIDE CLEFT

SECTOR GASLIGHT

An attractive face twenty five metres right of the wide cleft. The face is about twenty metres long and has a big Yew growing out of the left side near the top and another Yew four metres right of this, again growing out of the rock.

32   Gaslight   VS   5a

Climb the obvious crack four metres right of the second, big Yew and behind a Holly. At the top bulge, move left and climb the good continuation crack.

About twenty five metres further right is:

SECTOR NIGHTSHADE

A rather gloomy small wall with two shorter wall left and right.

33   Nightshade   VS   4c

Climb the wall at its highest point between the two trees growing out of the crag.

The crag continues as a line of shorter walls up to four metres high. After forty metres is a bigger wall between a sheaf of Hazel and a big Yew.

This is:

SECTOR MOONLIGHT

No recorded climbs.

Thirty metres further right is:

SECTOR TWILIGHT

A very attractive buttress with a prominent overhang. Sunny and open now due to felling.

34   Twilight   VS   5a

Climb the continuous crack on the left of the buttress to the left of the prominent overhang.

35   Neetabulb   E1   5c   *

Start two metres right of Twilight at a short crack. Climb the wall above the crack to a break in the overhang. Climb this direct to the top.

Across right is a detached face with an easy gully behind it.

36   Parasol   S

Climb the obvious crackline in the face of the detached block. Step right at the top.

Six metres right, beyond a block-filled chimney is:

SECTOR SHADOW

An extensive area with a fine wall at the left end and a higher but more broken right-hand end. This sector ends at a corner which has been drystone walled.

37   The Shadow   VS   4c

Climb the left hand wall on fine rock starting with a layaway on a small nose of rock.

Forty metres right a Yew grows from a jumble of large blocks.

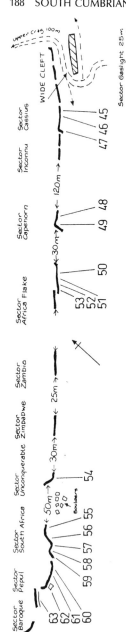

Fairy Steps – Lower Crag (left)

SOUTH CUMBRIAN LIMESTONE

SECTOR AMBRE SOLAIRE

This Sector has a big Yew at its left end. Further right on the ground is a large, square, flat block. This Sector is now more open and sunny due to felling.

38 Ambre Solaire VS 4c/5a
Climb the wall to the right of the big Yew moving up rightwards to finish up doubtful rock right of a stump.

39 Goleu E1 5c
Start at the large, squareblock on the ground. Climb the curving, small corner above the block to the overhang. The overhang is difficult. (PR).

Ninety metres further right the path opens out into a pleasant clearing of what used to be dank woodland. The crag is in this clearing and faces South West.

SECTOR GLOOM

This is a pleasant open face of excellent rock ten metres high. The main feature is a shallow corner in the centre whilst at the left side is a short, pink wall bounded on the right by an impressive face with some blocks at the base. The sector continues around to the right and ends beyond an impressive small buttress of clean rock with a fine overhang. The route names reflect its former condition before the wood was thinned.

40 Dusk HVS 5b
Start directly below the bulge at the left end of the crag to the right of the short pink wall and a slanting crack. Climb strenuously over the bulge on poor holds to a good flake. Move right at the top to finish.

41 Gothic Wall NL 6b   ★★
A desperately fingery climb. Start below a slim right-slanting crack below and left of the obvious flake on Dark Ages. Climb this crack and transfer with great difficulty into another slim vertical crack on the right. A tendon-popping move leads up to better holds and a less difficult finish at a small Ash tree.

42 The Dark Ages E2 5c   ★★
A hard route particularly for the short. Start just left of the central corner crack. Climb the wall leftwards on sketchy holds to a prominent flake. The steep wall leads on gradually improving holds to the top.

43 Gloom VS 5a   ★
A really good route up the corner finishing either right or left of the overhang, altenatively the overhang can be climbed direct on good holds.

44 Umbra HVS 5b/c
Climb the rounded arete just right of Gloom. A very hard rock-over is followed by a thin crack. Swarm up the face left of the Yew.

CLIMBS LEFT OF THE WIDE CLEFT

An area of deeply gashed and vegetated rocks starts to improve within twenty metres of the wide cleft. Two large Yews growing close to the rock are passed.

SECTOR CASSIUS

A pleasant, but shady sector with a obvious, slabby wall of excellent finely sculpted rock and a prominent layback corner on the left four metres left of the second Yew.

45 Pernambuco HS
Climb the wide crack starting three metres right of the second big Yew. The crack trends leftwards to the top.

Just around the corner to the left past the second Yew is:

46 Cassius S
Climb the fine slab just left of the big Yew.

47 Morocco Crack VD
Climb the slim layback crack.

Immediately left is:

SECTOR INCONNU

A good steep buttress presenting two steep faces separated by a left to right easy rake. No recorded climbs.

A series of problem walls follow until the rocks gain height and an overhanging chimney/crack is reached One hundred and twenty metres right of Sector Inconnu.

SECTOR CAPEHORN

A right-facing cave/corner identifies this sector.

48 Horn A Plenty S
Climb the undercut groove to the right of the cave/corner.

49 Capehorn VS
Climb the Cave/corner.

Thirty metres further left is:

SECTOR AFRICA FLAKE.

This is the fine steep wall of excellent rock which has a prominent down-pointing flake shaped like Africa in the centre of the right-hand wall. A receding but fine stepped arete separates this first wall from a second, less fierce wall of excellent rock.

50 Black Africa Flake E1 5c
A climb at the top end of E1, awkward and surprisingly strenuous. Climb the right side of the Africa Flake.

51 White Africa Flake VS 4b   ★
Climb the left side of the Africa Flake.

52 Apartheid HVS
Climb the thin crack a few metres left of the flake.

53 Kudu VS 4a
A potentially lethal route which ascends the right-slanting edge of the huge detached blade of rock forming the left end of the central part of Africa Flake Wall. Start up the chimney and swing boldly onto the front face. Good holds and deep-stirrings lead to the top.

From the second wall and after seventy metres is a clean face with a huge boss of roots below it. This is:

SECTOR ZAMBIA

A clean face with a large Ash growing on a ledge on the left at half height.No recorded climbs.

Twenty five metres further left is:

SECTOR ZIMBABWE

A steep clean buttress with a slim, single-stemmed Yew growing beside it. To the right is a deep chimney.No recorded climbs.

Thirty metres further right is a tall buttress with an unmistakeable right-slanting flake crack.

SECTOR UNCONQUERABLE

54   Right Unconquerable   VS   ★
Start at a big block below the flake. Climb the V-crack and the right-slanting flake to the top.

Cross a jumble of blocks and after fifty metres the next continuous face of rock is:

SECTOR SOUTH AFRICA

55   Vorster's Groove   HS   4b
Start two metres left of the short arete below a cracked corner. Climb the corner and exit right.

56   Game Reserve   HVS   5b
Climb the long, slim crack two metres left of the corner. Very awkward and deceptively steep.

57   S. African Lawn Tennis Association   HS   4b   ★
Start below the cracked wall to the left of the arete.Climb the thin cracks to a gnarly stump. Move back up and right to finish at the arete.

58   Preston's Of Bolton   S
Start one metre further left at a wide crack in a corner. Climb this and the undercut rib above.

59   Simonstown   VS
Ten metres left is a deep cracked corner with a bulge at the top. Climb the crack direct.

Moving left of the deep cracked corner is an area of steep rock shaded by large Yews and a massive Oak which grows out of the crag at mid-height.

SECTOR PEPUL

To the left of the big Oak is a steep rounded buttress which is seamed by two grooves. The left groove trends up to a bleached, dead Yew which hangs down the face. Further left is a huge block which presents a pleasant face leading to a ledge and cracked slab above. The sector finishes with an attractive slab split midway by a long ledge.

60   Betel   E1   5c   ★
Start below the first groove just left of the Yew Tree growing hard against the face left of the big Oak. Climb the technical groove to a good handhold. A hard move gets one established in the upper groove which is climbed to a Yew and a lower off.

61   Pepul   VS   4c   ★

Start at the foot of the second groove left of the big Oak. Climb the left-trending groove towards the bleached, dead Yew. Move up and right over the overhang on good holds. Finish up the cracked rib to the left of a tree-filled groove.

62   Two Timer   S

Start at the front face of the huge block. Climb this to a ledge and crevasse. Step across this and climb the fine cracked slab above.

Two metres left of the huge block is a massive Yew in front of an easier angled face, split at mid height by a long ledge which has a Yew growing on the left end and a slim Holly to the right.

63   Final Score   S

A very pleasant climb. Start below the shallow obvious groove in the upper slab above the ledge. Climb the steep wall via flakes to the Holly. Climb the easy groove above.

Moving left for 17 metres past broken rocks leads to a rib with a leaning wall extending leftwards. The left end of this leaning wall consists of a semi-detached flake of rock forming a "Flying Buttress" for want of a better term. This is:

SECTOR BAROQUE

No recorded climbs.

6   TYNE AND WEAR

This large area dominated in the North and East by the urban sprawl of South Tyneside is a most unlikely climbing area. The climbing here ranges from large Sandstone quarries near Stanley and Consett, to small outcrops of Magnesian Limestone on the coastal strip. The area suffers from its proximity to the superb Sandstone Crags of Northumberland in that these are just too far for a short evening and secondly they are so good that anything else, including the crags described here could (and will) be deemed a "bag of ---" in comparison. The inclusion of the crags however does not need excuses as there is a demand for climbing here as witnessed by the number of climbers seen on the crags. Causey Quarry is the most famous and popular with most people and Hownsgill Quarry could well develop beyond its present popularity if its bolt-protected climbs are increased. The Cove, just North of Marsden Rock is well-worth anyones' attention and as the ultimate outdoor gym, should be on the agenda of anyone hoping to break into the eigth-grade. Cleadon is a pleasant spot to while away an evening with rock of finger-rasping roughness and some tough problems. Houghton Graveyard with its twenty metre, leaning walls of good, though dusty limestone is presently a top-rope venue which could see modern developments very shortly. Further South, the tranquil riverside at Durham gives us Kepier Crag, a minute, but popular Sandstone Wall with a host of problems.

HOWNS GILL QUARRY   O.S. SHEET 88   TYNESIDE   G.R. 097 489

SITUATION AND CHARACTER

Howns Quarry lies between Consett and Castleside in County Durham, some 15 miles South West of Newcastle.

The old sandstone quarry lies in the wooded valley of Howns Gill and due to its sheltered position and its vertical and overhanging nature, it can be climbed on even in poor weather. The crag faces West and has a height in excess of 25 metres in some places.

At the South end of the Main Crag a huge cavern has been quarried out, leaving a rock facade and a series of pillars supporting the face. Further sheltered climbing is provided on the walls and supporting pillars inside the cavern in the form of low-level traversing. There are also several high and low-level traverses on the Main Crag.

The sandstone varies in quality and great care should be exercised in the placing of protection as due to the softness of the rock this cannot always be relied upon. Indeed this and the monolithic nature of the rock has led to pegs being used for protection in several places.

A disturbing feature at Howns Quarry are shale bands between the layers of sandstone, at the top of the crag and extending to a depth of 9 metres in places. This problem is in some way alleviated by the presence of vertical cracks and grooves splitting the shale bands and providing a relatively simple but fairly adventurous exit to the top. If in doubt, rig up a long tether using a second length of rope and either exit using this for assistance or lower off. Many climbs on the Shale Wall have been equipped with cemented bolt lowering or abseil points which means that the shale beds do not need to be climbed.

N.B. Route heights are given for topping out and may be considerably shorter if the bolt lowering points are used.

APPROACHES AND ACCESS

From Consett, follow the A692 towards Castleside for about 1 mile until the Stanefordham Arms public house is reached. On the opposite side of the road a track is followed through allotment gardens to a parking place and a good Public Right Of Way leads across fields to the clearly visible Howns Gill Viaduct. Passing under the viaduct, the path divides and the left-hand path is followed into the wooded left (West facing) side of the valley and after just over 100 metres the quarry becomes visible on the left. All of the paths in the valley and those leading to it are Public Rights Of Way and the walk takes little more than five minutes from the parking.

HISTORICAL

The climbs are the work of Malcolm Lowerson and friends and probably date back to the 1980's or even before.

THE CLIMBS

The climbs are described from left to right and section by section, working from left to right.

Main Crag is composed of **5** Sections:
Initial
Corner
Rising Wall
Shale Wall
Sandwich Corner
Graffiti Buttress

Quarry Basin is composed of **2** Sections:
Pond Wall
Rake Wall

MAIN CRAG

INITIAL CORNER SECTION

Two walls which converge to form a 9 metre corner.

1   Pup   4m   VD

Start at the left side of the left wall below the first, broken crack. Climb the crack passing an overhanging block at 3m.

2 Fang 6m MVS 4c
Start a few metres right below a wall with an undercut base. Climb the wall using two rectangular slots and finish up the block with the serrated edge.

3 Doggy Bag 9m E1 5c
Start as for Fang. Climb up to the two rectangular slots below the small overhang and step right to reach a pocket in a horizontal crack. Climb up with difficulty to reach the two vertical slots on the wall. Climb to the top avoiding the corner.

4 Choker 8m MVS 4c
Start at the foot of the corner. Climb the corner for a couple of metres then move onto the left wall. Make an ascending hand-traverse left and finish up the block with the serrated edge as for Fang.

5 Cold Nose Corner 9m VS 5a
Climb the corner.

6 Dog End 9m E1 5c   ★
Start just over 1m right of the corner and beneath a weakness in the small overlap. Climb the steep wall direct making an awkward move at 5m. The centre of the smooth wall above is climbed on small holds.

7 Distemper Wall 9m VS 5a
Start as for Dog End. Climb the steep wall, but trend right to reach thin cracks lines which are followed to below the right-hand side of the small Oak tree at the top.

8 Foxy 9m HVS 5b
Start just over a metre left of the arete and below a recess in the bottom half of the wall. Climb the wall to the small recess below the overlap. Gain the twin cracklines above and climb, trending to the left to finish at the same place as Distemper Wall.

An easier start is to climb the arete until it is possible to traverse left to reach the twin cracks above the overlap. This reduces the overall standard to MVS.

RISING WALL SECTION
This wall extends rightwards from the arete and forms a 15 metre corner at its junction with the next section, Shale Wall.

9 Bloodhound 11m HS 4b
Climb the arete, starting on its right side.

10 Aniseed Trail 15m HS 4b
Start one pace right of the arete. Climb the wall to gain a horizontal ledge at 4m. The widening ledge is traversed right into the corner up which the climb finishes.

11 Dogs Dinner 10m HVS 5b
Start 2m right of the arete. Climb over the overlap to the ledge. Small finger holds on the wall above bring a horizontal crack into reach. Move up and left to the top.

12 Paws 14m HS 4b
Start 3m right of the arete. Climb the wall to gain the horizontal ledge by an awkward mantelshelf. Traverse into the corner and finish up this.

13   Watch Dog   12m   E1   5b   ★
Start 4m right of the arete. Climb the unpleasant wall to the ledge via a letter-box pocket. From the diagonal crack on the wall above, move left and up to reach the horizontal crack. Strenuous climbing leads straight up over the block overhang at the top.

14   Lapdog   15m   VD
Climb the corner passing an Oak sapling at half-height.

15   Walkies   20m   HVS   5b   ★
A left to right Girdle of Initial Corner and Rising Wall Sections. Start as for Fang. Climb up to the two pockets and traverse right into the corner. Continue traversing at the same level to the arete, rounding this to gain the horizontal ledge on Rising Wall. Follow the ledge into the corner with an awkward move crossing the break.

SHALE WALL SECTION

This is the next section of wallwhose base lies within the confines of a long pitlike depression extending rightwards from the corner of Lapdog. Shale Wall is almost 40m long and up to 27m high at its highest point. It has prominent alternating sandstone and shale beds in the top quarter of the face. These can be climbed but a spare rope used as a tether for lowering off is recommended. The slope above is blessed with many trees.

N.B. Recently the installation of bolt abseil stations at many points below the shale beds has made climbing on this wall a much more attractive proposition.

The wall has many features and very few of these are sufficiently distinctive for the purposes of describing the routes.However with the descriptions and a quick inspection from the top of the bank forming the outer side of the pit, it is possible to pick out the complexities of the routes.

16   The Snarl   20m   HVS   5b
Start 2m right of the corner of Lapdog at some red paint splashes. Climb the wall which is undercut at the base keeping just right of the paint splashes to reach a niche below a small overhang. Move up and right into a shallow, square recess and out of it to the right via shot marks moving left. Finish by stepping right onto a good ledge. Finish by moving left and upwards for 2m and climb direct through the Shale beds to a notch in the Sandstone band above.

17   The Growl   23m   HVS   5b
Start a little over 4m right of the corner below an overhanging nose just out of reach above the pink-painted name "Dougie". Pull up with difficulty on the right then move back left above the nose.
The thin crack is climbed before pulling right to a small ledge in a V groove at 8m. From here, step left and climb into a shallow recess and continue straight up to a roof-capped sentry-box at 15m. Climb out of this to the left to the good ledge of The Snarl.

Moving right within the confines of the long pit, a contorted Ash tree is a feature, growing from the steep bank in front of the crag. On the crag face opposite this at 3m is a diagonally-aligned fin of rock below the overlap.

18   The Eyrie   26m   E1   5c
Start below a V groove which splits the overlap almost 3m above

the ground about 2m left of the diagonal fin of rock. Climb this groove and the crack above to a small ledge at 9m. Traverse right for a short distance until it is possible to climb the bulging wall until a step right can be effected onto a sloping ledge at 15m. Climb up and right to the bolt lowering point on The Whimper.

19 The Whimper   26m   HVS   5b
Start just over 1m right of the V groove, below a prominent diagonally-aligned block beneath the overhang. Climb directly up the wall via this, passing a small bulge. Continue up the slightly overhanging wall, passing to the right of an unusual rounded "boulder puddingstone" to reach a ledge at 15m. Climb the wall above via a shotmarked groove or by the groove to the right to reach a bolt lowering point.

20 Mad Dog   27m   E2   5c
Start in front of the contorted Ash and below the diagonally-aligned block beneath the overhang. Climb over the overhang and traverse right to gain the bottom of a vertical crack. Climb the crack to a good ledge. Move up and right onto another ledge and gain bolt lowering point.

The slim wall between the crack of Mad Dogs and the left -hand one of the twin cracks taken by The Bark and The Bite respectively is ascended by Plague Dogs.

21 Plague Dogs   15m   E2   5c   ★
Start below the wall to the right of the vertical crack of Mad Dog. Surmount the overhang at 3m with difficulty onto a small ledge and climb the bulging wall to reach the large ledge at 12m. Move up and right as for Mad Dog to Bolt lowering point.

22 The Bark   27m   E3   6a
Start right of Plague Dogs at a chest high overlap with blue paint marks below it. Above, is a small ledge with twin cracks leading up from it. Climb onto the ledge at its right-hand end. Step left and climb the slightly overhanging left-hand crack to a ledge. Move up and right as for Plague Dogs to bolt lowering point.

23 The Bite   27m   E2   5c
Start as for The Bark. From the ledge, climb the right-hand crack to the large ledge above a triangular overhang. Follow The Bark to the recess and bolt lowering point.

24 The Howl   26m   E2   5c
Start 3m right of The Bark below a block which protrudes from beneath an overhang 14m up the face. Climb up past very thin, twisting cracks where the overlap diminishes and step right and up to a small recess. Climb the crackline to the protruding block and use this to surmount the overhang. Gain the V recess above and exit diagonally right to a bolt lowering point. Alternatively move left into the recess of The Bite and lower off.

25 Hound Trail   31m   VS   5a
Start 2m right of The Howl at a 1m high vertical crack. Climb up for 2m and move left to a small pocket recess. Climb the vertical crack of The Howl for 2m to a narrow ledge. Traverse left for 2m until aledge above is gained. Continue traversing left to a large ledge and move into the recess of The Whimper and lower off.

26   The Whine   26m   E2   5c
Start 2m right of Hound Trail below a small, tapering, hanging corner just above head-height. Climb the wall left of this corner to a narrow ledge and follow the crack lines from its right-hand end direct to where the wall overhangs (P.R. in situ). Step left and climb the weakness in the overhang trending up left via a ragged crackline and shallow groove. Move right to a bolt lowering point.

27   The Bitch   26m   HVS   5b
Start as for The Whine below the hanging corner. Climb up to the corner and follow two parallel cracks leading to a bulging, cracked block. Gain the narrow ledge above direct or by moving first left then traversing right. Climb the wall above into a large V recess. Exit the recess through the roof on the right to a ledge. Bolt lowering point or climb up then traverse left to reach an exit groove and the top.

28   The Wolf   25m   HVS   5b
Start 2m left of the first arete on the right below a recessed groove whose walls diverge. Climb the groove to a small ledge and continue up the recessed groove using the right-hand of the parallel cracks to some overhanging blocks. Climb the blocks to a ledge on the right. Climb the wall above and groove moving left to a bolt lowering point.

29   Hardpad   23m   VS   5a
Start in the corner to the right of the first arete. Climb the corner for 11m until it is possible to move left onto a small ledge on the arete. Finish as for The Wolf.

30   Vixen   23m   E2   5c
Start 2m right of Hardpad and just left of the second arete at a vertical crack. Climb the crack and where it ends continue direct to another short, vertical crack which in turn leads to a bulging wall (peg runner). Move up and rightwards to a bolt lowering point under the big roof visible beneath the top arete.

31   On The Leash   73m   E2
A Girdle of Shale Wall finishing across the left wall of Sandwich Corner Section. Start as for Snarl, 2m right of the corner with the tree halfway up it.

1   25m   5b
Follow The Snarl to below the overhanging ledge and move right onto The Growl. Descend this for 2m to the ledge in the V groove. Climb up right onto The Eyrie and continue rightwards below the bulging wall to the round block on The Whimper. Follow this to a large ledge and peg belay.

2   18m   5c
Climb down the crack of Mad Dog to its foot and traverse right and up into the crack of The Bark. Traverse right to below the protruding block on The Howl. Hanging belay.

3   15m   5c
Traverse right onto The Whine below the weakness in the overhang (peg runner) and continue right with difficulty to reach the tapering ledge which is followed right to a small ledge on the arete. Belay.

4   15m   5c
Descend the corner of Hardpad for 3m and move right across the

wall onto Vixen which is followed to beneath the overhanging ledge (peg runner). Move round the arete and traverse past a peg runner to finish up Teacake Corner.

32   Dachshund   35m   5c
A low-level Girdle of Shale Wall below the level of the overlap.

SANDWICH CORNER SECTION
This section includes the short narrow wall just right of the second arete which terminates in Teacake Corner. Rightwards from Teacake Corner are four cave entrances in a line whose intervening pillars support an unattractive face above. Climbing on the first pillar marks the end of this section's climbing.

33   Sandwich Cake Wall   23m   E2   5c
Start below the centre of the left wall of Teacake Corner. Climb the wall on diminishing ledges then hand-traverse strenuously left to the arete below the overhanging ledge. Climb onto the ledge and move up left to bolt lowering point below big roof of Vixen. Lower off or follow the arete above to the top.

34   Teacake Corner   20m   HS   4b
Bridge the corner to a large ledge on the right. Continue up the corner via another ledge and escape rightwards at the top.

35   Teabreak Wall   20m   HS   4b
Start 2m right of the corner. Climb the dirty crack in the bulging wall to the large ledge and finish as for Teabreak Corner.

36   High Tea   20m   HVS   5b
Start 2m right of Teabreak Wall on the inside edge of the cave entrance. Climb the wall below the roof of the cave entrance and traverse out and up the overhanging wall to reach the large ledge. Finish up Teabreak Corner.

37   Cake Walk   21m   VD
Start on the front of the first pillar to the right of the cave entrance. Climb the front of the pillar passing an anchor inscribed in the rock and move left over the top of the cave entrance to gain the large ledge. Finish up Teacake Corner.

GRAFFITI BUTTRESS
Four cave entrances below an area of loose rock and shale, separate Sandwich Cake Corner Section from the buttress whose lower face is daubed with painted names.To the right of Graffiti Buttress are another four cave entrances, not to be confused with those in Sandwich Corner Section. Four rock pillars lie between these cave entrances and provide excellent, strenuous climbing.

The cave entrances lead into an amazing gallery supported by pillars and the place as a whole provides many all-weather problems and traverses.

38   Undercoat   17m   HS   4b
Start on the right-hand side of the fourth cave entrance to the right of Sandwich Corner Section. Climb up the recessed, left edge of the wall moving right past a small roof and up onto a ledge. Traverse right along the ledge and gain and climb a large corner.

39 Topcoat 17m MVS 4c
Start 2m right of Undercoat below an arete. Climb the arete to a
sloping ledge and from here gain the large ledge and finish up the
corner on the right as for Undercoat.

We now move right onto the lurid front of Graffiti Buttress itself:

40 Watercolour Corner 17m HS 4b
Start 2m right of the arete in a recessed corner. Climb the corner to
the top.

41 Daubers' Delight 20m VS 4c
Start on the right side of the knife-edged arete, 2m right of the
recessed Watercolour Corner. Climb up the wall to the right of the
large nose on the arete at 6m and pull onto the top of it. Continue
up the arete until a traverse can be made onto the large ledge of
Watercolour Corner. Finish up the corner.

42 Nom De Plume 21m VS 4c
Start 1m right of the knife-edged arete by an Oak tree. Climb up the
cracks passing a recess to reach a roof at 11m. Step right and pull
onto the ledge above. Climb the big, V-groove through the shale
bands to finish.

43 Initial Wall 23m VS 5a
Start 4m right of Nom De Plume below a thin, vertical crack in the
centre of the buttress. Climb up the crack to a ledge at 4m. Continue to a smaller ledge and on up past a small recess to a long
ledge at the start of the Shale bands. Traverse left along the ledge
to the big, V-groove of Nom De Plume and finish up this.

44 Doodler 23m VS 5a
Start below an overlap at head height. Climb the thin cracks above
the overlap to the right end of a ledge at 4m. Climb the wall above
up a staircase of small ledges to a small roof. Move up right into a
V-groove which is climbed to the ledge below the shale bands.
Climb these trending right to the overhang then go up the V
crackline to reach ledges leading to the top.

45 Heavy Make-up 15m E2 5c
Start 3m right of Doodler below a vertical crackline that ends at 6m.
Climb the vertical crackline through the bulging wall (2 Bolts in-
situ). Pull up on a good jug to reach holds on the wall above. Climb
the shallow corner up to the Shale bands. Move right or left to
lowering points.

46 Brushline 23m HVS 5b
Start as for Heavy Make-up below the vertical crack. Climb the
crack until a Hand-traverse can be made rightwards to its edge
below a bulge with a slim, shot-mark. Climb the bulge and crack
above to a ledge at 12m below Shale bands. Trend right past two
roofs to the top.

*The next routes are described in relation to the next four cave
entrances and the four pillars between them.*

47 Heavy Breathing 15m E3 6a   *
Start at the foot of a rib 2m right of Brushline. Climb up the inside
edge of the first cave entrance right of Graffiti Buttress and move
left onto the outer edge of the roof. Move back right to beneath the
corner in the roof and pull into it with difficulty continuing straight

up to the Shale bands. Lowering point in the large recess.

Alternative Start: Climb the outer edge of the cave entrance to the roof (5c)

The next two climbs are on the first pillar to the right of the cave.

48 Obscene Phone-call 15m E3 6a   *
Climb the left, inside face of the First Pillar to the roof (Bolt Runner). Pull round right onto the face and climb straight up to the Shale bands.Lowering point in recess.

49 Corinthian 18m HVS 5b
Climb the crack on the front of the First Pillar to the recess at the top. Climb up and left out of the recess to a small, narrow ledge below another shallow recess. Move up right via a break in the overhanging wall and reach a ledge. Climb the Shale bands via cracks or lower off.

The next routes are all located on the Second Pillar which is right of the second cave entrance. This pillar has "Monk" daubed in green paint on its front face.

50 Hercules 18m VS 5a
Climb the left-hand face of the Second Pillar pulling onto the ledge at the top. Climb the overhanging wall above to reach a large ledge where the Shale bands start. Lower off or climb up through the bands and into a groove which leads to the top.

51 Lipstick Traces 15m E2 5c   *
Climb the front face of the Second Pillar moving to the left edge to pull onto a ledge at 7m. Move up left to traverse above the second cave to reach holds on the wall right of Corinthian (Bolt runner). Pull up strenuously to reach the Shale bands and lower off.

52 Samson 17m VS 4c
Start at a vertical crack on the right outside edge of the pillar. Climb the crack to a ledge at 3m. Continue straight up to a recess and then trend left to a large ledge below the Shale bands. Lower off or finish up through the bands into a groove and the top.

53 Delilah 17m VS 5a
Start 1m right of Samson, below a vertical split in the pillar. Climb the split to a crack which leads to a roofed, V-groove. Exit right from the groove onto a ledge in a corner. Climb the corner through the Shale bands to the top.

Across the third cave entrance is the Third Pillar which has an obvious niche and a lurid protestation that "Dopey's OK".

54 Rising Dawn 12m E5 6b
Start at the arete to the left of the niche on the left wall of the pillar. Climb the arete on its right-hand side and move up diagonally right to gain a pit-prop (Bolt runner). Move out left to cracks in the bulge and by means of a vertical shot-mark to the left of the cracks, gain a good hold. Move back right and up to lowering chains.

55 Edge Of Darkness 12m E4 6b   *
Start at the arete as for Rising Dawn. Climb rightwards into the niche and up onto a sloping ledge. Climb the overhanging wall past a slot and move right onto the right-hand wall of the pillar above the fourth cave entrance making some strenuous moves on poor holds to reach easier ledges. Bolt lowering point.

56   Caveman Capers   12m   E3   6a   ★

Start on the right-hand face of the Third Pillar below and right of the painted name; "GAS". Climb up and left to the roof then using a horizontal finger crack, swing out to reach good jugs below the hanging corner (Bolt runner). Climb the corner with difficulty to reach good ledges. Bolt lowering point.

Alternative Start: Climb the outer edge of the pillar direct to the roof starting just left of "GAS".

57   Wildman   12m   E2   5b   ★

Start as for Caveman Capers. Climb up for 3m and traverse to the left outside edge of the pillar below Caveman's corner. Follow a series of handholds up to the left on the overhanging wall to a small inset block, above and right of a bolt runner. Pull up past the block and move up right to a ledge. Bolt lowering point.

The Fourth Pillar is the last pillar to the right of the fourth cave entrance.

58   Still Life   12m   HVS   5b

Start at the bottom left edge of the wall. Climb the left edge of the wall moving into the centre below the overhang. Make a long reach for holds above and pull onto a large ledge. Move left and climb the broken buttress above to finish.

59   Fresco   12m   VS   5a

Start as for Still Life. Make an ascending traverse up to the right to a small ledge on the right-hand edge of the wall. Climb the edge below the overhang, then swing round onto the right wall (without putting a foot on the ground). Reach for a small crackline and pull onto the large ledge above. Climb the broken buttress to finish.

60   Neo-Classic   7m   S   4a

Start 2m right of Fresco on the front face. Climb onto the large ledge then climb the right-hand side of the arete to the top.

61   Rainbow's End   48m   E2

A left to right Girdle traverse of Graffiti Buttress. Start as for Initial Wall below the thin, vertical crack in the centre of the buttress.

1   18m   5c

Climb the crack past the large ledge to the small ledge at 6m. Traverse right below the V-groove of Doodler, crossing Heavy Make-up below the bulging wall and meet Brushline at the arete. This is followed to a belay below the Shale bands.

2   15m   5c

Climb down into the hanging corner of Heavy Breathing and traverse right above the first cave to reach Corinthian below the shallow break in the overhanging wall. Continue rightwards, crossing above the second cave to reach the ledge on the Second Pillar. Traverse rightwards around the pillar and move up 2m to belay.

3   15m   5c

Climb down and traverse over the third cave. Move right up to good ledges which are followed to the arete.

QUARRY BASIN

The climbs are on the crag above the pond on the South side of the wooded basin below Graffiti Buttress. This section, whilst composed of good compact rock is now quite dirty from lack of use. **The routes are described from right to left.**

POND WALL
The following routes are on the wall immediately above the pond and which is bounded on its right by a corner of easy-angled rock.
62 Tadpole 9m HS 4b
Start in the corner by the pond. Climb up the easy-angled, right wall to a ledge. Climb the wall above moving left at a protruding block-like feature and follow the vertical broken edge to the top.
63 Newt 12m S 4a
Start as for Tadpole. Climb the corner for 3m then move onto the left wall below the right-hand side of an overhanging, triangular block. Pull up to the right of the block and continue up the recessed wall via ledges to the top.
64 Toad 13m HVS 5b
Start 2m left of the corner of Newt. Climb the wall to reach a short, thin vertical crack leading to the left side of the triangular block. Pull up to the left of the block onto a ledge. Traverse 2m left and climb the steep wall to a ledge. Trend left to finish at a small tree.
65 Dragonfly 13m HVS 5b
Start 3m left of the corner. Climb the slightly overhanging wall to below a small bulge. Pull up past this on the right, to below an overlap. Move up left to gain a ledge and continue to another ledge. Climb the steep wall above to yet another ledge and finish to the left of a small tree.
66 Mosquito 13m MVS 4c
Start 4m left of the corner and below the left end of the overlap. Climb up to and above the overlap to reach a ledge. Finish as for Dragonfly.
67 Horsefly 13m S 4a
Start 6m left of the corner at a small corner below the right-hand end of the rake. Climb the corner to gain the rake. Move into a larger corner and follow this to a ledge on the right. Climb the wall above to a small overhang and pull over this to finish.

RAKE WALL
This is the wall to the left of Pond Wall. Rake Wall is split by the grassy rake sloping up from right to left.
68 Whirligig Wall 13m VS 5a
Start 2m left of the small corner of Horsefly below the right end of the rake. Climb the short wall to the rake. Move left and go up the wall to reach the thin vertical crack in the lip of a small overlap above. Pull up the crack and trend right into the middle of the wall. Move up into a small corner and climb the little overhang to finish.
69 Crowfoot Crack 13m S 4a
Start 5m left of Horsefly. Climb the short wall onto the rake and move up and climb the thin crackline running up the edge of the wall above. Finish up ledges.
70 Kingcup 8m VD
Start on the rake, 2m left of the thin crackline of Crowfoot Crack.

Climb the wall trending right to join Crowfoot Crack at the first of a series of ledges leading to the top.

71   Duckweed Wall   6m   MVS   4c
Start as for Kingcup. Ascend the wall direct, surmounting an overlap before moving up to finish to the right of a tree.

72   Liverwort Wall   4m   HS   4b
Start 2m left of Kingcup. Climb the wall via an overlap to finish to the left of a tree.

KNITSLEY QUARRY   O.S. SHEET 88   G.R. 120 482

SITUATION AND CHARACTER.

A small quarry of good quality Sandstone about 3 miles by road from Howns Gill. The quarry which faces West is sheltered and a suntrap in Winter. Unlike many quarries, it has a pleasant rural feel to it. This is helped by the lack of rubbish and litter. The climbing in the quarry is restricted to the Main Wall which is up to 6 metres high and 20 metres long although possibilities do exist in the bay to the right of the Main Wall. It is well worth an evening visit or can be combined with a trip to Howns Gill, but go to Knitsley first, when fresh.

APPROACHES AND ACCESS

From Castleside follow the A692 into Consett and turn right at a crossroads with traffic lights into Delves Lane. Follow this road through the built-up area for just over a mile until a crossroads is reached just beyond an industrial site on the right-hand side of the road. Turn right into a minor road signposted to Satley on the C1619 and go downhill to Knitsley Bottom where a sandstone bridge parapet is crossed. Park on the wide verge here and enter the quarry by squeezing between the parapet at its S.E. corner and a fence. Time from car is 20 seconds!

HISTORICAL

All of the routes were climbed and recorded by Stu Ferguson in June 1989.

THE CLIMBS

The Main Wall is grossly undercut at the left-hand side, whilst the middle of the Wall is split by an obvious right-facing flake. The right-hand section is a steep wall with stepped overlaps near the top. A good arete is the final feature. The climbs are described from left to right.

1   Undercut Wall   6a
Climb the severely undercut wall at the extreme left-hand end, left of the obvious curving corner.

2   Shallow Corner   4c
An attractive though dirty, curving corner is climbed.

3   The Left Arete   5a
Start as for Shallow Corner. Climb the arete immediately right of the corner.

4   Overhang Crack   5b
The large overhang of the severe undercut left-hand end has two short walls beneath it. From the left wall beneath the overhang move out right to gain and climb the crack splitting the wall above the overhang.

5   Overhang Direct   6a
From under the overhang use a flake to surmount the roof to the right of Overhang Crack via the horizontal break above. Climb the wall above direct.

6   The Hand Traverse   5b
Climb up to the right-hand end of the big overhang and Hand-traverse the horizontal break. Finish up Overhang Crack.

7   Central Flakes   4c
Climb the obvious layback flake in the centre of Main Wall. Old peg runner high on right face.

8   Right Wall 1   5a
Climb the wall direct, 2m right of Central Flakes.

9   Right Wall 2   5a
Climb directly up the steep wall at the left end of the stepped overlaps.

10   Right Wall 3   5b
Climb the wall passing through the centre of the stepped overlap.

11   The Right Arete   4c
Climb the obvious arete on mainly good holds.

12   Low Level Traverse   5a
This is a traverse of the Main Wall with many variations.

CAUSEY QUARRY   O.S. SHEET 88   TYNESIDE   G.R. 204 560

SITUATION AND CHARACTER
A very old Sandstone Quarry just North of Stanley has recently been incorporated into a walks and picnic complex featuring the nearby Causey Arch, the first single arch railway bridge in the world, built in 1727.

This now very pleasant development is the setting for the climbing at Causey Quarry and makes it a very important venue for climbers in the Tyne and Wear area.

The crag faces North -West and has a maximum height of twenty metres. It consists of a Main Face with shorter wings at either end.

The Sandstone is massively bedded and sound, although there can be some loose rock at the top of some of the climbs. Run-off from the shale slopes above the face at times can make the rock dirty. Trees at the top of the face provide belays but some of these are in a poor state due to abuse from climbers and the public. In general, the holds are good and the climbing tends to be strenuous.

For the lone boulderer the crag has much to offer both in up and down problems and in a wealth of strenuous and technical traverses. Due to its sheltered location of the crag is a four season venue.

Causey Quarry

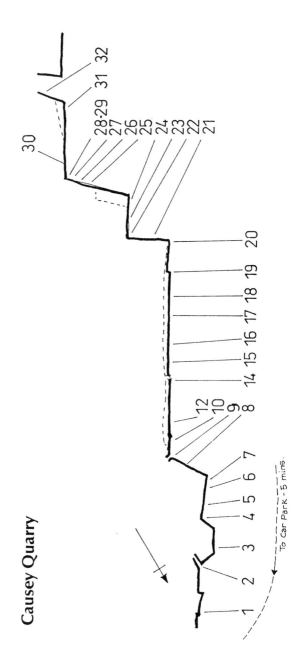

To Car Park - 5 mins.

APPROACHES AND ACCESS

Follow the A692 South out of Gateshead, passing through Sunnyside. Two miles beyond Sunnyside turn right into the Causey Park picnic area opposite the Causey Arch Inn. Park in the picnic area car park and descend on foot following signs directing one to Causey Arch and the gorge, to reach the crag in five minutes by Left Wall.

HISTORICAL

Records of climbing at Causey were hard to come by until the Thompsons produced the chapter on Causey for the Northumbrian M.C. guide.

However according to the strong oral tradition of the North-East certain links exist between Causey and the early Crag Lough Group. The quarry itself was discovered by Nev Hannaby and he visited it along with other members of the group including the late Albert Rosher, Eric Rayson and Geoff Oliver. This group according to Geoff Oliver mainly used the quarry as a "gymnasium". but it is certainly possible that some of the routes were climbed in this period.

The climbing of the recorded routes is open to a deal of speculation, but it is likely that some of the harder lines "evolved" as free climbs from being partially aided. Ed. Thompson senior and Ed. Thompson junior made the first ascent of the excellent High-Level traverse; The Haunt. The Dangler was almost certainly free climbed in 1969 according to reliable sources.

Karl Telfer climbed the bold Sandman in the mid-seventies and the difficult Perplexity was the result of a "stringing together of pieces", following Paul Linfoot's fantastic effort in the early 80's of climbing it to above the overhang before moving up the Dangler finish. This climb has stopped many a top-rope attempt by some very talented climbers. The early 1980's also saw the audacious Mauler Roof succumb to the "handsome" George Haydon. The creation of the picnic area has certainly changed the face of climbing at Causey and the crag has reached respectable maturity.

THE CLIMBS

The climbs are described section by section from left to right.

LEFT WALL

This is the short wall at the extreme left-hand end of the quarry. It has three large trees growing at the top and it ends on the right at a corner rising out of a small, cave-recess.

1   Wall Route One   6m   S

This pleasant climb start at the middle of the Left wall just right of a small, left-facing corner. Climb the face passing the main horizontal break and continue up the upper wall on a "staircase" of good handholds.

2   Black Crack   7m   VD

Climb the corner via the cave on good holds, passing a wedged block.

EASY BUTTRESS
This is the protruding buttress which has an abundance of ledges.

3   Easy Buttress   7m   M   ★
Climb the buttress via its frontal arete, moving right at the start onto the top of the obvious "pull-up" block. Easy climbing leads to a finish through a cleft at the top. Well-worthwhile.

RIGHT WALL
This wall immediately right of and slightly set back from Easy Buttress ends at the undercut, broad arete/rib taken by Dusky Maiden.

4   Spider Crack   7m   S   ★
Start on dirty ledges immediately right of Easy Buttress. Follow the open corner to the base of the crack which is followed, slanting right near the top. Finish by moving steeply left. Increasing interest and a good finish.

5   Wall Route Two   7m   HS   4b
A good steep climb. Start just right of Spider Crack where a narrow, vertical crack splits the face. Climb the improving crack moving left near the top to finish as for Spider Crack.

Direct Finish: VS   4c
At the top of the crack, climb through the bulges, moving slightly left to finish at trees.

6   Dusky Maiden   9m   S
Start 1m right of Wall Route Two. Mount easy ledges rightwards then climb the short wall on the right to a ledge below the broad-fronted rib which is undercut. Climb the rib on good holds. Technically easy but lacking in protection.

QUARRY WALL
This is the short steep wall just right of the blunt arete of Dusky Maiden and at right angles to the Main Face. Quarry Wall has two facets on either side of a sharp-edged prow at four metres.

7   Quarry Wall   12m   VS   4c   ★★
Start below a thin crack in the upper left-hand facet. Climb a short, wide crack and surmount the cracked bulge above. From a comfortable, pointed block ledge ascend the crack to a break. Traverse right for 1m and climb a bulge on good holds.

8   Overhanging Wall   17m   HVS   5a
Start below the overhanging, right facet of Quarry Wall at a short, right-slanting crack at head-height. Climb this crack to a ledge and pull up steep rock to a small hold above. Move right into the obvious, crack in the wall just left of the corner. Follow this and where it ends move left to finish up Quarry Wall.

9   Crack And Chimney   18m   S
An aimiable thrutch but quite good. Climb the crack in the angle of Quarry Wall and Main Wall. The chimney once reached leads to the top.

MAIN WALL
This is the showpiece of the quarry, up to twenty metres high in places.

This impressive wall is split by the vertical crackline of Mangler running up the face at its highest point whilst left of this is the Mauler Roof at the top of the face. To the right of Mangler, a long overlap provides some interesting climbs. The Main Wall provides good bouldering, especially many traverse problems and eliminates, most of which are 'pumpy'.

10 The Mauler 20m E3 5b   ★★
A 'pushy' route with some adventurous moments. Start 2m right of Crack And Chimney at a short rib. Climb the rib to a ledge just below an overhang. Using handholds above the bulge, traverse right for about 3m past a small hole under an overlap to a ledge. Move left and up the wall to below the large; Mauler Roof. Look wistfully at the roof and swing thankfully right until it is possible to pull through a break in the overhang. Traverse left to finish.

11 The Mauler Roof 20m E5 6b   ★
Climb The Mauler and finish up the obvious roof.

12 The Mauler Direct 20m E4 6b
Climb the wall to meet the main roof from the end of the initial traverse right. Finish as for The Mauler.

13 The Mauler Direct And Roof 20m E5 6b   ★
Climb The Mauler Direct and The Mauler Roof.

14 The Mangler 19m HVS 5a   ★★
A minor classic! Steep, positive, protectable where it matters and never too hard! Start below the obvious crack running the full-height of the face. Climb up to a sentry-box, keeping to the left. Continue up the crack, keeping to the right at the top.

15 Perplexity 19m E5 6c   ★
Aptly-named! Start 2m right of The Mangler. Climb directly up the wall to the overhang. Climb this direct at its widest point on small holds and make very hard moves to gain a resting ledge above. Move straight up the wall above on small holds.

16 The Dangler 19m E3 5c   ★
Start 2m right of Perplexity. Climb the thin, interrupted cracks in the wall, to reach the roof. Climb the roof using the obvious nose on the left and move left to a resting place. Climb up and right to a groove which is followed to the top.

17 Hangover 9m E1 5b   ★
Start 3m right of The Dangler below a thin crack which ends in a block overhang. Climb the short, awkward wall to reach the crack. Follow this through the overhang and finish more easily.

18 Letter-Box Wall 9m E1 5b
Start 3m right of Hangover, at a very short, vertical crack at head-height. Climb the wall to gain the letter-box at 4m via an awkward move. Continue up the wall finishing straight over the bulge or to the left at a cracked overhanging corner.

19 Corner 9m HVS 5a
A dirty climb without much direction. Two metres right of Letter-Box Wall is a short corner. Follow this then climb the steep, dirty wall above.

20 The Arete 8m HS 4a   ★
A good and technically easy but steep climb which should not be taken too lightly. Climb the arete.

To the right of the arete are two large corners: Hanging Corner and Telstar Corner.

21   Wall Route Three   9m   S
Climb the irregular crack in the centre of the left wall of the corner. Move left and up onto a detached flake. Finish left.

22   Hanging Crack   12m   MVS   4b   *
Climb the crack in the corner until a small ledge is gained. Traverse right and finish up the obvious Causey Crack in the right wall.
Variation Start: VS   5a
Climb the wall just right of Hanging Crack via a mantelshelf and a wall on poor holds. Move slightly left to better holds leading into Hanging Crack.

23   Causey Crack   12m   VS   4c   **
This very fine climb starts below the middle of the right-wall of Hanging Corner. Climb onto a small ledge at 2m and pull onto a sloping ledge on the right. Climb the crack above via a small square-cut niche.

24   A Means To An End   10m   VS   4c
Start at the right hand end of the right wall of Hanging Corner where the face is severely undercut. Climb onto a ledge and move right onto the arete which is followed to the top.

To the right is the second big corner; Telstar Crack. The left wall of this provides some easy but good climbs whilst the steeper right wall is a bit "hairy-chested".

25   Diagonal Direct   8m   HS   4b
Start below the right wall immediately right of the roofed-undercut at a rock step. Move up and left to a wide crack. Climb this then move right into Diagonal. Follow this to the exit ledge on the left and step back right and climb the cracked wall above a semi-detached pedestal flake.

26   Telstar Direct   15m   VS   4c   *
Climb the obvious vertical crack in the wall just left of the corner.

27   Diagonal   9m   D
Start at the top of the muddy slope below the main corner. Climb diagonally leftwards across the left wall on good ledges.Finish easily above Causey Crack.

28   Telstar Crack   18m   S   *
Climb the corner crack to the roof and finish by an airy traverse left beneath it.
Direct Finish: VS   4b
From the top of the crack continue through the overhang on undercut jams and layback moves.

29   Right Hand Wall   18m   VS   4c   *
Start as for Telstar Crack. Climb Telstar Crack past a ledge at 4m and continue to a blunt-topped flake on the right wall at half-height. Traverse right to a small ledge above the overhangs and pull left into a line of short cracks trending leftwards. Finish strenuously to the right of the roofs just right of the top of Telstar Crack.

30   Right Wall Direct   18m   E1   5c   **
Start at the foot of the right wall, 3m right of Telstar Crack. Climb

the wall leftwards to the recess below the overhang. Pull through and join Right Wall. Steep, strenuous and good.

31 Sandman 14m E3 5c   ★

Start at a small recess at the right end of the lowest point of the right wall. Climb a short corner to the large overhanging nose which forms the right edge of the wall. Climb the roof and climb the left side of the nose to a ledge. Move up then around the arete to finish by a block on the right.

Up to the right of the start of Sandman is a muddy gully with a dirty wall above and left. This has been prone to some rockfall and caution is advised.

A route, White Light Revisited starts just right of Sandman and ascends the wall bearing right to a ledge below tree routes. The finish is via an easy overhang – HS but not recommended!

32 White Traverse 11m VS 4b

An esoteric experience. Start from the top of a block 4m up the left gully wall. Climb up dirty rock until a hand-traverse leads left to below the small corner up which Sandman finishes. Climb this moving left.

To the right of the muddy gully is a very grim area of rock and three veg! Two climbs have been recorded:

Green Crack (5a) and Dirty Wall Corner (4c) both are fairly strenuous and need either cleaning or forgetting.

GIRDLE TRAVERSES

Two good Girdle Traverses exist at Causey Quarry:

33 The Low Level Girdle Traverse 5b   ★★

Either direction. Many variations.

34 The Haunt 46m VS 5a   ★★

An excellent high-level girdle. Start as for Quarry Wall.

Pitch 1 13m

Climb Quarry wall to final bulges. Traverse right 1m and step down to gain a good hold which enables a move round the overhanging rib to be made. Go across the top of Overhanging Wall and into the upper reaches of Crack And Chimney.

Pitch 2 15m

Move down Crack And Chimney until a delicate move up and right can be made to gain holds running right beneath the big overhang. Traverse right until below the final bulging section of The Mangler and move right across the wall (strenuous) until the groove of The Dangler can be gained. Continue traversing at the same level along a loose, horizontal, hand crack to exit on top.

Pitch 3 9m

Move down to the prominent, thin tree at the top of The Arete and descend this route for a couple of metres. Traverse right to gain the large hanging ledge crossing it to Causey Crack. Descend Causey Crack (arrange protection high in crack) and from just above the niche and hand traverse right to the finish of Diagonal.

Pitch 4. 9m

Cross the wide ledge and make an awkward move into Telstar Crack. Traverse delicately right to gain the small, exposed ledge in the middle of the right-hand wall. An awkward short descent leads to a small footledge (protection in crack and chockstone). Reach the top of a big block on the right and pull strenuously to a ledge which leads onto easy ground.

On the other side of the stream is a small outcrop which is not popular. The obvious arete is Xenon (E1 5b). The crack left of this is Easy Crack (VD). A number of short problems exist to the right of the arete (3c-4c).

Other quasi-climbing activities are possible hereabouts, one of these is: The Bridge Jump – Causey Arch, described as a "tight-filler".

THE COVE: MARSDEN   O.S. SHEET 88   TYNESIDE
O.S. G.R. 394 662

SITUATION AND CHARACTER

This delightful seaside cove surrounded by generally overhanging walls of excellent limestone is located about three quarters of a mile North of the famous Marsden Rock. It is a pleasure to climb here as the rock is clean and the landings are the best of anywhere: luxurious, deep, clean shingle.

The cove consists of two inlets separated by a jutting buttress of overhanging rock. The south inlet, the one nearest Marsden has some excellent problems coming out of three caves on the south side. Roofs, overhanging walls, traverses galore. Possibly one of the best bouldering venues in the North-East.

The rock is brecciated Reef Limestone of the Magnesian Limestone group and provides wonderful holds at all angles and it is this that gives the bouldering its diversity and challenge.

The seaward walls of the cove are up to 7m in height and some easier climbs could be made using a rope if that was felt necessary. The top of the faces can be a little loose in places, although this should be immediately apparent. "Topping Out" whilst possible tends not to be the norm and down climbing and or jumping ensures optimum rock time.

APPROACHES AND ACCESS

Coming South from the Tyne Tunnel or North via the A19(T), turn onto the A194 for South Shields. At the first roundabout, turn right onto the A1300 and stay on this road until a roundabout with a clock in the centre is reached. Continue straight on following signs for Marsden. After about a mile, the Marsden Inn is passed on the left and one carries straight on beyond this junction to eventually turn left onto the coast road. As soon as one reaches the brow of the hill and South Shields comes into view, pull over to the right hand side of the road and park in the long parking lane adjacent to the wide expanse of grass known as The Leas.

Strike directly across The Leas towards the sea and pick up a good gravel track with a metal barrier fence alongside. Follow this fence Northwards until it comes to an end. At this juncture, descend bearing left down an easy path which leads into the cove. The cove

THE COVE – LONNEN QUARRY–CLEADON CRAGS

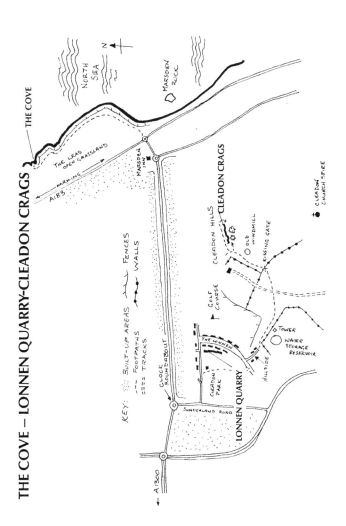

is easily identified by the presence of chalk on the holds and also by a big block below the H.W.M. near the South side.

CLEADON CRAGS   O.S. SHEET 88   TYNESIDE
G.R. 386 640 and 391 630

SITUATION AND CHARACTER

The climbing on the crags collectively known as Cleadon is spread between two main areas:

Lonnen Quarry and a small outcropping of excellent rock 300 metres South-East of the old windmill on Cleadon Hills. There are other tiny faces in the area but these do not warrant description.

Lonnen Quarry is the most popular and its location in Cleadon Park Recreation area surrounded by houses and football pitches is reminiscent of the crags at Cavaillon in Southern France but there the similarity ends!

Lonnen Quarry is a series of faces of Magnesian Limestone up to 5 metres high facing West-South West with a not unpleasant outlook and a mere one minute walk from the parking. The grass extends up to the foot of the crags and provides excellent landings. The climbing is excellent ranging from less than vertical walls on tiny holds through to vertical and overhanging walls on bigger flatter holds. The finishes to the climbs at the left end are clean, but all the finishes on Black Wall require care, although an unusual and tenacious Ivy mass forming a moustache along the top edge provides something "to get your fingers into". This seems to work for everyone and provides a bit of adventure. The climbs are graded for an 'on sight' ascent and even taking this into account, they may seem a bit harsh to visitors. Locals are at a distinct advantage here as the rock particularly on Broken White Buttress is difficult to read and familiarity makes the climbs seem easier. Great care should be taken to avoid glass broken by the other idiots who infest such places.

Cleadon Crags, the other venue provides some tough overhang problems on Dancing Buttress and a dozen good, clean wall climbs on Main Wall.

The climbing is shrouded by trees and whilst good, is not as popular or as accessible as Lonnen Quarry.

APPROACHES AND ACCESS

Approaching from the North via Tyne Tunnel or from South on A19(T), take A194 for South Shields. At first roundabout, turn right onto A1300 and stay on this road until the roundabout with a clock in the middle is reached. Turn right onto Sunderland Road and go along here for about 100 metres when some trees will be seen ahead on the left. This is Cleadon Park. Turn left immediately before the trees and go up the minor road with the park on the right. After passing the school on the right, the playing fields and Lonnen Quarry will be visible on the right. Park alongside the houses opposite the playing field. The crag is easily reached from the car in about one minute. To reach Cleadon Crag it is necessary to follow the base of Lonnen Quarry to the right until a good made up path is reached. Turn left along this and mount a curved set of concrete steps to pass between the bungalows and meet the Lonnen. Turn left and then turn right into Hillside which leads up past a little outcrop; Golf Course Crag on the left. This provides a few very short climbs and traverses. The big wall surrounding the Water Storage Reservoir is followed uphill until paths lead to the Old Windmill. Pass the Old Windmill and follow the wall until it bends. Cleadon Crag lies on the top of the slope opposite just above the trees and is best approached from above. Time from Lonnen Quarry about 10 minutes.

HISTORICAL

The first recorded climbs at Lonnen Quarry were made by Mike Blenkinsop in 1974. Blenkinsop climbed both the Left and Right Walls amongst others. Paul Stewart pushed standards somewhat with his ascents of Thin White Crack and The Dancer and also Naybrew which at the time of its ascent in 1975 must rank with the hardest in the whole area. The development of the Black Wall area is also the work of Paul Stewart, particularly good is the fine arete of The Rat and the steep wall of Improvisor. Many other problems have been created by the many who use the area for "Evening Training" and the necessity to upgrade many of the routes says a lot for the talents of the First Ascentionists pre- sticky rubber.

THE CLIMBS

LONNEN QUARRY

SPLINTERED WHITE BUTTRESS

This is the clean and attractive face at the left-hand end of the quarry nearest the road. The climbs are described from left to right.

1   Small Wall   4c
Climb the wall at the extreme left end of the buttress.

2   Small Crack   4a
Climb the right-trending crack.

3   Short Wall   5b+
Climb the brown-stained wall via a hard mantelshelf.

4   Short Crack   4b+
Climb the crack which initially trends left.

5   Left Wall   5b   **★★**
Start at the foot of a "staircase" leading up and right. Climb this to a good hold below a little overlap. Using small holds above for the hands, step left onto a sloping ledge and pull over using a finger pocket to finish near the arete.

5a   Left Wall Direct   5c   **★**
Gain the little overlap and pull over rightwards to finish up and diagonally right.

6   Golden Years   5c-6a   **★**
Reasonable until right at the top, then the grade is for the long and the short. Start just left of Central Groove. Climb the obvious slim, brown wall just right of the initials N.M.E. painted on the face. Reaching a long brown pocket near the top is the crux.

7 Central Groove 4a
Climb the prominent grooveline passing a good ledge at 2m. Finish up the steep groove or swing right onto the arete for a 4b 'one star' finish.

8 Right Wall Eliminate 6a+
Start directly below the thin streaks of pink paint at the top. Climb the wall direct to these without use of holds on the arete to the left or on Right Wall.

9 Right Wall 5a+ ★★
Starts just left of a triangular rock scar at head height. Climb the impending wall and finish up the concave wall above.

10 Entre chiens et loups 5b ★
Start just right of the triangular rock scar. Climb the overhanging scoop to a good hold. The blunt face above is climbed direct using a good undercut.

11 Left-Hand Variation 4b ★
Start 2m right of the triangular rock scar at a slabby, left-slanting gangway. Climb the ganway to reach the good undercut of the previous route and finish to the right of this.

12 Original Route 4b ★
A good route. Start below the obvious thin crack 4m right of Central Groove. Climb the crack without recourse to holds on the flakes to the left. Finish up the shallow groove at the top.

13 Le ventre de l'architecte 6a+
Climb the wall immediately right of Original route. A poor layaway hold is of some assistance in surmounting the belly. Finish direct.

14 Hidden Wall 5b
Start at a faint rib midway between Original Route and Depression. Climb the rib with the crux being to get established in a shallow scoop in the rib. Finish direct.

15 Depression 4b
Start below a depression at head-height where the fossiliferous rock abuts against beds of smoother, banded rock. Climb into the depression and climb directly to easier angled rock above.

16 Grooveline 4c
Directly above the smooth, banded rock is a V-groove. Climb awkwardly up the smooth rock to gain and climb the groove. Care with finish!

17 Pock Wall 4b
Climb the crozzly wall 1m right of the smooth rock, to finish just left of a masonry wall at the top.

18 The Corner 4a
Climb the distinct corner crack.

19 The High Girdle 5b ★
Starts at the left-hand side and girdle to the right just below the top.

20 Lower Girdles 5c-6a
A variety of ways exist in both directions and can be made harder or easier depending on the line.

SMOOTH WHITE BUTTRESS

The slim buttress to the right of The Corner. It is split by a thin crack with a wider crack a bit further right on the edge of the wall.

21   Clit   5b
Climb the left-slanting grooveline just right of The Corner.

22   Naybrew   6a
Climb the wall just left of the thin crack using a small down-pointing flake at the start.

23   Thin White Crack   5c   ★★
Climb the thin crack, the transfer across the discontinuity is the crux.

24   Ragged Crack   5a   ★
Climb the attractive crack on the right edge of the wall.

25   Smooth White Eliminate   5c
Start to the right of Ragged crack. Climb across the wall from right to left diagonally to finish up Naybrew.

26   The White Girdle   6a   ★
Traverse the wall at mid-height from left or right.

27   High Level Variations   5b

From Smooth White Buttress rightwards is a scruffy wall which has a number of easy lines. The first landmark of any significance is a good, short cracked arete with a steep corner to its right. A Hawthorn grows in the field in front of this arete.

THE BLACK WALL

This is an extended series of walls interspersed with corners and aretes which terminates some way right at a large tree growing hard up against the rock. Its name is something of a misnomer as it now has a more open aspect now that the scruffy Hawthorns hiding its front have been felled and the grass has established itself at the foot of the face where once was rubbish and glass.

28   White Arete   4b+
Climb the prominent, cracked arete on its left-hand side to a steep, awkward and insecure finish.

29   Minstrel Show   4b+
Climb the steep wall to the right of White Arete. Very enjoyable.

30   Black Corner   3b
Climb the corner which isn't too black and is easier and better than it looks.

The wall immediately right has a band of overhangs at mid-height. The rock on the right-hand side of these is loose and should be treated with care.

31   Arch Wall   4a
Start 1m right of Black Corner. Climb the steep wall to a hole near the top. Step right to finish.

32   Archbishop   4c   ★
Start in a small, right-facing corner right of Arch wall. Climb up to and over the overhang to finish up the white wall above.

33   Patriarch   5b
A potentially dangerous climb due to loose blocks. Climb the loose

overhangs between Archbishop and the slim corner of Arch Enemy.

34 Arch Enemy 4b+
A strenuous and enjoyable climb. Ascend the slim corner at the right end of the overhangs, 4m right of Black Corner.
The wall to the right is steep and looks quite loose and yellow. It is however a lot better than it looks and provides some of the best climbing on the buttress. A steep crack in the upper wall is a feature.

35 Chodflinger 4b
This charmingly-named climb starts at a protruding block at chest-height, 1m right of Arch Enemy. Climb the impending wall above, to finish at a slight break at the top.

36 Chod Crack 4b   ★
Start 3m right of the Archbishop Overhangs at a yellow recess below a prominent crack in the upper wall. Climb the recess and wall to reach and climb the crack. Good holds throughout.

The next two climbs have a common start:

37 Supervisor 5b
Start at the yellow recess at the left-hand end of the overhang guarding the upper wall as for Chod Crack. Pull out of the recess rightwards on good holds then instead of moving right as for Improvisor, continue direct up the slight bulge immediately right of Chod Crack.

38 Improvisor 5c   ★★
A thrilling expedition for such a small crag not to be taken lightly. Start at the yellow recess as for Supervisor. Pull out of the recess rightwards on good holds then move right to gain a small, vertical finger crack. Hard moves up the wall above and left of a fresh rock scar completes this hard climb.

38a Improvisor Direct Start 5c
Start midway along the overhang barrier between the start of Improvisor and the arete of Visor to the right. Ascend the overhang first left and then right onto the wall above to finish as for Improvisor.

39 Visor 5a
Start 3m right of Chod Crack at the right-hand end of the overhanging barrier and below the prominent arete. Layaway up the end of the overhanging barrier and climb the arete taking care with holds. The finish is steep.

40 Revisor 4c   ★★
Start just right of the arete below an open scoop. Reach up to gain a projecting ledge and climb onto it. Climb the scoop above trending right to the top.

41 Black Plague 4c
Start just right of the projecting ledge of Revisor. Climb the right-slanting slab to a black patch. Climb the wall above to finish.

42 Diamond Dogs 5a
This interesting traverse starts as for Visor and follows a line diagonally rightwards to finish on good holds at the top of the overhanging arete of The Rat.

43   The Rat   5a   ★★
An impressive climb. Start directly below the black, bulging arete 3m right of Visor. Climb the rounded pillar to a little cave then attack the bulging arete direct. Good holds.

44   Black Cat   5a
Start in the corner just right of The Rat. Climb the corner moving right. At the top, move left to finish up the overhanging corner just right of The Rat.

45   Piler   5b   *
Start 3m right of Black Cat below a block which protrudes just above head-height. Gain this block and stand on it. Traverse right at mid-height for almost 3m to finish up a slab just right of the bushes at the top of the crag.

46   Piler Direct   5b
Start by climbing a groove just right of Piler, to gain a bird-limed niche above. Finish up the groove above with care.

47   Piler Superdirect   5c
Start 2m right of Piler below an undercut flake below the right-hand end of the top overhang. Pull up on the flake and finish up the corner at the right-hand end of the overhangs.

48   Black Niche   4c
Start 2m right of the undercut flake where a rib leads up to a black, roofed niche. Climb into the niche and step left to exit as for Piler.

49   Bin Man   4b
Climb the wide-open scoop to the right of Black Niche.

50   Black Wall Girdle   5a   ★★
Traverse the buttress from White Arete to finish as for Bin Man. Low or High Level alternatives exist.

51   The Great Girdle   5a   ★★
A combination of all the Girdle Traverses gives a long and arduous expedition.

CLEADON CRAGS

From the old Windmill, follow the wall until one can strike across to the wooded slope opposite. The climbing is on the partly-hidden escarpment below the top edge of the wooded slope. The buttresses can be reached by easy jungle-bashing from the left-hand end or by means of a good path running along the top to the far end wher a descent can be made.

LEFT-HAND BUTTRESS

This is the extreme left-hand buttress which is clean though short and provides some easy climbs and an interesting Girdle.

DANCING BUTTRESS

The prominent jutting overhang of perfect rock, rising from a rock ledge at 1m.
The buttress was so-named because of the comical leg-kicking that was a feature of the First Ascent.

1 The Dancer 5c
Climb the overhang at the left-hand end. Fine to start, desperate to finish.

2 The Necromancer 5c
Climb the overhang in the centre. Nothing to it!

3 Dancing Groove Prickly 3c
The groove on the right is full of brambles. It used to be climbed.

INTERMEDIATE BUTTRESS
This indeterminate short wall of good rock extends for a further 25m right of Dancing Buttress. Here are possibilities for various easier problems. It terminates at the right by a left-trending gangway, right of which is the best buttress on the crag; Main Wall.

MAIN WALL
This is the steep, rectangular wall of perfect rock just over 4m high. It has a wide grassy landing-pad below.

4 Gangway 2c
Climb the easy, left-trending gangway.

5 Gangway Crack 4b
Climb the left-trending crack just above the start of the gangway.

6 Pegged Crack 4c
Climb the more prominent left-hand one of two parallel vertical cracks.

7 Urckwind 5a
Climb the right-hand, fainter crack.

8 Poacher 5c
An eliminate which ascends the blank wall just right of Urckwind.

9 The Wurlitzer 5a ★
Climb the wall just left of the central, slim groove, to finish via a good pocket hold.

10 Slim Chance 4b ★
Climb the fine, slim groove in the centre of the wall.

11 Ronnie Lane 4a
Climb the wall midway between the slim groove and the obvious crackline to the right.

12 How Come? 4b
This climb squeezes a way up the wall just left of the obvious crack. Climb the wall to pass an awkward mantleshelf.

13 Slim Crack 4a
Climb the slim crack.

14 The Eliminate 4a
Climb the wall right of Slim Crack.

15 The Arete
An easy ascent or descent.

16 Main Wall Girdle 4b ★
An interesting, either way Girdle with a choice of levels.

THE RECESS
The area to the right of Main Wall.

17   Recess Slab   4b

18   Hanging Groove   4c
Climb the obvious line.

19   The Overhang   5a
To the right of Recess Slab is an overhang which is climbed direct.
Further right again is:

RIGHT-HAND BAY

20   Bay Crack   4a

21   Baby Blue   4a
Climb the wall to the right of the crack.

22   The Corner   3c

23   Girdle Traverse   3c

HOUGHTON GRAVEYARD – HOUGHTON LE SPRING
O.S. SHEET 88   G.R. 345505

SITUATION AND CHARACTER

Houghton Graveyard is within the urban area of Houghton-Le-
Spring only a couple of miles South-West of Sunderland. The crags
are found in a former graveyard on the North-East side of the town
only a hundred metres from the roar of the A690 Dual Carriageway
to Sunderland.

Definitely Gothic this one. An unreal place of manicured grass and
overturned headstones with ivy-wreathed walls of pallid rock glo-
wering across the stillness above squalid littered-strewn banks
sloping down to the living world below.

The faces of Magnesian limestone, part of an ancient reef deposit,
are up to twenty metres high. The climbing is restricted to the best
and most impressive faces which are also the first encountered as
one enters the graveyard. The rock on these two faces is good,
better than it looks, but it does suffer from a powdery deposit,
almost as if the rock gave out its own salts. This soon disappears
with use. The rock is very compact and does not run to strong
features or cracks, this plus the unrelenting steepness and small
holds and pockets means that the climbing is very hard indeed.
Protection is absent and systematic bolting could make this place a
good venue for climbers from further afield as well as locally.

APPROACHES AND ACCESS.

From the main roundabout below the A690 Durham to Sunderland
road, exit onto the B1404 for Seaham and take the first left turn
almost immediately into Elizabeth Street. Follow this uphill to a
crossroads and go straight ahead. (The crag is now visible on the
hill behind the allotment gardens.) Take the first street on the left,
Ironside Street and at the end, turn right into Sunderland Street.
Drive up the hill to the end of the street and park near Hillside
farm, the detached house at the end. A path leads uphill to the old
cemetery gate. Turn into this and follow a short path into the

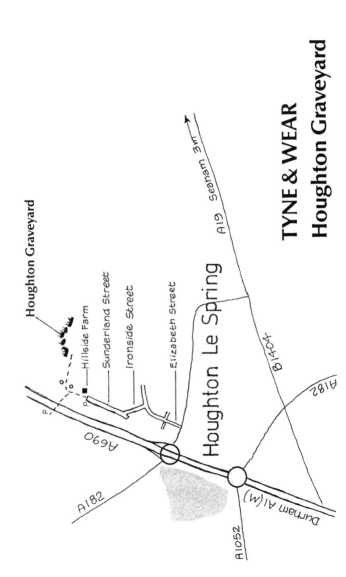

Houghton Graveyard

TYNE & WEAR
Houghton Graveyard

graveyard. The first crag on the left is Lower Wall whilst above and behind is the Main Wall.

It is possible to park at the top of the hill on the A690 on the Sunderland side of Houghton "Cut" and cross the road to reach the graveyard.

HISTORICAL

Many of the routes were first climbed by Gavin Ellis and John Boyle particularly worth mentioning are Abiotrophy and Revenge Of The Bodysnatchers. Michael Gardner and Dave Stainthorpe were also prime movers and contributed the fine Pegasus and Pinning The Tail On The Donkey. Also involved in the development were T. Gallagher, T. Smith and N. Wilson. Stephen "Woody" Fleming made a unique contribution with his very bold lead of Roasting The Ox.

THE CLIMBS

There are two sections: Main Wall and Lower Wall. The climbs are described from right to left starting with Main Wall.

MAIN WALL

This is an impressive face up to 20 metres high. It is uniformly steep. The right-hand side of the face forms a slabby corner with a conspicuous black bulge on the left wall.The short right-hand wall has a fine arete bounding the right side of this. To the right again the crag loses height as a bank is ascended. Most of the routes are top-roped and good anchors are available on trees above the crag. The top of the Main Wall is reached by scrambling up the wooded bank to the left of the Main Wall and above the Lower Wall. The striking crack seaming the left end of the face has not been climbed.

1   The Sepulchre   NL   5b/c
Start below the right hand side of the steep slab up the slope at the extreme right-hand end of Main Wall. Climb the slab left of the Ivy mass.

2   The Cat Crept Into The Crypt   NL   5b/c
Left of Sepulchre on the steep slab is an obvious crack. Climb the slab just right of this.

3   Roasting The Ox   E1   5b   ★★
Start below the corner left of the narrow wall and the obvious arete. Go up the corner until moves on the right wall can be made towards the arete. Follow the left wall making occasional use of the arete. On the first ascent a long sling was hung down the very top loose section. A very bold route indeed.

4   My Little Pony   NL   6a   ★★
Start just left of the foot of the corner. Climb the wall to mid-height and move left through a weakness in the wall. Move back right and climb the wall above.

5   Good Friday   NL   5c/6a   ★
Start to the left of a black bulge at the base of the crag about 5m left of the corner. Climb up the wall to the left of the bulge then move slightly right to ascend the wall passing a small overlap halfway up.

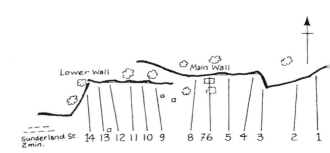

TYNE & WEAR   Houghton Graveyard

6   Myrrh   NL   5c
Climb the obvious curving scoop until near the top it is possible to move left. An alternative finish exists at the same grade, up the wall before the traverse left at the top.

7   Pegasus   NL   5c   ***
Start as for Myrrh below the obvious scoop. Climb up the scoop until a traverse left can be made onto a blunt arete. Finish straight up the wall above. Sustained.

8   Pinning The Tail On The Donkey   NL   5c   **
Start at a lower level than the other routes to the left of a small memorial plaque. Climb the wall to the left of centre to a ledge. Continue up the wall above at its steepest part trending slightly left near the top.

THE LOWER WALL
Just left of the Main Wall and below are two walls divided by a deep chimney. The left wall is a steep slab whilst the right wall is a very steep wall offering technical climbing up to 12 metres in height. Most of the routes finish below the top as the rock deteriorates. Tree anchors are plentiful on the top and the slope to the left of the Main Wall gives access to the top of the Lower Wall. The climbs are described from right to left.

9   Immortalised In Stone   NL   5b
Start at the right-hand end of Lower Wall a couple of metres left of a right-curving overlap. Climb the wall to an obvious pocket, move left then right above this to finish at a jug. A short climb.

10   Evensong   NL   5c   *
Start a couple of metres left of Immortalised In Stone below a very shallow right-facing "corner". Climb the "corner" finishing at two large jugs.
Just left of the "corner" is a vague groove/overlap sloping up to the right.

11   Seven Sisters   NL   5b/c   *
Climb the vague groove until at the capping bulge, move left and finish up the fingery wall above to finish below the loose rock.

About 6 metres further left the top of the crag is crowned by a big tree.

12   Abiotrophy   NL   6b/c   ★★★
Start directly below the big tree at the top of the crag.
Climb the wall direct until a desperate move on a small undercling leads over a small roof. Another hard move is made to gain the large finishing pocket.

13   Revenge Of The Bodysnatchers   NL   6b   ★★★
An extremely sustained route on good rock. Start below the steep wall midway between Abiotrophy and the deep corner on the left. Climb the wall by delicate fingery climbing which gives way to a series of snatches to reach a good flat hold, 3m below the top. The next moves to gain a big pocket are the crux.

14   Bushwhacking   NL   4c
Start below the big tree to the left of the arete which is the left side of the central corner/chimney. Climb the slabby wall.

KEPIER WOODS   O.S. SHEET 88   G.R. 291 441

SITUATION AND CHARACTER
Situated alongside the riverside path about one and a half miles downstream of the City of Durham, this small outcrop of good quality sandstone provides excellent, strenuous problems up to six metres high.
Its location is in lovely woodland and Its sheltered situation ensures all-year climbing on rock that is fairly clean and quick to dry.

APPROACHES AND ACCESS
From Durham centre follow the A690 in the direction of Sunderland and take the Belmont exit. At the sharp bend at the top of the sliproad and just before crossing the A690 on the flyover, turn sharp left into a car park. Descend the tarmac path and turn right at the bottom on a path (downstream) past an old quarry. Kepier Wall is on the right. Time from car is five to ten minutes.
On foot from Durham City: Follow downstream path at the end of Providence Row (off Claypath). This leads via stiles and through fields to Kepier Wall. Time by this route is about twenty minutes.

HISTORICAL
The Kepier Wall has long been a venue for climbers from the Durham colleges and Dave "Dids" Bowen climbed here prior to the publication of the first edition of The North Of England Guide. It was he who introduced Stew Wilson and friends to Kepier. This team climbed and recorded the routes for the first guide fully aware of the fact that most of the routes had been done before, with the possible exception of Maggy The Whip. Alan Short from Belmont claimed Short's Crack Subsequent generations have left no stone unturned.

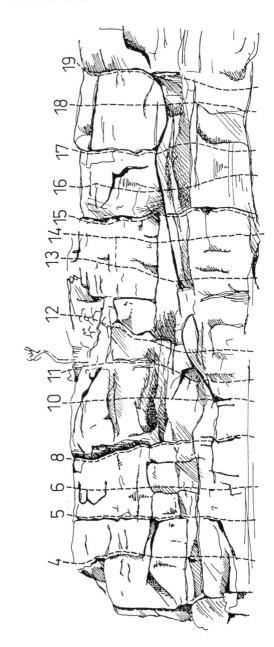

KEPIER WOODS

THE CLIMBS

These are described from lefy to right as one faces the crag. A small face just left of the obvious descent chute at the left end of the main wall gives:

1   Dids   4a
Climb the thin crack.

2   Dids Two   4b
Climb the undercut wall just right of the crack.

The following climbs are on the Main Wall:

3   Crucial Knee Jam   5a/b
Climb the arete at the left end of Main Wall, using a hand or knee jam.

4   Hard Labour   4c
Climb direct to and up the thin flake crack. If started from Work-shy, the grade goes down to 4b.

5   Workshy   4c   ★★
Climb the obvious crack after a bulging start.

6   The Grafter   5a
Climb the wall between Workshy and the arete on layaway holds.

7   Don's Arete   5b   ★★
Climb the arete just left of the wide crack of Ferret on rounded layaways.

8   Ferret   4b
Climb this crack, the widest on the wall.

9   Double Mantelshelf   5b
The first mantelshelf just right of Ferret is the hardest.

10   Wall And Overhang   5c
Climb the wall and overhang just right of the mantelshelf.

11   Bobbery John   4b
Start just right of Wall And Overhang. Make fingery moves into a corner which starts at head- height. Finish on good holds to the left of the Beech tree.

12   Fitchen   4a
Climb the right-trending "dog-leg" crack on rounded footholds. Finish right of the tree.

13   Hob Hole   5a   ★
Climb the wall which has an obvious pocket.

14   Ledge Climb   4a
Climb the wall between Hob Hole and Teabreak Crack.

15   Teabreak Crack   4c   ★
Climb the thin crack direct.

16   Teabreak's Over   6a
Climb the wall right of Teabreak Crack past a bulge on sloping finger holds. Worrying!

17   Maggy The Whip   5a/b   ★★
Climb the undercut wall to gain twin cracks above.

18   The Gaffer   6a
Climb the wall between Maggy The Whip and Short's Crack

19   Short's Crack   4c   ★★
Climb the fine crack at the right end of the wall.

20   The Sneck   6b
Climb the nose to the right of Short's Crack.

Traverses
Kepier Wall has many good traverses and routines: High Level
Traverse: Hands on or near the top of the crag. Mid Level Traverse:
Hands at level of second overhang. Low Level traverse: Hands at
level of first, main break. Very Low Level Traverse: Hands on
undercut base beneath first overhang and no higher than first flat
shelf.

TYNE AND WEAR – MINOR CRAGS AND BOULDERING VENUES

JESMOND DENE   O.S. SHEET 88   G.R. 254672
Jesmond Dene is a well-known local beauty spot in the centre of
Newcastle less than a mile to the East of the A6125. The climbing in
this little stream-filled valley is on small walls of reasonable sandstone with the accent on steep or technical problems. No records
have been kept of the problems as far as is known, but it is a
popular spot with local climbers.

ELDON SQUARE WALL
The Eldon Square Leisure Centre is blessed with one of the best
artificial walls in the country. It is a Bendcrete Wall and has a variety
of interesting features; overhanging walls, panelled walls, arches
and free-standing boulders. It offers something for climbers of all
standards. The proximity of cafes and good shopping can make this
a good, Winter venue even from far-afield.

THE STAITHES   O.S. SHEET 88   G.R. 395573
Stretching Westwards from under the Wearmouth Bridge are a
series of walls and buttresses up to 15m high consisting of poor
quality Magnesian Limestone, but mainly man-made walls of a
variety of materials. These have been climbed on for many years by
Wearside climbers and were first developed by Paul Stewart, Bill
Wayman, Dave Stainthorpe, Ian Weetman and Alan Moist; who is
totally to blame if this information is duff.

The walls look out onto an interesting urban landscape and provide
good (if different) climbing.

Section 1: Lies underneath the bridge and is a slab of poor rock
best top-roped. The scoop in the centre is 4c. Watch out for
U.F.O.s from the bridge high overhead!

Section 2: Now for some real climbing. Choose your poison; Limestone, Gritstone, Sandstone or concrete with added refined tor-
tures of Jamming, laybacking or face climbing.

This section contains The Main Wall which extends for over 100
metres at a height of around 6 metres. An obvious line goes up on
good holds via two drainage pipes (inhabited!) at 4b. Scoop Direct
is 5a+ and goes up this feature on small, positive holds. The Pillar
takes the left arete of the pillar to finish on pinchgrips and a
mantelshelf. This is 5c. A good route and well- worth the effort is

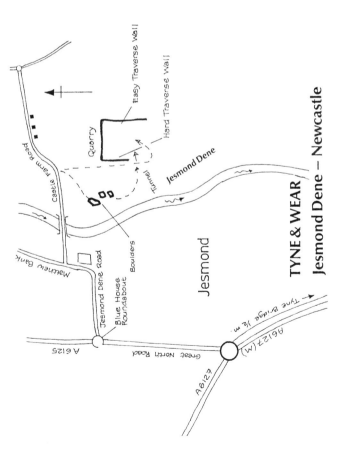

The Low-Level Traverse, over 100 metres long and 5c.

Section 3: The next section has an impressive, central crack which is named Grand Parade. It goes at HVS 5b and has good gear placements. This is very popular. The Rusty Walls area has a corner somewhat in the 'Green Death' idiom. This has been soloed at 5c with an exciting and contorted layaway finish. A 5a takes the wall up to the first iron girder taken 'a cheval' to a mantelshelf finish.

Section 4: These unique concrete slabs provided some good friction climbs but it is reported that they have now been severely chipped by a Local Authority Outdoor Activities Association reducing the grade to Severe. (What a fine example to set to newcomers to climbing!)

ROWLANDS GILL VIADUCT   O.S. SHEET 88   G.R. 180600

Situated on the A694 in-between Rowlands Gill and Winlaton Mill is is the Derwent Walks Country Park. The viaduct crossing the picturesque River Derwent has climbing on the legs on the North and South banks of the river. There is a good car park/picnic site just off the A694. Follow the path rightwards from the car park to Derwent Walk and turn left onto this to reach the viaduct. The North Bank is the first bank you come to.

NORTH BANK

Leg nearest river has a difficult crack (5b/c) with some protection pegs in place. Belay and abseil from a block under the arch after 15m.

The second leg from the river has a crack which can be jammed or the face can be climbed. Belay and abseil from blocks under the arch where some pegs and tat may be in place (check first or carry replacements!)

SOUTH BANK

Bouldering on all the legs, but the traverses on the third leg from the river are best as they are protected from above by the arch and at the sides by trees. A good place for a rainy day.

THE MOTORWAY BRIDGE (Chester-le-Street/Great Lumley)
O.S. SHEET 88   G.R. 299508

This Sandstone-clad support for the A1(M) as it crosses the Breckon Hill Beck, is around 50m long and 5m high and provides a wealth of problems and fingery traverses from 5a to 6c. To get there follow the B1284 from the East (Lumley Castle) side of Chester-le-Street, going uphill past the golf course. Immediately after the "Z-Bends" turn left down a road marked 'Except For Access'. After 150 metres pass the Smith's Arms pub and 50 metres beyond is the bridge. Very, very popular with local climbers and a good place to meet people. Night climbing is also popular here (if you have a car with a fully-charged battery!).

BELMONT VIADUCT   O.S. SHEET 88   G.R. 298449

Belmont Viaduct crosses the River wear only two miles downstream of Durham City centre and close to the Kepier Wood crag. It must surely be one of the most impressive of its type in England and comprises nine elegant arches spanning a hundred metre gorge. Each arch is supported by a slender pillar composed of Gritstone blocks. The top of the central pillar is 40 metres above the river. The situation is picturesque and rural and the routes are all located on the same face which faces South-West. The fact that it catches the sun for most of the day and its sheltered location in the gorge means it can be climbed on all the year round. There are three serious climbs on the viaduct and these were first climbed by John Moulding, Fred Stevenson, Norman Armstrong and Steve Booth-royd in the early 80's.

The first route is A Taste Of Experience (E4 6a) which starts at the foot of the South face of the Central Pillar from a ledge at 5m above the river (reached by abseil or wading!). An old aid version climbed directly up the pillar on bolts but the free version starts at the foot of the right arete of the pillar as one faces in. Climb the right arete and after 9m, traverse left and follow the face direct (bolt runners from aided ascent-check these!) to a large ledge at 22m. Belay. Above the ledge the difficulties ease somewhat and the thin crack offers natural protection. The finale is a jutting parapet with a rounded finish if you can't find the hidden jug.

Total Perspective Vortex is a straightforward but "mind-blowing" A2 on bolts. This starts from the belay ledge at the top of the first pitch of A Taste Of Experience and follows the underside of the arch.

Walking On Air (E2 5c) is one of the most exposed trips in the area and is a 'Free Version' of Total Perspective Vortex. It starts from the belay ledge of A Taste Of Experience and follows the arch, with the toes just above the lip in places, hence the name. The crux is the first move off the belay ledge. The route finishes directly up the wall from a huge bolt about 5m left of the finish of Total Perspective Vortex. Pre-placed protection pegs have been removed but it is recommended they be replaced even though the route can be protected with small wires between the blocks. The grades have not been confirmed by subsequent ascentionists.

PITTINGTON   O.S. SHEET 88   G.R. 331447

A long outcrop of Magnesian Limestone of generally poor quality up to 15m high. the crags face West from a hillside above the village of Pittington about 4 miles east of Durham City. Leave the A1(M) at the Durham/Sunderland junction and follow the A690 North until a minor road to Pittington can be followed. In Pittington, at a sharp right-hand bend in the road, carry straight ahead (ie left) up a narrow road to a cul-de-sac where cars can be parked, taking care not to block driveways. The crag is a 5 minute walk on a Bridleway straight ahead. This divides into numerous chalky paths. take any of these to the right to reach the crag.

There are two areas used by climbers the first is called The Window Cave Area and Wailing Wall Area further right as one faces the rock. The Window cave Area consists of basically two walls set at right angles the axix being a short corner at the top of a grassy bank. The long left wall has a protruding and overhanging buttress at the left-hand end above a small Hawthorn and there is one known routes on this overhanging wall. Dire Straits (N.L. 5c) ascends the wall just right of the central curving crack. To the right of this overhanging buttress the walls step back at a deep chimney; The Chasm which is climbed by a thin crack in the left wall and left arete to give: Le Chasm Des Miserables (N.L. 5a) and via its over-hanging right wall to give: Lunge Beyond The Edge (E1 5b) which finishes on the front wall just left of Bullitt. The long wall to the right of this seems to be composed of better rock, at least until the top is reached. The first route to the right of The Chasm is Bullitt (N.L. 5b) which follows the thin crack with a small niche at mid-height, just right of the chimney. Just to the right of Bullitt are two, very thin, vertical cracks. this gives: Twin Cracks (HVS 5a). Further right the wall is split by a deep, right-curving chimney: The Chim-ney (V.D or S by L.H. finish.) Kant (VS 4c) ascends the deep chim-ney and block just to the right of The Chimney then it moves out onto the clean upper wall to the right of the upper chimney/crack. The Corner is a short and loose climb (VD). The wall to the right of The Corner is followed rightwards for several metres until a black overhanging corner is reached. Starting in this corner it is possible to traverse left and gain the left-hand arete which is climbed. This is: Amen Arete (HVS 4c/5a). Patric's Pleasure (VS 4c) moves left at the arete to climb the wall to the left.Two old pegs may still be in place to protect both of these routes.

Further right is a smooth looking wall; Wailing Wall with some good, sharp cracks in its upper half. The centre of this wall is identified by a blocky overhang at mid-height, with a vertical crack, splitting the wall above.The first route starts below the left end of the blocky overhang. Festerhaunt (VS 4c) – Climb up to the left-end of the overhang, step right and pull over the overhang (crux) and finish up the wall to the left of the long, vertical crack. Dead Hedgehog (N.L. 5a) – Start at a thin crack directly below the right end of the block overhang. Climb the crack and wall above, tren-ding left slightly. climb the overhang and easier vertical crack above.

Wailing Wall (N.L. 5b) – Start a couple of metres right of Dead Hedgehog. Climb the very steep wall to a "letterbox" hold to gain the left side of the prominent ledge. the wall above is followed direct. There may be some old wooded wedges in place. The routes are the work of M. Sweeting, B.Green and M.Davis whilst at Durham University in the mid 70's. Later routes were the work of Jordan Tinniswood in 1991.

ROGERLEY QUARRIES   O.S. SHEET 92   G.R. 024373

These disused Limestone quarries are behind the small estate of houses at the West end of Frosterley in Weardale, just North of the A689. Following the A689 West from Wolsingham, through Fros-terley, a minor road on the right, 300 metres beyond the left turn to Bollihope is followed uphill. Cars can be parked near a sharp left-hand bend or better still near the main road. The quarries are to the West and East of this minor road . The best quarry lies to the East behind a small housing estate. Climbing here was popular in the early 80's and many climbs up to HVS were made, especially on the wall to the right of the tunnel which goes beneath the minor road and which joins the West and East quarries. The venue may still be of interest to climbers, but it should be pointed out that sections are dangerously loose and that the walls are not overhanging and so very hard routes may not be plentiful.

ICE CLIMBING IN TYNE AND WEAR

A small icefall can build up in the little bay on the right on the approach to the Kepier Wood crag. This can give up to 12m of vertical ice; Grade 3. The best ice-climbing however is found in Weardale between Wolsingham and Stanhope at the quarries on Bollihope Common O.S. SHEET 92 G.R. 984350 and at Parson's Byers G.R. 005366. Two hundred metres in from the entrance to the quarry is a 30m pitch of Grade 3, whilst 300 metres from the entrance is a steep, 15m pitch.At the end of the quarry, a stream gives an interesting, but short Grade 4.

7 THE DURHAM DENES

Denes are the local name given to deeply-incised valleys which dissect the coastal plain and run from West to East. The climbing is found on various Magnesian Limestone crags and buttresses throughout the length of the valleys and does involve some walking. The two main denes are to be found a few miles North of Hartlepool. Castle Eden Dene is a local Nature Reserve and climbing is viewed as a threat to the environment. This superb valley has a lot of rock and one cliff in particular; Jacob's Ladder provides some of the longest routes to be found on Dolomitic Limestone in the North. Nevertheless, climbers continue to operate here whilst maintaining a low and eco-friendly profile. Nesbitt Dene has three separate areas and Jack Rock in particular has all the attributes to make it an attractive, modern venue. It is very steep and compact, stays dry and is out of the public eye. It is ironical that the streams are in a worse condition now than 'in the pre-conservation days.

THE DURHAM DENES

The relatively high land of the Durham coastal strip to the East of Durham city and between Seaham and Hartlepool is dissected by a number of West to East trending streams which have incised, with the help of glacial meltwater, a series of deep valleys. The thick beds of Magnesian limestone have been exposed in these valleys forming very steep crags up to forty metres high.

The two valleys or denes as they are known locally, where climbing development has taken place in the past are: Nesbitt Dene and a little further North; Castle Eden Dene. The Magnesian Limestone is tremendously variable, but certainly no worse than parts of Whitestone Cliff. Indeed some of the rock is excellent, pocketed limestone.The faces are impressive however and this coupled with lack of protection meant that even the most modest routes were adventurous undertakings. Modern climbers, using modern methods may (or may not!) consider these crags worthy of some attention. Few have heard of the places , fewer still have visited them or climbed the crags. It might be a different story if it was elsewhere than in this non-climbing area.

CASTLE EDEN DENE   O.S. SHEET 93   G.R. 417387 and 432394

SITUATION AND CHARACTER

Castle Eden Dene is a fine valley well-worth walking through. It has been compared with Dovedale. Not so many years ago it was fairly wild with the upper valley around Gunner's Pool, difficult of access. The situation has changed and a militant conservationist approach dictated that good paths were necessary for the "Middle Classes" to become more aware of their heritage and natural history. Paths were driven through and now droves of "aware" people can visit, without much effort the places that twenty years ago were the haunt of Roe Deer, poachers and the local rockclimbers. The crags that have seen development lie in two main areas:

In the Lower dene just upstream of Dungy Bridge and in the Upper dene upstream and downstream of Gunner's Pool.

The climbing is generally steep and with good holds in the form of pockets with the rock being much sounder upstream of Gunner's Pool in the Trossachs Gorge. The crags on the North Side of Trossachs Gorge are composed of excellent rock and are sunny and quick to dry.

APPROACHES AND ACCESS

The Dene has several access points but the crags are most quickly reached from specific points.

LOWER DENE: Leave the A19 at the Castle Eden exit and follow the road past the Castle Eden Inn. Turn right onto the Blackhall road and drive East for less than a mile. Turn left and follow a road to park near St. James Church. The dene is entered on the right and a steep path follows the bottom of this tributary dene downhill for about half a mile until the main stream is crossed at Castle Bridge. Following the main stream in a downstream direction the first crag on the left is Seven Chambers Crag. This is a continuous escarpment on the North side of the valley ending at a point above Dungy Bridge. On the opposite side of the beck at this point will be seen a large crag with a cave entrance: Pegjellima's Cave. Following the path downstream a large boulder beside the path called The Devil's Lapstone provides bouldering and also marks the presence of Lapstone Crag.

UPPER DENE: This can be reached by following a footpath upstream at the junction of the two streams just upstream of Seven Chambers Crag, but it is perhaps easier to enter the Upper Dene from the East end of Edderacres plantation, reached by taking a track on the right hand side of the road half a mile beyond the right turn onto the Blackhall road (see Lower Dene approach). Follow this track alongside the golf course and pass under the A19 road. bear right and follow the North side of the stream to reach the Trossachs Gorge after about six hundred metres.

Access is no problem, but the authorities view climbers as a threat to the environment. It is possible to enjoy a day's climbing here without seeing a soul but it is as well to be discreet and avoid damaging the environment. It is ironical that for all this sanitization one can no longer find the fish in the beck that were plentiful before the twin-developments of Peterlee and this Nature Reserve.

HISTORICAL

The first climbers to visit the dene were Ken Jones, Stew Wilson, Pete Long, Tony Rice and Vic Twist. In 1965 the first routes climbed were on Seven Chambers Crag, with Vic Twist climbing the protectionless off-width Great Corner. The Gambler and Moonraker were climbed in the same year by Stew Wilson and Kenny Jones. The discovery of the biggest cliff in the area; Jacob's Ladder above

Gunner's Pool created a challenge that could not be easily ignored.

The featureless left wall was aided by Vic Twist and Bill Tait whilst the Central Wall was eventually pieced together by Pete Long, Jones and Wilson to give the serious Guano.

The right-hand arete of the wall was an obvious prize and Stew along with Terry Johnston claimed this in 1966, the result being the impressive Archangel.

Upstream, the Trossachs Gorge with its slabby North wall and overhanging South Wall gave up some good routes: Bill Tait climbed the excellent Nothing and Wilson added a companion route, Striptease Wall to its left. The big slabs upstream of here were climbed by the same team whilst Kelvin Neal produced The Necker. Kelvin turned his attention the the overhanging South wall and after top-rope ascents led the very steep and bold Original Sin.

LOWER DENE
THE CLIMBS
These are described from left to right crag by crag.

SEVEN CHAMBERS CRAG
The first rock encountered on the North (left) side of the stream after descending from St. James Church and crossing Castle Bridge. Seven Chambers comes nearest the path at the Great Corner. The base of the crag to the right gradually rises away from the path and the face gains in height. The Seven chambers are hewn in the foot of the crag to the right of the Great Corner where the path under the crag climbs a steep bank. The right-hand end of the crag is most impressive and features a big unclimbed open-book corner.

1   Great Corner   12m   E1   4c   *
Start at the foot of the right-angled corner visible just above the path. Climb the off-width which gives a brutal experience.

Some distance right up the bank are some caves.

2   The Gambler   12m   HVS(A)   4c
Start at a cave to the left of a flat-topped pinnacle. Climb the steep wall using 2 pegs for aid. Climb a steep wall above to a vegetated finish.

3   Moonraker   16m   HVS(A)   4c
Start at a right-facing corner/flake. Climb this and the wall on the left (peg for aid). Finish up steep, vegetated rock.

Several metres further right and directly above three large boulders near the path, the crag has a barrier of overhangs at shoulder height.

4   The Swallow's Nest   19m   S   *
Good rock and protection make this a relatively attractive climb.
Start at the right-hand end of the overhangs. Climb the slabby wall on good holds to a small cave. Climb out of the cave and ascend the wall behind the draping branches of a big Yew.

PEGJELLIMA'S CAVE CRAG
Just downstream of Seven Chambers the crag on the right (South) side of the river opposite Dungy Bridge has an obvious large, bivi

cave in the right-hand side of the crag. There are some big, steep crack lines running the full-height of the face but the only route is a low-level traverse leftwards from the cave mouth which makes use of a line of large pockets: Owl Traverse (S).

Downstream, beyond Dungy Bridge the large boulder on the left is called The Devil's Lapstone. It provides short problems on excellent rock. On the same side and immediately above The Devil's Lapstone is another small crag:

LAPSTONE CRAG

This is well-weathered and only about nine metres high but provides a couple of reasonable climbs.

5 Van Eyck's Wall 9m HS 4b
Start at the left side of the crag where a steep wall is overhung by trailing branches. Climb the wall delicately on small holds.

6 The Swag 9m S
This pleasant climb starts at the centre of the crag. Pull onto a shelf (stalactite thread) and climb the bulging wall on good holds to a ledge. Climb the final wall with help from a Yew.

BUTTONHOLE SLAB

This outcrop in actually in the Upper Dene, but it is more easily reached from Castle Bridge by following the path beside the main stream in an upstream direction for several hundred metres until two large boulders are reached on the left of the path. Above and to the right is:

7 Buttonhole Slab 12m S
Start below a small buttress of conglomerate with a pleasant slab to the left at a niche reached by scrambling. Step left to avoid the bulging conglomerate and climb the slab in the corner. Step left and delicately climb the slab into an ill-defined groove to the finish.

From here it is about five hundred metres upstream to Marshmallow Wall, a gently overhanging wall of pocketed dolomite on the South side of the beck. The path goes immediately below it. Just upstream of this is Jacob's Ladder, Gunner's Pool and The Trossachs Gorge.

UPPER DENE

The climbs are described crag by crag from left to right.

THE TROSSACHS GORGE

This is the first area walking downstream from the A19. The path skirts the gorge on either side but it is quite simple to enter on foot. Facing downstream, the sunny left wall of the gorge consists of steep, slabby walls of rock, now vegetated but formerly cleaned. These attain a height of twenty five metres. The right wall is a bluff of very overhanging pocketed rock, some of which is good. Roofs and traverse lines are in abundance and it is an excellent area for all-weather traverses.

Downstream, the gorge narrows to produce a unique rift over twenty five metres high which can be straddled at its base. This rift is bridged by a metal suspension bridge which gives excellent views of the gorge and the big cliff; Jacob's Ladder.

LEFT WALL

At the upstream end of this slabby wall is a deep, right-facing corner.

8 Something 12m HVD ★
Start at the foot of the right-facing corner. Climb a runnel to a tree. Back and foot up the chimney and pull out left onto the arete. Finish up a short wall.

9 Extra Something 15m HS 4b ★
A pleasant and delicate face climb. Start as for Something. Climb the runnel to the tree. Ascend the right wall of the chimney and continue up a crack past a bulge. The delicate slab on the right is followed to a tree.

To the right is a steep slab with a mossy streak on it.

10 Old Stranton 18m VS 4b ★
Excellent rock when you find it. A good climb. Start just right of the mossy streak by climbing the slab to a tree. Continue up a short rib to a small tree. Step right and climb a pleasant slab, moving right slightly to finish.

11 Yew Turn 25m HS 4a ★
A very pleasant climb on reasonable rock. Start to the right of Old Stranton. Climb the wall direct on good holds via a huge Yew tree. Finish at a crack containing a jammed block, as for Old Stranton.

12 The Sting 25m VS 4b ★
Open climbing on good rock. Start 4m right of Old Stranton below and left of a small cave at 4m. Climb the wall to the left of the cave and follow holds directly up the wall to an overhang. Climb the overhang (crux) and reach the top.

To the right is a face of excellent rock, covered in Ivy. Just right of this is a ledge below a fine wall reached by scrambling up some 8m. The wall is identified by a fine flake crack at its right-hand end.

13 Gnat 7m VS 4b
Start at the extreme left end of the wall from the ledge below a clean strip of rock below the left fork of a hanging Yew. Climb the wall to the left of a very shallow scoop to a tree. Lower off.

14 Moss Mania 7m VS 4b
Climb the very shallow scoop in the steep wall right of Gnat. Lower off the hanging Yew.

15 Lucky Lemon 7m S
Start directly beneath a thin tree on a ledge at 6m. Climb the wall to the right-hand end of a narrow ledge. Nice climbing leads to the slender tree.

16 Striptease Wall 11m MVS 4b ★★
A fine wall climb on positive holds. Start at the foot of the steep wall, 2m left of the fine corner, flake crack. Climb on small holds to a horizontal break. Move up past a small overlap to a little Rowan and finish direct to a tree.

17 Nothing 14m HS 4b   ★★
Climb the fine crack in its entirety. Varied and well-protected climbing on superb rock.

18 The Necker 14m HVS 4c
A steep and commiting wall climb with some dubious rock. Start a 2m right of Nothing. climb the wall with small wires for protection.

19 Dirty Trick 12m VS 4c
Start 14m right of Nothing below a break in the upper bulge which is in the form of a left- pointing flake. Climb to the bulge and through the break. Climb direct to a big tree.

20 The Devil's Rising 62m VS 5a   ★
An unusual and exciting expedition particularly if the stream is running high. This canyon descent starts above the first waterfall at the upstream end of the narrowing gorge. Traverse the left wall at a constant level to a short corner. Descend this almost to water level and straddle the gorge until more holds appear. Continue on the left wall over the next waterfalls and continue on excellent rock throughout to exit in the amazing cauldron below the arete of Archangel on Jacob's Ladder.

RIGHT WALL
The right wall of The Trossachs Gorge is grossly undercut, with overhanging walls and roofs above.

21 Sweet P.A. 14m A2
Climb the centre of the first wall on the right side of the gorge. Poor placements.
At the left end of the continuously overhanging wall is a weakness near the top in the form of some left-slanting flanges. Right of this at the top of the crag is an overhung bay or recess.

22 Devil's Advocate 14m E3 5b
Start directly below the overhung bay. Climb the intermittent corner up to the bay then finish by traversing right beneath the roofs. Steep and poorly protected.

23 Original Sin 12m E3 5c   ★
Audacious and bold. Start 2m right of a thin tree growing at the top of the crag and below the obvious flanges which are the means of escape at the top. Climb steeply up the overhanging wall to a poor resting place. Climb left on good holds until a move up right gains a large pocket (thread). Climb powerfully up left on the flanges until the crux brings the top to hand.

24 Aeschylus 8m VS 4c
This awkward and poor climb starts some metres downstream below a crack which opens out into a groove. Climb onto a ledge above the stream and climb the crack, moving right to a small ledge on the right wall. Finish up the wall.
The next crag Jacob's Ladder is best reached by following the path above the North side of The Trossachs Gorge and at the suspension bridge, bear left and descend an easy chimney via steps to reach Gunner's Pool.

JACOB'S LADDER

The most impressive piece of rock by far in the area. Jacob's Ladder presents a big overhanging face rising forty metres above Gunner's Pool. The left end of the face is a monolithic sweep of white rock climbed by Suicide Wall whilst the middle of the face is somewhat grassy. The rock just left of the right-hand arete of Archangel must surely present a challenge for high standard free climbing as must Suicide Wall?

25   Suicide Wall   31m   A2   ★
Start at a big, dirty flake from the shingle at the left side of Gunner's Pool. Climb this flake and peg the prominent thin flake in the wall above. A diagonal break leads right to a stance on a small ledge. The left-slanting gangway is free climbed until the wall above via a letterbox can be climbed with aid.

26   Guano   40m   E1   5a
A powerful, serious and intimidating climb up the big central wall identified by a cave at the top. Start from the shingle beach below a right-slanting flake. Climb the flake and wall above on suspect rock until a traverse right gains a ledge and tree. The steep wall above leads to an easier slab and the cave. Stance and peg belays (not in place). Climb the corner above the left side of the cave to the top (Peg runner not in place).

27   Archangel   30m   VS   4c   ★★★
The best route in the area. It follows the fine arete on the right of the main face. Start in the dark cauldron round the corner from the main face below a steep slab of pocketed rock right of the arete. Climb the slab moving leftwards to the knife-edged arete. Climb this to a bulge and good resting place beneath a bigger bulge (thread). Climb the bulge on its right side and continue up a shallow groove in an awe-inspiring position. Swing strenuously right to a tree and the top.
Another climb Diminishing Returns VS 4c climbs the dirty wall of the cauldron right of the start of Archangel. It finishes up a prominent crack.

Downstream of Jacob's Ladder the path soon passes under a steep honeycombed wall which has a deep corner on its right:

MARSHMALLOW WALL

This wall has a maximum height of ten metres of excellent rock. The finishes above this are insecure. Anchors at the top of the good rock would protect the upper vegetation fron erosion.

28   Scrugg's Wall   12m   NL   5b   ★
Start below the middle of the steep wall left of the blunt overhanging left arete of the corner.
Climb the wall and thin crack on jugs and pull over onto an easier angled wall above. Finish with care.

29   Marshmallow Diedre   12m   HVS   5a   ★
Climb the corner(peg runner not in place) and continue delicately up the wall and into a dirty scoop on the left. Finish up this.

NESBITT DENE   O.S. SHEET 93   G.R. 472370, 465370 and 443377

SITUATION AND CHARACTER

The most Southerly of the Durham Denes and a wilder proposition than Castle Eden Dene. The paths are narrow and the vegetation dense. Exposures of Magnesian limestone occur throughout the length of the valley but only three areas have seen any development. These are:

1   The Lower Dene, sometimes called Crimdon Dene.
2   The Middle Dene just South of Benridge.
3   Jack's Rock in the Upper Dene below the village of Hesleden.

APPROACHES AND ACCESS

Approaches are given with the separate areas. Access is no problem as Public Rights Of Way exist for the crags in the Middle Dene and at Jack Rock. The climbs in Crimdon Dene have caused no problems and the approach described should be adhered to.

HISTORICAL

The crags in Nesbitt Dene were first climbed upon by Stew Wilson and Steve Gretton in May 1963. They climbed Josiah and Hezekiah and later with Ken Jones, Charisma was added.

Stew and Stan Shout made a nocturnal ascent of Nightmare in October 1964 and Neil Stewart climbed Churchill. The routes on Jack Rock were climbed in 1966. Wilson climbed Lavaredo Wall and Jack In The Corner and Geoff Harper added Bramble Wall.

THE LOWER DENE: CRIMDON DENE

Crimdon Dene is best approached by turning left (West) off the A1086 at the Seagull Inn and parking on the side of the road one mile further on where a marked Public Footpath descends into the Dene via Benridge Farm. Follow the path which can be muddy, past the farm and a couple of small lakes to reach a disused railway line. Turn left and follow the old line through a cutting until it crosses Crimdon Beck.Scramble down the side of the bridge parapet to the left (East) and follow the beck downstream to reach the first crag; Ramp Crag on the left after two hundred metres.

RAMP CRAG

A sunny, open crag of brecciated Reef Limestone providing a few steep and easy but exciting climbs. The rock is in the form of protruding blocks and needs careful handling.

THE CLIMBS

These are described from left to right ie. from the upstream end.

1   The Ramp   31m   HVD   ★
An easy ascending left-trending traverse.
Start fom a small ledge in the centre of the crag at 4m.Traverse horizontally leftwards across the face for 9m to where the face curves round beyond a rounded rib. Ascend diagonally upwards to finish at a large tree.

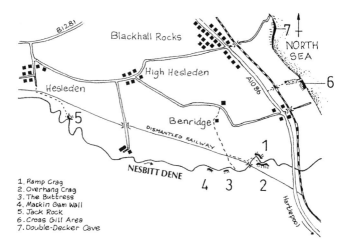

Blackhall Rocks

B1281

High Hesleden

Hesleden

Benridge

DISMANTLED RAILWAY

NESBITT DENE

A1086

NORTH SEA

Hartlepool

1. Ramp Crag
2. Overhang Crag
3. The Buttress
4. Mackin Gam Wall
5. Jack Rock
6. Cross Gill Area
7. Double-Decker Cave

2 Mortuary Wall 11m MVS 4a   ★
Steep and interesting. Start fom the ledge 4m above the stream in
the centre of the crag. Move diagonally upwards to the right on
good holds for 3m to a recess (runners). Step left to below the
obvious break at the top of the crag. Climb through this groove
direct on good holds.

3 En Hiver 11m HVD
Start as for Mortuary Wall. Traverse horizontally right for 4m to a
small tree. Climb direct to a small cave on good holds and exit
above with care.

*Continuing downstream for a short distance and just beyond a steep
bend in the stream, the Overhang Crag is on the South side of the
beck.*

THE OVERHANG CRAG

This has a very big roof at its left-hand end. The walls on either side
of the roof are composed of a harder and much more compact
limestone than the Ramp Crag.

THE CLIMBS

These are described from left to right ie. starting at the downstream
end.

4 Charisma 8m HVS 5a   ★
A good strenuous climb. Start just right of a bulging rib at the
extreme left end of the crag left of the roof. Traverse left above a
pool to the rib. Climb the bulge into a concave recess and follow
the bulging rock above to a tree.

5 Bulger 8m A1
Start below the overhanging wall 3m right of the rib of Charisma.
Climb two bulges to finish near Charisma. (4 pegs). Will definitely
go free!

6 Churchill 12m A3   ★★
A very fine aid climb with difficult placements which climbs the
Main Overhang. Start from the right side of the roof at a vertical

wall. Climb the wall free, to gain the roof. Follow a line of expanding flakes until improving rock leads to the lip.

7 Josiah 10m HVS 5b ★★
Start 6m right of the narrow, vertical first wall of Churchill at a conspicuous barrier of roofs above head height. Pull over this barrier on indifferent holds to a resting place. Move right onto the clean rib and climb this direct to an overlap. Step left with difficulty to gain a protruding ledge and finish at a tree.
Direct Finish: (5b) From the resting ledge above the initial roof, climb direct up the shallow groove to finish direct onto the projecting ledge.

8 Nightmare 14m VS 4b ★
Start to the right of the smooth wall right of Josiah wher a slight rib meets the stream.
Climb the rib to a loose ledge and step up to the right (thread). Climb direct on awkwardly- placed holds to a small overlap. Step left and finish up a groove to a tree.

9 Hezekiah 11m VS 5b
Start at the extreme right end of the crag where a bulging and friable wall rises out of a deep pool. Traverse left just above the deep pool (crux). From the centre of the face, the wall above is followed to the top.

10 The Primrose Way 40m VS 5a ★★
A left to right girdle of the crag.
Start at the foot of the narrow, right-slanting wall as for Churchill. Climb this and swing round the rib on the right. Gain the resting ledge of Josiah via a strenuous hand traverse. Move right and step delicately across the rib to gain the obvious ledge which crosses the smooth wall to reach Nightmare by the thread runner. Finish up Nightmare.

THE MIDDLE DENE: NESBITT DENE

This is approached as for Crimdon Dene, but at the disused railway line, cross over and follow good paths down into the dene to arrive at some brick buildings. Continue upstream until the valley narrows and a slim buttress is found just above the stream on the South side.

THE BUTTRESS

This is the first decent bit of rock encountered. It has a short corner at the top and provides one climb:

11 Pagan's Penance 12m HS 4b ★
A good climb on sound rock. From the toe of the buttress, easy but steep rock leads to a steep groove. Climb this exiting up a steep wall on the left.

MAKIN' GAM' WALL

A few metres upstream on the same side is a wonderful little crag of good rock about 8m high. It is in the form of a petrified wave and could produce some first-class high-standard bouldering and micro-routes.

12   Makin' Gam'   8m   A1
Start from a table-like platform under the centre of the roof. Climb the obvious right-slanting line to finish through a buttocks-like cleft at the top. (4 pegs).

A few metres upstream on the other side of the stream is a big, loose buttress with one climb going up the wall just left of the central, overhanging area: The Temptress (VS 4c).

THE UPPER DENE: JACK ROCK

This imposing prow of generally good quality overhanging rock up to twenty five metres high stands atop a bank above a meander.Facing South-West it is sunny and dries very quickly, even in winter. Of all the crags in this area it certainly could produce a good arena for "Sport Climbing" It is best approached from the village of Hesleden by continuing along the road past Benridge for a further two miles. In Hesleden, turn down East Terrace just beyond the Primary School. Cars can be parked near the disused railway line. Follow the railway line in an Easterly direction for about one hundred metres until a field boundary on the right can be followed above the wooded edge of the dene. Follow this boundary until it bends then strike down into the dene twenty metres beyond this bend. The crag lies directly below on a meander in the stream. It is easily recognised by its fierce appearance and its position high above the stream. Time from Hesleden: Ten minutes.

THE CLIMBS

These are described from left to right facing the crag.

13   Bramble Wall   15m   VS   4b
Serious and poorly protected. Start just left of the point where the undercut base of the crag peters out. Climb a small V- groove and follow vague depressions up the wall to the top.

14   Lavaredo Wall   25m   VS   4c   *
Start at the foot of an easy, left-trending gangway 4m left of a cave at the right end of the crag. Climb easily up the gangway to an overhanging corner. Pull out left and gain the top of the corner. From here move up a steep wall via a suspect block to gain a short slab of superb rock up which the climb finishes.

15   Jack In The Corner   8m   HVS   5a   *
Start 3m left of the cave below a thin crack in the overhanging wall. Climb this wall to gain the corner which is followed more easily to the top.

BLACKHALL ROCKS   O.S. SHEET 93   G.R. 471390 and 476380

SITUATION AND CHARACTER

Blackhall Rocks is eight miles North West of Hartlepool and lies between Castle Eden and Crimdon Denes on the coast. The rocks rise to a height of fifteen metres but finishes are awful and so the best use of the area is for bouldering.

The rock at the level of the beach is excellent pocketed dolomite, not up to the same standard as The Cove at Marsden but similar. Here the accent is upon long pumpy traverses and short overhanging walls and roof problems all with excellent landings.. The headlands are riven with caves and whilst some are rather dank, others offer roof problems of all difficulties. There is a lot of rock and so two areas have been selected as representative. Both offer good bouldering and are easily reached. The most Northerly area is Double-Decker Cave whilst Cross Gill is a half mile further South.

APPROACHES AND ACCESS

CROSS GILL AREA: Follow the A1086 coast road past Crimdon Dene and park a couple of hundred metres past the Seagull Inn. On the East side of the road a path leads across a field to pass under the railway line via a short tunnel. After passing under the railway line, descend directly down a steep valley to the sea. This is Cross Gill and as one nears the beach the walls of the gill become rocky. Facing the mouth of the Gill from the seaward end, the rock face on the left provides good problems on sound rock and further left a large cave has problems on both sides of it.

DOUBLE DECKER CAVE AREA

Continue on the A1086 past the Seagull Inn for a further mile until a crossroads is reached. Turn right and follow the narrow road through houses until it passes under the railway and swings steeply left continuing through open fields to a parking place above the very steep "Dead Man's Bank", named after the fate of the old seacoal gatherers who tried to push their too- heavily laden bikes up the bank.

Descend the bank and turn right at the bottom and follow the beach passing a small gill whose steep walls of good rock provide excellent problems up to 5c, until a cave-riven headland is reached. At the far side of this isThe Double-Decker Cave which has an archway running across it.

Many problems involve gaining the top of this arch at various points. To the left of Double-Decker Cave an overhanging shallow cave provides good sport and the prominent arete on the left; Stepped Arete goes at a loose Severe. The headland to the right of the Double-Decker cave contains a prominent concave,slabby scoop. This is The Fisherman's Seat (VD). The right wall of the Fisherman's Seat is Pater Noster (VS 4c).

An excellent sea-level traverse (Castle Traverse 4b), starts on the steep wall below and right of the Double-Decker Cave. Climb this until level with the Fisherman's Seat and traverse right, crossing the scoop. Beyond, the traverse is regained and followed to a flat shelf. Walk across this and swing right across the wall to the right.

HARTLEPOOL HEADLAND   O.S. SHEET 93
G.R. 532 338; 532 337; 531 336; 527 334

SITUATION AND CHARACTER

Situated on Hartlepool Headland overlooking the sea, the varied faces of mainly man-made origin provide excellent bouldering in the form of short walls up to 6m high and a host of difficult and strenuous traverses.

In one or two places the walls are constructed of monolithic blocks of gritstone and these provide routes of up to 12m with in-situ peg protection. The situation is most pleasant and am afternoon or evening can be combined with all the pleasures that a seaside location can give.

APPROACHES AND ACCESS

Hartlepool Headland is well-signposted from all directions and basically only has one main road leading onto this peninsula (more accurately it is a tombolo; an island of hard Magnesian Limestone attached to the mainland by a spit of sand). Follow this road until the bus station is reached. At the bus station, turn left into High Street and park near Verrills Fish and Chip shop beside the imposing church of St. Hilda.Walk South from here to reach the Fish Sands via Sandwell Chare which is an arched gate through the mediaeval walls leading onto the beach. From here onwards, the coast can be followed in an anticlockwise direction via a prom- enade above and below which are all the bouldering locations.

HISTORICAL

A valuable training amenity for local climbers before the advent of indoor walls. Most of the routes were climbed and recorded by lads from the local Henry Smith School in the 1960's and 70's. Richard Kirby added the peg protected routes on the big wall just North of the Heugh Breakwater in 1987.

FISH SANDS AREA

The bouldering here is located on either side of Sandwell Chare, the arched gate leading onto the beach. To the left are buttresses on dolomite blocks which provide routes up slabs onto the top of the town wall.

The best wall hereabouts is immediately right of the gate and this vertical wall of beautifully pocketed limestone provides some fairly extended problems rising from the silky, white sand of the beach.

To the right of this wall and just left of the set of steps leading down onto the Pilots Pier from The Harbour public house, is a fine groove; Hells Groove which can be climbed at 5b. The arete and wall to its right is 5c.

BLOCK SANDS WALL

Following the promenade anticlockwise from the Fish Sands one passes under a canopy (finger- traverses!) to arrive at a paddling pool with a wall behind it at a higher level.

This wall provides many vertical problems as well as a "super-traverse" which goes at about 5b/c and is not often completed in one push. The traverse is usually done from right to left with the crux near the right-hand end. The Kirkham Hotel is directly above.

HEUGH WALL

To reach Heugh Wall, ascend the steps at the right-hand end of Block Sands Wall and turn right passing above the Heugh Wall until a slope opposite the end of the War Memorial Gardens leads down onto the shingle beach below the wall.

This is the biggest wall on the Headland and appears to be concave in profile. It is made up of huge blocks of Gritstone and holds are found both on the edges of the blocks and on the faces so climbing is almost like on a crag.

The routes are described from left to right and are all about 12m high and exceptional lead training. All have in-situ peg protection which should be inspected before use.

1   Don't Stop The Dance   12m   E2   5b   ★★
Two in-situ peg runners (red and blue tat). Start directly below first peg. Climb to the first peg then gain the second peg before moving slightly right to gain the top.

2   T.N.T.   12m   E2   5c   ★★
Start 2m right of the pocket at one third height. Traverse to the pocket (Friend 2) and then move up to a peg runner (red tat). Climb direct to the top. A direct start is possible at 5c.

3   Brain Drain   12m   E1   5b   ★★
Start as for T.N.T. Trend right to a peg runner (white tat) then up to a second peg runner (purple tat) and finish direct.

4   Hot Tuna   12m   E3   5c/6a   ★★
Start almost 5m right of Brain Drain below a peg with yellow tat. Move up to a rippled jug and trend left (wires for protection) . Climb strenuously to the peg above (crux) and finish direct.

5   Infected   12m   E3   5c   ★★
Start 6m right of Hot Tuna. Move up to a peg then right to another peg. Climb up and slightly right to a good jug and finish direct.

Moving right beyond the foot of the access slope and crossing slippery rocks one comes to another wall of dolomite blocks just right of the line of the top of the slope.

6   Nostromo   12m   HVS   5a   ★
Start on a steep wall below a left-facing shallow corner above a long ledge halfway up the wall. Climb the steep wall to the ledge. Ascend the corner and move right onto the wall to finish at the railings.

7   Stan's Route   12m   HVS   5a   ★
Several metres right of Nostromo an obvious buttress protrudes from the sea walls. This is part of the old cliff-line reinforced with concrete. Start below the centre of the buttress. Climb the wall on pockets and ledges until a delicate move gains the easier slab above. finish up the bulging capstone above.

THE BATTERY WALLS

These walls lie a further 100 metres further round from Heugh Walls and beyond the lighthouse. The walls, a mixture of fissured concrete, gritstone and natural limestone all rise out of the promenade and provide excellent bouldering.

CONCRETE WALL 1

Starts in the corner under the slope above which is an old cannon and a memorial to the First Soldier Killed On British Soil in the Great War.

Various vertical lines making use of cracks in the concrete and drain holes. The best is a layback up a thin concrete edge at 5c.

EASY WALL

At the end of Concrete wall 1 is a wall of sandstone blocks. Up and down routes up to 4b and several good traverses.

HARD WALL

Just right of Easy Wall is a similar but harder wall whose right-hand end consists of a wall topped by a concrete slab. Climb up and down anywhere from 5b to 6a. The traverse is a testing 5c.

FRACTURED WALL

To the right of the Hard Wall is a concrete wall with a 5c and two 6a problems following the only breaks.

BOG WALL

A few metres right of Fractured Wall, facing across an open area of promenade which formerly housed a bandstand. It consists of overhanging and dirty limestone topped by a slope on the left and a series of grooves and wall in the middle. The right-hand end is limestone topped by yet another slope. Many problems exist from 4c to 5c.

8   TEESDALE

The majestic valley of the River Tees upstream of Barnard Castle along with the high moors to the South West, extending across to the A66 at Bowes Moor host a variety of crags. The most famous of these is Goldsborough Carr, whose long history of climbing includes such names as Bentley Beetham. Goldsborough provides superb climbing of all standards on excellent Gritstone with a choice of orientations to suit the wind and weather. Holwick Scar provides climbing on Dolerite, similar to Crag Lough on the Roman Wall, but unfortunately access is difficult. An unusual venue is Catcastle Quarry which has one of the best routes in the North of England; Black Cat. To the North of the river, Gritstone outcrops again at Pallet Crag whilst Limestone climbing can be sought near Middleton-in-Teesdale on Jack Scar. The scenery of Teesdale is varied, even spectacular at High Force and this in itself makes a visit worthwhile.

CATCASTLE QUARRY   O.S. Sheet 92   G.R. 013 164

SITUATION AND CHARACTER

Situated on the South side of the Rigg above the pleasant valley of Deepdale, one and a half miles South of Lartington, these open faces of quarried gritstone are a very attractive venue. The quarried grit up to eighteen metres high faces South. The Western end of the quarry is best and the face above the Westerly of two pools contains a gritstone classic; Black Cat.

The rock at Catcastle is variable but this is only a problem when combined with a lack of protection. The monolithic nature of the rock however does make protection hard to arrange on some climbs. This accounts for the number of climbs that have been top-roped rather than led.

APPROACHES AND ACCESS

The quarry can be approached in two ways, either from the minor road which crosses the Rigg between Bowes and Cotherstone or via a shorter walk from Lartington. The longer approach has the advantage in that Low Crag and Deepdale Crag can be visited en route.

Lartington is reached on the B6277 from either Cotherstone or Barnard Castle and at the junction in the village by the church, take the minor road going West. Follow for about a mile to a T-junction and turn left. Go uphill for less than a mile and park on the roadside where a bridleway leads over Crag Hill via Low Crag and Deepdale. The disused Catcastle Quarry lies about 300 metres East of Deepdale Crag and near to a Caravan Site.

The short approach is to leave Lartington on foot. From the road junction by the church, follow a track signposted to Catcastle Quarry which leads along the disused railway line, Southwards.

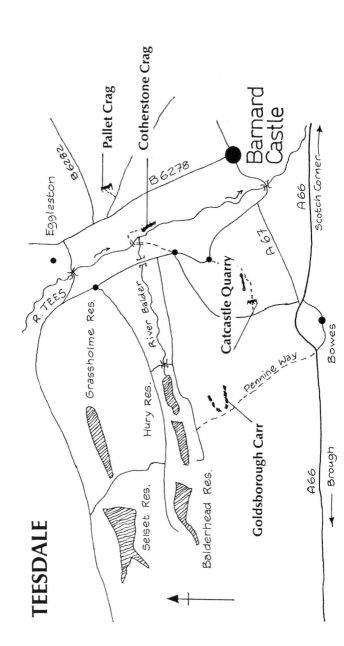

The permission of the Quarry owner who lives in a caravan in the trees above the working quarry should be sought to climb in the old quarry. Many do not observe this courtesy if approaching from Deepdale, but access is usually granted and a civil approach should prevent problems arising.

The disused quarry is reached by walking through a small caravan park just before a demolished viaduct.

HISTORICAL

The first recorded route at Catcastle Quarry was the prominent arete; Brigantes' Retreat, at the right-hand end of the Western pool climbed by Geoff Milburn in May 1962. More recently Tris. Kenny climbed Conquss and Nick. Clement added Choss Wall. The rest of the routes climbed between 1981 and 1983 are the work of Paul Carling, the best being the magnificent Black Cat.

THE CLIMBS

The quarry consists of several walls set at angles to each other.

The West end is a steep wall taken by Swamp Crack whilst right of this are walls behind the left-hand pool which culminate in the steep, cracked wall above the right-hand end of the pool taken by Black Cat.

Next to the right is the easy arete of Brigante to the right of the pool. The wall to the East of this arete has the prominent Rubic's Groove whilst right again is an easy descent. Beyond the easy descent is Choss Wall. The climbs are described from Right to Left. Maximum height is 18 metres.

1   Choss Wall   5c
Climb the short wall right of the descent route.

2   Conquss   HS   4b
Start below cracks, 2m left of the easy, stepped arete. Climb the cracks.

3   Gritstone Bugaboo   E1   5b
Start left of Conquss below a faint weakness in the blank wall. Climb the faint weakness to a horizontal break (peg runner; not in situ). Make a hard move onto the glacis above and finish up the groove.

4   Mantichore   HVS   5b
Climb the thin parallel cracks to a prominent ledge. Finish up the arete.

5   Rubic's Groove   E2   5c   ★
Climb scrappy rock to a ledge, move left and climb the prominent V-groove.Poorly protected.

6   Brigantes' Retreat (Milburns' Route)   HVD
Climb the slabby rib just right of the pool. Traverse left and climb the arete to finish.

7   Black Cat   E1   5b   ★★★
One of the best climbs in the area. A magnificent route which on its own justifies a visit from far away. Well-protected. Start at the right hand side of the pool and traverse left to a ledge 3m above the water. Climb round onto the face and follow the thin crack to the top.

The next two routes are best reached from above by abseil. Fence posts can provide anchors or good nuts can be arranged a long way back at the top of the descent. Those unable to climb out will be faced with either a long and thorny traverse or a swim in the foetid waters of the pool.

8   Science Friction   E2   6a   ★
Start on a ledge beneath the overhanging corner to the left of Black Cat. Move right and up to a sapling and flat holds. Move slightly left and make a series of trying moves up to an in-situ peg runner. Finger traverse left and finish behind the tree.

The wall to the left impends. At the left-hand end is a feature reminiscent of a face in profile. The "face" has a prominent white "eye".

9   Face Route   NL   5c
Climb the profile of the "face" until level with the "eye". Move left and climb the wall just right of the left edge.

The next five climbs lie on the clean, prominent wall to the left (West) of an area of vegetated rock. All can be reached by descending the grassy rake in the Western corner of the quarry, however the next two climbs are best reached by abseil.

10   Overlord   NL   5b   ★
A strenuous, unprotected route with some suspect rock. Start at the steepest point of the buttress at a line of weakness. Climb the weakness until the wall steepens. Move left to a dusty ledge. Move up right and Hand-Traverse right into an open bay. Climb the left wall above to friendly, hand jams and a not-so-friendly finish.

11   Icarus   NL   5a
Climb the friable crack behind the Rowan tree, it becomes easier towards the top.

12   Warlord   NL   5c
Start at the short crack to the right of Icarus. The crack leads to a diabolical Hand-Traverse into Icarus.

From the bottom of the grassy rake a short traverse across easy rock leads to a grass ledge some 4m above the pool.

13   The Wilderness Years   VS   4c   ★★
Start from the grass ledge. Climb the triangular, rock cone above the ledge and move onto a ledge above (thread runner in shot holes). Step left around the arete. Move up and exit with difficulty from beneath the prominent tree.

14   Twizzle   NL   5c
Start at the bottom of the rake below two, short, sharp aretes running up into a small roof. Wide bridging enables a poor hold to be gained above the roof. Using this and even wider bridging gain a ledge via a mantelshelf. Move right then back left to finish directly above the start.

15   Intro Slab   D
Near the top of the rake is a solitary Birch tree. Climb the clean slab below this.

16   Swamp Crack   HS   ★
Climb the prominent crack in the dank, left wall of the quarry. This is excellent when dry!

DEEPDALE ROCKS   O.S. SHEET 92   G.R. 010163

SITUATION AND CHARACTER

These four, pleasant Gritstone buttresses up to 7metres high give limited bouldering and short lines where a rope may be useful. The rocks face South in a wooded location and are part of the same outcropping as Catcastle Quarry which is only a further 300 metres East.

To the West on the South side of Crag Hill on a Public Right Of Way is Low Crag, a buttress of Gritstone which has a pleasant Severe climb on it.

APPROACHES AND ACCESS

The crag can be reached by a pleasant, four minute walk West of Catcastle Quarry through woods following the rocky edge. Alternatively the long route of approached as described for Catcastle Quarry avoiding the Caravan Site can be followed. Cars can be parked North of Nova Scotia! The crags are on Public Rights Of Way and there are no access problems.

HISTORICAL

The recorded routes are the work of Paul Carling.

THE CLIMBS

The present climbing is located on the left hand, most Westerly buttress. Just right of a short, easy chimney is:

1   Rooster Booster   6m   VS   5a   ★
Climb the blind crack in the wall via a series of nice moves.

2   Winter's Tale   6m   E1   6a   ★
Start just right of Rooster Booster. Climb a line of holds which leads strenuously round an overhang. Turn the last overhang on the left.

COTHERSTONE CRAG   O.S. SHEET 92   G.R. 018 198

SITUATION AND CHARACTER

Cotherstone Crag is a small outcrop of variable quality sandstone on the North Bank of the River Tees about four miles North West of Barnard Castle.The crag faces South West and is in a lovely situation in woodland adjoining the river. The crag has never been particularly popular on account of loose rock but the new routes have been cleaned from above and should provide better climbing with a re-clean as many have not had second ascents. Loose rock can be a problem but should disappear from the more popular routes with a bit of traffic. Avoid the crag after prolonged rain as it can be dirty due to run-off.

APPROACHES AND ACCESS

From the West side of the River Tees in Barnard Castle, take the B6277 in a North-Westerly direction to Cotherstone. In Cotherstone, leave the village green and follow a lane opposite the pub to a field, where parking is possible. Continue on foot, crossing the River Balder via a bridge and then crossing the River Tees, again by a footbridge. Turn right across a field following a Public Right of Way. The crag is visible at the far side of the field. During periods of low flow, it is possible to reach the crag via the river's edge but during high flow, a gully at the far end can be descended from the path above. The gully is reached by following the Public Right of Way above the crag until it crosses a drystone wall at a stile. The descent is slightly further on, on the other side of a wire fence, which must not be damaged. The crag is on land owned by the farm on the hill above, next to the caravan site. Climbers are tolerated and access is no problem. The farmer however was not impressed when the wire fence above the crag was broken down.

HISTORICAL
Nothing is known of the early history of the crag, although the line of Solidarity was originally pegged. The climbs recorded in the first edition of the North of England guide were the work of Paul Ingham and Tony McClean. In 1981, Paul Carling added a further thirteen climbs, the best of which were Sandshoes, Solidarity and the excellent Phreatic Wall.

THE CLIMBS
The climbs are described from left to right.

LEFT-HAND BUTTRESS
This is the small buttress at the left-hand end of the crag.

1   Gibsneeze   8m   VD
Ascend the crack in the centre of the buttress.

MAIN WALL
The main part of the crag alternating fairly continuously, steep walls and grooves.

2   Grotty Groove   11m   S
Start at the left end of Main Wall below a shallow groove. Climb this and the overlap. Move left up another groove to finish.

3   The Stang   9m   NL   5c
Climb the groove to the left of Lynesack to below a roof. Step up left to a ledge and move back right with difficulty over the overlap. Climb the steep corner to a Yew.

4   Lynesack   9m   S
Climb the crack containing a Yew, passing an overhang at the bottom.

Some metres right is an easy line with dangerously loose rock.

5   Pete's Arete   11m   HS   4b
Start below a crack left of the dangerous, easy line. Climb the crack to start and move onto the steep arete on the left.

6   Peathrow   9m   S
Start below the crack as for the last route. Climb the pleasant crack to the top.

7 Terminal Encounter 9m S
Start to the right of the dangerous, easy line below a groove capped by an overhang. Climb this, passing a Yew and at the roof step left round the corner, taking care with a loose block and pull up the wall to an earthy ledge. Climb twin cracks until good holds on the right lead to the top.

8 Sandshoes 9m E2 5c   ★★
A steep wall climb. Start below the arete right of Peathrow and the dangerous easy line. Climb the arete until a hard, unprotected move right into the centre of the wall gains a scoop above. Move left and climb the obvious flake above.

9 The Arcanum 11m S   ★
Start just left of an ivy mass on the wall and behind a mass of branches.Climb a series of good ledges trending left until steep moves right lead to a downward pointing sapling. Move slightly left into an earthy niche below a large Yew and climb the continuation groove above.

10 Nibor 11m HS
Start at the foot of an obvious left-facing groove which is often wet. Climb the groove to the top and pull over on a mass of tree roots to finish.

The wall to the right of Nibor is split by a thin crack leading to a small overlap. To the left of this crack is an arete.

11 Electra 11m E1 5c
Climb the arete between Nibor and Solidarity with trying moves to reach a tree. Swing up into the tree and follow the jam crack to finish up Solidarity.

12 Solidarity 11m E2 6a   ★★
Climb the thin crack by a series of technical moves and pull over the overlap. Easier climbing above leads to a large Oak at the top. Well-protected but some dubious rock.

13 Spider Corner 12m VS 4C
A good climb. Start below an obvious corner which becomes a short chimney near the top. Climb the corner to a small ledge and enter the chimney. An exit is made to the right onto the arete.

14 The Polack 11m HVS 5b   ★
Climb the the obvious V-groove/corner past a PR. A bold move right gains a jam crack behind an impending block. Scramble off or abseil descent.

15 Staindrop 11m MVS
A steep climb which starts just right of the obvious groove of The Polack. Climb up and rightwards on incut holds to where a steep section leads to a short groove. Climb the groove passing a tree.

16 Dire Straits 12m HVS 5b   ★
Start below an obvious corner which is normally wet. Climb this with a well-protected crux at half-height. Excellent when dry.

17 Gimcrack Groove 12m HVS 5b
Right of the groove of Dire Straits is an arete split at its base by a short, overhanging groove. Climb the arete and groove on the left. Continue more easily past a tree on the left of a roof. Well- protected.

18 Ug   12m   HS
To the right is a steep wall which has a jam crack leading to a tree at the top. Climb the steep wall to a ledge. Follow the crack on jams to the tree.

A rockfall in this vicinity makes the following climb less attractive.

19 Sharnberry   11m   HS
Climb the scrappy groove just right of a wet corner. Climb awkwardly over a horrible, loose overhang and continue up a groove to a loose, earthy finish. A Sport Climb.

20 Depeche Mode   11m   HVS   5a
Start below a thin crack leading to a small roof at three metres. Climb the crack and turn the roof on the left. Move back right to a ledge. The slabby ramp finishing up a dirty wall and groove. Runners can be placed in a chimney to the right.

To the right is an impressive, steep and relatively clean wall with a short, wet wall on its left.

21 Dane Geld   8m   VD
Climb the short wall direct or step right at half-height and finish up the corner.

22 Phreatic Wall   12m   E2   5c   ★★★
An excellent climb up the impressive wall. Start to the left of the crack of Nidip and hand-traverse to the left arete. Climb the arete until a hard move right (runner in tree and poor Friend placement) leads up a steep wall to a ledge. A fall just below the ledge could be serious. Finish up the crack on the left. A direct start is possible.

23 Nidip   9m   HS
Climb the crack in the right side of the impressive wall to an earth ledge. Continue straight up to the top.

24 Keverstone   8m   VD
Climb the square groove.

25 Stoned Woman   11m   HS
Start below the centre of the buttress right of the square groove. Climb the slab to the overhang which is climbed to a niche. Another overhang is passed on the right. Finish up a wide crack behind a tree.

26 Marwood   7m   VD
Climb the cracks on the last buttress.

PALLET CRAG   O.S. Sheet 92   GR 025 228

SITUATION AND CHARACTER

Pallet Crag consists of a more or less continuous edge of gritstone on a spur (Scroggs) of the Langley Beck two miles East of Eggleston. The crag faces North-North-East and has a very pleasant outlook. The prominent feature of the crag is a fine buttress of excellent quality rock which contains the best routes. To the left and right of the protruding main buttress are walls and slabs with some good but now, possibly dirty climbs. It is useful for a short day or evening and the routes on the main buttress are well-worth seeking out.

APPROACHES AND ACCESS

Take the B6278 for Eggleston from Barnard Castle and follow this for approximately five miles. Turn sharp right onto the B6279 about one mile short of Eggleston and follow this for approximately one and a quarter miles. Park on the left verge near a right hand bend with a wood on the right. The crag is visible over to the left above the little valley of Langley Beck. Do not attempt to climb the wall as access may be compromised. Instead, go through a gate on the Eggleston side of the bend. A track leads immediately to a shallow quarry, continue over rough land to reach the crag.

The crag is on land belonging to the Raby Estate who tolerate climbers. Although problems relating to vandalism (not by climbers!) have occured in the past.

HISTORICAL

The crag has been climbed on for a number of years by local climbers, but the origin of the ancient bolt on Kermit is unknown. Kermit was climbed by Paul Ingham whilst Roy Small climbed Miss Piggy in 1982. The other recorded climbs are the work of Paul Carling, Nigs Reader and Nigel Jones although some may have been climbed before.

THE CLIMBS

The climbs are described from left to right facing the crag.

1   Day Of Action   6m   D
Climb the obvious groove at the left-hand end of the crag.

2   Talisman   6m   HVS   5a
Climb the wall just right of Day Of Action.

3   The Swan   6m   HS   4b   ★
Climb the obvious curving crack to the right of Talisman.

The next climbs are on the Main Buttress which protrudes from the hillside.

4   The Hollow Hills   12m   VS   4c   ★★
Start left of the start of Miss Piggy/Kermit, on the left wall of the buttress below an obvious hanging flake. Climb a groove and ascend the obvious, hanging flake until a hard move can be made to gain a ledge on the left. Move right to finish.

5   Miss Piggy   14m   HVS   5b   ★★
Climb the blunt arete until stopped by an overhang. Step left onto a ledge and enter the shallow groove above. The upper buttress once gained, is climbed by its left arete to the top.

6   Kermit   14m   HVS   5b   ★★
The original route of the crag and still the best. Bold and exciting climbing but never too demanding. Climb the blunt arete as for Miss Piggy until stopped by the overhang. Move right beneath the bulge and pull over onto the wall above. Climb the upper buttress just left of the right-hand arete. The right wall of the buttress may have been climbed. Evidence of an ascent has been apparent but nothing has been recorded.

The crag to the right of the main buttress is a slabby wall, bounded on the right by a distinctive overhanging groove.

7   Shady Lady   9m   HS   4b
Climb the slab to the left of the overhanging groove. to a ledge.
Finish up the broken crack.

8   Little Mary   9m   VS   4c   ★
Climb the distinctive, overhanging groove to a ledge. Step right and
climb the cracked overhang.

9   Cracked Arete   9m   HS   4b
Climb the arete to the right of Little Mary, finishing leftwards on
Little Mary.

10   Dunroamin   6m   D
Climb the slab to the right of Cracked Arete.

11   Happy Hernia   6m   D
Climb the slab to the right of Dunroamin.

GOLDSBOROUGH CARR   O.S. SHEET 92   G.R. 954175

SITUATION AND CHARACTER

A pleasant outcrop of good quality gritstone in a similar mould to the
popular Slipstones Crag. A remote but idyllic situation which is
nevertheless close to the road.It is ideal for a family excursion or an
evening's bouldering with some excellent and very hard problems.

The crag is situated on the top of the table-topped Goldsborough.
Where the 'Carr' came into it is uncertain, a carr being an area of
wetland usually with Alders etc. It consists of a discontinuous line of
buttresses and boulders about half a mile in circumference around
the summit.The climbs are not very long,about 12 metres at the
most,but suitable climbing for both beginner and expert can be
found. Climbs vary between cracks and corners. In the modern
idiom there are steep 'pumpy' walls and gymnastic overhangs. A
choice of orientation makes sunshine(?) or shade an option. With
regard to grading, it is not easy to give an overall grade to short
problems but generally speaking a lower adjectival grade is given if
the hard moves are near the ground and you can jump off easily. At
Goldsborough, routes frequently ease higher up or have gear higher
up, so a high technical grade does not necessarily always justify a
high adjectival grade.

APPROACHES AND ACCESS

Goldsborough is best approached from Teesdale but it can be
reached from the West, by leaving the A66 at Brough and following
the B6276 past Windmore End and continuing for seven miles to a
right turn at the end of Selset reservoir. Follow this minor road,
ignoring junctions until a left at a junction leads to Hury. Pass
through Hury and after about three quarters of a mile, turn right and
cross the River Balder at the East end of Hury Reservoir. Turn right at
the next junction and follow the narrow road through West Briscoe.
Continue until at a left-hand bend the road goes uphill, climbing the
side of the fell with Goldsborough clearly visible on the left. A
parking place on the side of the road will be found and the North-
West buttress is reached by a short walk.The approach from Cotherstone in Teesdale is easier. Follow the B6277 going up the dale

from Cotherstone and turn left on a minor road to East Briscoe just before the main road crosses the River Balder.Continue through East Briscoe and West Briscoe as described

HISTORICAL

Goldsborough Carr has been climbed on for many years. Bentley Beetham the "Father of Borrowdale Climbing" came here regularly in the 1930's, in fact the Mountaineering section of Barnard Castle School where he taught was called the Goldsborough Club. No records of their exploits appear to have been kept.More recently visits by the more adventurous!!members of the Eden Valley M.C. resulted in most of the easier climbs prior to 1980.The best of this era were Fiddler Arete by Stew Wilson and Dave Bowen's Fiddler On The Roof. Unknown to the Eden Valley lads, Paul Carling from Barnard Castle and Nigs Reader were also active.The latter adding Motivation in 1980 whilst Carling contributed many fine problems such as Enigma, The Thornbird and Long Reach prior to 1982. Ian Cummins and Nick Clements made what they thought were first ascents but after checking the dates, it was Carling who stole the show. However Ian added the bold Green Nigel in 1983 and Nick Clements climbed the Scoop and Barney Boys in 1986.Nick Clements also climbed the direct start to Motivation naming it The Obsessed, he then moved right from here and claimed Viola. I hope he will forgive the merging of the two routes to provide Viola The Obsessed. Stu Ferguson made an ascent of Reader's Motivation in 1986 thinking that "Topal" was a new route. Stu also added Flymantle; a serious route. Nothing much remains now, but the line just right of Hubris will be hard.

THE CLIMBS

The climbs are located on the North-West Buttress which is the first rock reached on the walk up from the parking and on the South Side which is around the corner. The climbs are described from left to right.

NORTH-WEST BUTTRESS

1   Flymantle   5m   E2   5b
Climb the wall just left of Flakeaway to gain the right side of overhanging block. Hand-traverse out to the lip of the overhang and mantleshelf onto the top. Worrying!

2   Flakeaway   5m   VD
Climb the flake crack at the left side of the buttress and finish up a short crack just right of a large overhanging block at the top of the crag.

3   Scoon Crack   5m   S   4a
Climb the wall and crack to the left of the arete.

4   Scoon Arete   4m   MS   4a
Start just left of the arete and finish up this.

5   Wall Of Errors   5m   VS   5a   ★
Climb the wall just right of Scoon Arete with a difficult start.

6   Crackaway   5m   MS   4a
Climb the obvious wide crack right of Wall Of Errors.

7   Pocket Wall   5m   VS   4c   ★
Climb the wall right of Crackaway to gain pockets and the top.

8   Bentley's Arete   5m   VS   4c
Climb the imposing arete starting to the left and finish on either the right (easier) or left wall.

A vegetated central section now follows.

9   Briscoe Crack   5m   VS   4c
Start to the right of the system of ledges at a short crack. Climb the crack and move leftwards over an overhang to finish just left of a small prow at the top.

10   Howgill Wall   6m   VS   4c
Start below the bulging wall just right of Briscoe crack. Climb the short wall and a detached flake to gain a ledge. Move left then right up steep rock and finish over the summit bulge.

11   Pitcher Crack   5m   MS   4a
Climb the crack to the left of the rib which is found in the funnel/gully on the right side of the face.

12   Hagworm   5m   MVS   4b
Start right of the gully at a finger of rock below a prow. Climb the finger direct and move left to a ledge. The left side of the prow is climbed on good but awkwardly-spaced holds.

13   Friar Wall   5m   HS   4b
Climb the wall just right of the prow.

14   Tuck   3m   D
Climb the wide crack in the right side of the buttress.

Ten metres further right is an undercut slab with an overhang above it.

15   Wriggle Up   3m   HS   4b
Gain the undercut slab from below (hard) and move left over the overhang.

16   Blockton Way   3m   S   4b
Gain the right side of the slab and move right to finish.

17   Block And Tackle   3m   S   4b
Climb the overhang just right of the slab.

18   North-West Girdle   S   4b
Start at Flakeaway and traverse right to finish up Tuck.

SOUTH SIDE

BUTTRESS ONE

This is the buttress at the left side of the South Side. It is identified by a large flake leaning against the crag.

19   Y Crack   4m   VD
Climb the Y crack at the left side of the buttress.

20   Finger Crack   4m   HS   4c   ★★★
Climb the second crack which leans to the left. A lecture in fingerwork.

21   Ravock Chimney   4m   VD
Climb the obvious V chimney just right of Finger Crack. Hard to start.

A giant block holds the next two routes and some minor problems

22 Enigma 6m E1 6a   ★★
Start to the right of Ravock Chimney at a steep wall with a shallow groove. Pull onto the wall on the right of the groove, using the right arete and poor left handhold. Contrive to enter the groove on the left which is followed to the top.

24 Cotherstone Reiver 5m E1 5c
Gain the foothold on the wall left of Corner Crack by a precarious layback move and reach for the top.

25 Corner Crack 5m D
Climb the corner to the left of the flake leaning against the crag.

26 Flake And Crack 5m S 4b   ★
Climb the flake and the steep crack above.

27 Hubris 6m E1 5c   ★
Pull round the overhang right of Flake And Crack and finish up the wall above.

28 Cenopod Corner 5m VD
Climb the wide crack in the corner to the right of the overhang. This is the right hand of two right-facing corners.

29 Saturnalia 5m HVS 5b
Climb the wall right of Cenopod corner.

30 Hunder Crack 6m MS 4a
Towards the right end of this buttress are twin cracks to the left of an overhanging block. Climb the main (left hand) crack and the broken wall above.

31 Crawlaw 5m VD
Start as for Hunder Crack. Climb the main crack then move right and hand-traverse along the overhanging block to a short corner. Finish by a mantelshelf.

BUTTRESS TWO

A small buttress about eighteen metres right of Buttress One and separated from it by broken rocks.

32 Mawmon 5m S 4b
Climb the left arete of the small buttress to a ledge. Climb the wall above.

33 Stewart's Wall 5m VS 5b/c
Climb the short wall and overlap in the centre of the wall right of Mawmon. Finish directly above.

34 Yoke Sike 5m HS 4a   ★★
Climb the corner crack and the overhang on good holds. Climb the wall above to the top.
Variation Start: 4c
Climb the arete to the right of the corner.

35 Yawd Sike 5m MVS 4b   ★
Climb the steep wall two metres right of the corner. A long reach is an advantage.

36 Brown Rigg Flake 4m VD
Climb the flake crack at the right end of the buttress. A low traverse of Buttress Two has been done.(5c).

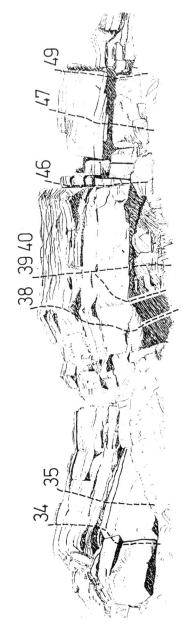

Goldsborough Carr

Buttresses 2 - 4

BUTTRESS THREE
The finest buttress on the crag which is just right of Buttress Two. It presents an impressive, roofed-prow with climbing on all three facets.

37   Battle Crack   5m   S   4a
Climb the undercut crack at the left side of the buttress.

38   Motivation   9m   HVS   5b   ★
The left side of Buttress 3 is undercut.Pull up at the obvious iron intrusions to reach good holds.Go straight up and right using small holds to finish on the arete.

39   Viola The Obsessed   10m   HVS   5c
A good route. Start below the overhung arete right of Motivation. Climb this on pockets and heelhooks and traverse the overhang along the break rightwards to finish up the final wall of Fiddler On The Roof.

40   Fiddler On The Roof   10m   E1   5c   ★★
A fine and intimidating pitch for such a small crag. It has stopped many in their tracks. The loss of a hold has caused an increase in difficulty. Start below a break in the middle of the roof a few metres right of the arete. Climb up to the roof and cross it using flakes that are not always good. A hold on the lip enables the upper easier, but not easy, wall to be climbed.

40a   Cotherstone Cheese is Fantastic   E3   6b/c   †
Climb roof via pocket just right of Fiddler

41   Green Nigel   12m   E2   6a   ★★
Pull round the roof as for The Thornbird and follow the ramp-line leftwards to finish delicately straight up,to the left of the green seepage line. A very fine climb.

42   The Thornbird   10m   E2   6a   ★★★
The outstanding route of the crag. Start six metres right of Fiddler On The Roof. Climb onto a ledge below the roof. Climb around the roof(hard)trending right on poor holds to reach a good jug. Continue directly up the wall to a faint crackline running up the steepest part of the buttress. Pull round the bulge at the crackline and finish steeply above.

43   The Long Reach   10m   E1   5c   ★★
A good route if you have the reach.Vexing if you do not! Right of The Thornbird gain the undercut arete left of Legless and climb this using layaways and a long reach to gain a ledge. Continue up the overhanging arete above.

44   Legless   10m   E2   6b   ★
Climb the bottomless groove right of the arete with difficulty to reach a grass ledge. Reach a jug just right of the arete, pull onto the wall and climb the arete to good finishing holds.

45   Gut Reaction   10m   HVS   5b
To the left of Tute Crack, gain the undercut arete using a hold on the wall to reach the ledge. Continue up the centre of the wall just left of Tute Crack.

46   Tute Crack   5m   S   4b
Abutting the right side of Buttress Three are three cracks. Climb the left crack to a ledge on the left and finish up the steep corner above.

BUTTRESS FOUR

The short but steep wall that separates Buttress Three fom the other impressive buttress; Buttress Five. Buttress four is undercut at its base.

47   Lockout 5m   VS   4c
Climb the undercut base just left of centre an ascend the steep wall above on small holds.

48   Borstal Breakout   6m   E1   6a
Start three metres right of Lockout and climb the undercut base onto the wall above. Finish directly up the wall.

49   Loup's Arete   5m   HS   4b
In the right arete of the buttress is a corner. Gain the corner with difficulty and climb it on good holds. It is possible to traverse the rounded break below Lockout. (5c).

BUTTRESS FIVE

An impressive buttress with an undercut base.

50   Maggie's Wall 5m   S   4a
Climb the wall left of Fiddler Arete, starting from the block and following the easiest line.

51   G String   12m   VS   5a
A Girdle of Buttress Five.Start on the block below Maggie's Wall and traverse right to Fiddler Arete and cross the front of the buttress to finish on the right.

52   Fiddler Arete   6m   HVS   5a   ★★
An excellent climb with a hard start. Climb the fine, left arete of the buttress.

53   Fiddler   6m   HVS   5a   ★
Climb the overhung base of the buttress just right of the arete. Climb the wall above and move left to a ledge on the other side of the arete. Finish up the wall above.

54   Fiddler Direct   6m   E1   5b   ★
The logical finish. Start as for Fiddler and climb the overhanging wall direct.

To the right of Fiddler there is a short prominent ledge just above the undercut base. The next two climbs utilise this ledge.

55   Barney Boys   6m   E2   6a
Gain the left-hand end of the ledge directly by a semi-mantleshelf. Move up boldly to finish up the right-hand side of the neb of Fiddler Direct.

56   The Scoop   6m   E2   6b
Enter the shallow scoop to the right of the ledge. Continue more easily straight up.

57   Thin Finger Special   7m   E1   5c   ★★
A brilliant problem. Climb the thin undercut crack just left of the cave to an indistinct finish.

58   Jumping Jack Flash   6m   HVS   5b
To the right of Thin Finger Special is an overhanging arete. Use flat holds to reach a jug on the lip. Swing out strenuously and climb the wall above more easily.

BUTTRESS SIX

The small, clean-cut buttress to the right of Buttress Five.

59 Plagiarist 4m HVS 5c ★★
Another brilliant little problem. Gain the front of the buttress using a small pocket. Reach the break and exit above awkwardly.

60 Bass Special 4m VS 5a ★
Climb the cracked right-hand end of the wall right of Plagiarist.

60a Scream HVS 5b
Climb direct up overhanging scoop right of Bass Special.

61 The Balder 4m HS 4b
Start on the ledge right of Bass Special. Hand-Traverse left to finish up the arete. A low traverse exists beneath Bass Special. (6a).

BUTTRESS SEVEN

The very small buttress at the right end of the South Side. It has two wide cracks which slope up to the right. It hosts a handful of pleasant problems.

62 Adverse Camber 5c
Start on the left side of the buttress. Climb the difficult mantelshelf without the aid of an ancient, chipped handhold.

63 Gap Factor Nine 4c
Start left of the arete and move round right and up, with a difficult move to exit left.

64 Diagonal Crack D
Climb the lower of the two cracks and finish with a mantelshelf.

65 Diagonal Direct 4a
Ascend the centre of the face to finish with an awkward mantelshelf.

66 Milk Snatcher 5b
Start at the small footledge right of Diagonal Direct and stand on it with difficulty. Step left and up to a ledge and the finish.

67 Kel's Problem 6a
Climb the wall just left of the right edge using a "bullet scar" to pull onto the wall. Continue above the break. A good low traverse exists below Kel's Problem. (6a).

HOLWICK SCAR   O.S. SHEET 92   G.R.902 269

SITUATION AND CHARACTER

This escarpment of Igneous rock is a part of the Great Whin Sill which faces North-West across Upper Teesdale in the village of Holwick.The faces provide steep and often strenuous climbing on good rock which is not as smooth and frictionless as similar climbing on Crag Lough on the Roman Wall. Most of the routes follow crack and grooveлines and these are plentiful. Recent neglect has left these once cleaned buttresses in a somewhat vegetated state. It is hoped that this situation will change.

APPROACHES AND ACCESS

The crag is best approached from Middleton-in-Teesdale which is only 4 miles South East of Holwick. From Middleton cross the River

Tees on the B6277 going South. Take the first right which is the minor road leading to the village of Holwick. Park in the village. The crags are now clearly visible one field away and dominating the scene. To reach the crag, it is necessary to walk to the West end of the village, where at a bend in the road, a Public Bridle Way leads off to the left. Follow this for a short distance to where it divides and a branch of the Public Bridle Way goes up through the escarpment in the direction of Selset reservoir. Access has been a problem at Holwick for many years, the landowners, the Strathmore Estate have been unwilling to help in any access negotiations, and the tenant farmer who lives in a house opposite the crag is a violent man who has been known the threaten climbers with real injury if they continue to climb. It is a pity that such a fine outcrop is denied the climbing community and it is hoped that climbers will continue to visit the crag and respectfully and without resorting to the cheap tactics of the tenant eventually see the situation resolved 'de facto' as it should be.

HISTORICAL
The crag has a recorded history of climbing that goes back over thirty years to the days of the Yackley M.C inspired by Tony Gooding. The Cleveland M.C. also played a part in the development.The crag was documented in a small guide produced by the Yackley M.C. and again in the Rock Climbers Guide to the North of England (Pointer 1980).

THE CLIMBS
These are described from left to right as one faces the crag.

GREAT BUTTRESS
1   "A" Chimney   15m   D
Start 6m up the wide, grassy gully on the left-hand side of the crag. Climb blocks in the corner until it is possible to enter the chimney proper. Straight up to a grassy ledge then trend rightwards to the top. Belay on a Yew tree.
Variation finish   S
From the top of the chimney step across onto the right wall and climb over a loose spike to finish.
2   Spiral Staircase   18m   D
Start at a corner 6m up the wide, grassy gully. Follow the obvious line rightwards to a series of ledges and a tree (belay).Move down right to a platform, then into a groove. Follow this until a traverse right leads to a short chimney and the top.
2a   Carol's Delightful Hand   D
A better finish. From the tree belay climb the obvious line to the top. Finish up a short chimney.
3   Left Escalator   24m   HS   ★
Starts 4m right of Spiral Staircase in a wide groove with a pinnacle on the right.
1   12m   4a
Climb the wide crack on the left of the groove to a tree belay on Spiral Staircase.

2   12m
Move down and right to a platform, then into a groove. Follow this until a traverse right leads to a short chimney and the top.

4   Right Escalator   12m   VS   4c
Start at the foot of the wide groove. Climb the pinnacle and make an awkward step left into a groove (delicate). Finish at the tree belay on Spiral Staircase.

5   Derision Groove   24m   VS
Start to the right of the pinnacle at a black groove.

1   12m   5a
Climb the groove to a sentry box. Belay high in a crack on the left.

2   12m
Bridge up the sentry box and pull across left on excellent holds to join Spiral Staircase.

6   Master's Groove   26m   VS   ★
Start at the lowest point of the buttress 2m right of Derision Groove.

1   11m   4b
Climb easily to a grass ledge on the left. Ascend the left hand crack and move right to a big ledge and tree belay.

2   15m   4c
Step back left above the crack and climb a steep groove. continue up the V-groove surmounting an overhang to finish on grassy ledges.

7   Surprise   28m   S
Start at the protruding rib of the buttress 2m right of Master's Groove.

1   12m
Climb the rib direct to a ledge and and tree.

2   16m
Move right behind the tree and make a series of awkward moves up the steep gangway to the top.

8   Rigor Mortis   23m   VS(A)
Start 2m left of the obvious, deep chimney; Great Chimney. Climb a steep crack to a niche at 4m. Three aid pegs lead to an easier finish.

9   Great Chimney   23m   S   ★
Start at the foot of the obvious chimney. Climb this over chockstones and move left over blocks at the top overhang to reach the top. A fine climb.

10   Cascade   25m   VS   4b
Start below a groove little more than a metre right of Great Chimney. Climb the groove to a resting place on the right at 6m. Swing left across the groove using a flake. the bulge above is climbed on good holds and a prominent block is passed towards the finish.

11   Strathmore Crescent   28m   S
Starts 7m right of Great Chimney just beyond a thin crack which widens into a groove higher up. Climb diagonally leftwards up the wall for 3m then traverse left into a groove. Follow the groove to a ledge and rickety spike. Step right past the spike to another ledge.

Climb the rib and groove to exit right over blocks to a grassy ledge and a tree.

12   Central Climb   28m   S
This climb finds a way up the wall between Great Chimney and another obvious chimney; Charlie's Chimney. Climb the wall from left to right to finish on a ledge with an Ash tree.

13   Sentinel's Stride   28m   HS
Start below the gangway which goes up the wall to the left of the deep-cut Charlie's Chimney.

1   15m   4a
Climb the wall for 4m then make a delicate move up right to the gangway. Climb this into a chimney and step across onto a large, grass ledge.

2   13m   4a
From the ledge, step back across the chimney and into a shallow groove. Move up to a horizontal crack and regain the gangway by a swing to the left. Climb over a pinnacle to the top.

14   Charlie's Chimney   21m   VD
Climb the obvious deep chimney.

15   Groundhog   10m   HVS   5a
Start at the foot of Charlie's Chimney. Climb the groove on the right wall of the chimney. Exit onto a grass ledge halfway up the chimney. Poor protection.

16   Chimney And Slab   14m   D
Start 2m right of Charlie's Chimney below another chimney. Climb the chimney and exit right onto a slab. Climb this to a tree. The corner above is climbed to the top.

To the right the crag is at its lowest height and has an bay bounded on the left by a corner crack.

17   Interrupted Crack   21m   S
Climb the corner crack to a good ledge. Climb the continuation crack above to an awward exit onto a slab. Finish above the tree as for Chimney And Slab.

BISHOP'S BUTTRESS
This section contains some of the best climbs on the crag. The imposing face provides greater steepness and continuity than anywhere else on the crag.

18   Stroll On   23m   HVS   5a   ★
Start at a little niche in the projecting corner of the buttress just to the right of interrupted Crack. Climb up and out of the niche and pull round the rib onto the wall on the right. Climb straight up for almost 5m and move back left onto a large ledge. From the right-hand end of the ledge move up a mossy wall to finish up a difficult, corner crack.

19   Thrombosis   28m   HVS   ★★★
An exciting, strenuous and spectacular climb. Start at the little niche as for Stroll On.

1   15m   5a
Move up and out of the niche onto the right wall. Climb this on

good holds until a traverse can be made to a stance and belay in the narrow chimney; Bishop's Chimney on the right.

2   13m   5a

From the chimney, move up and back onto the wall above the traverse line. Move up to holds which are followed leftwards to a spike. Move up past the spike and traverse right to reach and climb the obvious, flake crack.

20   Bishop's Chimney   18m   HS   ★

The steep, narrow chimney in the right-angle of Bishop's Buttress.

1   9m

Climb the corner to a large platform at the foot of the chimney proper.

2   9m   4a

Climb the chimney facing right. An awkward move over chockstones leads to the top.

21   Sabre Cut   12m   HS

Start 3m right of Bishop's Chimney below a steep, narrow crack. Climb the awkward and strenuous, narrow crack.

To the right of the last climbs and about 6m left of the drystone wall, is a pinnacle, with a recess to the right of the pinnacle.

22   Straight Up   12m   VS   4b   ★

Climb the steep narrow crack which runs up a corner in the left-hand side of the recess.

23   Yackley Chimney   14m   D   ★

Start at the foot of a clean-cut chimney at the back of the recess. Climb the left wall until the chimney proper can be entered. Climb this to block belays on the left.

Various other climbs exist in the area above the drystone wall but are not recorded. Beyond the drystone wall is a tall buttress with a climb following a series of grooves:

24   G-String Grooves   VS   4c

Climb the grooves, the first of these is prominent and smooth.

25   Sarongster   88m   HVS   ★

An excellent left to right high-level Girdle. Start as for Left-Escalator.

1   12m   4a

Climb the wide crack on the left of the groove to a tree belay on Spiral Staircase.

2   19m   4c

Traverse right to Derision Groove and continue past Master's Groove to a good ledge on the arete. Make an awkward move onto Surprise and continue to a stance and belay below the roof of Great Chimney.

3   16m   3c

Move out of the chimney rightwards, passing the prominent block on Cascade. Enter the groove of Strathmore Crescent and follow it to the top. Tree belay.

4   12m   4a

Descend the last pitch of Sentinel's Stride to a grassy ledge and nut belay.

5   9m   4a
Traverse delicately right to a tree belay on Chimney And Slab.

6   20m   5a
Move down and rightwards and traverse onto Stroll On to a peg
runner below the final crack. Continue rightwards to another peg
runner on Thrombosis. Traverse right and finish up the flake crack as
for Thrombosis.

JACK SCAR   O.S. Sheet 91   GR 947275

SITUATION AND CHARACTER
Pleasantly situated above Hudeshope Beck in Teesdale amidst
woodland, this gorge of variable quality limestone provides some
excellent climbs as well as some rather more overgrown ones. The
crag faces East and can be shaded in Summer. A visit in Spring or
Autumn can be most rewarding. The climbs described have been
cleaned but with the passage of time all may require a 'brush-up'.
There is much scope here for new routes.

HISTORICAL
Nothing is known about the history of climbing at Jack Scar but the
cave is mentioned in Northern Caves and in all probability caver/
climbers have been responsible for the pegging that took place on
the free climb; Hunger. All the recorded climbs are the work of Paul
Carling and Roy Small who visited the crag in 1982.

APPROACHES AND ACCESS
Leave the B6282 in Middleton-in-Teesdale, travelling west and turn
right just before crossing the Hudeshope Beck onto an unclassified
road. This runs North along the East bank of Hudeshope Beck.
Follow the road until it crosses the stream and becomes an unmetalled track. Park just before the bridge. Follow the track until an old
quarry is reached. All of the climbs lie on the East side of the stream.
If the stream is high, wellingtons could be useful. There are no
access problems. A Public Right of Way exists on both sides of the
beck.

THE CLIMBS
These are described moving upstream and then when necessary
from left to right unless otherwise stated.

RESURGENCE WALL
This is the long wall opposite the quarry. There is only one climb
here at present.

1   Cholera Corner   18m   VS   4c
Climb the obvious corner just left of the spring rising at the base of
the wall. The overhang is more solid than it first appears.

*Further upstream, the gorge narrows and a traverse can be made on
the West bank. Just upstream is an earthy wall, the only climb here
takes the central crack.*

2   Avoid The Rhino   10m   HS   4a
Climb the wide crack direct on good holds to an interesting finish. Descend to the left (facing crag).

Around the corner upstream is Undercut Buttress. Two prominent cracks run down the wall. The left-hand crack fades out six metres above the ground and provides the line of Hunger. The right-hand crack is unclimbed.

3   Hunger   24m   E2   6a   ★★★
A superb, steep expedition. Pull onto the wall just left of a faint weakness and move right and up to the overhanging crack (peg runners). Climb the crack until it is possible to hide in a niche before doing the right thing and pulling out of it direct. Move left to finish. Descend to the right (facing the crag).

The gully and wall to the left provide four climbs, **these are described right to left.**

4   Botanic Man   14m   S   4b
Climb the V-groove in the left wall of the gully to reach a tree close to the top. Swing into the tree and exit left.

5   Creaking Jesus   14m   HVS   4c
Climb the left fork of the Y-crack on the wall.

6   Daddy Cool   14m   E1   5c
Climb the wall between Creaking Jesus and Bilharzia to reach a thin crack. A long reach is an asset.

7   Bilharzia   12m   MVS   4c   ★
Climb the clean-cut groove on the left of the wall. Only difficult to start.

To the left of a short series of shattered grooves and gullies is a clean wall with a grey streak down the centre.

8   Borrowed Time   12m   E1   5b   ★
Climb the indefinite line to the right of the grey streak until the wall steepens. Step left and back right and enter the scoop above. Climb the flake on the left to a large tree.

9   Extra Time   12m   E1   5b   ★
Climb the thin crack to the left of the grey streak to a narrow ledge. Move up steeply to the break and gain the wall above. Descend via the gully on the left.

Some distance upstream, flanked by shattered grooves and aretes is one final, solid, overhanging buttress.

10   Moss Groove 11m   VD Climb the corner to the right of the main buttress.

11   The Janissary   10m   E1   5b   ★
Climb the right-hand side of the face of the buttress to reach a crack in the overhang. Move up left strenuously to finish. Rock needs care in the upper half.

12   Paladin   10m   VS   5a
Easier than its neighbour. Climb the left-hand side of the wall until below the overhang. Turn this on the left and finish up the arete above.

Lamb Hill Quarry

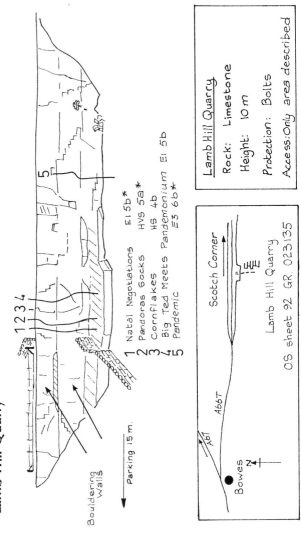

1 Natal Negotiations   E1 5b*
2 Pandoras Socks   HVS 5a*
3 Cornflakes   HS 4b
4 Big Ted Meets Pandemonium E1 5b
5 Pandemic   E3 6b*

Parking 15 m.

Bouldering
Walls

Lamb Hill Quarry
Rock: Limestone
Height: 10 m
Protection: Bolts
Access: Only area described

Scotch Corner

A6T

Lamb Hill Quarry

A67

Bowes

N

OS sheet 92 GR. 023135

LOUP'S CRAG   O.S. Sheet 92   Barnard Castle   G.R. 966 178

SITUATION AND CHARACTER

An outcrop of excellent quality gritstone visible to the east from the South side of Goldsborough. Loup's crag lies just inside the firing range and close to a small conifer plantation. The climbing is mainly short cracks and hand-traverses mainly in the lower grades. No climbs have been recorded as yet and it is best combined with a session at Goldsborough.

APPROACHES AND ACCESS

The crag lies within the Battle Hill firing range and should not be approached when the red flags are flying. There are no problems of access at other times. Approach direct across the moor from the South side of Goldsborough.

EGGLESTONE BURN CRAG   O.S. Sheet 92   G.R. 987 264

SITUATION AND CHARACTER

A generally poor quality sandstone gorge with one excellent, solid wall split by two cracks. The existing climbs will probably require re-cleaning or some traffic at least.

APPROACHES AND ACCESS

One mile from the Moorcock Inn in Eggleston on the B6278 towards Stanhope, is a Water Authority Pump House on open moorland. Park nearby. Descend the gully immediately below the Pump House being careful not to damage the drystone wall which must be crossed. The wall with the existing climbs quickly comes into view on the left. The gorge is a popular scramble with walkers and there appear to be no problems with access. A Public Right Of Way can be followed Southwards into the gorge from a point three hundred and fifty metres North of the Pump House.

HISTORICAL

The two recorded climbs were first climbed by Paul Carling and Roy Small in July 1983.

THE CLIMBS

1   Rowan   12m   HVS   5b   ★★
A very good climb. Climb the right hand crack with a move round the roof at four metres. Sustained hand and finger jamming with good protection leads to a tree and abseil descent.

2   Exegesis   15m   HVS   5b
Easier than its neighbour. Climb the left crack with one hard move above the first horizontal break. Move left near the top on large holds and suspect rock to exit either right or left of a large tree.

WINTER CLIMBING IN TEESDALE

There is very little snow and ice climbing in Teesdale although in a hard Winter, climbing can be found. This is particularly useful for training or for when blocked roads in the area preclude trips further afield.

1   In good conditions the North side of High Force provides entertainment at about Grade 1/2 in unusual positions, traversing above the pool from the footpath to finish up the gully.

2   A good, steep icefall sometimes develops in the far corner of the quarry behind the lorry park up the road from the High Force Hotel. (G.R. 879 290)

3   Excellent ice, with about four to six good lines often forms in the quarry South of Middleton in Teesdale at Moor Rigg (G.R. 947 247). These are vertical with short, overhanging sections and are usually top-roped.

4   White Force (G.R. 852 280) near Forest in Teesdale can provide a good climb in a remote, mountain environment. Being a stream course, it requires a protracted period of low temperatures to come into condition. When formed, it provides over ten metres of steep water-ice finishing up a chimney which leads to twenty metres of mixed snow and ice at an easier grade. The exit may cornice and the chimney is the last section to freeze. It is possible to check it out with binoculars from the High Force to Langdon Beck road.

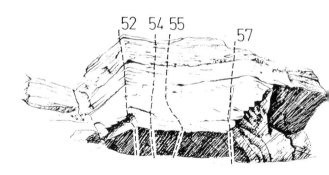

Goldsborough Carr   Buttress 5

9   THE CLEVELAND HILLS

The term the Cleveland Hills is chosen to define the scope of the area. These are the line of shapely hills facing North-East over the Vale of Cleveland between Great Ayton and Swainby. They constitute the best part of The Lyke Wake Walk and also feature in The Coast To Coast Walk.These hills contain a clutch of Sandstone crags, not the same Sandstone as that in the Eden Valley or Northumberland, but coarse, Jurassic Sandstone which weathers like Gritstone and has numerous iron intrusions and encrustations. The crags are a sample of the crags which make up the area known as The North York Moors and are amongst the most popular with Teesside climbers. The treatment of the crags is definitive in that all known routes are described and this represents an honest attempt to set the record straight in terms of grading and quality. In the past these fine little crags and the local users have suffered as a result of a grading system in which HVS could mean anything up to E3. The crags described, all have something different to offer. Scugdale is a fine place for bouldering whilst The Wainstones and its neighbour, Ravens Scar has some serious and extended routes equal to the best outcrop routes anywhere. The crags are friendly and the outlooks wonderful. What more could you want?

PARK NAB – KILDALE   O.S. SHEET 94   G.R. 609085

SITUATION AND CHARACTER

Park Nab is on a Western spur of Kildale Moor in the Cleveland Hills, part of the North York Moors National Park. It faces W.S.W. at an altitude approaching 300 metres and commands far-ranging views across the Vale of Cleveland. The near views to Great Ayton Moor and Captain Cook's Monument are particularly fine and add to the charm of the situation.

The crag in common with others hereabouts is composed of Middle Jurassic Sandstone which is a superb climbing rock made more interesting by the presence of pockets and small intrusions of iron which provide sharp edges and narrow slots.

There are a number of stakes at the top of the crag and it is used by groups. A special plea to all top-ropers. Please extend all anchors over the edge of the crag to avoid the continuance of erosion that threatens this charming spot.

The climbing at Park Nab is nowhere more than 10 metres high but the average height is less, making it a popular place for solo climbing.

The crag is very compact and yet a range of features endow it with a unique character which when combined with its setting, makes it well-worth a visit.

APPROACHES AND ACCESS

Park Nab is best approached from Stokesley by following the A173 in the direction of Great Ayton for less than a mile to take the minor road on the right leading to Easby. In Easby take a left fork signposted to Kildale. About a mile before Kildale, the road goes under a railway bridge and Park Nab can be seen up on the right. Take the next junction on the right and follow this road uphill and through a gate. Parking is at the end of the wall on the right and the crag is reached by an easy uphill walk of less than five minutes. Dogs must not be taken to the crag.ß

HISTORICAL

The first records of climbing here go back to the 1930's when the "Bergers", a group of local climbers from the Teesside area, inspired by Arthur Barker and his brother made some ascents. The 1950's was the next phase of development by J.Fletcher, J.Hickman, A.E.Rout and N.A. Thompson.

The 1960's saw an upsurge in interest in climbing in the area generally and John Adams made the ascent of the serious Pessimist and Dynamo.

The steep line of Dangle was contributed by M.Binks.

Another 'Leading Light' of the time was Chris Woodhall who contributed The Pinnacle Face in 1972.

Shere Khan, the most difficult route on the crag and a test-piece by the standards of any area was the work of Nick Dixon who "boldly went forth....." after Ian 'Squawk' Dunn had stripped the face of its ironmongery.

Ian Dunn also provided a direct start to Shere Khan and the difficult arete of The Twister. He then mopped Parallel Lines and Picture This.

Not much remained and in a sweeping up operation Stu Ferguson climbed the difficult Gazeuse in May 1988.

THE CLIMBS

These are described from left to right.

1   Gazeuse   6m   E1   6a
Climb the wall on the extreme left of the crag using peg scars to gain a rounded finish.
Just right of this is:

2   Harvest   6m   E1   5c
Start at a 2m rib at left end of crag below an overhang.Climb this and the arete above.

3   Dangle   7m   E2   5c   ★
Start at sme place as Harvest. Climb the rib and move right. climb the overhang direct passing a square pocket.

4   Lion's Jaw   7m   E1   5b
Start 2m right of Dangle at a left-facing 2m high corner. Climb the corner and the wide crack above.

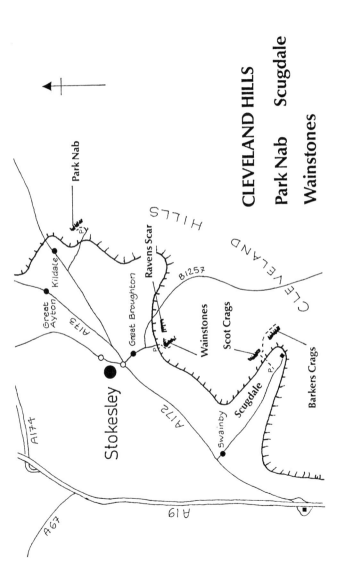

CLEVELAND HILLS

Park Nab   Scugdale

Wainstones

The crag now cuts into a little recessed area whose steep left wall has a thin, tempting crack.

5   Zero Route   5m   HVS   5a   ★
Starting from a ledge, gain and climb the thin, curving crack.

The more broken back wall of the recess now gives some worth-while easy climbs:

6   Cook's Gully Left Chimney   9m   D
Start in the corner right of Zero below a protruding rib in the gully. Climb the rib and buttress above. Pleasant and traditional.

7   Cook's Gully Table Climb 9m   M   ★★
Start 1m right. Climb the twin- cracked recess and buttress above.

8   Castle Climb   11m   VD   ★
A good traditional climb done in two pitches and taking a stance on the big ledge below the final steep wall of the buttress. Start as for Table Climb. Ascend to a ledge on right at head-height, then pull onto a good flake above. Move right and up to the big ledge. Traverse right to the arete via a good footledge. Reaching the handholds is hard for the short but the finish up the arete is memorable.

9   The Keep   11m   VS   4c
Start below the right-hand side of the flake used by Castle Climb. From blocks, gain the thin crack on the right side of the flake. Move up and through a little V- notch above. Finish up the wall left of Castle Climb's arete.

To the right is a recess with "1953" inscribed in the right wall.

10   Grumble And Grunt   9m   HVS   5b   ★★
The name says it all-- well almost! Start in the 1953 recess and struggle up the bottomless chimney above, passing a chockstone.

Moving right from the recess is a short rib, below and right of a jutting roof. Four bolt holes in the wall above and left of the roof testify that "rabbits" possibly made the first ascent of this wall.

11   Shere Khan   10m   E6   6b   ★★★
A desperately hard climb since the disappearance of a flake. Start at the short rib below and right of the four bolt holes. Ascend the rib past a horizontal break and use the holes to gain the arete on the left by some perplexing manoevures. Once gained, the arete proves to be very hard. The top horizontal break is reached and the upper arete of Castle Climb is followed to the top. Squawk's Direct: The upper arete can be gained direct (6b)

12   Styx   8m   E1   5b   ★
An excellent climb, fairly hard in the grade. Start from the top of the large block below the obvious Twisting Chimney. Climb the narrow left wall of the chimney, moving out left to an iron intrusion. Move directly up to the horizontal break then climb the middle of the upper wall. A more direct start leads from the foot of Shere Khan and up rightwards to the iron intrusion (5c)

13   Twisting chimney   9m   D
Climb the twisting chimney passing a capstone near the top.

14   Twister   8m   E4   6a
Climb the right arete of Twisting Chimney on the Twin Cracks side.

Park Nab

The wall to the right is split by two parallel vertical cracks which provides a very good climb:

15   Twin Cracks   6m   MVS   4b   ★★
Climb the twin cracks past a small Holly at the top.

16   Dynamo   6m   HVS   6b
Start immediately left of a pillar dedicated to "Phil". Climb the steep wall leftwards with difficulty to gain and stand on a small, horizontal ledge. Finish up the rib above.

17   Lady's Gully Left Crack   6m   HVD
Climb the crack to the left of the "Phil" inscription.

18   Lady's Gully Right Crack   6m   S
Immediately right. Climb it.

19   The Fat Slag   6m   HVS   5b
Climb the wall immediately right of the right-hand crack.

To the right, is an impressive pillar; the Pinnacle. This reclines against the crag and has two faces separated by a steep arete.

20   Pinnacle Crack Left Hand   6m   D
From a staircase of blocks, climb the short, left-curving crack to finish up an open groove above.

21   Pinnacle Crack Right Hand 6m   S
Mount the staircase of blocks left of the pinnacle and climb the aggressive-looking wide crack above passing a wedged block.

22   Pinnacle Face   8m   E2   5b   ★
From just right of the arete, climb past the initials "CP" and climb the face direct using the arete on the right whenever the need arises.

23   Chairman's Climb   8m   HVS   4c   ★
Start 1m left of the arete below a wide crack. Climb this to a ledge. Follow the steep wall to the right of the arete using the arete for the left hand.

24   Chockstone Chimney   6m   VD   ★
Start 1m right of the wide crack of Chairman's Climb. Climb a wide, stepped crack and deeper chimney above. Awkward.

The steep wall at right angles to the Pinnacle on the right, is split by parallel, twin cracks.

25   Parallel Lines   6m   HVS   5a
Uninspired but providing excellent protection. Climb the left hand crack via a bulged recess to finish direct.

26   Wallbar Buttress   6m   S   4a   ★★
Ascend the square rib between the two cracks on mainly excellent holds. Steep and sustained.

27   Picture This   6m   HVS   5b   ★
Start from a block immediately right of Wallbar buttress and below a vague arete which rises from a ledge at 3m. Climb to the ledge and finish up the arete above.

28   Scoop Chimney   6m   VS   4b
Climb the vertical pod to reach an open gully above which are two corners, either of which provides an awkward and dirty finish.

To the right of this chimney is an attractive final wall which at its right-end is vertically split by the aptly-named Long Bow.

29   Pessimist   6m   E5   6a   ⋆
Climb the left-hand arete of the wall immediately right of Scoop Chimney.

30   Hara Kiri   6m   HVS   5a   ⋆⋆
Start below a thin, vertical crack on the front face just right of the arete of Pessimist. Climb the crack to the first horizontal break. Traverse right for 2m and ascend the wall directly on good side-holds. A long reach gains the top. The wall below the finish gives a Direct Start at 5b.

31   Long Bow   6m   HS   4b   ⋆
Climb the bow-shaped crack to an alcove from whence the top is reached.

32   Bowstring   6m   VS   5a   ⋆
Climb the string which has unfortunately snapped!

33   The Bitter End   6m   E1   5b   ⋆
Start 2m right of the bow-shaped crack from a block. Pull up the wall to reach a "letterbox" for the left hand. finish up the wall above.

34   The End   6m   VS   5a
Climb the right-hand arete of the crag.

35   The Girdle   62m   HVS   5a   ⋆⋆
One of the better small crag girdles. Start as for Dangle below the left-end of the roof. From the roof, hand-traverse rightwards. Beyond the arete, Zero Climb is crossed into Cook's Gully Left Chimney. Now follow Table Climb rightwards and pull right round the prominent arete above Shere Khan. The horizontal break across the Styx Wall is traversed either as a foot or hand-traverse into Twisting Chimney. Cross Twin Cracks and maintain a constant level rounding the Pinnacle to the ledge of Chairman's Climb. Cross into the upper scoop of Scoop Chimney and move right onto the traverse of Hara Kiri. Continue into Long Bow and either finish up this or continue across The Bitter End to The End (5b).

THE WAINSTONES   O.S. SHEET 93   G.R. 559034

SITUATION AND CHARACTER

This deservedly popular venue is well-known to North-Easterners and should be better known further afield, such is its attraction.

The Wainstones occupy an elevated position at 360 metres on a Western spur of Hasty Bank one of the distinctively shaped Cleveland Hills which rise abruptly out of the flat plain barely ten miles South of Teesside.

Viewed from the village of Great Broughton, on the route of approach, the "Stones" appear as a group of pinnacles in a notch in the right-hand skyline of Hasty Bank but this is only a part of the whole, as by far the most interesting faces, those overlooking Bilsdale, cannot be seen.

The Wainstones provides a wide range of climbing both in terms of style and spread of grades on Jurassic Sandstone of superb quality which outcrops in the form of a continuous edge as well as a plethora of good, big and not so big boulders. As a bouldering venue, these rocks are superb and a short break in the rain or a mild winter's day can see them in good condition, indeed the frictional property of the rock is so good that the easier routes can be done when wet. The harder climbs in common with many others on sandstone are bold and technical and "traditional" gradings by 'locals' should be viewed with suspicion. Miss Muffet at Hard Severe 4a being one example!

The Wainstones can be very busy at weekends and groups of beginners can be hazardous both to other climbers and to the state of the rock as evidenced by the worn state of some climbs due to the practice of abseiling. A midweek day or fine evening is the best time to sample this delectable crag.

APPROACHES AND ACCESS

The Wainstones are best approached from the South via the A19 and A172 to Stokesley or from Teesside and the North on the A19/A174/A172.

Leave Stokesley on the B1257 and go through Great Broughton from where the rocks are visible on the right-hand skyline of Hasty Bank which is the distinctive flat-topped hill. Two approaches are possible beyond Great Broughton the first is more direct and climbs paths on the Broughton side of the hill through mixed woodland whilst the other route involves a longer, though very fine walk along the top of Hasty Bank from the car park on the summit of the B1257 at Clay Bank.

The direct approach involves turning right off the B1257 at a steep left hand bend in the road about a half mile South of Great Broughton. The metalled minor road leading directly towards the hills is followed for a further three-quarters of a mile to where it becomes unmetalled at a junction. Cars should be parked beyond the right turn on the wide verge.

The forest track leads uphill from this point and beyond a gate bears right. At the obvious bend in the track continue directly up the hillside on a series of steps to reach the next wide track. At this juncture, turn right and follow the good track to the next junction and turn left to cross the boundary fence at a stile on the right a little further on near two shale banks. These banks and the prominent grassy spur lead up to the Wainstones to arrive below the outer pinnacle; the Needle. To the left is the Broughton Face separated from the Steeple and Needle by the rocky defile called the Sheepwalk which is part of the Coast To Coast Footpath.

To the right of the Needle is the Bilsdale Face overlooking many picnic spots amongst the array of large boulders.

HISTORICAL

According to local legend, a Danish chieftain was slain at the rocks and the name Wainstones may derive from the Saxon verb wanian which means "to lament". That early climbers frequented these rocks is evidenced by the number of ancient inscriptions to be found in some unlikely places including routes claimed as first ascents, this century.

In 1906, E.E. Roberts visited the Wainstones and wrote: "Odd visits do not count. Some idle shepherd boy may have climbed there before me."

In 1912, Canon Newton and the brothers, C.E. and D. Burrow visited the rocks and their friends G and E. Creighton cycled from York to join them.

In 1928 the Barker brothers started to visit the rocks in the company of of the "Bergers", a small group of keen, local climbers who were looking for a local practice ground after sampling the delights of climbing in the Lake District. The Barkers were responsible for many of the earliest recorded routes, amongst them were; Wall And Ledge, The Bulge and Bench Mark Crack. Another local family involved in the early ascents were the brothers C.S and T.H. Tilley. In 1939 J. Devenport and A. Parker produced Groove And Crack on Ling Buttress.

The 1950's saw A. Evenett lead Little Bo Peep and C. Fielding's superb, Sphinx Nose Traverse in 1954 was something of a watershed. In 1955 B. Mankin's Steeple Face must stand out as something special for the time. In 1959, Terry Sullivan was very active in the area and his Central Climb was a fine addition, but not so fine as Ali Baba which although requiring pegs was a powerful and intimidating route climbed in 1960. In the same year, Sullivan added Sesame to the collection of climbs on Garfit Buttress. 1965 was a good year for Garfit Buttress and the major line of the crag; Ali Baba was led completely free by Tony Marr. Hartlepool climbers, Stew Wilson and Steve Gretton invested some time in the Garfit Buttress routes and finished off by girdling the buttress to give Turkish Delight. Another Hartlepool lad active at this time was Stan Shout and his not inconsiderable talents led to the creation of Concave Wall. Also in 1965 the line which was to become Terrorist was top-roped by Geoff Harper and Stew Wilson.

The late 70's saw Ian "Squawk" Dunn arrive on the scene and his Peel Out was mistakenly taken to be the work of John Redhead. Paul Ingham and "Squawk" had their sights on Terrorist and this became reality in September 1979. Terrorist pointed the way to future climbs in the area in and Ingham went even further in his search for difficulty with Psycho Syndicate possibly the hardest route in the area. This was in the early 80's. It would seem that the crag was more or less "worked out" for the later part of the decade produced one route; Cissam, wrung from Garfit Buttress by Tony Marr in July 1986.

THE CLIMBS

The Wainstones presents two escarpments, the Broughton Face and the Bilsdale Face. Two pinnacles; the Steeple and the Needle are at the axis of these faces. The Needle being the outermost pinnacle.

The climbs are described from left to right, buttress by buttress commencing with climbs on the North-West or Broughton Face and its Eastern continuation; Oblique Buttress, then on the South-West or Bilsdale Face.

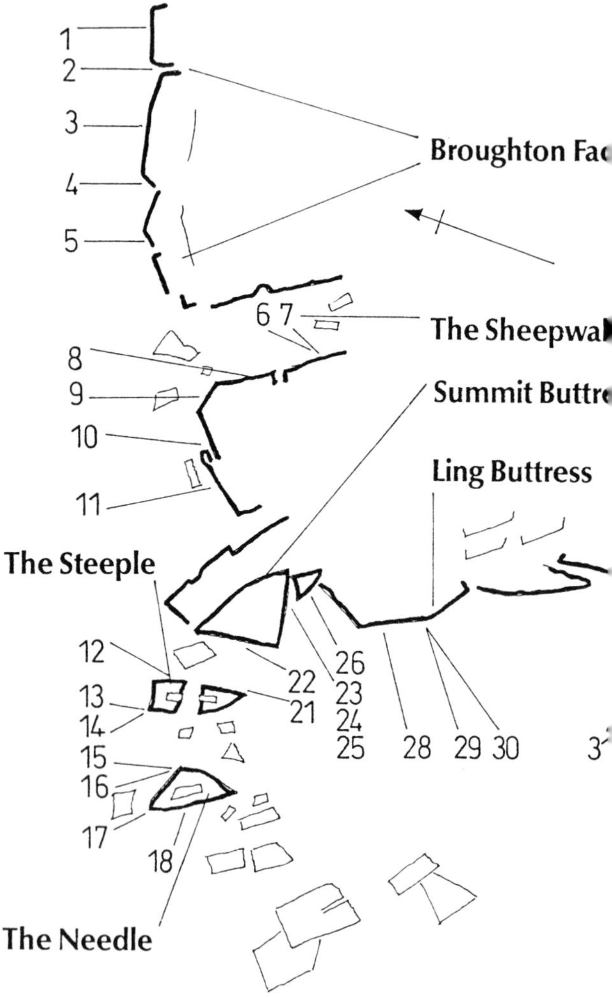

1
2
3
4
5

Broughton Fac

6 7
The Sheepwa

8
9
10
11

Summit Buttr

Ling Buttress

The Steeple

12
13
14
15
16
17
18

22
21
26
23
24
25
28 29 30
3

The Needle

THE WAINSTONES

Garfit Buttress

...sdale Buttress

Main Wall

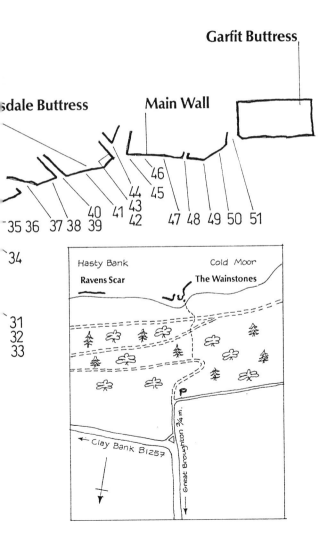

46
44 45
43
40 42
35 36 37 38 39 41   47 48 49 50 51

34

Hasty Bank   Cold Moor

Ravens Scar   **The Wainstones**

31
32
33

← Clay Bank B1257

Great Broughton ¾ m.

THE BROUGHTON FACE

This steep face of rather lichenous rock bends through ninety degrees into the narrow, rock strewn defile known as the Sheepwalk. The opposite side of this corridor consists of another steep wall which extends Westwards before bending through ninety degrees at a blunt rib. The short wall following the blunt rib ends at an easy corner beyond which is easy, blocky ground extending rightwards to the pinnacles of the Steeple and Needle.

1   Broughton Ridge   8m   MS
From the extreme left-hand end of the face, move diagonally right to gain and climb the rib overlooking the crack with the Benchmark near it. Finish on a grassy ledge and scramble off.

2   Bench-Mark Crack   6m   S
Climb the obvious off-width crack which has a Bench-Mark on its right wall.

3   Psycho Syndicate   7m   E6   6c/7a   ★★★
Start 2m right of Bench-Mark Crack below a peg-scarred wall. Climb the wall. The hardest climb in the area.

4   Tiny's Dilemma   8m   VS   5a   ★★
Start in a cracked corner, 4m right of Psycho Syndicate. follow the corner until near the top a step left can be made onto a good foothold. Continue up the wall above to finish just left of the block overhang.

To the right of the corner is a steep slab inscribed "PJ".

5   Rookery Nook   9m   VD   ★
A fine climb with an elegant finish. Start just right of the "PJ" slab at a short chimney. Climb the short chimney and move left on a ledge above the slab. Keep moving left until the block overhang above can be turned via the slab on the left. Finish at the same point as Tiny's Dilemma. Direct Start: Climb the centre of the "PJ" slab at Mild Severe.

Two poor routes have been made just right of here. Milky Way(MS) climbs the steep face above the initial chimney of Rookery Nook and Evening Wall (S) follows the green wall to the right.

Now we turn into:

THE SHEEPWALK

The climbs are all on the South side.

6   Green Wall   5m   VS   4c
Start at the left end of the wall and just right of an overhung recess. Climb the green and dirty wall which is a bit better than it looks.

7   Sheep Walk Slab   8m   HD
Start as for Green Wall. Gain flat footholds and traverse horizon tally right to a chimney. Finish up the chimney.

8   Flake, Wall and Crack   6m   HS   4b
A much better climb than it looks, in fact its quite good. Start from an embedded flake just right of the chimney/crack. Pull up onto a good ledge, step left and finish up the converging cracks above.

Two metres right is a blunt rib with a metre high block below its right-hand side.

9   Solomon's Porch   7m   HS   4b
Another good clean climb. Rather strenuous. Start from the top of the metre high block below the blunt rib. Pull up right to a hold and swarm onto the ledge above. Climb the bulging nose of the buttress to the left of the cracked corner of Lurch.

10   Lurch   6m   HS   4c
Climb the cracked corner starting 1m right of Solomon's Porch.

11   Humpty Dumpty   6m   HVD   ★
Start 2m right of Lurch from a "finger-shaped" block lying left of an overhung recess. Climb the short slab to its top. The face above is steep but a nice hand-crack provides good holds.

The wall at right angles to Humpty Dumpty has an unenticing easy groove just right of the initials "JSS" This is Novitiate which is Moderate.

THE STEEPLE

This pinnacle is cleft by a fine chimney, but first, two metres right of Novitiate is:

12   Steeple Groove   7m   HVD
Climb the steep groove above two blocks and finish up the Steeple by the inscription; W. Bennison.

13   The Steeple Face   7m   E2   5b   ★
Steep and scary. Start from the lowest rocks on the N.W. (Broughton) side of the Steeple. Climb over inscribed blocks to the top of a flake. The steep face above is ascended using the right and left edges as required.

14   The Steeple Chimney   8m   HD   ★
A good chimney climb if that's not a contradiction! Start as for The Steeple Face. From the blocks move right to enter the chimney which provides a tight squirm in relative safety.Finish on top of the Steeple.

There is another route on The Steeple called Chop Yat Ridge. A description is included in the Summit Buttress section.

THE NEEDLE

This is separated from the Steeple by a Needle Gap which is partially blocked by enormous blocks.

15   Main Route   9m   HD   ★
A serious route. Start at the slabby base of the Needle under a huge block on the Broughton side. Climb the slabby arete to a small ledge level with the top of the huge block. Move left and climb the South side of the top block via a sloping foothold. Descend with care.

16   The Needle Girdle   11m   S
Start as for Main Route. Follow this to below the top block and follow the obvious ledge/crack line below the top block.

17   North Route   7m   E1   5a   ★★
Strenuous climbing on mainly big, though flat holds and with a bad landing. Start 2m right of Main Route a a thin flake crack, just left of a big, flat-topped block. Climb up the flake and make a long reach for a bracket above. Keep pulling until the ledge below the top block is gained and easier now pull up the sharp edge of the top block and gain the top.

18   The West Face   7m   E5   6b   ★★
Start below a horizontal pegged crack less than 2m above the
ground. Ascend direct into the scoop and climb above with difficulty. The horizontal peg-scarred crack is a good problem traverse
(6a).

*The next buttress, Oblique Buttress is well to the left (East) of the
climbing on the Broughton Face going towards Ravens Scar.*

OBLIQUE BUTTRESS
This isolated buttress lies about 100 metres N.N.E. of the
Broughton Face along the continuation of the edge.

19   Physical   8m   HVS   5b
Climb the obvious groove at the right end of the buttress.

20   In The Nick Of Time   8m   E2   5c
Climb the steep wall to the left of Physical.

THE BILSDALE FACE
This faces South West and has fine views down Bilsdale. The
Bilsdale Face whilst almost a continuous edge is best described as a
series of six walls and buttresses with conveniently located easy
descent gullies separating these features. The six sections working
from the Steeple left to right are: Summit Buttress; Ling Buttress;
The Sphinx; Bilsdale Buttress; Main Wall and Garfit Buttress.

SUMMIT BUTTRESS
This buttress abuts against the South side of the Steeple. Summit
Buttress has two faces, a gently overhanging face adjacent to the
Steeple and to the right of a prominent triangular roof is a steep
wall facing down Bilsdale.

21   Chop Yat Ridge   8m   HS
Start at the foot of the ridge of The Steeple adjacent to the overhanging face of Summit Buttress.Climb the ridge of The Steeple for 3m
to a horizontal crack move right to below a steep wall which is
climbed on small holds.

22   Birdlime   8m   E3   5c
Start below the overhanging West face of Summit Buttress from the
top of an embedded block. Climb the face on sidepulls trending
right to a pocket. The wall above is climbed trending to the left.

*The next climb starts from the foot of the big gully right of the
overhanging nose of the buttress.*

23   Little Bo-Peep   9m   VS   4c   ★
This sustained climb starts below the gully with the huge capstone.
Climb onto a 2m high block at the foot of the gully and from it, step
left onto the left wall of the buttress. Move up then make a difficult
traverse left for 2m to a juggy ledge. A hard step up gains the top.

24   Miss Muffet   8m   HVS   5a
This "traditional" Severe is somewhat mean. Start as for Little
Bo-Peep but instead of traversing left, follow the slim, right-
trending groove to a steep finish.

25   On Form   12m   E2   5b
A right to left traverse of Summit Buttress. Start as for Little

The Wainstones – Bilsdale Face (Left end)

Bo-Peep. Climb Little Bo-Peep to reach the little, juggy ledge and move left on the continuation break above the steep start of Birdlime finish up this.

26   Cantilever   8m   HD
Start at the foot of the gully below the huge capstone. Climb onto the top of a 2m high block and then from a pile of smaller blocks, bridge out onto the right wall and gain the ledge above and right of the capstone by means of an ungainly wriggle. The steep crack in the corner on the left leads to the top.

LING BUTTRESS

This is the fine, slim buttress to the right of the gully with the huge capstone. Ling Buttress has a short, overhanging left face over-looking Summit Buttress whilst the side facing out over Bilsdale is seamed by cracks and grooves.

27   Peel Out   8m   E4   6b
Start below a curved overlap in the overhanging left left wall about 1m left of the arete. Climb the wall and fnish up easier rock above.

28   Ling Buttress   9m   S   4a   ★★
A fine climb with plenty of variety. Start at the steep rib on the left edge of the front face of the buttress below and left of an obvious tapering slab within a groove. Climb the rib and step onto the slab within the groove which is followed to a step left at the top onto another higher slab. Finish up the steep wall to the left of the upper arete.

29   Groove And Crack   9m   S   4a   ★
Start 2m right of Ling Buttress at a little corner. Follow the corner to gain a flake edge above and left of the inscription "Barton". From the top of the flake edge move left into a groove and follow this up and left to finish up a crack in the headwall. The holds on top are awkwardly placed and good protection should be considered.

30   Ling Corner   9m   S   4a
Follow Groove And Crack to the foot of the groove, step right onto a slab then follow the right- hand arete of the buttress to the top.

THE SPHINX

An imposing buttress whose distinctive profile leaves one in no doubt as to its identity. The West face is steep and compact and has a distinctive pod at 4m whilst the East face provides some easier fare on excellent rock including a truly delectable traverse on the horizontal break seaming the face. The nose itself is has a triangular roof split by a very thin crack.

31   West Sphinx Climb   12m   E3   5b   ★★★
A tremendous pitch requiring careful choice of protection. Start 1m right of the lowest point of the buttress below a big, triangular roof at 6m. Climb the left-trending slabby rib to the left edge of the triangular roof. The concave face above is climbed direct past a horizontal crack (runners) and a big pocket. From the pocket, move right to finish at the same place as The Sphinx Nose Traverse.

The Wainstones – Bilsdale Face

28 31 40 41 45 46 47 48 53

Direct Start   5c
Start directly below the obvious horizontal pod 3m left of the normal start. Climb up to the pod then leave it before moving right to join the normal route at the left edge of the big triangular roof.

32   Black Knight   11m   E3   6c
Climb the nose of the Sphinx direct, starting up The Terrorist and moving left. Two pegs protect the crux (not in place).

33   Terrorist   12m   E5   6a   ★
Very hard climbing; a test of finger strength. Start at the same point as West Sphinx Climb at a faint rib below a narrow, hanging corner leading up to the right-hand side of the triangular roof. Ascend the rib and narrow corner to a small overlap, just right of the roof. Moving up and slightly right on small holds, gain the Sphinx Nose Traverse. Climb the face direct just right of the Sphinx "eye".

34   East Sphinx Direct   7m   HVS   5a   ★
A good steep climb with the crux in its lower half. Start from an embedded block below a thin, vertical crackline in the centre of the East face. Climb the crack to gain an "iron" pocket. A long reach to flat holds is followed by a wider crack.

35   East Sphinx Climb   6m   D
A pleasant route. Start from a wedged block in the bottom of the gully to the right of the East face of the Sphinx. Traverse left on good holds to finish up the wide crack above the Direct.

36   The Sphinx Nose Traverse   12m   S   ★★★
A unique and fascinating climb in a wonderful position, one of the best outcrop Severes anywhere. Start as for East Sphinx Climb from a wedged block in the bottom of the gully right of the East face. Follow East Sphinx climb to the wide crack then follow the fine traverse leading leftwards to the Nose. Handholds are small but good and there are a few good gear placements. To finish, move left onto the Nose and climb this direct.

Another traverse exists on the Sphinx, this is: Traverse Of The Gods (E3 5c) which follows a left to right line crossing the West Face via the horizontal crack below the top pocket on West Sphinx Climb and the East face via a finger traverse on the footledges of the Sphinx Nose Traverse. To the right of the gully bounding the East face of The Sphinx and at a higher level is a ledge above which are three, short climbs Pip, Squeak and Wilfred which use the vertical cracklines.

BILSDALE BUTTRESS
This is 5 metres right of The Sphinx. Its left-hand end is a smooth wall which is in fact the outer face of a massive flake which is separated from the bulging, barrel-shaped right-hand side of the buttress by an attractive, easy groove; Jackdaw Gully.

37   Jackdaw Wall   6m   E2   5c
A contrived route avoiding any of the holds that would appear to be of some use. Start below the smooth, left wall and below a small right-facing flake edge at head height. Layback this finger edge and climb the smooth wall above moving slightly left.

38   Jackdaw Ridge   7m   MS
Start from a little pedestal at the foot of the prominent arete which is the edge of the huge flake. Climb the arete until one can move along a ledge on the left wall above Jackdaw Wall. Finish up this wall.

39   Jackdaw Gully   8m   D   ⋆
A very good line. Climb the prominent groove.

40   Christopher   9m   HVS   5a   ⋆⋆
A super route with a delightful sequence on the crux. Start at the foot of Jackdaw Gully. Climb this until the steep right wall can be climbed on breaks to an overlap. Step boldly right and gain the slabby groove which leads to the top.

41   The Bulge Super Direct   8m   E3   6a   ⋆
This excellent, desperate problem used to be graded VS. It involves some very curious moves and has kept countless people amused for at least three decades. Start 1m right of Jackdaw Gully below a short, V-groove. Climb the wall just right of the groove bearing right to a good hold at 5m. The upper slab is gained and climbed direct with ease.

42   The Bulge   10m   VS   4b   ⋆
Start from a block 2m up Dusty gully at the right end of the buttress. Climb direct to good holds above a steepening and traverse left for 2m to finish up the slab just right of Christopher.

43   The Bulge Direct   8m   HVS   4c
Start as for The Bulge. Climb to good handholds above the steepening then make a long reach to rounded holds and use these to gain the slab above. Finish up the slab.

44   Dusty Rib   9m   MS
Climb the rib which splits Dusty Gully.

Immediately right of the unpleasant descent route of Dusty Gully is:

MAIN WALL

This fine face, one of the attractions of the crag has two facets the right-hand facet being a narrow concave slabby wall.

45   The Slab Climb Variation   10m   S   ⋆
A good route. Start immediately right of Dusty Gully from atop an embedded flake. Climb the left edge of the slab to an overlap and surmount this. Finish up the wall above.

46   The Slab Climb   10m   S   ⋆
Not particularly hard but serious as it lacks protection. Start from a big block, 1m right of the embedded flake. Climb the pleasant slab on sloping holds with a mantelshelf move on the way. Reach the upper ledge and finish up a small corner.

47   Central Route   10m   HVS   5b   ⋆
A tense one move crux! Start as for The Slab Climb, but move diagonally right to a good foothold just left of the big crack of Wall And Ledge.The steep slab above is climbed by a tricky mantelshelf facing right. Climb direct to the top.

48   Wall And Ledge   12m   HD   ⋆⋆
A classic climb with comforting holds almost all the way. Start fro on top of a block below the big crack. Follow the crack which

trends to the right to gain a pedestal on top of a flake. Move up and left onto the upper ledge and finish up a shallow groove.

49   Ridge Route   12m   HS   4b
Start at the foot of the undercut arete to the right of Wall And Ledge. A steep pull up the bulge on good holds gains the ridge above. Follow this to a junction with Wall And Ledge at the pedestal flake. Finish as for Wall And Ledge.

50   Concave Wall   12m   E1   5b   ★
Start just right of the undercut arete. Climb over a flat ledge and continue up the slab above to good holds in the horizontal break. Continue direct to the top.

51   Mousehole Gully   13m   D
Climb the gully separating Main Wall from the impressive Garfit Buttress.

GARFIT BUTTRESS

This tall, final buttress has an impressive S.W. face capped by intimidating bulges. To the right is the less stern S.E. face and a short wall at the back of the buttress reached by scrambling up the broken rocks below the S.E. face has two routes.

52   Lemming Slab   12m   E5   5c/6a
Harder for the short. Start in the centre of the S.W. face. Climb straight up to stand on the second of two little ledges. Make a difficult pull up and left to good holds and use these to pull leftwards round a rib. Finish up the easier-angled narrow face above.

53   Ali Baba   12m   E3   5b   ★★★
A fine bold route which feels "big". Start at the right-hand end of S.W. face below a shallow, scooped corner. Climb the shallow corner on flat and sloping holds to the overhang. Pull out to the left and move back right. Long reaches conclude the trip.

54   Cissam   12m   E3   5b
Start as for Ali Baba. Climb the corner but break out right at 3m and move up to a ledge. Move back left and climb the blunt arete just right of the finish of Ali Baba.

55   Sesame   12m   E2   5b
Start as for Ali Baba. climb up the shallow corner until the obvious break leading onto the S.E. face can be followed. Move right to the wide, vertical crack and finish up this.

56   Turkish Delight   14m   E2   5b/c   ★
A very scenic right to left Girdle of Garfit Buttress. Start at the right -hand side of the S.E. face from the top of a block below and right of the wide upper crack. From the block, move left onto the face and climb Garfit Face to below the wide crack up which it and Sesame finish. Move left and pull onto the S.W. face (Sesame in reverse). Cross the S.W. face by the easiest line moving under a small overlap. Move left round the rib overlooking Mousehole Gully and follow a green crackline to where the face on the right can be climbed via a good flange.

57   Garfit Face   9m   HVS   5a
Start as for Turkish Delight from the top of a block. Move across the

face leftwards to gain and climb the wide vertical crack up which Sesame finishes.

58   Lofty's Ease   5m   S
Start as for Garfit Face from the top of a block. From the block, move up and right until the short, back wall of the buttress can be climbed just right of the arete.

59   Tom Thumb   4m   D Climb the short wall at the back of the buttress by the easiest line.

THE WAINSTONES BOULDERS

No visit to the "Stones" would be complete without climbing on the boulders that lie below the main escarpment of the Bilsdale Face.

Further right of Garfit Buttress is Garfit Quarry which provides numerous problems including a good traverse and the Central Crack (6b).

RAVENS SCAR

To the N.N.W. of the Wainstones beyond Oblique Buttress the fine crag of Ravens Scar faces out across the plain towards Teesside. This crag suffers from lichenous rock and takes time to come into condition but in fine weather it provides climbing that ranks with the best of any outcrop. The crag has over fifty routes and some very hard test-pieces of which the best are: Screwy (E4 6b) which climbs a thin crack, bulging wall and arete to the left of an obvious overhanging corner which gives:

Satchmo (E2 5c). Three metres right of Satchmo, Stratagem (E5 6b) forces a route up the front of the buttress to finish up a slanting crack at the top.

Beyond a sandy gully to the right is the tallest part of the crag.

Hooker (E2 5c) goes up the wall to the left of the groove in the right-hand arete (Harlots Groove, an excellent VS).

To the right of this face is an obvious open groove, Waterslide.

Fever Pitch (E3 5c) climbs the groove right of this, to a bulge. The horizontal crack on the right gives access to a blunt arete and a fine thin crack to finish.

All of the above are of three star quality.

Ravens Scar

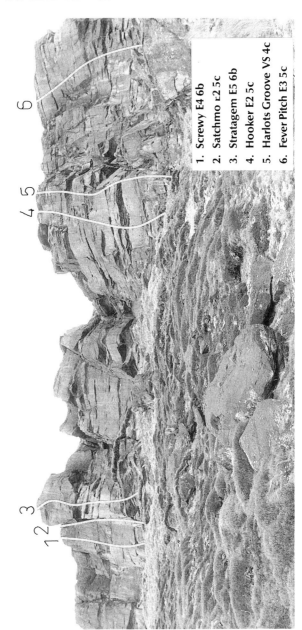

1. Screwy E4 6b
2. Satchmo E2 5c
3. Stratagem E5 6b
4. Hooker E2 5c
5. Harlots Groove VS 4c
6. Fever Pitch E3 5c

SCUGDALE: SCOT CRAGS AND BARKER'S CRAGS
O.S. SHEET 93   G.R. 518004 and 523003

SITUATION AND CHARACTER

Scugdale is one of the Western dales of the Cleveland Hills about 13 miles South of Middlesbrough. The crags, small outcrops of good quality Jurassic Sandstone with iron intrusions all face S.S.W. at the head of the dale above Scugdale Hall and reach a maximum height of 12 metres.

Scot Crags is the most popular of the two mainly due to its greater accessibility and multitude of excellent short climbs in the easier grades and for this reason it can get a little crowded on fine weekends. Barker's Crags on the other hand, has never been as popular as evidenced by the lack of wear and tear, but rising standards and the need for steeper rock have given some of the fearsome little walls in the Amphitheatre and New Dimensions Sections something of a reputation. The fact of the matter is, that if these were in Northumberland you would have heard about them from "Geordie".

Visitors from outside the area may in the past have been surprised at how hard the easier climbs were, indeed all the climbs require a determined and energetic style and an attempt has been made to rationalise previous grading anomalies which may have given the casual guidebook reader an idea that these were rocks for beginners only.

APPROACHES AND ACCESS

From the A19 at Cleveland Tontine to the South or from Teesside to the North, take the A172 and follow this to the village of Swainby at the foot of the dale. Swainby has three pubs, a shop and a small camp site. Just beyond the South end of the village, take the left fork for Scugdale and signed as a No Through Road. This narrow and potentially dangerous road should be followed carefully up dale for almost three miles until limited parking is available just below the stile leading up an obvious path to Scot Crags. Access is not a problem, but large groups should go elsewhere (Eston Nab?) and on no account should dogs be taken to the crag.

N.B. Approaches to Barker's Crags can be found in that section.

HISTORICAL

Scot Crags, Barkers Crags and Stoney Wicks were most probably first climbed upon in the 1920's and 30's by the Barker brothers from Teesside. In the late 1930's however A.W. Evans visited the crags with some regularity and was probably responsible for many of the popular routes such as Razor Rib, Drunken Buttress and the steep Main Mast Crack. In the period coming up to the mid-sixties, many climbers were operating on these popular little crags, but it was always considered to be merely "practice for the real thing" and as a result the activists were usually reluctant to record their efforts Leading up to this period, we know that R.B Wharldall, J. Carter and J. Elliott were active. Eric "Spider" Penman spent some time on these rocks in the early 60's and amongst other things, climbed The Deviator.

In the mid-sixties the Cleveland scene was very active and the only source of information was the "Coffee Bar" in Linthorpe Road, the regular meeting place of local climbers.

Many claims and counter claims were made for various first Ascents and rival factions had their own heroes. Fred Lightfoot and John Chambers led a small band of activists and were probably responsible for the Pingers routes at Scots. In 1965, Stew Wilson and Geoff Harper on the same day, led Pulpit Direct without the aid. In the same year these two claimed the first leads of the three unled routes on Barker's. Geoff with The Chute and Stew with Leaning Wall and Sculptured Wall. The Seventies however saw a rise in standards and a systematic look at all the crags in the area. Tony Marr was certainly responsible for much of this development and stands out as one of the prime movers of climbing in the area. His contributions spanning a quarter of a century of first ascents. Eve was climbed by Marr in 1975 whilst two years later on Barkers Crags he added Easter Edge. The excellent Snatch Arete was climbed by Marr in 1978. About this time another climber, Paul Ingham appeared on the scene. Paul was "rock hungry" and enthusiastic and soon he had a string of fine ascents to his name. Finger Jam and Sculptured Arete, this latter a route of the early 80's, are typical of these. New Dimensions is another route of 1977, climbed by Alan Taylor, it became something of an inspiration and led to the further developments at Barkers. In the same year Alan Taylor and Tony Marr came up trumps with their ascent of The Shelf, a popular test-piece at Scot Crags. An outstanding ascent was made at Scots in the early 80's and even by todays standards must rank as a very hard climb; The Serpent was the route and I. Carr the climber. The latter developments at Barkers have fallen to the practised hand of Richard Davies, a commited technician who in April and May of 1987 contributed some scary and technical climbs such as Dreams With Wings.

SCOT CRAGS

THE CLIMBS
The climbs on Scot Crags are located on numerous isolated blocks and walls extending over a distance of less than 200 metres from the far left end to the fence at the right-hand end. The buttresses have been named in the traditional manner, and whilst this is useful in the majority of cases it can cause confusion where boundaries between them are indistinct.

Starting from the left end, 13 separate sections are named and described with climbs numbered from left to right.

For additional ease of identification the following brief resume of the buttresses at the point of arrival at the crag is offered and climbs can be selected by referring immediately to the appropriate section:

The approach path as described,arrives at the rocks at its most popular part where flat, sandy areas between huge blocks provide good places for picnics etc. From this arrival point the view to the left encompasses Buttress 9 with its right-curving chimney: Scugdale Chimney. Leaning against Buttress 9 on its left-hand side are Buttresses 8: Pisa and 7: Drunken Buttress which are in reality two huge blocks. A big Holly tree is visible from the arrival area with the Pingers Wall of Buttress 11 on its left whilst right of this is a small Oak tree and further right is the taller Buttress 12: Razor Buttress.

Walking left of Scugdale Chimney the most impressive face above a jumble of boulders is Buttress 6: Adam and Eve Buttress. Just left of this is an obvious tall pillar with a bulbous top: The Prow: Buttress 5. To the left of the Prow are Buttresses 1-4.

BUTTRESS 1: RAIKES BUTTRESS

This is at the extreme left-hand end of the escarpment above Raikes farm. It has an impressive block roof at half-height at its right-hand side.

1   Auntie's   6m   HVS   5a
Climb the extreme left-hand arete of the buttress on its right-hand side.

2   Uncle's   6m   VS   5a   ★★
Start just right of Auntie's. Move up and diagonally right to three pockets. From these, gain the runnels above.

3   Straight And Narrow   6m   HD
Start at the toe of the buttress. Climb rightwards to good ledges. Mount the slab rightwards to finish up runnels at the top.

4   Easy Stages   6m   M
Start below and right of the big roof. Climb the blocky rib to the top.

Twelve metres right across heather is a small buttress with a protruding nose at 3m:

5   Mounting Block   3c
Climb the nose direct.

Seven metres right is a slab with a short, cracked corner just left of an overhang at the top of the face:

6   Nutcrackers   5m   D
Climb the cracked corner of the slab.

Just right is:

BUTTRESS 2: THE PARSON'S NOSE

Easily recognisable on account of the prominent, protruding nose on its right-hand side. Its left wall, facing across a recess is steep and smooth.

7   Jivers' Wall   5m   HS   4c   ★
Start below the centre of the left wall in the recess. Climb this direct on small holds.

8   Bop Route   5m   S   4a
Start from a sloping block below the right-hand arete of the steep wall in the recess. Climb the right-hand side of the arete and finish up a cracked groove.

9   Zoot Route   5m   S   4a
Start below and just left of the prominent, Parson's Nose on the front face of the buttress. Climb the steep wall and sloping corner just left of the nose.

A walk to the right of thirty metres brings one to the next buttress.

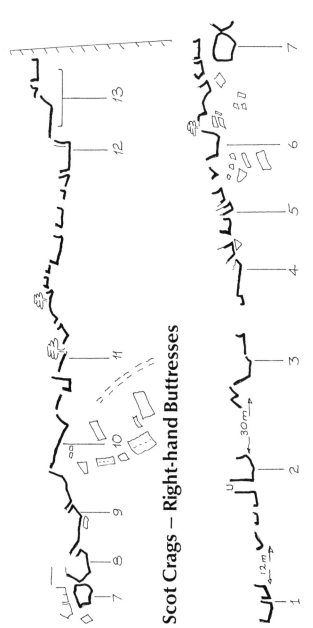

Scot Crags – Right-hand Buttresses

Scot Crags – Left-hand Buttresses

BUTTRESS 3: SCOT BUTTRESS

This attractive buttress has a steep left wall, reminiscent of Jivers' Wall, facing across a square alcove. This is separated by a fine steep arete from a front face which is seamed by a wide vertical crack and a wide diagonal crack.

10 The Vallum 5m S 4a
Climb the wall direct just right of a wide corner crack at the left hand end of the steep wall in the square alcove. Finish at a wide crack in the face above.

11 Hadrian's Wall 6m S 4b ★
Start at a right-slanting, diagonal crack in the left wall. Foot traverse this break until creases in the wall above lead to the top.

12 Corner Direct 7m HS 4a ★★
Not a corner! Start just left of the arete of the left wall. Pull right onto a good ledge- The Nook- and climb the arete direct with long reaches between the breaks.

13 Nook And Cranny 7m HVD
Start as for Corner Direct. Climb into the Nook and move right to a flake crack up which the climb finishes.

14 Highland Fling 7m HVS 5a
Start below and right of the flake crack of Nook And Cranny below a bulging rib. Step off blocks and move left up the rib which is then climbed direct.

15 Bawbee Crack 7m HVD ★
Climb the wide, vertical crack 1m right of Highland Fling. Take care with a moveable "Bawbee".

16 Blaeberry Crack 7m D ★
Climb the right to left diagonal crack to finish as for Bawbee Crack.

17 Blaeberry Buttress 6m M
Start at the arete, 2m right of Blaeberry Crack. Climb the arete, moving left on good holds at half-height.

18 Scot's Girdle 12m MVS 4b ★
A right to left Girdle traverse. Start to the right of Blaeberry Buttress and move left at mid- height, to finish up The Vallum.

Walk 9 metres further right to reach:

BUTTRESS 4: ROMULUS AND REMUS

This is easily recognised by its fine steep slab facing down the dale. A deep block-filled chimney; Tiber Chimney separates Romulus from Remus which is narrower and has a big ledge at half- height.

19 Wolf Wall 6m S ★
Start at the left side of the steep, slabby wall just right of a block ledge leading up to an easy corner. Climb the wall via a long reach to a good hold. Good holds lead to the top.

20 Woodpecker Wall 7m S 4a ★★★
A superb climb on small but sufficient holds. Start just left of the rounded front of the buttress. Climb the wall on horizontal breaks until a "ladder" of good pockets leads to the top.

21 Romulus 7m S 4a ★
Climb the narrow front of the buttress just left of Tiber chimney.

22   Tiber Chimney   7m   M
The unpleasant chimney is climbed direct.
23   Decline And Fall   9m   S   4a   ★
Start at the foot of Tiber chimney. Climb the chimney for 4m then move right onto a break above the undercut base of the slab on the right. Traverse right on this and climb the right edge of the slab.
24   Remus   7m   VS   4c   ★
Start just right of Tiber Chimney at the nose of the lower half of Remus. Climb a left-slanting flake edge to a big ledge. The upper face is taken on the front or by a vague arete to the right.
To the right of an easy gully is:

BUTTRESS 5: THE PROW
Just right of the easy gully immediately right of Romulus and Remus, and at a higher level, starting from the top of a 2m high boulder is a steep face with an off-width crack in the angle. The wall at right angles to the off-width crack is in fact the outer wall of the huge flake of rock whose front is a jutting prow: The Prow. A steep chimney separates The Prow from another steep wall.
25   Halyards   6m   MS
Start from the left-hand end of the ledge at 2m. Climb the left arete to a steep finish.
26   Little By Little   5m   S   4a
Start 2m right of Halyards. Climb the wall via a scoop and two curving, blunt flakes.
27   Main Mast Crack   5m   VS   4c   ★
Climb the off-width corner crack. Sustained and hard.
28   Stewker   6m   E1   5b   ★
A tall man's climb. Much, much harder for the short!
Climb the steep wall just right of Main Mast Crack via a very long reach to a letter-box near the top.
29   The Prow   7m   E1   5a   ★★★
A bit of a meaney, so take care! Climb the slim face of the Prow by a variety of frictional- shinning moves and some expenditure of nervous energy.
30   Galley Chimney   7m   M
Climb the chimney past a big block.
31   The Heads   6m   HS   4b
Start below the arete of the right, inside wall of Galley Chimney. A long reach brings excellent holds on the inside wall. Finish direct.
32   The Bulkhead   6m   HS   4b   ★
Start on the front wall just right of The Heads at a thin crack. Climb the crack which steepens at the top.
To the right of The Bulkhead is a small buttress with a sharp arete, this is Adam.

BUTTRESS 6: ADAM AND EVE
Adam is the small buttress with the sharp arete just right of The Bulkhead whilst at a lower level on the right is Eve. Eve is a more complex block, it has a short wall facing Adam across the gully

which gains height as the slope steps down to the right. A fine arete separates this face from the impressive up-dale face.

To the right of the up-dale face is a jumble of huge blocks forming a good, cave cum shelter. Included with this buttress are the line of rocks above the cave, an isolated pillar of rock: The Pulpit and above and behind The Pulpit is a small buttress called The Choir.

30   Jill's Delight   D
Climb the arete of Adam, starting from a little rock "doorstep".

On the back of Eve and facing Adam across the gully are:

31   The Fig Leaf   5m   HS   4c   ★
Climb the short wall on the left side of the back of Eve to finish in a recess above.

32   Curving Arete   6m   HS   4b   ★
Climb the curving arete just right of The Fig Leaf, starting immediately above a block-step leading to the lower part of the down-dale face of Eve.

33   Jack's Delight   7m   VS   4c   ★
Start at the lowest point of the buttress from on top of a rectangular block. Move up and left across the down-dale face to finish up its centre above a row of pockets.

34   Eve   7m   E1/E3   5a/5b   ★
Climb the fine arete of Eve. The grades refer to which side it is climbed on. The left side is easier.

35   The Serpent   8m   E5   6a   ★★★
One of the "test-pieces" of the crag, bold technical and scary! Start on the up-dale face of Eve from a ledge below a right-trending, thin crackline. Gain the crack and follow it until the wall above and left can be climbed using small pockets.

To the right of Eve is a cave formed by huge blocks. Above the cave are two short walls separated by a vile, chockstone crack.

36   Green Wall   3c
Climb the centre of the left-hand wall, below and immediately right of a small Holly. Strenuous.

37   Archer's Crack   4b
Climb the chockstone crack moving right at the top.

38   Clarance   5b/c
Start just left of the arete to the right of Archer's crack at an undercut wall. Climb the overlap and wall above.

To the right of these small walls is an isolated pillar of rock with an overhanging top block: THE PULPIT.

39   The Pulpit   E1   5c   ★
Start at a wide crack at the left-hand side of the front face. Climb the crack to gain a rightwards Hand-traverse below the top block. Traverse to the prow (runners in break and big thread below prow) and climb it to the top. A solo would attract a higher overall grade (E3). A Direct Start is possible. Another climb; Lazing On A Sunday Afternoon (E1 5c) starts as for The Pulpit and ascend the overhang at the start of the traverse right.

Behind and to the right of The Pulpit is a small buttress with two faces separated by an arete. This is THE CHOIR.

40   Hallelujah Chorus   6m   HVS   5b
Start in the chockstone gully to the left of the buttress. Climb the scoop just left of the arete without using boulders on the gully.

41   Anvil Chorus   6m   HVS   5c
Climb the left side of the undercut wall just right of the arete. Passing a bulge is the crux.

42   Haec Dies   6m   HVS   5b   ★
Climb the centre of the right-hand wall direct, starting from good footholds.

43   The Choir   6m   HVS   5b
Climb the right-hand side of the wall immediately left of rib. The difficulties increase towards the top.

We now come to those buttresses that are visible from the Arrival Area of the crag.

BUTTRESS 7: DRUNKEN BUTTRESS

This is the first of the two huge block buttresses leaning against Scugdale Buttress (Buttress 9).

Drunken Buttress is just across the gully from The Choir and it takes the form of a large tilted block 6 metres high with an undercut slab facing down valley. The wall to the right, facing across the valley is steep and covered with good incut "iron pockets"

44   Seamy Side   D   ★
Start at the left of the undercut on the slabby, down valley face at the foot of a fine arete. Climb the arete.

45   Hangover   HS   4c   ★★
A super severe with a pokey start. Start at the right-hand end of the undercut slab. Layback over the bulge into a shallow groove which leads pleasantly to the top.

46   Tippling Wall   VS   5a   ★★
Start below the very steep wall around to the right from Hangover and 1m left of the right-hand arete. Fine climbing leads on small but improving holds to the top break. Move left to finish or climb direct (HVS) to the top. The shorter bulging wall around to the right from Tippling Wall is initially featureless apart from a sloping "shelf" at its upper right-hand side. A good low -level traverse starts at The Shelf and moves left round the buttress at less than one and a half metres to Tippling Wall (6b)

47   The Shelf   E2   5c   ★
Start at two long blocks on the ground below the overhanging wall below The Shelf. Climb the wall to gain The Shelf. A difficult pull and step up lead (with some relief) to the top.

Sandwiched between the block of Drunken Buttress and Scugdale Buttress is another huge block is Pisa Buttress.

BUTTRESS 8: PISA BUTTRESS

This buttress has a steep but relatively narrow base which emerges as a wider face from behind the rear end of Drunken Buttress at the top. A steep crack marks the junction of Drunken and Pisa Buttresses.

Scot Crags Buttresses 8-11

48   The Plumb Line   S   4a
Climb the short, awkward crack at the junction of the two buttresses.

49   The Bob   S   4a
Start from the ledge above the finish of Plumbline. Climb the obvious arete on the left. This is on the emergent upper face of Pisa Buttress.

50   Gravity Wall   7m   HS   4b   ⋆
Start 3m right of Plumbline at the front arete of the buttress. Follow holds diagonally up and left until the wall can be climbed direct to finish.

51   Galileo's Gully   7m   S   4a
Climb the outside of the wide chimney whose right wall is Scugdale Buttress.

BUTTRESS 9: SCUGDALE BUTTRESS

This is the highest buttress at Scot Crag. It has two faces. The left hand face is just right of Galileo's Gully and has a wide vertical crack at the top. The right-hand face has the conspicuous curving cleft of Scugdale Chimney splitting it from top to bottom.

52   Tooth And Nail   8m   HS   4c   ⋆⋆
Start just right of Galileo's Gully at a steep wall below a bottomless, wide crack in the upper wall. Climb up to the crack and follow it on good holds to the top.

53   Hybrid   8m   HS   4b
Not an outstanding route. Start at the foot of Scugdale Chimney. Climb the left rib of the chimney until a left traverse can be made, below the level of the overhang, to gain the left wall. Move into Tooth And Nail and follow this to the top.

54   Supine   8m   VS   4c
Climb the arete of the buttress.

55   Scugdale Chimney   9m   HD   ⋆⋆⋆
Climb the right-curving chimney with an awkward step near the top.

55   Scugdale Chimney Eliminate   8m   VS   4c
Climb the chimney to where it trends right. MOve left and surmount the overhang and climb direct to the top.

56   Zeta Wall   6m   HS   4b   ⋆
Climb the discontinuous cracks in the steep wall 3m right of Scugdale Chimney. The finish is awkward.

57   Deviator   6m   VS   5a
Start 1m right of Zeta Wall in a small right-facing corner. Climb this corner and move left into a shallow scoop. Finish up the weakness above, left of the arete.

58   Nameless Crack   4m   S   4a
Climb the widening off-width crack immediately right of Deviator.

The attractive rectangular wall on the right is:

BUTTRESS 10: BARKERS' BUTTRESS

This buttress consists of an attractive rectangular face seamed by two horizontal cracks. A steep rib separates this face from a narrow face which has a slim crack splitting it near the top. At right angles to the slim face and immediately right of the obvious Barkers' Chimney is another steep wedged-shape wall.

59 Cub's Climb 5m VD 3c
Start at the extreme left end of the rectangular S.W. face below an obvious shallow corner at the top. Climb the wall and finish up the shallow corner.

60 Kitten's Climb 6m VD 3b ★
Start 2m right of Cub's Climb at a short vertical crack. Climb this and the wall above trending left.

61 Pup's Climb 7m VS 4c ★★
Start at the left-slanting flake right of the crack above the first horizontal break. Climb the crack and the wall above to finish at an obvious break at the top.

62 Bonzo 7m HVS 5b ★
Start 2m left of the right-hand arete by a pointed block. Climb the wall direct with a long reach to a good pocket below the second horizontal break. Finish direct.

63 Pet's Corner 7m MVS 4c ★★
Climb the wall just left of the right-hand arete. The nearer the arete the harder it is.

Beyond the arete is:

64 Whippet Wall 7m VS 4c ★
Used to be considered "thin"! Start 1m right of the arete. climb the middle of the slim wall to finish up a thin flake crack.

65 Barkers' Chimney 6m M
Climb the chimney in the corner past two blocks.

66 Cat Walk 6m VD
Start at the right-hand side of the steep wall right of Barkers' Chimney. Climb up the right -hand side until a ledge crossing the face can be traversed from right to left to finish at the top of the chimney. A direct start up the face just right of the chimney is possible at 4b.

67 Pluto 6m HS 5a
Rather contrived. Start at the right-hand end of the wall as for Cat Walk.Climb the edge of the wall to the top. The start is hardest and does not use the wide crack or blocks to the right for footholds.

68 Cerebrus Crack 4m S
Start on a ledge around the arete from Pluto. Climb the wide, right-trending crack.

69 Peke's Perch 4m MS 3c
Start 2m right of Cerebrus Crack at the foot of a short rib below a slim crack. Climb the rib and crack direct.

BUTTRESS 11: HOLLY TREE BUTTRESS
This next buttress is dominated by a large Holly which is threatening to take it over. The wall left of the Holly is steep and smooth. An overhanging nose projects above the tree whilst the wall to the right is split by vertical cracks. In the more broken rocks to the right, an Oak tree struggles for existence and further right across an open

gully is a small buttress with a conspicuous bulge at mid-height below a mantelshelf.

70   Pingers Left-Hand   6m   VS   5a
Start at the left edge of the wall. Climb direct to finish up a scoop at the top.

71   Pingers   6m   VS   5a   ★
Start below the middle of the steep slab below a two finger pocket. Climb the wall above the pocket to better holds and the top. An Eliminate: Pingers Right-Hand can be contrived at 5c (with a little imagination!)

72   Prickly Rib   7m   VS   4c
Start immediately left of the Holly. Climb the steep wall onto the sloping arete. Climb the rib above on its right-hand side to the top.

73   Holly Tree Chimney   8m   HVD
Start below a rib which runs up to the overhang just right of the Holly. Climb the rib until a slab on the left can be traversed from right to left. Finish up the wide chimney above.

74   Holly Tree Hover.   6m   VS   4c
Start below the middle of the wall to the right of the rib of Holly Tree Chimney. Climb the wall and crack above to the right of the jutting roof.
Harder Variations exist to the left (HVS) by pulling out over the overhang to the left. A sabre- toothed block below should be padded with rucsacs.

75   Saint's Wall   6m   VD   3c   ★
Start 1m right of Holly Tree Hover. Climb the obvious crack passing a niche.

76   Oak Tree Wall   6m   HS   4a
Start 1m right of the crack of Saint's Wall at an overhanging, short corner. Climb the corner to a ledge. The cracked scoop above leads to an awkward finish.

Across the gully to the right of an Oak is a small buttress with a distinctive bulge at mid-height.

77   The Mantelshelf   6m   VS   4c   ★
Climb the centre of the slab to the bulge. Pull up to the ledge above the bulge and mantelshelf onto it.

78   Humpty Dumpty   6m   S   4b
Climb the steep rib to the right of The Mantelshelf via a red jug and an awkward step. Do not use holds across the gully.

BUTTRESS 12: THE RAZOR

To the right of Humpty Dumpty the rocks are broken for 9m then there is a tall buttress with a stepped right-hand arete. This is The Razor. The right wall, to the right of the arete is cut across by a good ledge. To the left of The Razor is a short lower wall leading to a good platform. Above this platform is a short, upper wall.
The next climbs are start below the lower wall left of The Razor.

79   Cicatrice   4a
Start in the centre of the left, lower wall. Climb up to a thin crack at the top and an awkward finish.

80   Slashed Wall   VD
Climb the left-trending blunt flakes, 1m right of Cicatrice.
81   The Gash   D
Climb the V-corner 1m right of The Slash.
The next climb is on the wall above the last three climbs:
82   Tonsure   4a
Climb the centre of the upper wall to a flake crack. climb this
moving right.
The next climbs start below the front face of The Razor.
83   Sweeney Todd   7m   VS   5a   ★
Start just right of the V-corner of The Gash. Climb to a good ledge
at 2m. Climb the wall above on small holds.
84   Razor Rib   8m   HVD   ★★★
Start below and just left of the stepped arete. Climb up and slightly
left to gain and follow a left- curving flake to the top. The arete itself
can be climbed direct if preferred at S 4a. Laybacking the left-hand
side of the arete, "Archangel-style" gives Acres Wild (HVS 5a).
The next two climbs start from a ledge at half-height on the wall to
the right of the rib.
85   Suds   5m   HVS   5b   ★
Climb the thin left-hand crack above the ledge.
86   Tension   5m   E2   5c   ★
Climb the wall to the right on small holds. Seriously bad landing.

BUTTRESS 13: BEGINNERS' SLAB AND CURTAIN SLAB
These are the two slabby faces at the extreme right-hand end of the
escarpment before the fence. Beginners' Slab is well-worn and
enough to put newcomers off for good. Curtain Slab is to the right
of Beginners' Slab and can be climbed anywhere at around VD.
87   Alpha   7m   VD
Start at the left side of the slab just right of a block-filled chimney.
Climb the awkward wall to the bottom of a left-trending gangway
up which one can teeter to the top.
88   Beta   7m   VD   ★
From the right-hand end of the slab, move up and left to the middle
of the face and follow a vague, curving flake to the top.
89   Gamma   7m   HS   4a
Climb the right-hand edge of the slab.

BARKER'S CRAGS

THE CLIMBS

From a stile in the fence to the right of and above Scot Crags, a
good path can be followed up valley above the escarpment. The
escarpment is not continuous and the location of the buttresses is
very specific.

There are another seven buttresses or more specifically, sections.
These are from left to right going up valley; Buttresses 14- 20.

The first climb is located on an unnamed buttress about 70 metres beyond the fence. This is a small buttress with a distinct knife-edged arete.

90   Tales Of Harperly Hall   5m   5c
Climb the arete direct.

The first distinctive feature beyond the fence is a lone Oak tree growing by the drystone wall just below the level of the escarpment. Forty metres beyond the Oak, descend to the first section of continuous rock:

BUTTRESS 14: AMPHITHEATRE BUTTRESS

This section consists of a short wall with a big ledge: Pedestal Ledge, on the right arete at 4 metres. Around the arete to the right is the Big Amphitheatre which is a bay or indentation with a very steep right wall bounded on its right by a bulbous arete. To the right of this is the Small Amphitheatre which has a steep and impressive right wall. The extreme right arete has an overhanging pillar front with right again a deep chimney. A fine sharp arete bounds this chimney on the right.

91   Green Chimney   VD
Climb the left-curving off-width crack at the extreme left of the first short wall.

92   Problem Wall   4m   5c
Climb the steep wall right of Green chimney.

93   Outer Wall   5m   S   4a
Start 3m down the slope from Green Chimney. Climb the steep wall just left of the upper arete rising from the Pedestal Ledge.

94   Pedestal Crack   4m   HVD
Climb the very thin flake crack 1m right of Outer Wall to the ledge.
Go round The Nose into Big Aphitheatre.

95   Walled In   4m   5b
Climb the steep wall of The Nose.

96   Who Nose   4m   HD
Climb sloping holds to the right of The Nose onto Pedestal Ledge.

97   Pedestal Chimney   D
Climb the "not a chimney" crack 1m right of Who Nose.

98   Pedestal Wall   6m   HS   4b
Climb Pedestal Chimney to the ledge and move right onto the wall on the right. Finish by an exposed mantelshelf.

99   Flake Chimney   5m   VD
Climb the chimney 2m right of Pedestal Wall via a prominent, vertical rock fin.

100   Flake Chimney Wall   6m   HD
From the foot of Flake Chimney, gain a ledge on the right wall at shoulder height. Traverse diagonally right and finish steeply up the crack above.

101   Long Chimney   6m   S
Start in the prominent, cracked corner left of the fine, lichenous right wall. Climb the corner which is hardly a chimney!

102   Easter Edge   5m   5c
Start 4m right of Long Chimney just left of the undercut front of the

Barkers Crag – Little Amphitheatre

buttress and below the steep upper arete. Climb the overhanging, concave wall to better holds just before the arete.

103   Fairy Tale High   5m   6b
Start just right of Easter Edge below a bulging wall with a pocket at chest-height. Climb the wall.

104   He Nose, You Nose   5m   5c
Climb the right-hand arete direct 1m right of Fairy Tale High, gaining a good flake edge.

Moving right into Little Amphitheatre:

105   Alcove Cracks   6m   S
Climb the recessed groove via twin cracks.

106   Alcove Chimney   7m   S
Climb the deep, corner chimney.

107   Alan's Wall   7m   E1   5b
Start 2m right of Alcove Chimney below a crozzly wall bounded on the right by a curving rib. Climb the wall just left of this rib.

108   Captain Kirk Where Are You?   7m   E1   5c   ★
Climb the groove left of Snatch Arete with a hard move to reach the overhang. Step left to finish.

109   Snatch Arete   7m   E2   5c   ★★
Climb the extreme right-hand arete of Alan's Wall on its left-hand side.

Around the arete to the right is a deep chimney:

110   Pioneers' Chimney   7m   M
Climb the deep chimney.

111   Empty Illusions   7m   5c
Climb the underside of the fin of rock which forms the right side of the chimney.

112   Ancients' Ascent   6m   VD
Start to the right of the fin of rock which is the N side of Pioneers' Chimney. Climb the slab using the left edge as a handhold.

Regain the track on the moor above the escarpment and follow this for a further 60 metres till above the end of a small wood. Twenty metres beyond this wood, the edge rises to form a little slab facing down the valley. Here is:

BUTTRESS 15

113   One For The Road   5m   D
Climb the right edge of the slab.

114   Chaser Chimney   5m   D
Climb the chimney round to the right.

Another "Not really worthwhile" face is 30m further on this has a flake at its right-hand end:

115   Last But One   5m   VD
Layback the flake.

Thirty metres of "sub-Alpine" blocks and chasms leads rightwards to yet another, better, small buttress:

BUTTRESS 16

This consists of a steep wall facing down the dale, separated from a jutting prow by a twin- cracked corner.

116   Flake Wall   VD

Climb the centre of the flakey wall.

117   Joshua's Nose   HVD

Climb the rib at the right end of Flake Wall.

118   Bilberry Cracks   S

Climb the twin-cracked corner.

119   Only A Diff.   5c

Climb the front of the overhanging wall to the right of Bilberry Cracks.

120   Dangerous Game   5b

Climb the arete just right of Only A Diff.

121   Gossip   4c

Climb the flake 3m right of Dangerous Game on the right-hand wall.

Directly below this buttress is a deep-sunken track concealed in the bracken. Descend to this and cross it then pick up a continuation track above the escarpment. The next section is identified easily by a lone Oak tree growing in a rocky cleft above the escarpment. This is:

BUTTRESS 17: ARCH AND ATTIC

122   Arch Gully   7m   M

Climb the obvious gully, arched by a massive block.

123   Fallen Arch   5m   HVS   5a   ★★

Climb the overhanging hand-crack just right of the gully.

124   Attic Gully   5m   M

Climb the block-filled corner and exit on the left.

125   Footloose   5m   5c

Start 4m right of the hand-crack below an undercut black flake in the middle of the leaning wall. Move up and leftwards to finish via a short flake crack and sloping ledge.

Thirty metres right from Footloose is a steep block with a wide vertical cleft above a horizontal break. This is:

126   Hogmanay   4c

Climb up to and into the cleft. Struggle to the top.

127   First Footing   D

Climb the arete immediately right of Hogmanay.

Across a 2m wide gully is:

128   Black Corner   VD

Climb the black, left-hand rib on good holds. Confusing name!

129   Black Wall   5b

Climb the wall 2m right of the rib. The start is the hardest.

130   Timeless Divide   4c

Climb the wall 3m right of Black Wall.

Twenty metres further right is some of the best climbing at Barker's Crags:

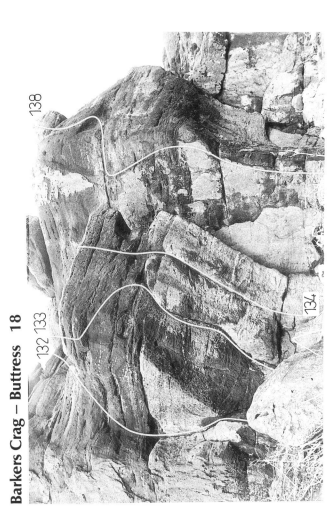

Barkers Crag – Buttress 18

BUTTRESS 18: NEW DIMENSIONS

An impressive, leaning wall of excellent rock which compares favourably with the more famous walls in Northumberland. Its a pity there isn't more of it. The buttress is cleft in two by a deep chimney wide enough to allow independent routes on its walls.

131 Leaning Wall   8m   HVS   5b   *
Start at the left arete of the left-hand buttress below an open, black scoop (The Chute). Climb the wall just left of the little corner and move diagonally from right to left up flakey holds on the steep left face.

132 The Chute   7m   HVS   5a
Start as for Leaning Wall but from the little corner, move up the black scoop to finish on the right.

133 Finger Jam   7m   E3   6b   **
Start below the overhanging front face, 2m right of The Chute. Climb the thin, overhanging, finger crack moving out left at the top to finish in the scoop of The Chute. Direct Finish: The obvious direct finish over the nose.

134 New Dimensions   8m   E4   6a   ***
Start 1m right of Finger Jam below a thin crack with a vertical slot just out of reach. Climb this and the wall above.

135 Stone Free   9m   E4   6a
Climb the outside, overhanging left arete of Chockstone Chimney.

136 Chockstone Chimney   10m   D
Climb the chimney separating the two leaning walls.

137 Sculptured Wall   10m   E1   5a   **
Start at the foot of the right wall of Chockstone Chimney below a left-trending flake. Climb this and the wall above on generally good holds. An unforgiving place to fall off!

138 Sculptured Arete   12m   E4   5c   **
Start as for Sculptured Wall. Climb this until at a hole, one moves right towards the arete. Follow the left-hand side of the arete until a traverse right onto the front wall leads to an awkward finish left of the top block.

139 Heartbeat   12m   E3/4   5c   **
Climb the right-hand side of Sculptured Arete moving left from the top break to finish up the groove on the arete.

140 Dreams With Wings   12m   E5   6b   ***
Start in the middle of the overhanging wall right of Sculptured Arete. Climb the wall with the crux at 6m above a poor landing.

141 Night Entry   12m   VS   4b   *
Start at the right-hand end of the overhanging wall right of the chimney below a corner cleft. Climb the cleft and the edge of the buttress above finishing to the right of the top block.

142 Rum Doodle   12m   VS   5a
Climb the layback crack to the right of Night Entry. The exit from the crack is awkward. Finish as for Night Entry.

Thirty metres right of Rum Doodle is:

143 A Sack A Day   5m   4c
Climb the arete of this isolated small buttress.

One hundred metres further right is:

BUTTRESS 19: CINDERELLA BUTTRESS
This consists of three small buttresses. Cinderella is the left-hand and biggest with the two ugly sisters to its right.

144   Beware The Thunder   5m   5c
Climb the wall to the left of the overhang left of the nose up which Cinderella goes. A long reach is an advantage. Finish by trending right.

145   Impressionless Lust   7m   6a
Ascend the centre of the overhang between Beware The Thunder and Cinderella. Finish up Cinderella.

146   Cinderella   7m   D
Climb the nose of the buttress.

147   Ugly Sister 1.   5m   VD
Climb the left-hand side of the second buttress.

148   Ugly Sister 2.   5m   VD
Climb the left-hand side of the third buttress.

Fifty metres right is the final buttress:

BUTTRESS 20: THE VIRGIN

149   The Virgin   6m   4c
The left wall is ascended.

150   Flaked Out   6m   5b
Start just right of The Virgin. Climb up to a flake and finish more easily.

151   Obsessions Of The Mind   6m   6a
Start on the right wall of the buttress, right of the arete. Climb the right wall and gain a hold on the arete on the left. Pull across and straddle the arete moving up to better holds and finally the top.

152   Right Wall Route   5m   S
Climb the wall of the buttress right of Obsessions Of The Mind.

Stoney Wicks is a further one hundred and twenty five metres right from The Virgin. Here, on perfect rock are twenty short climbs from M to HVS. Well worth a visit.

10   SWALEDALE

Swaledale is one of the most glorious of the Dales. The climbing in Swaledale is mainly on Limestone but Healaugh Crag, better known as Crag Willas provides excellent quality Gritstone with a potential for hard climbs exceeding the now famous Slipstones Crag in Colsterdale.

Swaledale as a climbing venue has mainly been used by climbers from the immediate locality, Teesside and County Durham.

The lower dale, just West of Richmond has the most popular crag; Hag Wood, but it is North-facing and not as pleasant to climb on as Applegarth Scar. The steep crags above Wainwath have a lot of potential for future prospectors and Kisdon Scar has already succumbed to the Hilti and if this proves to be a succesful venue, it will be creamed off into the Yorkshire Limestone Book Of Very Big Numbers.

HUDSWELL CRAG   O.S. SHEET 92   G.R. 154005

SITUATION AND CHARACTER

Located about one mile West of Richmond in lower Swaledale facing North on the South side of the river. Hudswell Crag is part of the same escarpment as the more popular Hag Wood. The quality of the rock is variable and the finishes can be loose and dirty. Having said this, some of the routes when clean, provided good climbing. There is much scope for development.

APPROACHES AND ACCESS

Follow the A6108 West out of Richmond. Just beyond the cemetery on the right and a caravan site on the left, turn off the road on the left and park in the parking place by the footbridge over the River Swale. Cross the bridge and follow a Holly hedge by a derelict wall up the hill in an upstream direction. The crag is just in woodland at the end of the field.

HISTORICAL

The routes at Hudswell were climbed in the Spring of 1973 by a group of Darlington-based climbers including Tony McLean, R. Gay and G.R. Davidson. Betablocker was climbed by Paul Carling in November 1984.

THE CLIMBS

The climbs are described from left to right facing the crag.

1   Graham's Route   6m   S
Climb the prominent chimney at the extreme left end of the crag.
Three parallel cracklines are the next notable feature.

2   Betablocker   12m   HVS   5b
Climb the central crack to finish up a loose groove and earth bank.

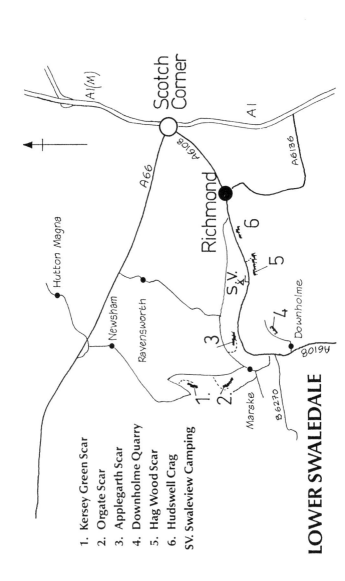

1. Kersey Green Scar
2. Orgate Scar
3. Applegarth Scar
4. Downholme Quarry
5. Hag Wood Scar
6. Hudswell Crag
SV. Swaleview Camping

LOWER SWALEDALE

3   Conifer Corner   12m   VD
Climb the prominent corner past a Yew tree. Finish up an easy crack and belay well back.

Thirty metres further right is Graffiti Cave.

4   Missile Groove   20m   VS   4c
Start 9m right of Graffiti Cave below a crack and groove. Climb the crack and groove and step left to pull over a block. follow the loose, Ivy-clad wall to the top.

5   Grey Delight   18m   VS   4b
Start at an easy corner below a cave. climb the corner to the cave then bridge until a step right can be made onto a rounded foothold. traverse right and move up to a ledge and tree.

6   Urban Gorilla   11m   S
Start 8m further right at the foot of a blunt arete. Climb the arete to the top. It is easier but inferior to start up the groove on the left.

7   The Main Overhang   18m   A2
Start 30m right of Urban gorilla below the obvious roof.

8   White Light   21m   VS   4c   ⋆
Start to the right of The main overhang below a series of overhanging grooves. Climb twin cracks and move left to gain a ledge. Continue with difficulty to a niche beneath the final overhang, then traverse left around the arete and finish up the wall above.

9   Knife-Edge Groove   15m   HS
A good climb with a loose finish. Start 28m right of The main Overhang at a prominent, flake crack. Climb the flake for 6m and traverse right to finish up a short corner.

HAG WOOD   OS Sheet 92   GR 134010

SITUATION AND CHARACTER

This is the most important crag in Swaledale. Hag Wood is a limestone escarpment up to 20 metres high with a selection of good climbs mainly in the middle grades, but with some interesting harder climbs.

The crag faces North north west and is at the top of a steep wooded slope overlooking the Swaleview Caravan site on the A6108 about two and a half miles West of Richmond.

The Limestone of Hag Wood is quite massive in structure but has some interesting cracks and grooves. On some climbs, crystalline pockets provide essential holds. Protection is usually plentiful but care should be taken in the choice of placements particularly behind flakes.

Hag Wood crag due to little traffic and the fact that it was mainly developed "from the bottom up" has more than its share of loose rock but this is manageable. The finishes to some climbs require caution as the steep finishes are composed of large blocks in a steep shale slope. Fortunately large trees abound and these can be used as anchors and for abseil descents (recommended). Local climbers could well consider putting in an odd afternoon to trundle blocks from the finishes to the climbs. Where this has been done, the finishes are no problem. In the future fixed lowering points from twin bolts could serve the purpose of alleviating stress in the leader and protecting the unstable tree-covered slope above the crag from unnecessary erosion. This would in no way detract from the routes as the finishes certainly have little technical merit.

The climbing is very enjoyable providing you are not expecting too much. It is equally possible to climb here in winter if you are prepared to suffer a little. The best time to climb is on a fine evening when the crag enjoys the sunshine.With a bit of "spade-work" and traffic the crag will be a very good venue.

APPROACHES AND ACCESS

Follow the A6108 westwards up Swaledale from Richmond for one and a half miles before crossing the River Swale. Continue for another mile until a couple of muddy laybys are encountered below the steep wooded hillside on the left. The entrance to the Caravan site is a little further on, on the right.

From the second layby a variety of paths are followed steeply uphill to reach the crag. As the crag is not extensive, follow the base to the left-hand end to locate the first routes. Time from layby to crag is about five minutes.

HISTORICAL

The original explorers were John Deighton, John Brighton and Dave Lloyd who in 1962 climbed some of the easier lines. In 1966/7 Chris Craggs and Pete Ackroyd added Garlic Groove, Nix, Cleavage and Cobs Corner. Colin Binks climbed Karumba and Holy Moses, whilst Neil Stuart added The Blade (later climbed free by Fred Stevenson) and the spectacular Limbo.

In 1974, Bruce Perry and members of the Cleveland M.C. added more climbs, the best of which were Levon, Indian Sunset, Razor Face and Only A Rose. They also free-climbed Twilight Crack which had previously required aid. Peter Dyson added Jubilee, Cat Walk and the excellent Twilight Groove, whilst Tony McClean completed the Girdle Traverse.

A lull followed until 1982 when Nigel Preston added the fine D-Rider, Hag Wood's first Extreme. In 1983 Paul Carling repeated D-Rider thinking it to be a first ascent and went on to add Pocket Billiards. Just A Carrot was another of Carling's projects and this was also climbed and claimed by Stu Ferguson some months later as Bum Under. Stu protected the climb with a peg, which is still in place. Paul Carling also climbed Dust and Tears which warranted the E3 grade for seriousness if not for difficulty and is probably unrepeated. Roy Small found Dry Grasp and in 1985 Stu Ferguson brought matters up to date with Criminal Infusion and a direct finish to Twilight Crack. Whilst checking for the present guide Stew Wilson added The Rose And The Ramson. Remaining lines are few, but who knows? The scoop to the right of Holy Moses must be a distinct possibility!

THE CLIMBS

Climbs are described from left to right. Descents can be made at

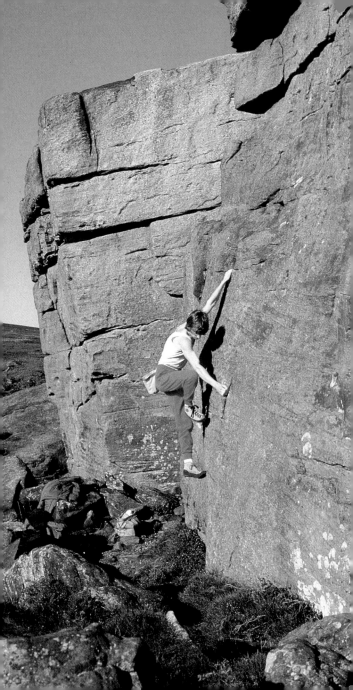

the left end of the crag or down a large gully; "The Rubbish Chute" which is at the right hand end of the crag to the right of Levon. It is better however to abseil off routes from the many trees at the top.

The climbs at the extreme left end of the crag are on a short, steep wall.

1 Yankee Doodle 5m S
Climb the crack which starts at chest height. The finish is awkward.

2 Letter Box 6m VD
Climb the wider crack in the centre of the wall moving left to finish.

3 Littler Eliminate 6m S
Climb the wall just right of the central crack.

4 Minority 6m VD
Climb twin cracks towards the right-hand side of this first wall.

5 Pocket Hole Corner 6m S   ★
Climb the steep right-hand corner.

6 Pocket Billiards 7m VS 5a   ★
Climb the arete to the right of Pocket Hole Corner, on a series of delectable finger pockets. Finish slightly right between two trees.

7 Garlic Groove 9m MVS 4b   ★
Start just around the arete. Climb the V-groove past a small tree with increasing difficulty.

8 Shield Groove 9m HS
Starts two metres further right below a large flake. Climb the groove to the large flake and continue up steep rocks to the top.

9 Perron 11m S
At the right-hand end of the wall is a chimney. Climb the thin just left of the chimney with difficulty to a ledge and sapling. Step left and climb the front of the buttress to a Yew and finish direct.

10 Swinging 8m D
Climb the chimney.

11 Crystals 11m S
Climb the wall just right of the chimney and move right at a steepening on pockets, to finish up a corner.

12 Cality 11m S   ★
Climb the steep corner-crack to the right past a ledge at seven metres. A good climb.

13 Crastifit 11m VD   ★
Starts three metres right at a chimney behind an Elder. Climb the chimney past chockstones. Step right at mid-height and finish on good holds.

14 Tower Traverse 15m VD
Starts behind a 'tower' at the foot of the crag. Climb the back of the tower, step onto the wall and follow a series of ledges leftwards to finish.

15 Dandelion Crack 12m VS
Start on the wall immediately behind the tower. Climb the left of two thin cracks to a small ledge. Continue up the crack past loose blocks to the top.

16 Babel 12m VS 4c
Climb the right-hand crack behind the tower to an awkward

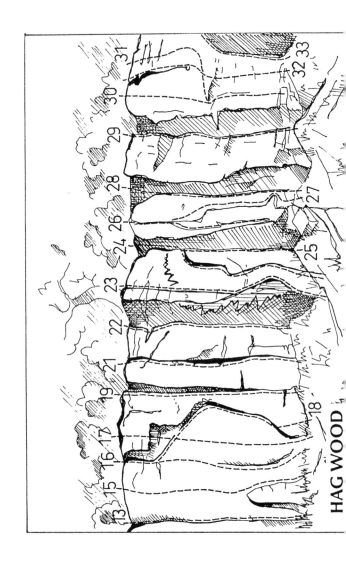

HAG WOOD

mantleshelf below an overhang. Move slightly right and finish up the V-groove of Barkad the rib to the left of this groove is slightly easier.

17   The Blade 14m   HVS   5b
Three metres right of the tower is a thin crack. Climb this via a shallow cave and so to the top with difficulty.

18   Barkad   15m   VS   4c   ★★
Starts at the right side of the wall. Follow pockets for 6 metres. Traverse left past a large thread to a cave. Climb up a steep little wall to a ledge and finish up the V-groove of Babel. A very minor classic.

19   Rack Crack   14m   HS   4b   ★
Climb the prominent, straight off-width crack just to the right.

At the right hand end of this wall is a prominent chimney with a horrifying-looking finish. This is Limbo.

20   Holy Moses   15m   VS   4c   ★
Start at a crack 3 metres left of the chimney and climb it to a small sapling. Move up and delicately left round a bulge and into a slight depression. Climb to a small ledge with difficulty and traverse into a crack, following this to the top.

21   Holy Moses Direct   14m   HVS   5a   ★
Better than the original. Start up the thin crack to the left of the original and join Holy Moses at the slight depression. Move up to the ledge and finish straight up the wall above, moving slightly left at the top.

22   Limbo   17m   VS   4b
Climb the prominent, deep chimney, into and out of a cave. Finish left at a prominent Beech. Much better than it looks.

23   Dust And Tears   17m   E3   5b   ★
Accepts the challenge of the friable, red arete to the right of Limbo. A serious climb with sparse and suspect protection. Scramble up to the ledge at the base of the arete. Pull over the overlap on pockets and go left to a good hold (small wire placement) and a semi-rest. Move back right to climb the final, steep groove to a Yew.

24   The Criminals   15m   HVS   4c
Start right of the red arete in the middle of the next wall and follow the shallow groove via a crack until a bulge can be ascended. Move rightwards and up to a small Yew. Move rightwards into a corner and follow this to the top. A serious climb.

25   Cleavage   14m   MVS   4b   ★
A good route up the obvious corner. To the right of this corner a large block lies below the crag marking the starts of the next two routes.

26   Dry Grasp   14m   HVS   5a
Start to the left of Slow Drifter below a fierce, undercut crack. Climb this and the scoop above to below a groove (thread runner). Climb the groove moving right near the top to finish up Slow Drifter.

27   Slow Drifter   14m   VS   4c
Starts at a steep crack above the big block just right of the undercut crack. Climb the steep crack to a large, dangerous flake. Bear left past a small tree to finish.

28   Ginger Crack   14m   HVD
Climb the corner crack to the right with care.

29   Acid Head   15m   VS   4c   ★
Start below the next corner which has a fine crack with a pronounced bulge. Climb this with some difficulty.

30   Jubilee   14m   VS   4c
Start below the left side of the next wall on the right. Climb the wall
until a line of pockets leads diagonally right above the bulge. Finish
directly up the front of the buttress to the tree.

31   Cats Cradle   15m   HS
Climb the initial wall of Jubilee to a ledge. Traverse right using
holds over the bulge (thread) to reach a tree. Finish directly up the
groove above.

32   Catwalk   14m   VS   4b
Start at a shallow groove just right of the previous climb. Climb the
groove past a bulge. Trend right to small trees and finish up the
arete on the left.

33   Crows Nest   14m   VD
To the right of the wall is a slender pinnacle in a corner. Enter the
chimney behind the pinnacle from the left wall, passing a small
tree. Continue to a vegetated finish.

34   Caw 14m   VD
Climb the crack on the right side of the pinnacle.

To the right of the pinnacle is a large Elm below a groove.

35   Rookery   12m   S
Climb the rib on the left of the groove to a loose block. Step off the
block and traverse leftwards to the top of Crows Nest.

36   Midnight Groove   14m   HS   ★
Climb the groove behind the Elm and the continuation crack.
Climb the overhang with help from a good handhold and finish
above.

The big wall to the right of the Elm host some fine climbs.

37   Twilight Crack   15m   E1   5b   ★
Start below the superb finger crack on the left side of the big wall.
Climb up to the start of the crack and climb it with difficulty to a
niche. Move rightwards and climb over a block to finish above.

Direct Finish   E2   5b   ★★
A much better finish is to climb straight up the Hanging groove
above the niche. This produces a superb climb.

*To the right of the start of Twilight Crack is an easier line up a series
of dangerous flakes. This is not recommended.*

38   Twilight Groove   15m   HVS   5a   ★
Starts in the centre of the big wall at a shallow chimney/groove.
Climb the groove to a small cave. Climb the steep wall on the left
and surmount a bulge on doubtful blocks. Move up and left or
right to a sapling to finish.

39   D-Rider   15m   E2   5c   ★★
A good sustained route up the groove and wall to the right of
Twilight Groove. Make a difficult pull around a small overhang and
move left to a ledge. Climb the groove on the right to the second
horizontal break. Step right onto a small ledge and before courage
runs out, climb the wall above to give an exciting finish.

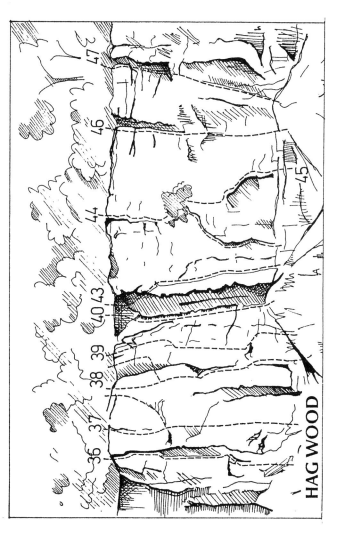

To the right the very big corner is:

40   Cobs Corner   14m   S
Climb the corner to a dirty finish.

41   Claim To Fame   14m   S
Climb the fine crack in the right wall of Cobs Corner and finish as for the latter.

42   Cob Piece   14m   MS
Start below the arete to the right of Claim To Fame. Climb the wall using holds on the arete. Finish as for Cobs Corner.

43   Cobs   15m   S
Climb the wide crack to the right of the arete and finish as for the others.

The wall to the right has some of the longest climbs on the crag. This wall decreases in height until it meets the descent gully: the Rubbish Chute.

44   Tiny Dancer   19m   VS   4b
Start just right of the crack of Cobs at a thin crack. Climb the thin crack to the top of a large flake. Move up for three metres and step right to a Yew. Finish up the easier groove above.

45   Razor Face   19m   VS   4c   ★
Starts below a thin crack leading to a point just right of a Yew growing out of the face. Climb the crack with difficulty, struggle through the Yew and saunter up the groove. A good effort.

46   Indian Sunset   19m   VS   4c   ★
An attractive climb which follows the groove above a large, reclining tree. Climb the groove past a large thread on the left. A commiting move is needed to reach a crack leading to a ledge and tree. Finish up the corner above.

47   Levon   14m   VS   4c   ★
Start just right of the groove of Indian Sunset below a crack. Climb the crack which is followed by some thin climbing up steep rocks to a ledge. Step right to finish.

The Rubbish Chute; a deep, muddy gully blocked by a rock step is some fifteen metres further right. The crag continues in a vegetated state and the next climbs are on the cleaner wall to the left of the Rubbish Chute.

48   Kimney   15m   VD
Start six metres left of the Rubbish Chute below a shallow chimney which does not quite reach the ground. Climb the chimney. Care with loose rock.

49   Work Out   14m   S   ★
Start just left of the Rubbish Chute below two shallow corners, both of which fail to reach the ground.Climb the left-hand of the two corners.

To the right of the Rubbish Chute is a fine, isolated buttress which continues rightwards is a line of walls and corners gradually diminishing in stature.

50   The Rose And The Ramson   13m   E1   5b   ★
Start just left of the toe of the buttress below the overhanging slim face. Climb the slim face to a cluster of pockets. Move up with

difficulty past a tiny pocket to a break (runner). Move up onto the arete with difficulty. Continue up the arete overlooking the Rubbish Chute to the top. Care with holds at top.

51 Karumba 15m HVS 4c ★
Start at the toe of the buttress. Move diagonally rightwards to a small tree. Move diagonally leftwards and climb the front face of the buttress just right of the arete with a paucity of both footholds and protection to a large tree.

52 Only A Rose 13m VS 4c ★
Another good climb, but take your pruning knife. Start to the left of the fallen block directly below a fine, thin crack which splits the upper wall. Climb the steep face to the small tree. Continue with difficulty up the thin crack.

Lamumba Finish HVS 5b
A good steep finish. Climb the wall just right of the thin crack past a peg runner.

The steep wall to the right has another peg in it this marks the line of Just A Carrot.

53 Just A Carrot 15m E2 6a ★★
A strenuous climb that has become dirty. Climb the wall to the right of Only A Rose trending right slightly to the first horizontal break (peg runner). Make a long reach off a pocket and undercling (or if short, jump!) for the second break. Move left and make a final hard move to the top.

To the right of the isolated buttress is a corner.

54 Stinger 15m S
Climb the corner and after four metres quit this for the arete on the right to reach the top.

55 Intruder 14m S
A dangerous route on account of loose rock. Start four metres right of Stinger below another corner. Climb the corner via a bulge which has large holds.

56 Criminal Infusion 15m E2 5b
Takes the sustained and poorly protected wall to the left of the block-filled chimney – The Gallows. Climb straight up the centre of the wall following shallow grooves to gain a sloping ledge with difficulty. Move left around a block and go directly up the right-hand break in the overhanging wall.

57 The Gallows 15m S
Hanging death! Climb the block-filled chimney on the right passing a bulge. The exit on the right is easier but very dangerous on account of stacked blocks so exit left. A route to avoid.

58 The Happy Wanderer 17m S
Start below a tall pillar a few metres right of the chimney. Climb the crack to the left of the pillar and from the top move left under the overhang and climb up a corner. Step right and finish up a slab. Loose:

60 Girdle Traverse HVS 4c/5a
A poor left to right girdle traverse exists which can be varied at many points. It is spoilt by much wandering and has never been popular – a good thing as on a crag such as this it would interfere

with other climbers. It should also be said that the stances and belays should be chosen with great care on account of loose rock. Start at Pocket Hole Corner.

1   Climb Pocket Hole Corner and step right at mid-height. Move right and descend Garlic Groove until a flake can be reached by some upward moves. Continue to the wide chimney of Swinging and move around the corner. Traverse into another corner – Cality – and ascend this for a short distance before moving right to a small ledge and peg belay (not in place).

2   Traverse right passing A series of shallow caves to reach the off-width crack-Rack Crack. Move diagonally downwards (Holy Moses reversed) to reach the foot of the big chimney of Limbo.

3   Traverse around the corner and reach and follow the shallow groove of Criminals. Climb this route almost to its top and move right past a small tree into the corner of Cleavage. Continue at this level to the next corner and belay (Ginger Crack).

4   Descend Ginger Crack to a ledge and tree near the bottom. Move around the corner and climb the wall diagonally rightwards to a small tree. Continue to a stance and belay by a large pinnacle in the corner.

5   Traverse right across the wall and swing into a groove with a large tree at the bottom – Midnight Groove. Continue right across the big wall and finish up Twilight Groove.

APPLEGARTH SCAR   O.S. SHEET 92   G.R. 116 016

SITUATION AND CHARACTER

A Limestone crag situated on the Northern side of Swaledale about three-quarters of a mile North East of the village of Marske. The scar forms the Western end of a line of crags extending West of Richmond. It faces South at an altitude of 250 metres and catches the sun for much of the day. One result of this is a fair amount of vegetation both under and on the crag. However, the trees do provide good belay and abseil anchors.

The climbs are concentrated in two sections of the crag, the Left-Hand Section and the Right-Hand Section, separated by a stretch of broken vegetated rock some 50 metres in length. There is a wide variety of features providing steep climbing on corners, walls and cracks up to 15 metres in height. Descents are possible at either end of each section, although abseiling from trees may be more convenient in places. In common with many other limestone crags, loose rock can be found so care should be exercised when swinging from jug to jug.

APPROACHES AND ACCESS

Applegarth Scar is on private land but climbing is permitted. The Coast to Coast path passes immediately below it. To reach the crag follow the minor road from Marske towards Richmond and park on the steep hill less than a mile from Marske. A gated lane (Public Bridleway to West Applegarth) leads South towards the Swale. At the first gateway turn left between stone walls into the pasture

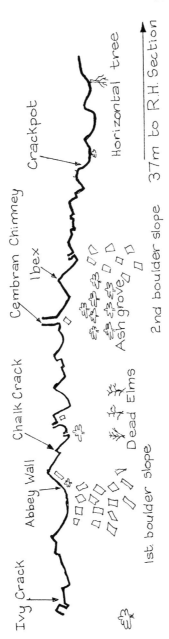

APPLEGARTH SCAR – Left Hand Side

below the scar which is soon visible in the trees up to the left. Time from the road is less than ten minutes.

HISTORICAL

The scar has seen activity for a number of years and the first recorded climbs were those of Ernie and Ruth Shields and Dave Staton in the 1960's.
These formed the basis for the first edition of this guide. No new development has taken place, but new approaches to steeper Limestone may render this guide obsolete very quickly.

THE CLIMBS

These are described from left to right.

LEFT HAND SECTION

The major feature visible is a large corner groove (Cogden Crack) with a large cracked slab to its left above a jumble of fallen blocks; the First Boulder Slope. Some 20 metres to the left of here is a shallow square-cut groove next to a small sycamore tree.

1   Ivy Crack   12m   S
Climb the left side of the shallow groove to a small ledge holding a sapling. Finish more steeply on suspect rock.

The next climbs lie several metres further right across the First Boulder Slope where the crag cuts into a fine, big corner with an upstanding block below the slabby, left wall.

2   Abbey Wall   14m   VD   ★
Start just left of the big block. Climb the centre of the cracked slab to a ledge at 7m. Move left and follow the crack to the top.

3   Cogden Crack   13m   MS   ★
Climb the slab immediately left of the large corner. From a small tree, move left to finish at the same place as Abbey Wall.

Immediately right of the corner is a fine overhanging wall of excellent rock.

4   Chalk Crack   13m   VS   4b   ★★
A really good route. Start 5m right of the big corner and right of the overhanging wall at a small V-shaped corner. Climb this by bridging and laybacking.

5   Hale   12m   S
Start 4m right of Chalk Crack and at a lower level below a slanting off-width crack. Climb this crack to a large ledge then climb the shattered crack above. Scramble off to the left.

From here the crag continues rightwards, but no routes have been made until one arrives at a small grove of trees, predominantly Ash, growing around the base of the crag. A large, square block bars access to a wide chimney just left of a steep, white wall.

6   Cembran Chimney   14m   D
Climb into the chimney from the left-hand side of the large block and ascend the wide cleft above.

7   Cembran Rib   14m   S
Start 5m right of Cembran Chimney by a block at the foot of a fine

arete. Climb the arete bearing right until a cracked break leads up the right side of the arete to a loose finish.

8   Ibex   12m   VD
Climb the wide crack in the next, very big corner to the right.

9   Tached   12m   VD
Start 5m right of the big corner, to the right of an arete and below a wide, chockstone chimney. Bridge up the outside of the chimney and move onto the left-hand rib near the top. Loose.

10   Hackerside   12m   S
Start at the same point as Tached, but climb the wide corner-cleft immediately right of Tached.

11   Oxnop   12m   HVS   5a
Start 3m right of and down the slope from Hackerside below a vertical fin of rock which runs up to a crack. Climb the fin of rock (shaky!) to gain a sentry-box. Climb direct past Ivy to a Yew tree.

12   Bents Dale   12m   MVS   4b   ★
Start 8m right of Oxnop below a big, Open-Book corner. Climb the corner, passing a bleached stump at 4m. Lower off the tree at the top. (Care with blocks hereabouts).

13   Bonsai   12m   MVS   4b
Start 3m right of Bents Dale in a short corner below a stepped corner. Climb up the short corner and into the corner containing the Bonsai tree. Climb this corner and the one above on the left to finish.

14   Gunnerside   12m   S
Round the arete to the right is a recessed groove with a tree at 4m. Climb this loose groove choosing one of a number of possible lines.

15   Crackpot   12m   E1   5b
Start just right of Gunnerside below a bottomless, cracked groove which overhangs at 4m. Climb the cracked groove to the bulge. Surmounting this block is the crux and care must be taken as both holds and protection assumes its stability! Move right onto sounder rock and finish at a large Ash.

16   Myrin   11m   VD
5 metres right is a corner just right of a Yew growing out of the face at 2 metres. Climb the corner avoiding the Ivy on the right.
Moving right again one passes under a short, white corner with an obvious fragile flake on its right wall. Just right of this is an undercut crack.

17   Dinnertime Special   6m   VS   5a
Climb the undercut crack.

RIGHT-HAND SECTION
This section which has some very attractive and generally shorter climbs is reached by walking rightwards past an obvious horizontally growing tree at the end of the Left-Hand Section and continuing under small walls for about 40 metres. The rocks gain height in the region of a cluster of small Elms which grow hard against the crag.

18   Applegarth Chimney   9m   D
Start 6m right of the cluster of Elms below an instantly recognisable chimney. Climb the square- cut chiney which is bridged by a large tree

APPLEGARTH SCAR – Right Hand Side

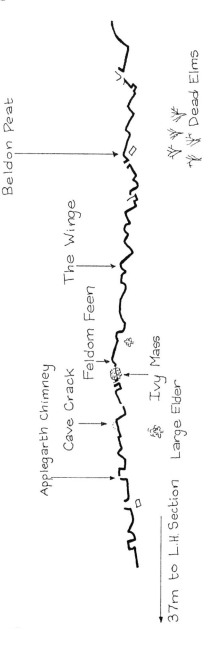

19   Starkie's Route   9m   MVS   4b
Start in a V-corner 3m right of Applegarth Chimney. Climb the fine-looking corner and after 5m step right onto a small ledge and continue to the top.

20   Cave Crack   12m   S   ★★
Around the arete to the right is a fine corner with a small, cave at its base. Climb this excellent corner.

21   Park Top   9m   S   ★
Start just right of the next arete below a wide, flake crack. Climb this to finish at a Yew.

22   Clap Corner   9m   S
Start 4m right of Park top at the foot of a corner which appears promising. Climb the corner and the deteriorating continuation to the top.

An Ivy mass hides the next wall on the right.

23   Feldom Feen   10m   VS   4b
Start in the narrow corner by a sapling, just right of the ivy mass. Climb the corner.

Around the next arete are two Ivy masses on either side of a steep wall.

24   Cumma Crack   10m   HS   4b
Start from a ledge of blocks below a cracked recess jus left of the right-hand Ivy mass. Climb the cracked recess to tree belays on the top.

Five metres right a huge dead Elm projects from the face at two metres.

25   Munn End   9m   VD
Climb the open groove behind the huge, dead Elm.

26   The Winge   9m   VS   4c
Climb the fine, slim corner/groove 2m right of Munn End.

A twin-stemmed Ash grows out of the face at head-height.

27   Wham Bottom   9m   S
Start just left of the big Ash. Climb up the grooved recess to finish at a Yew.

28   Blades   9m   S
Climb a left-slanting, thin, cracked groove 3m right of the Ash. Finish at a Yew.

29   Barf Side   10m   VD
Start 2m right of Blades where an open corner is blocked at its base by a 3m pillar of rock. Climb either side of the pillar (right is best) past a possible thread. climb the blocky groove above passing a broken bough.

Eight metres further right and beyond a clean corner crack is a large, detached flake, to the right of an Ivy mass.

30   Brownsey   11m   VS   4b
Start in an orange recess below the off-width crack to the left of the large flake. Pull up steeply to gain a recess below the crack. Climb the crack and finish up the wall above.

Moving right, around the nose of the detached flake, one comes to a recess with a right-slanting chimney.

31 Clogger 12m VD
Start from a ledge at 2m below the recess. climb into this and follow the line of the slanting break taking care with dangerous blocks.

The next feature of the crag is a massive square-cut block perched on a ledge two metres above the base of the cliff. A fine corner lies behind it.

32 Beldon Peat 9m S
Climb the corner direct.

33 Wegber Crack 9m HVS 5a   ⋆
Start below a prominent crack in the wall behind the big block. Climb the crack to a ledge on the right arete and follow this to the top. Stepping off the block reduces the standard.

34 Conny Tammy 7m S
Start below and right of the huge block at a corner with a double-edged wide crack. Climb the corner.

35 The Fleak 7m VS 4b
Start around the next arete right in a steep corner above a sizeable Briar Rose. Climb the corner.

36 Swang Gully 7m M
Start up the slope 8m right of the Briar Rose. Climb the corner and gully above, passing a tree and taking care with loose rock.

ORGATE SCAR   O.S. SHEET 92   G.R. 096020

SITUATION AND CHARACTER

Orgate Scar faces S.W. across Marske Beck, a Northern tributary of the River Swale. It forms part of the same outcrop of limestone as nearby Applegarth Scar and Kersey Green Scar, indeed all three could be visited in one day. Orgate Scar is about half a mile long and has a fine open aspect.

There are many fine lines and this would be a major crag if access were easier. Visitors to the crag need to be wary of the grades of climbs as access difficulties have hindered systematic checks. Stakes have been installed at the top of the crag.

APPROACHES AND ACCESS

The crag is most easily approached from Marske by following the minor road in a N.E. direction uphill onto Marske Moor. After crossing a cattle grid, the road is followed for a further three-quarters of a mile until a Public Right Of Way in the form of a Bridle Track leaves the road (Cordilleras Lane) on the left-hand (West) side. Follow this Bridleway trending generally Southwards until the top of the scar can be approached by heading South when the Bridleway descends towards Marske Beck. This approach is the least prominent of a number of possible approaches and should establish the climber on the crag with enough time to get some climbing done. Since the First Edition of this guide in 1980, climbers have met with increasing access difficulties. There appears to be no particular reason by way of bad behaviour. Shooting interests could well be at the heart of the matter. Hopefully the B.M.C may be able to intervene and formulate some agreement for the general climbing community. If asked to leave, do so and report the matter to the B.M.C locally.

HISTORICAL
The first recorded climb was Impede by Ernie Shield, J. Tomlinson and M. Martin and was mentioned in the Cleveland M.C journal of 1964. In 1970 Robin Gay added Feather Light Flakes whilst Gossamer groove was the work of J. Hancock, Paul Ingham and Tony McLean in 1971.
Nothing much happened until 1973 when D. Hume, M. Moseley and Glenn Bennett climbed Chockstone Chimney and whilst not a good climb, it led on to further developments by the same team. Paz was climbed on New Years day 1974 by Bennett and K. Shackleton. In 1975, Tony McLean climbed Evel Knievel and further developments in the same year by two newcomers, Dave Knight and Pete Ramsdale notably Snooky William. 1976 started well with Dave Knight adding Boston Dangler whilst Bennett climbed the fine corner of Andrex Ferrari. Tib Wall was top-roped and later led by Dave Knight who also added Julia Dream and Sniff. The story seems to end here due to long-standing access problems. It is hoped that this pleasant place will again be accessible to climbers.

THE CLIMBS
These are described from right to left.
A pinnacle, Moomintroll Pinnacle is a feature of the right-hand end of the crag and further right is a wall descending the fell and barring access to Limekiln Wood. Hume's Gully to the right of the Pinnacle provides a descent at the right-hand end of the crag whilst a chimney next to Gone For A Beagle is the descent from climbs on the Central Area. At the left end of the crag are several gullies providing useful descents.

PINNACLE AREA
This is the wall behind Moomintroll Pinnacle.

1   Fait Accompli   18m   S
Traverse the wall behind the pinnacle, starting up the left wall of Hume's Gully. Follow the horizontal break to a tree and ascend the dirty groove above (Chossalot).

2   Boilerman   8m   S
Climb a loose corner 9m left of Hume's Gully.

3   Chossalot   8m   S
Climb the dirt groove left of Boilerman.

4   Blue Funnel   11m   S
A good climb up the chimney in the corner, right of the Ivy-covered wall.

MOOMINTROLL PINNACLE
The pinnacle at the right-hand end of the crag.

5   Mjollnir   6m   S
Climb the centre of the face nearest the crag. Loose at top.

6 Paz 12m VD
From the base of the pinnacle ascend a short corner on the left and mantelshelf at 3m before climbing the left face via an obvious crack at the top.

7 Nine Point Rose Divot And Crown 12m S
Start as for Paz. Climb the corner then move right up the arete.

8 Hunt Of The Giant Mameluke 12m VS 4b
Start as for Paz. Climb the corner to the mantelshelf then move right and climb the face direct via a sharp-edged flake. Finish above a rounded mantelshelf.

Descend from the pinnacle via the right-hand face to a large ledge.

THE CENTRAL AREA

This is the area between the large, Ivy-covered wall just left of Moomintroll Pinnacle and a stone wall which comes up to the crag at its midpoint. At the top of a scree shoot at the right-hand end of this section is a descent chimney cutting through the crag at its lowest point.

9 Stairway To Hell 12m VD
Start halfway up the scree shoot. Climb onto a ledge at 2m then move up a similar distance to another ledge. Traverse left and up the wall to the top.

The next climbs are to the left of the descent chimney.

10 Moribundus 30m VS 4b
A traverse. Climb the left arete of the descent chimney to footholds on the lower horizontal break. Traverse left to the chimney of Yo-Yo then pull out left and Hand-traverse the wall of Evel Knievel to a good ledge around the arete. Move down and left and finish up the Z-crack of Impede.

11 Gone For A Beagle 5m S
Climb the thin, vertical crack just left of the descent chimney.

12 Jam Jar 5m S
Climb the obvious crack 6m left of the descent chimney.

13 Big Dipper 8m S
Climb the thin crack just left of Jam Jar.

At the left-hand end of this wall is a chimney; Yo-Yo.

14 Jack The Gripper 9m VS 4c
Start 2m right of the chimney. Ascend rightwards for 3m to reach a ramp. Climb this to the top.

15 Grip The Jacker 9m VS 4c
Start as for Jack The Gripper. Ascend the wall direct.

16 Yo-Yo 9m VD
This good climb follows the chimney at the left end of the wall. The start is hardest.

17 Evel Knievel 14m VS 4c
Start below a bulging crack, 3m left of Yo-Yo. Climb the crack and scoop to a flake. Finish left round the arete or over the overhang above. This is more sustained and loose.

In a bay to the left, is a wide crack behind a fallen block:

18   Impede   20m   VS   4b
Climb the wide crack into a cave. Traverse left and climb past a tree to finish up the crack and awkward chimney above.

19   Andrex Ferrari   17m   VS   4c
Climb the crack and groove in the corner to the left of Impede.

20   Leaning Meanie   18m   HVS   5a
Climb the crack in the wall left of Andrex Ferrari to a mantelshelf at 6m. Step right into the corner and climb this to a ledge before moving back left into the middle of the face. Climb the face trending right to the top.

21   Seacliffe Enchantress   18m   VS   4a
Climb the arete left of Andrex Ferrari. A bulge near the top is loose and hard to protect.

22   Chockstone Chimney   17m   VD
Climb the obvious chockstone chimney to the left. Pass the chockstone on the inside or the outside (harder).

23   Feather Light Flakes   17m   VS   4b
Start beneath a triangular pedestal 2m left of Chockstone Chimney. Gain the pedestal by a series of mantelshelves and a flake crack. Ascend twin cracks to a loose finish.

24   Gossamer Groove   18m   VS   4c
Start at a small tree at the base of the crag left of the arete to the left of Feather Light Flakes. Move up left until a mantelshelf leads to a bulging flake which is followed to a groove and a loose finish.

25   Owake   18m   S
Climb the second corner left of Gossamer Groove which has a tree at its base.

To the left of Owake, the path rises to a crest above which there is a crack in the face:

26   Boston Dangler   11m   VS   4c
Climb the crack in the face behind the tree. Jam to the slight bulge and finish strenuously above.

27   Q.C.   14m   VS   4b
Start beneath a smooth wall left of an obvious chimney. Climb the wall past a mantelshelf at 4m. Move right into the chimney and follow it until the left face can be regained and followed on loose rock.

28   Snooky Two   14m   S
Climb the crack to the left of a pillar left of Q.C. Step right and climb direct to finish.

To the right of the drystone wall which runs up to the crag, is a smooth wall; Tib Wall.

29   Rainbow Blues   12m   S
Climb the tower to the right of Tib Wall moving onto a ledge on the left arete at half-height. Move right and up to finish.

30   Julia Dream   12m   VS   4a
Climb the wall just left of the arete of Rainbow Blues.

31   Tib Wall   17m   HVS   5a
Climb the smooth face right of the drystone wall via mantelshelves. Gaining the overhang is the crux. Unprotected.

32   Snooky William   15m   VS   4c
Start just left of the wall. Climb the thin crack to a ledge and beyond to another ledge. The crack is followed through a bulging wall to just below the top. Traverse left around a block to finish.

33   Woodstock   13m   S
Start below a crack in the right wall of the second corner left of the drystone wall. Climb the crack and move left below the overhang and into the corner which is followed to the top.

34   Jaycee   9m   VD
Climb the obvious gully of the second corner and finish on the right wall. A series of gullies breach the crag and provide descents.

35   Snufkin   5m   S
Climb the centre of the left-hand wall of the right-hand gully.

36   Sniff   8m   VS   4b
Climb the wall to the left of Snufkin.

37   Desperado   8m   VD
Start below a groove in the right wall of the second descent gully. Climb the groove, finishing left of a crack containing a tree. Loose blocks!

There are three crack systems up the front of the buttress to the left of the second descent gully.

38. Chalkless Chimney   8m   VD Climb the chimney containing two cracks and finish up the right-hand crack.

39   Linda's Core   8m   VD
Climb the central crack.

40   Pe De Rools OK   8m   VD
Climb the left-hand chimney which is just right of the third descent gully. This chimney contains two cracks and the right one provides the finish.

41   Snoopy And The Red Baron   9m   S
Start below the buttress between the third and fourth descent gullies. Climb the crack 2m right of the arete to a halfway ledge. Follow the right-hand crack over a bulge to the top.

42   December 1963   6m   VD
Start below the buttress left of the drystone wall at the left end of the crag. Climb the wall direct.

KERSEY GREEN SCAR   O.S. SHEET 92   G.R. 083044

SITUATION AND CHARACTER

Kersey Green Scar faces N.E. and E across the little valley of Rake Beck on the moors to the North of Swaledale. The crag is part of the same band of limestone which outcrops continuously along the edge of these hills attaining prominence at Applegarth Scar then again at Orgate Scar just N.W. of Marske. Kersey Green Scar is about 4 miles N.W. of Marske.

The crag has a maximum height of 20 metres but 15 metres is more normal. The climbing on the crag tends to be steep and loose rock does require care in places. The more popular routes are reasonably clean and further traffic should see the crag improving. Trees growing at the top of the crag provide good anchors. There is still scope for development on the crag.

APPROACHES AND ACCESS

The crag can be approached from either Marske or the A66, 3 miles beyond Greta Bridge in the direction of Scotch Corner. From the A66 turn onto the minor road and go through the village of Newsham. Beyond the crossroads in the centre of the village, and going in the direction of Barningham, a left turn onto a minor road leading to Marske is taken. This road leads gradually uphill for 4 miles onto Newsham Moor and after Long Green, it is unfenced. Continue due South on this unfenced road for a further 2 miles and turn left at the next crossroads. Park on the verge a further mile along the road where it meets the valley above Rake Beck. Follow the valley downstream to reach the scar taking care with boundaries.From Marske follow the minor road North over Marske Moor which crosses Rakes beck after about 6 miles. The crag is on land owned by Barningham Estates, but the farmer is happy to let climbers use the crag providing they keep a low profile ie. small groups only, no litter, no noise and particularly no dogs. The Estate would not be happy about this arrangement if climbers caused any aggravation whatsoever.

HISTORICAL

All of the climbs at Kersey Green Scar were recorded by Peter and Elizabeth Dyson, Peter Ball, Bruce Perry, Mark Griffiths and Paul Carling. Some of the routes had no doubt been climbed before but of these there is no recorded history.

THE CLIMBS

The scar is not very extensive and so the climbs are described from left to right.

At the left-hand end of the scar is a small, shattered buttress with some Yew trees growing on it. 30 metres right of this are two grooves behind a large Elm tree:

1   Cosy Corner   10m   VD
Climb the left-hand groove.

15 metres right is a large wall with a massive Elm at mid-height:

2   Elm Tree Wall   15m   VS   4c
Start below the right-hand side of the wall at a crack. climb the crack for 5m to a small tree and continue up the crack to the top.

10 metres right is another steep wall:

3   Breathing   15m   VS   4b
Start 3m right of a clump of Elms. Climb the face for 8m to a ledge. Move right along the ledge and up the face a little way before stepping right to a loose crack in the arete which leads to the top. Serious.

4   Man Of Straw   15m   HVS   5a
Start 5m right of Breathing below a steep, corner crack with an Elder at its base. Climb the corner and first overhang and below the second overhang, Hand traverse a flat ledge to the right and pull

onto the wall above. Gain the arete and finish just right at a tree.

10 metres right is an attractive face with a small Yew at top left.

5   Irony   15m   VS   4b
Climb the steep wall to a ledge, passing an old peg over to the right. Continue up the crack in the top wall and pull over the top block.

6   Lightning   15m   MVS   4b
Combined with the top half of Irony, this makes a fine pitch. Start 1m left of the fist-wide crack in the corner to the right of Irony. Climb the overhanging rib on good holds and the short jamming crack above. Move up to the halfway ledge and finish up Irony.

7   The Ramp   15m   VD
Climb the right-slanting groove to the right of the fist-wide crack. This leads to the top passing to the left of a many-trunked tree.

8   Leaning Crack   20m   S
Start 5m right of Irony at a wide crack just left of an Elm cluster. Climb a block to where the crack widens. Move up to a sapling. The crack which now takes the form of a blocked chimney is climbed via its left side.

9   Hurst Chimney   15m   VD
Climb the obvious chimney 10m right of Leaning Crack.

5 metres right is an obvious wide corner crack breaking through overlaps.

10   Curlew   15m   S
Climb the right face of the corner crack to the top passing a tree 3m from the top.

5 metres further right is a square corner which becomes an open chimney higher up.

11   Helwith Groove   15m   MS
Climb the square corner to a sapling and continue up the chimney above.

15 metres further right is another prominent corner, capped by an overhang.

12   Kersey corner   15m   S
Climb the corner to the overhang and bear left and up a short crack to turn it. Step back right above the overhang and finish up the groove.

4 metres right is a corner with a short chimney at 6m.

13   Root Chimney   15m   MVS   4b
Climb the corner past an old stump. climb the chimney and exit from it with difficulty using a good, tree root. Step right to a tree and move diagonally left to gain a crack with another dead stump.

The next feature to the right is a corner with a very steep, clean right-hand wall.

14   Mortar Bomb Wall   15m   HVS   5a
A fine, sustained climb. Climb the lower wall by means of a flake and then a thin crack and move right to a peg runner (in-situ). From just right of the peg, climb the wall above to a tree and move left to finish.

Next we come to a grassy bay with a three-trunked tree and to the right again is a steep corner with a bulging, right wall.

15 Solid Air 15m MVS 4b
A very good pitch on good rock. Start from a sandstone plinth. Climb the corner crack and move slightly left to finish.

5 metres further right is a gully.

16 Jonah Wimp 15m HS 4b
Climb the right wall of the gully on good but dirty rock. Could be good with more traffic.

10 metres further right are the remains of a drystone wall.

17 Dill's Chimney 15m VD
Start 10m right of the drystone wall at a chimney. Climb the thin crack to a cave then follow the chimney above past a sapling.

The dirty corner 20 metres right of a fallen tree has been climbed to give:

18 Moss Corner 10m VD

THE TROUGH   O.S SHEET 92   Barnard Castle   G.R. 966 120

SITUATION AND CHARACTER
The limestone gorge of the Trough is visible from the A66 West of Bowes and runs roughly North to South, carrying the Sleightholme Beck. The area is popular with walkers and the gorge is on the Pennine Way.

The climbing is found on both the East and West banks of the gorge and is up to ten metres high. The limestone is of good quality although some of the faces are vegetated and these are best left that way as the gorge is a SSSI for lichens and mosses. There is room for more development on the clean, steeper faces but gardening must not stray onto the heavily vegetated areas for obvious reasons. The Force at the upstream end of the gorge is impressive and worth a visit. Caves in the Trough are documented in the Northern Caves series of guidebooks.

APPROACHES AND ACCESS
From Bowes which is just South of the A66, take the unclassified road South towards Gilmonby. Beyond Gilmonby continue uphill towards Sleightholme and after about three miles, park in a grassy layby just before a cattle grid. From here a Public Right Of Way leads North to the Trough, which is just visible from the layby.

HISTORICAL
The recorded climbs are the work of Paul Carling and Roy Small in 1982.

THE CLIMBS
The only recorded climbing lies just upstream of a huge, dead Pine which lies across the beck. Other possibilities exist however.

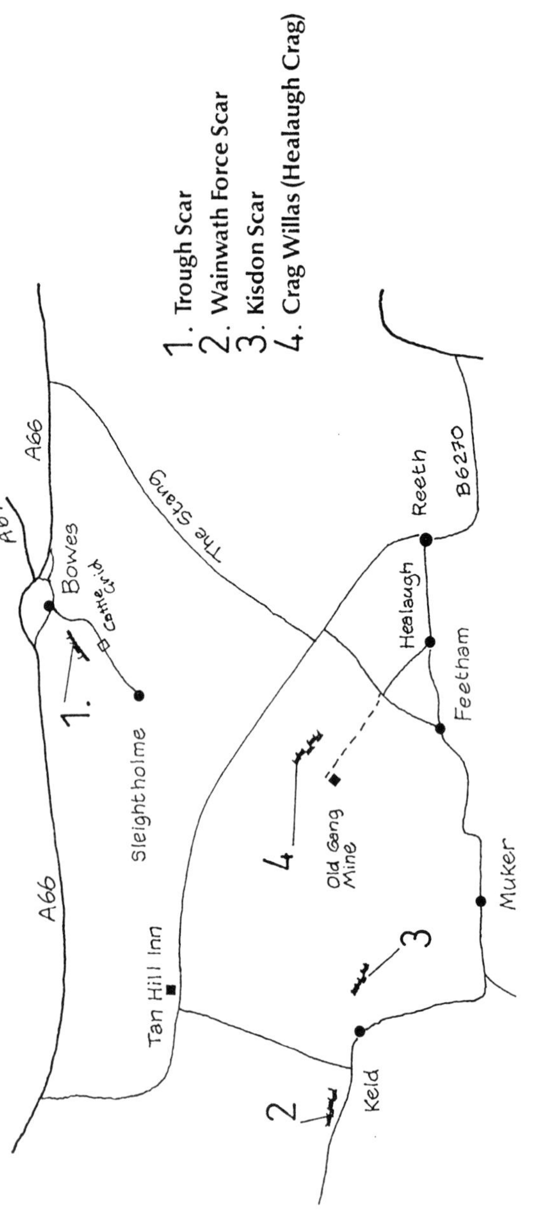

1. Trough Scar
2. Wainwath Force Scar
3. Kisdon Scar
4. Crag Willas (Healaugh Crag)
A66
A67
Bowes
Cattle Grid
The Stang
Reeth
B6270
Healaugh
Feetham
Sleightholme
Old Gang Mine
Muker
Tan Hill Inn
Keld
A66
1.
2
3
4

UPPER SWALEDALE

EAST BANK

This is the bank first reached.

1   Small Beer   10m   HS   4b
Climb the prominent corner ninety metres upstream of the dead Pine.

2   Near Beer   10m   E1   5b   ★
Climb the centre of the wall to the right of Small Beer.

3   Maltandet   10m   HVS   5a
Start to the left of Small Beer at a crack leading up to an overhang. Climb the crack to the overhang, move left and climb the wall above.

WEST BANK

4   The Crystal Voyage   10m   HVS   5b
Start below a scalloped at the right end of the crag, directly above the dead Pine. Climb the wall to exit in a recess.

5   Mother Night   10m   HVS   5b   ★★
A very good climb which takes the prominent arete to the left of The Crystal Voyage. Start on the left and finish on the right.

HEALAUGH CRAG (CRAG WILLAS)   O.S. SHEET 92   G.R. 978 012

SITUATION AND CHARACTER

Healaugh Crag (Crag Willas) is a small gritstone edge, magnificently situated at an altitude of 560 metres on Reeth High Moor above the Old Gang Smelting Mill. In the previous edition of this guidebook, it was referred to as Crag Willas, a name more correctly applied to the scatter of boulders three quarters of a mile West.

Healaugh Crag is about 4 miles North-West of Reeth in Swaledale and just South of Arkengarthdale facing South over over Old Gang Beck, once a scene of intense lead mining activity in centuries past. The moors are largely quiet now and the mining remains are being conserved by the Yorkshire Dales National Park. The flue from the smelt mill at Old Gang runs up the fellside and intersects the crag and this is useful in locating and describing the climbs.

The climbs are relatively short, no more than 8m high but the quality of the rock, magnificent, moorland setting and further scope for very hard developments must put it in the same league as Slipstone Crag in Colsterdale. It is an excellent place to spend a couple of days.

APPROACHES AND ACCESS

There are a variety of approaches to the crag. From Cumbria and the A66, the best route is to turn off the A66 near the end of the dual-carriageway 4 miles East of Brough and follow The Stang road which is signposted Scargill. This road crosses Stang Hope Moor and descends into Arkengarthdale. After crossing Arkle Beck, turn left passing the C.B. Inn and turn immediately right. The road crosses Turf Moor descending to a watersplash. Continue along the road over the next moor and a parking area is reached at the favourite picnic venue of Surrender Bridge. From Reeth in Swaledale, Surrender Bridge is reached following the B6270

up the dale to Healaugh. Go through the village and leave the B6270 by the first minor road on the right and follow this uphill before gently descending to Surrender Bridge, less than 2 miles from Healaugh.

From the Parking, the easiest way to the crag is to follow the good, wide track above the Old Gang Beck on its North bank until the ruins of the Smelting Mill are reached. Go beyond the ruins and strike up the fellside on the right trending back to the flue which can then be followed all the way to the crag. Time from Surrender Bridge is 30 minutes.

HISTORICAL

Initials carved on the crag are proof that hold-chipping was rife even in the Good Old days. However, those early rock pioneers left no records of their ascents. Their memorials are the mining relics which abound in the area. first to record his activities was D. Staton in the early 1960's whose routes included those on Miners Wall and Calver Face. These were published in the Cleveland M.C. Journal in 1964. Bruce Perry contributed climbs on the West side of Luckys-trike Buttress as the First Edition of this guide was in preparation.

In more recent times, Karl Lunt has climbed many of the existing routes and added some of his own the best of these being On The Level and Karl's Arete. Old Stager, Ronnie Kenyon returning to the scene of former crimes was given a "griddling" by Karl Lunt and Stew Wilson before going on to climb the pleasant, Mr Wobbly.

THE CLIMBS

The crag is described from left to right, section by section. There are six sections to the left of the flue and eight sections right of the flue. Minor bouldering sections left of the flue are described last of all.

SECTIONS LEFT OF THE FLUE

Left of the flue, at the extreme left-hand end of the crag there is a huge boulder with a low- angled slab facing the flue.

LOW-ANGLED SLAB

1   Look! No Hands   8m   M
The low-angle slab – wander at will.

On the opposite side of the block to the slab, a steep wall with parallel sloping breaks faces up- valley.

2   Tired Of Writing   5m   4a
Start at extreme left end of the undercut base. Climb the centre of the wall.

3   Helados   5m   4c
Step onto the undercut, left end of the wall and ascend the blunt rib above.

HEALAUGH CRAG (Crag Willas) Left Hand Side

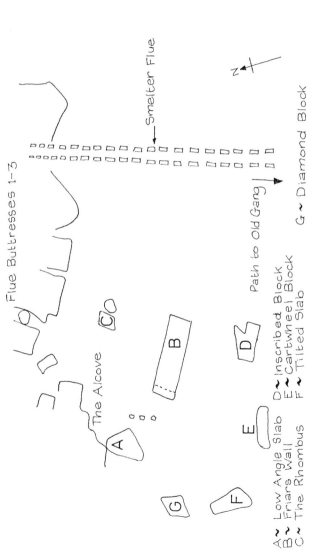

Smelter Flue

Flue Buttresses 1-3

The Alcove

Path to Old Gang

A ~ Low Angle Slab
B ~ Friars Wall
C ~ The Rhombus

D ~ Inscribed Block
E ~ Cartwheel Block
F ~ Tilted Slab

G ~ Diamond Block

4   King Kone   5m   5b   ★
Start 2m right of the undercut rib from a large block. Ascend the wall direct on awkward, slanting holds.

5   Mr Wobbly   5m   5a
Climb a shallow break, just left of the initials J.T. carved on the rock. Finish awkwardly via a thin crack.

6   On The Level   8m   5a   ★★
Near the right end of the wall is an open groove with J.T. carved on the rock. Ascend this open groove and make a rising leftwards traverse using the obvious parallel breaks. The going eases once the rib of Helados is passed.

THE ALCOVE
The area behind and right of the Low-Angled Slab.

7   Mivvi   7m   MVS   4a
Climb the blunt rib behind the Low Angled Slab to a ledge. The arete of the top block is laybacked and is bold but artificial.

8   The Dare's On You   7m   HVS   5a
Climb the chimney to the right of Mivvi and move out right to a ledge. A huge flake above and left has a slabby front. Step left onto this and ascend boldly to the top.

9   Gumby   6m   HVS   5b
Climb the front of the block, just to the right of The Dare's On You. Climb the curved rib above.

The right-hand side of the Alcove has a square-cut block buttress with a large ledge to its left.

10   Bruce's Arete   8m   HVS   5a   ★
Climb a short scoop to the large ledge. Move right and climb the front of the buttress just right of the left arete.

11   Don't Panic   7m   VS   4c
Climb the face right of Bruce's Arete using the right arete as a handhold.

FRIAR'S WALL
A few metres towards the valley bottom in front of Bruce's Arete is a huge block whose steep valley face holds a number of excellent problems. Care should be taken as some of the minute flakes are very fragile.

12   Friarfold   4m   4c   ★
Climb the wall 2m right of the left arete.

13   Fry Up   5m   5b   ★
The wall 3m right of the left arete has a vague flake line. Climb the wall immediately left of this.

14   Friar Tuck   5m   5a   ★
Start 1m left of carved initials M.C. Climb up and slightly left to good flake holds.

15   Hush   5m   5c   ★
Start immediately left of M.C. Climb wall using a pointed left hand hold to gain holds above a tiny undercut. Finish direct.

16   Ye Olde Friars   6m   5a   ★★
Start from a small ledge near the right arete. Move left using an obvious pocket and climb the wall above M.C.
17   The Gangue Way   6m   4b   ★
From the small ledge just left of the right arete, climb directly into the scoop above.
18   Gable End   6m   4b   ★
Ascend the right-hand arete.
19   The Pig   4m   5b   ★
The narrow, fluted wall right of Gable End is climbed near its right edge.

THE FLUE BUTTRESSES

These are the outcrops immediately adjacent to the point at which the flue meets the crag. For ease of identification they have been numbered: Buttresses 1, 2 and 3 are to the left of the flue whilst 4, 5, 6 and 7 are to the right of the flue.

BUTTRESS 1
20   Spot The Brain Cell   7m   VS   4c   ★
Gain a ledge on the left edge, traverse right and ascend the rib using a crack to its right.

BUTTRESS 2
21   Bong's Crack   4m   S
Gain and climb the crack high on the left side of Buttress 2.
22   Loopy   4m   VD
Climb the wide crack right of Buttress 2.

BUTTRESS 3
The buttress nearest the flue.
23   Dappy   4m   HS
Climb the awkward off-width crack left of Buttress 3.
24   Lumberjack   7m   E3   5b   ★
Start just left of the arete. Climb the right-hand side of the arete using the arete for the left hand.
25   He's O.K.   8m   VS   5a   ★
Climb a short crack immediately right of a small cave to the right of Lumberjack. The horizontal break is used to make a delicate foot traverse right for 1 metre. Climb the wall above to finish at a good flake hold.

SECTIONS RIGHT OF THE FLUE

THE FLUE BUTTRESSES

BUTTRESS 4
The first buttress right of the flue.
26   The Griddle   5m   6b
Should be re-named The Fiddle as no one is certain as to whether

HEALAUGH CRAG (Crag Willas) Right Hand Side

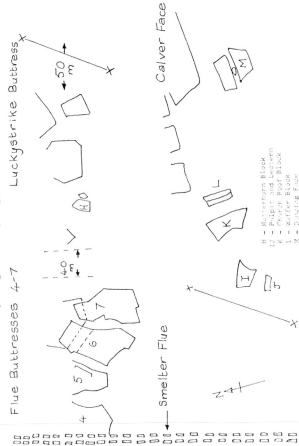

Flue Buttresses 4-7

Luckystrike Buttress

Calver Face

Smelter Flue

50 m

40 m

H – Matterhorn Block
IJ – Pulpit and Lectern
K – Church Roof Block
L – Wafer Block
M – Dancing Face

or not its been led! Climb the shallow, left-facing groove in the front of the buttress.

27   Magic Music   5m   5a
Ascend the right side of the arete to the right of The Griddle.

BUTTRESS 5

This is undercut on its right-hand side.

28   Karl's Arete   5m   5a/b   ★
Climb the left-hand arete with a blind reach left.

29   Fall Arete   5m   5a   ★
Pull over the overhang at the right-hand side and climb the rib above.

BUTTRESS 6

A most impressive tilted block with an overhang to match Kilnsey Main! To date there are no recorded routes here.

BUTTRESS 7

Another sizeable block which has only three routes on the short, back wall.

30   Lunt Goes Girlfriend Sitting   6m   VS   4c   ★
Climb the left side of the short, back wall immediately right of the arete.

31   Clover At Your Feet   5m   VD   ★
Climb the wall to a short, right-facing corner.

32   Twin Cracks   4m   VD
Climb the twin cracks to the right of Clover At Your feet.

LUCKYSTRIKE BUTTRESS

This isolated buttress is located some 50 metres further right of the Flue Buttresses. Several Boulders provide interesting problems in the intervening ground, notably Stepped Arete Block and The Matterhorn block which is below the West Side of Luckstrike Buttress.

Luckystrike Buttress has two faces: West Face, the steep West face and Miner's Wall, the slightly less-steep right-hand face. The Plumbate Face is a small isolated buttress below and right of Miners Wall.

WEST FACE:

33   Sach   7m   HVS   5b   ★
Climb the wall and overhanging crack on the left-side of the face.

34   Nikki   8m   E2   5c   ★
Climb the wall 2m right of Sach to the break. Finish with a difficult layback up the short, parallel cracks above.

35   Stewpot   8m   VS   5a   ★★
Right of Nikki is a ledge 2m above the ground. From here climb the cracks to the break then finish with a tricky move using a flake above.

MINERS WALL:

36 Luckystrike 9m S ★
Ascend the wall just right of the front rib.

37 Galena 8m VD ★
Climb the wall 2m right of Luckystrike.

38 Owre 7m D ★
Climb a shallow groove in the centre of the wall. Move right at the break and climb the wide crack.

39 Smelter 5m D
Climb the wall near its right-hand edge.

Plumbate Buttress: the small, isolated buttress below and right of Miners wall gives:

40 It's Up To You 5m S
Climb the left-hand, overhanging side of the Buttress.

41 Plumbate 5m S
Climb the right side of the buttress on sloping ledges.

CALVER FACE

A maze of boulders of varying sizes provide interesting problems in the 50 metres between Luckystrike Buttress and the final buttress.

Calver Face consists of an attractive steep face with a short but steep wall on the left, set at right-angles to the front face. An interesting twin block below the front face of Calver Face is called Dancing Face and this has a fine, steep slab on its front and a steep wall to the left.

42 Tito's 4m S
Climb the left-hand side of the short, left-hand wall.

43 Fiesta 6m HS 4b ★
Climb the wall 2m left of the arete. Pull over the overlap to the notch at the top of the crag.

44 Conqueror 6m S ★★
Start on the front face at a thin crack just right of the left arete. climb the crack to the horizontal break and finish up the twisting crack above.

45 Green Dragon 7m HS ★
Start 1m right of Conqueror at a left-facing, shallow corner. Climb this to the horizontal break, step right into a good crack to finish up this.

46 Marimba 8m HVS 5a ★★
Climb the centre of the wall, 2m right of Green Dragon to a horizontal break. Make a hard move into a shallow, left-leading scoop. Follow this to the top.

47 Upna Down 6m VD
Climb the right-hand side of Calver Face.

48 La Bamba 11m S
A girdle of Calver Face from left to right finishing as for Upna Down.

DANCING FACE

This steep-fronted block below Calver Face provides some excellent climbs.

49 Rondo 3m 4b
Climb the awkward-to-start crack to the left of the steep, slabby front.

50 Polka 4m 6b ★
Climb the smooth, slim wall to the right of Rondo.

51 Tarantella 5m 4c ★
Ascend the left arete of the wall moving in from the right.

52 Skiver 5m 4c ★★
Climb the centre of the slab moving in from the right. A Direct Start is possible on Skiver, gaining the slab by a very hard mantelshelf (6a/b).

53 Mazurka 5m 4b ★
Climb the right-hand arete.

A slab 30 metres right of Calver Face provides:

54 Strip The Willow 6m S
Climb the slab.

BOULDERS TO THE LEFT OF THE FLUE

To the left of the flue and below Friar's Wall are a collection of boulders which provide some interesting and generally easy problems. These are described from right to left or anti-clockwise.

INSCRIBED BLOCK

Lies on the valley side of Friar's Wall and seen from the latter, it presents a short, triangular wall. The valley face is bigger.

55 4a
From S.E. side climb over undercut rib and follow grooved scoop to top.

56 3c
1m left. Climb left-slanting gangway and finish with a swing left.

57 5a ★
Climb S.W. arete.

58 3b
Climb wall between the runnels.

CARTWHEEL BLOCK

Left (up-valley) of Inscribed Block. Cartwheel block presents a slabby, elliptical face to the valley.

59 3c ★
Start in recess at right end of block. Climb out of recess and Hand-Traverse a good ledge left to finish.

60 3c
Climb slab just right of centre.

61 2b
Start at up-valley end. Follow arete all way to other end with feet on the valley face.

TILTED SLAB

The next block to the left. It has a large slab for its up-valley face.

62   4a
Climb the steep, valley face stepping left or right at the top.

63   4b   *
Start 2m left at a right-slanting crack. Climb into corner and step onto upper slab moving right to top.

64   4a   *
Start 1m left at left-hand layback flake. Move onto "tongue" on right and finish direct.

65   3c
Climb the layback flake to the top.

66   2b
Climb the slab anywhere. A left to right traverse is quite good.

DIAMOND BLOCK
Behind Tilted slab about 8m away. The valley face has a diamond-shaped plaque on it.

67   **Diamond Left**   3c
Start 1m left of Diamond Face. Move left on undercuts to gain top.

68   **Diamond Face**   3b
Climb middle of plaque.

69   **Diamond Right**   2b
Start as for Diamond Face. Move right then up easy groove back left.

THE RHOMBUS
In the middle of the alcove behind Friar's Wall is a block with an attractive slab facing the valley.

70   **The Rhombus**   3b   *
Climb centre of slab.

DOWNHOLME QUARRY   O.S. SHEET 92   G.R. 113982

SITUATION AND CHARACTER
A small limestone quarry overlooking the A6108 Leyburn to Richmond road just North of the village of Downholme. The quarry faces West and so catches the afternoon and evening sun. The open aspect ensures that the rock dries quickly after rain. Much of the rock tends towards loose and for the most part is overlaid by a band of even worse quality rock. However, the Main Wall and the Introductory Bay are composed of excellent, rough rock and all the climbs are worthwhile.

APPROACHES AND ACCESS
A minor road leads East from the A6108 into Downholme village about three-quarters of a mile South of the junction with the B6270 road to Reeth. There is a small car park just beyond the Bolton Arms Public House on the left, behind a telephone booth. From the car park the lane curves round a corner to a gate on the left by a small barn some fifty metres distant. Go through this gate and

follow the level, grass track for about one hundred metres until Introductory Bay can be seen to the right. The quarry is on M.O.D land and there appear to be no access problems for individuals although the army levy a charge for users from Outdoor Centres

HISTORICAL
The quarry was unearthed by members of the Swaledale Outdoor Club who are responsible for the good state of affairs enjoyed by everyone using the crag.

THE CLIMBS
The first area encountered, Introductory Bay, consists of three short walls. The climbs are described from right to left. The descent is to the right.

INTRODUCTORY BAY
1   Pongoes   6m   S
Climb the prominent crack in the right wall of the bay.

2   Stumbler   5m   VD
Climb the corner which divides the right and central walls of the bay.

3   Brown Stane   5m   HVS   5a
Climb the centre of the central wall to an awkward finish.

4   Bumbler   5m   HS   4b
Climb the curving corner-groove separating the left and central walls.

5   D.E.W. Line   6m   E2   5b
Start just left of Bumbler. Climb the wall direct on small, widely-spaced holds.

6   Alistair   6m   E1   5b   ★
Climb the middle of the left wall via the zig-zag crack.

7   Crystal Tipps   6m   VS   4c   ★
Climb the curving flake cracks towards the left side of the left wall.

MAIN WALL
This is a short distance beyond Introductory Bay and is reached by descending into a rock- strewn depression. The climbs are described from right to left.

8   Tracer   6m   HVS   5b
Climb the centre of the narrow wall which is set at an angle to the Main Wall.

9   Big Boots   5m   D
Climb the well-polished corner which forms the right-hand boundary of Main Wall.

10   The Thwarting Of The Vamp Cow   6m   HS   4b
Climb the wall left of Big Boots via a shallow, rounded groove.

11   Fascination Street   7m   VS   4b   ★
Start 3m left of Big Boots at a short crack. Climb this and the wall above trending slightly right. Bold!

12 Line Of Fire 8m S ★★★
Climb the obvious crack 4m left of Big Boots. The start is steep but the climbing is excellent throughout.

13 Downholme Racer 9m HVS 4c ★
Start 2m left of Line Of Fire below an overlap. Pull over the overlap to a small ledge then continue up the wall above. Poorly protected.

14 Je cours tout seul 10m VS 4b ★★
Climb the wall 3m left of Line Of Fire to gain a left-slanting crack. Follow this to where it fades then reach right for a good hold. Trend left from here to finish.(One peg runner).

15 El Capitan 10m S 4a ★★
Start 3m left of Je cours tout seul, just right of a small overlap which has a straight crack above it. Gain the crack from the right and follow it to the top.

Four metres left of El Capitan is a flat, square block, embedded in the ground.

16 Sweet Pleasure 10m E1 5b
Start from the flat block. Climb the thin, right-trending crackline which sports two peg runners.

17 Never Enough 8m HVS 5a ★
Start 3m left of the flat block. Climb the easy wall to an obvious short V-groove. Pass this with difficulty and finish up the crack above.

18 Southern Death Cult 8m VS 4c
Start 2m left of Never Enough at a small overlap. Climb up to reach a prominent flake at half-height. Finish direct up the wall above.

Left of the Main Wall is an earthy slope of small rock steps and to the left of this is a small buttress with a corner groove in its centre.

19 Tank Tracks 8m D
Climb the stepped, right rib of the corner-groove.

20 Colonel Blimp 8m VD
Climb the central corner-groove.

21 General Accident 8m HS 4a
Start at the foot of Colonel Blimp. Climb the steep rib, left of the groove.

The quarry extends for a considerable distance beyond this point, however the rock quality deteriorates and the loose, upper band begins to impinge making exits risky.

KISDON SCAR O.S. SHEET 92 G.R. 898010

SITUATION AND CHARACTER
The largest crag in Upper Swaledale, situated a short distance downstream of the delightful hamlet of Keld. This riverside scar consist of an impressive South-facing, leaning wall up to twenty metres high. Unfortunately the rock is very blocky and inclined to looseness, often on a large scale. The trees which cap much of the wall contain large quantities of 'Hanging Death' and so a circumspect approach to new routing is advised. The river below has some superb swimming holes.

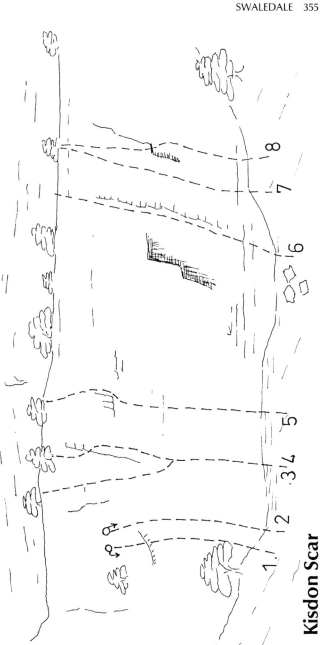

Kisdon Scar

APPROACHES AND ACCESS

There is limited parking in the centre of Keld but it is advisable to park by the Youth Hostel on the main road and walk into the village. Follow the Pennine Way south for a couple of hundred metres then branch left down to a footbridge over the River Swale. Follow the path on the other side of the valley as it swings right around a ridge. The crag is visible from here and its base is reached by a descent over steep grass followed by a short traverse.

HISTORICAL

It is quite likely that members of the Cleveland M.C. sniffed around this area looking for 'aid practice' in the mid-sixties. They certainly visited most of the other crags in the dale! The first definite route was the line of what is now Hard Rock, this was pegged by Chris Craggs and Dave Hobbs in 1968. Chris was so impressed by the potential of the crag that he rushed back twenty-two years later with Colin (The Hat) Binks for a free ascent of the route as well as to climb Rock On to its left. They noticed a line further left with spaced bolts and threads reputed to be the work of John Dunne. Chris and Colin abseiled down several other lines, some of which showed evidence of cleaning, but they were: 'obviously overly desperate'. They raised their hats and retreated in good order. In 1991 Chris Sowden and Tony Burnell began to develop some of the obvious potential setting Keld in Action. There remains a considerable amount of steep, blank rock and development will doubtless continue, albeit in the upper grades.

THE CLIMBS

These are described from left to right as one faces the crag.

1   The Tragedy of Bertie Pawle   Fr   6b
Climb the first of the two bolt-protected lines on the left-hand flat wall of the crag.

2   Feroz Khan   Fr   6b
Climb the second bolt-protected line.
Further right is a ragged crack which is the common start for the next two routes:

3   Soldier   Fr   7b   †
Climb the ragged crack then break out left before the impressive groove.

4   Keld In Action   Fr   7b   †
Climb the ragged crack and continue up the impressive groove.

5   Mrs Horneyold-Strickland Calls It A Day   Fr   7b   †
Start 6m right of Keld In Action. Follow the bolts!
Just right of the centre of the crag is a great, red corner; the scene of a recent rock fall and just right is a rib with bulges.

6   Dunne's Route   Grade Unknown
Climb the rib and bulges. Some of the best rock on the crag!
To the right re two groove lines:

7   Rock On   E2   5c
Climb the left-hand groove. An exercise in bridging.

7a   Rock Away   E3   6a
Break left out of the left-hand groove and climb a difficult corner containing peg runners.

8   Hard Rock   E3   6a
Climb the cracked corner and bulge by a chain-link bolt.

WAIN WATH FORCE SCAR   O.S. SHEET 92   G.R. 883016

SITUATION AND CHARACTER

Wain Wath Force Scar is situated in Upper Swaledale about one mile upstream of Keld.

The crag is on the North side of the river and faces due South enjoying full sunshine all day as well as the beautiful outlook over Wain Wath Force, a very popular picnic venue in Summer.

The escarpment is a long wall of limestone with a fair amount of loose rock which after cleaning provides good climbing. Trees along the top provide good anchors. A footpath, followed by the Coast To Coast Walk runs hard along the top edge of the crag. The left-hand end of the crag has a prominent cave which is the starting point for climbing. The average height of the crag is about fifteen metres and so individual heights are not given.

APPROACHES AND ACCESS

From Kirkby Stephen via Nateby follow the B6270 for about twelve miles passing the crag and Wain Wath Force on the left. Turn immediately left over Park Bridge and park.

The same place can be reached via upper Swaledale. From Park Bridge either follow the footpath Westwards along the top of the crag and continue above the cave until a descent can be effected by means of a grassy rake or alternatively from the road, cross the stepping stones in the river to reach the crag.

HISTORICAL

The crag was first climbed upon by members of the Swaledale Outdoor Club, in particular, Peter Dyson and Peter Ball aided and abetted by Nimmo Clarke. Paul Carling too left his mark here with ascents of The Day The Earth Moved and Desiree whilst Stew Wilson top-roped The Day For Moving Earth.

THE CLIMBS

The climbs are described from left to right facing the crag. A cave at the left-hand end of the crag is a good base for operations.

1   Duke   VS   4b
Start 18m left of the cave below an obvious corner. Climb this to the top of the crag.

2   Eridor   HVS   5a
Start 3m right of Duke below an obvious open groove. Climb the groove to the top of the crag.

3   Bruce's Route   HVS
Climb the crack in the immediate left wall of the cave throughout.
The remaining climbs are to the right of the cave.

4   The Day The Earth Moved   VS   4c   ★
Start at a large pedestal on the right wall of the cave near the back.
From the pedestal, climb the shallow chimney and finish up the
wall above moving right to a tree at the top.

5   The Day For Moving Earth   NL   5a
Start on the right-hand side of the right wall of the cave, below a
short jamming crack. Climb the crack and move right, passing a
loose block to gain a wider crack above. Follow this and the face
above to finish at a big Yew tree.

6   Samwise   S
Climb the obvious corner to the right passing an Ash tree.

*Forty metres further right is an obvious vegetated chimney which
could possibly be used for a descent:*

7   Will's Chimney   D
Climb the chimney.

8   Bilbo   HS   4a
Start at a corner below an overhang, just right of a large tree
growing out of the base of the crag 25m right of Will's Chimney.
Climb the corner to the overhang and avoid this by stepping left
onto the slabby wall by a small Rowan tree. Finish above.

9   Gondor   HVS   5a
Start 10m right of Bilbo below a large, open corner. climb the
corner to the first overhang then make a difficult and delicate
traverse right to finish up a corner to the right.

10   Dragon   VS   4b
Start 25m further right at an obvious corner split by a thin crack.
Climb the corner.

*Approximately fifty metres further right is another deep gully and
seven metres right again is an obvious V-chimney with a crack in the
back of it.*

11   Brown Chimney   S
Climb the V-chimney.

12   Shelob   S
Start 2om further right, just right of a large, fallen Elder below a
V-chimney. Climb the short wall to a tree then climb the V-
chimney.

*At the right end of the crag is a ruined stone building. Above and
slightly right is a large, block overhang halfway up the crag. Here is
found:*

13. Desiree   HVS   5a
Climb the wall slightly right of the overhang. Make a hard move
right onto a ledge then step up and traverse the wall on the left
above the overhang to a ledge. Move left along a break until it is
possible to exit at a tree.

SWALEDALE – MINOR CRAGS AND BOULDERING VENUES

EASBY CRAG
This is located on the banks of the River Swale, downstream of the
new bridge on the path to Easby Abbey. There are several climbs

but little has been recorded except: First Find (VD) which ascends the biggest buttress from water-level, moving right, then back left at the top.

Squeezeasy – a right to left Girdle starting at a chimney and finishing just right of the easy, Central Gully.

ROUND HOWE   O.S. SHEET 92   G.R. 161008

This broken and heavily vegetated Limestone crag has a few good lines and an impressive unclimbed buttress. It faces North above the River Swale and is reached by parking as for Hudswell Crag. After crossing river, walk downstream and cross a stile. The crag, a series of buttresses is in the woods above. There is much loose rock and the area is popular with the public so care is essential. Bay Of Pigs (VS 4c) is located in a corner bay at the right end of the crag. Climb the crack in the corner past a bulge to a ledge. Continue up the dirty corner above.

Towards the left end of the crag is an obvious descent gully with a prominent off-width crack in the right wall. This gives: The Snark (HS). The climbs are the work of Paul Carling.

MARSKE QUARRY   O.S. SHEET 99   G.R. 114991

This loose and generally unattractive Limestone quarry is located four and a half miles West of Richmond on the left-hand side of the A6108 just before the junction with the B6270 leading into the upper dale. Marske Quarry has two tiers of rock the Upper Tier is dangerous and rock dislodged can endanger people on the Lower Tier. A big layby gives access to the Lower Tier. The climbs were first recorded in 1971 by P.Ingham, M.Binks, G.Davison and T. McLean. The Upper Tier gave eight routes which are not described due to the instability of the rock and their lack of popularity in the intervening years.

CLIMBS ON THE LOWER TIER

1   Sunny Slab   8m   S
Climb the isolated slab to the left of the tier.

2   Little Vector   12m   HVS   5a   ★
Start 10m right of Sunny Slab below a short groove which is climbed to a traverse left to a loose spike. Gain the slab above and finish to the right.

3   Fossil   9m   VS   4c
Climb the obtuse angled groove. Trend right to finish.

4   Downholme Chimney   8m   D
The obvious chimney left of an alcove.

5   Gay Boys Groove   8m   VS   4c   ★
Climb the wall 5m right of the chimney and finish up an open groove.

6   Marske Corner   9m   VD
Ascend the left corner of the Alcove.

7   Zoot Allures   12m   VS   4c
Ascend the right corner of the Alcove.

8   Eezie Chimney   12m   D
Climb the left-hand of two chimneys to the right of the Alcove.
9   Ping's Chimney   12m   VS   4c
Climb the right chimney.
10   Pushover   8m   S
Climb the slabby arete 12m right of Ping's Chimney.
11   Friday Crack   9m   S
Climb the crack in the centre of the Lower Tier via an initial over-hang. finish on dirty ledges.

ELLERKIN SCAR   O.S. SHEET 98   G.R.961924

This imposing cliff is in Wensleydale and is situated about a mile to the North-East of Askrigg.

It is best aproached by following the minor road from Askrigg via Howgate to Nappa Scar. Permission should be sought from Mr. T. Metcalfe of Nappa Scar on Wensleydale 50342. Up to now permission to climb has always been granted. The crag consists of a Main Wall of smooth, compact limestone which has a quarried appearance. The left-hand slim crack is E1 5b whilst the fine corner on the right is VS 4c both routes are the work of P.Woodyer. Many more possibilities exist.

11   COLSTERDALE

Colsterdale is a lovely unspoilt valley to the West of Masham. The dale is a cul-de-sac and in 1980, The First Edition of this Guide pulled Slipstones Crag out of this particular bag. It is a long edge of impeccable Gritstone with literally hundreds of quality problems and short routes.

Slipstones has been a real success story and now it must stand with the best bouldering crags of the country.

SLIPSTONES CRAG – COLSTERDALE   O.S. Sheet 99   G.R. 138 821

SITUATION AND CHARACTER

This delightful gritstone outcrop is situated on the North side of Colsterdale about six miles West of Masham. Facing South, it receives sun for most of the day. The edge lies high on the moor with commanding views across the valley and as a consequence of its position, it dries quickly. The rock is blessed with numerous pockets and the wide variety of boulders and blocks of all sizes provide a plethora of exquisite problems complementing the equally superb routes on the 'edge' itself.

Slipstones is easily the best crag on the Eastern side of the North Of England guide area.

APPROACHES AND ACCESS

The crag is on open moorland and is approached from Masham by following a minor road West through Fearby and Healey. Just over half a mile (ignoring a right turn just beyond the village) beyond Healey the road forks and the right-hand branch is followed for a little more than a mile to a series of sharp bends. Several hundred metres beyond the sharp bends is an obvious parking place on the right. The track leading up to the crag is reached by walking along the road for a few more minutes until a gate on the right gives access to a good track crossing a field and ultimately gaining the open moor. The track, which is a Public Right Of Way leads to the left end of the crag.

HISTORICAL

"Yorkshire's Best Kept Secret", so says the Historical in the YMC Gritstone Guide of 1989. No mention is made of the fact that the crag appeared in the Rock Climbers Guide to the North Of England 1981, the first edition of the present guide.

The record needs to be set straight, history does not exist unless it is recorded:

The first person to record climbs on the crag was Martyn Berry with lads on camp from Pollington Borstal. From Martyn's original notes and sketches it is apparent that many of the easier lines up to Severe were climbed. Martyn passed on information to Allan

Allsopp in September 1958 for inclusion in a guide to West Yorkshire which was published by Walmer Brothers. Alan Allsopp
visited the crags and his comment was:

". . . Purely as climbing though, I don't think the standard (I don't
mean the technical level) is quite equal to that of most of the other
crags we have described in our guide . . . I would certainly be very
pleased to include a page or so . . . somewhat on the lines of 'Other
Crags'."

The crag was not included along with other West Yorkshire
gritstone crags in a whole series of guides including the YMC
Lesniak guide of 1982 because it was felt that it was more of a North
Yorkshire crag used by Teessiders and climbers from Durham and
of course it was North of the accepted Yorkshire Gritstone boundary of Nidderdale.

In 1959 Geoff Milburn, living in Richmond, used to cycle to
Masham to visit a girlfriend and on these visits he "discovered"
Slipstones and made the first ascent of Slanting Flake in July 1959.
Geoff took Peter Martin, the Biology teacher at Richmond Gram-
mar School to the crag in October 1960 and they climbed about
fifteen routes including Chockstone Overhang, Not-So-Tight
Chimney and Mantelshelf Crack. This led P.G. Martin to produce
his interim guide in 1965 which appeared in Climber magazine. This
guide recorded many of the easier climbs, repeating the Berry
routes of the '50's and was the work of the masters and boys of
Richmond School.

Ron Kenyon visited the crag with Stew Wilson in the late 70's and
repeated all of the old routes and many others most of which were
obviously climbed as evidenced by wear. The climbs were named
and graded and in all seventy one climbs were recorded in the
definitive guide.

The guide created a lot of interest and development proceeded
apace and was entirely the work of lads from Darlington and
Teesside.

Dave Stainthorpe climbed Stainthorpe's Wall in October 1980
whilst a few days earlier Paul Ingham produced Rock On. Also in
1980 Ian 'Squawk' Dunn climbed Squawk's Arete and later in April
1982 he led the fine Atomic seconded by Paul Ingham. Paul
Ingham's contribution to the crag are perhaps the most outstanding, to mention but a few of his routes: Paul's Arete, Ripper, Seven
Up, Impregnable and Leany Meany.

The mid 80's saw Slipstones established as the bouldering 'Mecca'
of the North-East and standards began to rise. Some route claims
were surrounded by some controversy and one of these, Sinbad
was claimed by its first ascentionists as HVS 5c. A subsequent
ascent by Ian Cummins established the grade at E3 6a.

Paul Ingham established the higest grades with his ascent of Layby
Arete in 1985 and Ian Cummins produced the extremely hard Sulky
Little Boys.

The YMC included Slipstones in their 1989 guide but this effort
merely pepetuated the confusion a wrongly titled photograph
created in the 1980 North Of England guide.

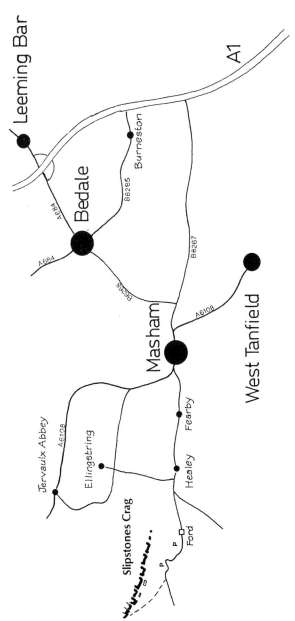

SLIPSTONES CRAG & COLSTERDALE

This edition hopefully sets the record straight and puts Slipstones where it rightfully belongs: in the North.

THE CLIMBS
These are described from left to right, buttress by buttress.

BUTTRESS 1
This is the isolated buttress 25 metres left of the main edge. It has a striking arete which is clearly visible.

1 Extremities 5m E2 5b
Climb the left-most wall on tiny finger holds. Fully unprotectable and a nasty landing.

2 Paul's Arete 6m E1 5b   ★★
The arete offers a superb introduction to the crag and is low in the grade.

3 Steve's Wall 6m E1 5b
Climb the wall to the right which eases towardsthe top.

4 Heather Crack 5m D
Climb the crack on the right of the buttress

BUTTRESS 2
This is the wall to the left of the large block boulder of Buttress 3.

5 Roofed Corner 5m D
Climb the corner on the extreme left of the buttress.

6 Overhanging Crack 6m VD
Climb the left-hand of the three cracks.

7 Undercut Double Crack 6m S
Climb the central crack with an akward start.

8 Not So Tight Chimney 7m S
Wedge the wider right-hand crack at the left of the buttress.

9 Space Truckin' 8m E1 5b
Climb the steep wall to the right finishing on thin flakes up the headwall. Hard.

10 Escalator 7m HVS 5b   ★
Climb the steep wall in the centre of the buttress.

11 Mantleshelf Crack 6m VD
Climb the wall to a recess at the top of the crag.

12 Staircase 6m M
The obvious gangway which slopes up left to the recess.

13 Mantleshelf Wall 5m S 4a
This is the left wall of the gully.Start at the obvious gangway of Staircase and move up right to finish with difficulty.

BUTTRESS 3
The large boulder with a slabby North face and overhanging South face. It offers some of the best climbing on the edge. The climbs are described beginning with the North face.

14 Left Edge 5m D

15 Petch's Groove 5m HS 4c   ★
The faint groove up the slabs centre.
16 Twenty Foot Crack 6m VD   ★
Climb the crack to the left.
17 Tranmire Arete 6m VD   ★
Climb the right hand arete of the slab.
18 Tranmire Crack 6m VS 4c
Climb the thin crack up the left side of the face.
19 Girdle Buttress 50m HVS 5a
Start up Tranmire Crack and follow the higher break rightwards around this buttress and buttress. Numerous belays will be required to prevent rope-drag and to protect the unfortunate second
20 Jenny Binks Wall 7m HVS 5b   ★
Climb the steep west wall of the buttress starting in the centre. Climb the well spaced horizontal breaks.
21 Easy Pickings 7m HS
Climb the wall to the right of Jenny Binks.
22 Beldin 8m E1 5b   ★★
Follow the gangway leftwards up the overhanging South face until a hard move allows the final short crack to be ascended. An excellent climb.
Direct Start: HVS 5b
Ascend the blunt nose on the left to join Beldin near the top The wall in between is 5c.
23 Gollinglith 8m VS 5a   ★★
Start to the right of the centre of the face and climb the overhanging crack and wall.
24 Zoom 8m HVS 5a   ★★
Start to the right of the arete within the marked recess.Gain the flake. Finish up the short crack. High in the grade and suprisingly strenuous.
Within the recessed, square cut alcove that separates Buttress 3 from Buttress 4, we find:
25 Atomic 8m E3 6a   ★★★
The undoubted classic of the crag. Start below the centre of the left wall. Climb to the break. Step left using tiny holds and pockets to attain a standing position (crux), then make for the top.
26 Barnley Crack 8m S
Climb the left crack in the back of the recess.
27 Barnley Wall 8m HS 4a   ★
Climb the wall at the back of the recess.
28 Ulfers Crack 8m VD
Climb the right-hand crack at the back of the recess.

BUTTRESS 4
The right wall of the recess forms the start of this buttress, which is capped by a roof just below the top. At the right-hand end the buttress turns in to another recess which is wider than the recess at the left end of the buttress.

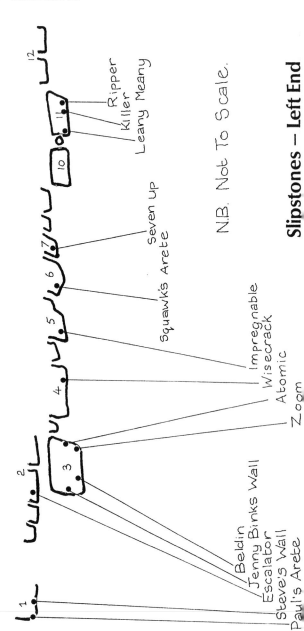

Ripper
Killer
Leany Meany

Squawk's Arete
Seven up

N.B. Not To Scale.

Impregnable
Wisecrack
Atomic
Zoom

Beldin
Jenny Binks Wall
Escalator
Steve's Wall
Paul's Arete

Slipstones – Left End

29   Forever Onward   8m   HVS   5b
Climb the right wall of the recess. The finish involves a long reach!

30   Timeless Divide   9m   HVS   5c   ★
Climb the right side of the arete, mostly on the wall and finish up the spectacular fin. A difficult problem.

31   Agra   9m   HVS   5b   ★★★
Start below and right of the roof and just right of the slab. Climb leftwards up the slab to the roof. The roof succumbs with difficulty.

Variation Start: **Agrete**   HVS   5c
Climb directly up to the finish of Agra.

32   Agra Right-Hand   8m   HVS   5b   ★
Start as for Agra. Climb direct to the roof. Move right below this before pulling round to the top.

33   Wisecrack   6m   HVS   5c
Start below the hanging crack. Climb this via a hard start.

34   Allan's Arete   6m   VS   4c
Climb the short arete at the right hand end of the face.

Now into the recess:

35   Shine On   5m   D
Climb the layback crack in the recess.

36   Mantle On   4m   S
Climb the wall at the back of the recess.

37   Groove On   4m   D
Climb the groove further right.

BUTTRESS 5

This is the buttress with the "impregnable" face just right of the easy descent. A prominent hole is visible 3m from the ground on the horizontal break.

38   Wall Climb   4m   D
Start below the centre of the wall of the left-hand side of the buttress within the recess. Climb the wall in the centre.

39   Block Arete   5m   S
Climb the arete on its left side.

40   Beta Blocker   6m   E1   5b
Climb the arete above the "motivating" flakes.

41   Impregnable   8m   E2   5c   ★★
Climb the centre of the face to the hole. Reach right and pull up to the break and finish more easily.

42   Get Nervous   8m   E2   5c
Climb the undercut arete with the crux at the bottom. Avoid escaping into Chockstone Overhang.

43   Chockstone Overhang   7m   S
Climb the undercut chimney on the right of the buttress. It proves strenuous and worthwhile.

BUTTRESS 6

This face has a blunt flake on the front.

44   Squawk's Arete   8m   HVS   5b
Climb the left arete of the buttress.

45   Undcut Flake   8m   S   ★
Climb the centre of the face to a ledge and finish up the short corner formed by the flake.

46   Dark Cleft   6m   D
Struggle up the chimney on the right.

BUTTRESS 7 and BUTTRESS 8.

Buttress 7 is the undercut face right of Dark Cleft. The two cracks are the vague divide between the two sections.

47   Forever Young   7m   E2   5c   ★
Follow the crease up the wall to the right of Dark Cleft with an awkward move at the top.

48   Seven Up   7m   E1   5b   ★★
Climb the imposing front face by launching off from the left arete. A fragile wafer provides interest near the top.

49   Fuser   3m   VD
Climb the layback crack at the division of the buttresses.

50   Wedge Down Crack   6m   HS   4b   ★
Climb the second crack using a wriggle technique.

51   Dennis in Darlo   6m   HVS   5b
Climb the centre of the squat wall just to the right.

52   Barren Waste   6m   E2   5b
Follow the right edge of the wall and use a 'telescopic' arm to reach the top.

53   Easy Groove   5m   D
Climb the groove on the right-hand end of the buttress.

54   Edge Route   5m   M
Climb the blocky end of the face.

BUTTRESS 9

This is the short wall behind the large, detached block that is Buttress 10.

55   Awkward Finish   3m   D
Climb the chimney on the left of the wall.

56   Roofed Chimney   3m   M
Climb the corner to the right of Awkward Finish.

57   Staircase Mantle   4m   D
Climb the next wall on the right.

BUTTRESS 10

This is the large detached block that is separated from the 'edge' by a wide gully.

58   Sowden   6m   VS   5a   ★★
Climb the left-hand arete of the front face using a flake crack in the wall on the right.

*The next five routes are described working **leftwards** around the block.*

59   Problem Wall   5m   HVS   5b
Climb the wall just left of Sowden.

60 Left Wall 5m VD
Climb the curving corner 3 metres left of Sowden.

61 Right Arete 5m VD
Start at the right-hand arete of the backside of the block which is a steep, undercut slab. Climb the arete.

62 Left Arete 4m VD
Climb the left arete of the slab.

63 Witton Wall 5m S
Climb a crack on the face (East) right of Left Arete.

*The next climbs are on the overhanging, front face, **right** of Sowden.*

64 Sinbad 6m E3 6a   ★
Climb the flake 2m right of Sowden which leads to pockets below the top.

65 Space Plucks 6m E3 6a   ★★
Climb the weakness 5m right of Sowden past an obvious slot.

BUTTRESS 11
This is the stretch of rock between the gully behind Buttress 10 and the recess further right.

66 Leany Meany 7m HVS 5b
Climb the left side of the leaning wall by starting from the left arete and moving up and right to a slot. Finish straight above.

67 Killer 7m E3 6a
The flake to the left of the blunt arete of Ripper provides a stiff start. Pull left and follow pockets up the wall.

68 Ripper 7m HVS 5c   ★★
Climb the grooved arete 6m right of Leaning Meany. Step from the boulder and follow the flakes. Precarious and thought-provoking.

69 Ripper Traverse 10m HVS 5c
Climb Leaning Meany to the break and traverse right to finish as for Ripper.

70 Half-Way Chockstone 5m D
Climb the chimney on the left side of the recess.

71 Central Bay Route 3m D
Climb the rocks on the right of the recess.

BUTTRESS 12
This buttress has a prominent, sentry-box crack splitting its centre and a pointed roof to the right.

72 Cummin's Route 5m HVS 5c
Climb the wall to the left of the crack.

73 Christopher Robin 6m HS 4b   ★
Climb the sentry-box crack.

74 Marr's Route 6m VS 4c
Climb the wall and overhang 3m right of Christopher Robin.

75 Moderator 3m M
Climb the chimney near the right-hand end of the buttress.

76 Little Gully 3m M
Climb the gully to the right of the buttress.

BUTTRESS 13 (The Siamese Blocks)

This buttress is composed of two large boulders close together, the right-hand one leans alarmingly over the path. There are a number of aretes.

77 Friday 13th 4m HVS 5b or 5c
Climb the left-hand arete on the left side at 5b or the right side at 5c.

78 Siamese Bridge 5m D
Bridge the chimney between the "Siamese" blocks.

79 Right-Hand Twin 5m HVS 5b
Climb the arete right of the chimney. It is easier than first impressions would suggest.

80 Strictly Personal 5m E1 6a   ★
Climb the right arete of the right "Siamese" block on the left side – Got it?

81 Brush Up 4m HVS 5b
Climb the right-hand wall right of the arete.

BUTTRESS 14

Further right is an isolated buttress with an impressive front face. The routes are still "Yorkshire's Best Kept Secret" until now.

82 String Vest 6m HVS 5c
Climb the shallow groove on the left-hand side of the face.

83 Aces High 6m HS 4a   ★★
Made famous in the 1981 North of England Guide photograph as Ellingstring. A gem of a route! Climb the centre of the face to the horizontal breaks. Finish direct or rightwards.

84 Trumps 6m VD   ★
Climb the right-hand arete to join the right-hand finish to Aces High.

BUTTRESS 15

This next section of the 'edge' has an obvious horizontal break running across the face.

85 Heather Wall 4m D
Climb the short, left wall of the buttress.

86 Pinnacle Chimney 5m D
Climb the chimney on the left.

87 Yaud Wall 5m HVS 5b
The shallow corner on the left side of the wall is climbed on good holds.

88 Ellingstring 5m VS 4b   ★
Climb the centre of the wall on unexpected holds. Well worth finding.

89 Gymnast 5m HVS 5c
Climb the undercut right-hand arete. A difficult struggle.

90 Girgle 9m VD
Traverse the low horizontal break.

Slipstones – Right End

NB Not To Scale.

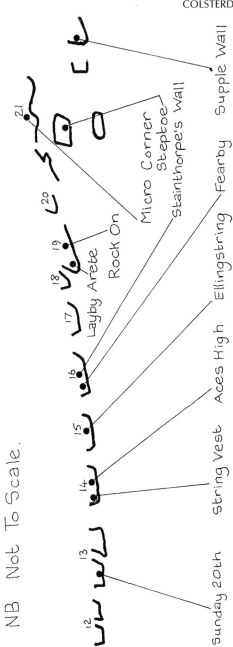

BUTTRESS 16

This buttress is identified by a series of small overhangs on the right-hand side.

91   Fearby   6m   VS   4b
Climb the left-hand side of the front of the buttress.

92   Stainthorpe's Wall   6m   HVS   5a   ★★
Climb the centre of the wall starting just right of Fearby. A variation start from under the overhang at 5c is possible.

93   Fascinationby   6m   E1   5c   ★
Climb up to the hanging groove from the rock scar.

BUTTRESS 17

This buttress has a horizontal crack across it at half-height, and a slab to the right.

94   Jug Handle Pull Up   5m   VD
Climb the left-hand arete.

95   Wall Centre   5m   HS   4a
Climb the centre of the buttress.

96   Happy Daze   5m   HS   4b
Climb the wall just left of the right arete.

97   Double mantleshelf   6m   VD
Climb the slab on the right of the buttress.

BUTTRESS 18

This is very small and has Easy Mantl   shelf – D.

BUTTRESS 19

This is a useful landmark, having a three-layered boulder in front of it.

98   Hand Traverse   6m   D
Start low down on the left of the buttress. Follow a crackline rightwards to finish in the centre of the face.

99   Layby Arete   6m   E2   6c   ★★★
Levitate up the arete, first on the right then swinging left to finish.

100   Layby   5m   HVS   6a   ★
Climb the thin flake crack which is often wet.

101   Little Baldy   5m   6c
Climb direct to the scar on Rock On using tiny holds for the left hand and NOT the Layby flake.

102   Rock On   4m   HVS   5c   ★
Start right again and reach a slot which aids further progress.

103   Rock Off   4m   5b
Climb the blunt arete on the right.

BUTTRESS 20

The next small buttress with easy routes.

104   Ten Foot Moderate   3m   M
Climb the crack on the left.

105 Two Chockstones 5m D
Climb the wide crack.
106 Left Wall 5m VD
107 Right Overhang 5m D

BUTTRESS 21
This consists of a series of three boulders progressing down the hillside.

Upper Tier:
108 Stomach Traverse Amusing
Crawl under the overhanging top of the buttress.

Middle Tier consists of three large boulders:
109 Curving Crack 3m S
Climb the crack on the right of the left-hand boulder.
110 Bert Wells 5m HVS 5b
Climb the short wall to the right.
111 Steptoe 5m HVS 5c
Climb the wall left of Tiptoe with the crux at the top.
112 Tiptoe 5m VS 4c
Climb the arete 5m right of Curving Crack.
113 Micro Corner 4m HVS 6a
Climb the obvious, blank-looking corner behind Tiptoe.
114 Bridge Chimney 3m D
Chimney up the gap between the two right-hand boulders.
115 Davies' Ramp HVS 6a
Start at the left arete of the right-hand boulder and follow the rampline diagonally right.
116 Slab And Mantleshelf 5m M
Climb the right-hand side of the right boulder.

Lower Tier:
The best of the three tiers giving a delightful slab which is easily spotted when approaching the crag.
117 Tommy's Dilemma 6m VD   ★
Climb the left side of the slab.
118 Gipsey Wham 5m VD   ★
Climb the centre of the slab

BUTTRESS 22
The final buttress containing a chockstone crack. The left side of the buttress is connected to the the Middle tier of Buttress 21.
119 Ten Foot Slab 3m D
Climb the connecting slab between Buttresses 21 and 22, just right of Slab And Mantleshelf.
120 Chockstone Pull Up 3m E1 6a   ★★★
A magnificent climb which takes the soaring crack direct.

121   Supple Wall   3m   6b
Climb the short wall to the left of the arete.
122   Sulky Little Boys   3m   6c
Climb the short arete on its right-hand side.
123   Slanting Flake   3m   S
Climb the blunt, rightward sloping flake on the right of the buttress.

Traverses:
124   Buttresses 3 and 4   HVS   5a   *
Start at the foot of Tranmire Arete and follow the highest break rightwards crossing both buttresses.
125   Low Level   Arduous   6b   ***
From Dennis in Darlo leftwards to finish at Tranmire Arete or the reverse.

BROWN BECK CRAG   O.S. SHEET 99   G.R. 125827

This small crag three-quarters of a mile West of Slipstones Crag is reached by following the minor valley beyond Slipstones up onto the moor. The escarpment is now on ones left and can be approached quite easily. Large boulders below the edge provide interesting problems.
The crag consists of several buttresses of a soft and lichenous Gritstone. It is nowhere more than five or six metres high, faces South and dries quickly.

HISTORICAL
The crag was first climbed on by Dave Paul and Steve Brown in the early 80's. Other Cleveland climbers involved in the development were Paul Ingham and Tony Marr.

THE CLIMBS
These are described from right to left and buttress by buttress.

BUTTRESS 1
1   Big Boss   MVS   4b
Climb the rib and bulge behind the Holly.
2   Top Man   S
Climb the right side of the rib to the left of the Holly.
3   Wichita Linesman   HVS   5a
Climb the undercut flake crack.

BUTTRESS 2
4   Escape   VS   5a
Climb the flake to the right of the arete.
5   Ingham's Route   E2   5c
Climb the overhanging arete with a ledge halfway up. Could be a nasty landing!

6 Transcendence E1 5c
Climb the flake just left of the arete to pass the overhang. A right-slanting ramp is the exit.

7 Phenomenonlogy E2 5c/6a
Climb the wall just right of the left-trending groove/ramp of Pella.

8 Pella VS 4c
Follow the left-trending ramp.

9 Let The Children Play VS 4c
Climb the wall and hand-crack above.

10 Childs' Play HVS 5c
Climb the wall just right of the ledge at the left end of the buttress.

BUTTRESS 3

11 Dealer VS 4c
Climb the slim face at the right-hand side.

12 Bahia HVS 5b
Climb the wall just left of the arete to finish on good holds.

13 Brown Boots HVS 5b
Climb the wall via pocket holds.

14 Big Boots VS 4c
Climb the wall to the right of the arete.

15 Dawn S
Climb the left arete.

BUTTRESS 4

This slim buttress is situated a further fifteen metres to the left.

16 Den VS 5a
Climb the right-hand arete on the left side.

17 Eric HVS 5b
Climb the front wall direct, starting on the left.

BUTTRESS 5

18 High Adventure HVS 5a
Climb up to the roof and leftwards into the chimney. Then follow the obvious hand-traverse and arete to the top.

19 Go Within VS 4c
Climb the wall below and just left of the roof passing a wide break.'

Further left are more small buttresses. A short walk further up the valley is a small quarry with other interesting lines.

FIRST ASCENTS

ARMATHWAITE

5.5.73	A Big Hand	S.Wilson, A.Yarrow.
	The first route on the crag and climbed in front of an appreciative audience.	
	Kingfisher	S.Wilson, A.Yarrow.
12.5.73	Glenwillie Grooves	S.W., A.Y. (shared leads).
	Direct	S.W. A.Y.
	The Bullgine Run	S.W., A.Y.(shared leads).
	The Crack Finish	A.Y. S.W.
	Ituna	S.W., A.Y.(shared leads).
	The ancient name for the River Eden. Both Slab start and Rib start ascended.	
17.5.73	Flasherman	A.Y., S.W.(alt.).
	Named after one of the team who found himself in a situation of extreme exposure.	
	Time And Motion Man	R.Kenyon, S.W., T.Dale.
	Nosescratcher	R.Kenyon, T.Dale.
	Joe Soap's Corner	A.Y. S.W.
30.5.73	Herbie	R.K.
1973	Princess Anne's New Ring	A.Y., S.W. (alt.)
	Climbed the day she was engaged to Mark Phillips.	
	Zephyr	A.Y., R.Whitsome.
	Codpiece Left-Hand	A.Y., S.W.
	Codpiece	A.Y., S.W. R.May (varied leads)
	Climbed using aid from two pegs. F.F.A. by J.Lamb in 1974.	
	Barnacle Bill	R.K., S.W.
	Two pegs used for aid. F.F.A. by J.Lamb in 1974	
	The Monkey Hanger	S.W., A.Y. (alt.)
	Stinkhorn	S.W., A.Y.
	Cally Crack	J.Lamb
	Named after the Caledonian pub in Carlisle-a climbers' venue.	
30.9.73	F.B.S.J.	S.W., R.K.
8.12.73	Douber	R.K., T.Dale.
9.12.73	The Schnuck	R.K., S.W. T.Dale.
	Interest was added when the large tree used as the only runner, slid down the rope towards the terrified belayers huddled on the middle ledge. Luckily nobody was hurt.	
1973/74	Andy's Slab	A.Hunter
	A great achievement and a route which sees few convincing ascents hence its other name: Once In A Blue Moon.	
12.1.74	Erection	J.Lamb, A. Liddell.
16.2.74	Blockbuster	R.K., Chris ?

1974	Dome Slab	J.L.

Photographs of this superb First ascent in Mountain gave Armathwaite some national publicity. Pete Whillance made an early Second Ascent.

1974	Cluedo	S.W. S.Butler.

Climbed by J.L. in 1975 and named Diamond Lil's

	Coombs Crack	S.W.
	Red Monkey	Mike Hetherington
	Red Lion	S.W.
	Red Spider	S.Miller.
	Victory V	Unknown.
	The Crescent	J.L. Mike Hetherington.
	Jelly Terror	J.L. M.H.
	Solitaire	J.L.
	Paper Moon	J.L.
	Pocket Solitaire	S.W.
25.3.74	Y-Front	P.Botterill, M.H.

A bold on-sight First ascent.

8.5.74	Free And Easy	P.Whillance, A.Greig.

Originally climbed with one aid point two days earlier. The name was a jocular reminder to observers that aid was not the name of the game.

17.9.74	Pickpocket	P.Whillance (solo)

After top-rope inspection.

28.9.74	Wafer Thin	P.W., A.Greig.

After top-rope inspection. An audacious lead!

18.1.75	Harry's Groove	R.K. "Jamie" Morton.
2.2.75	Victory V: Variation Finish	J.L., M.H., P.Botterill, H.Loughran
13.3.75	Flasherman R.H. Finish	P.W.
1975	Sailing Shoes	A.Hewison.
1975	Grey Duster	Unknown
18.3.75	Wafer Thin L.H. Finish	P.W.
26.3.75	New Moon	J.L.

This desperate problem was called New Moon Direct in that it straightened out New Moon, a Whillance route (10.9.74) which came in from the left. Other routes have superseded this. New moon as it is now, has probably not had an ascent since the 70's on account of a hold breaking off.

1975	The Exorcist	J.L.

One of the big ones! Jeff placed a protection peg on the F.A. He also climbed the route without, as did Ron Fawcett. The peg remains in situ and performs sterling service!

22.4.75	Cook's Crack	R.K.
	Cook's Left Hand	A.Beatty.
	Boomerang	A.Beatty.
	Aborigine	A.Beatty.
20.5.75	The High Level Girdle	P.W

This bold excursion was completed solo by Whillance on 1.7.75.

1975	The Scroll	Stuart Miller

This route has been omitted in order to preserve the fine inscription, a misquote from Walton's 'Compleat Angler.'

1975/76	Blue Lugs	J.L.

This was led by Jeff although few people were aware of the fact.

	Tramlines	Unknown
1975/76	Pickpocket Super Direct	P.Botterill.
	Erection Arete	J.L.
	Jeff's Wall	J.L.
1977	Blast Off	P.Rigby, D.Bowen.
	The Orbit	P.Rigby
	Moving Pictures	S.W. D.Bowen.
30.4.78	Close Encounters	R.K.
	Harry's Arete	R.K. Miss S. Thompson.
1979	Nurt's Way	R.K.
1980	Petit Mal	S.W.
	The Thirty Nine Steps	S.W
1985	Blanks' Expression	L. Blanks
1986	Moondance	S.W. Mrs. M.Wilson, A.Williamson.
	The Green Knight	S.W. Mrs M.Wilson.
	Gwalchmai	S.W. J.Wilson, T.Suddaby.
	John and Frog's Route	J Wilson, J.Hughes.

Almost certainly climbed by Lamb in mid 70's

	Cook's Apron	D.Hetherington, S.W.
	Cook's Tour	D.Hetherington, S.W.
August '86	Smiling Faces	M.Holden, D.Holden, M.Tomlinson.
	Meat Is Murder	M.Holden, D. Holden, M.Tomlinson.
	Astral Wall	M.Tomlinson, M.Holden.
	Kaleidoscope Eyes	M.Tomlinson.
1987	Soft Touch	A.Greig
	Beyond The Thunder Dome	Mark Hetherington
	Devil Moon	A.G., R. Parker.
	Plain Sailing	A.G.
31.1.87	Smear Or Die	A.G. R.P.
1.2.87	Limpet Lil	A.G., R.P.

Climbed by P.Botterill in '70's but not claimed.

	The Black Russian	R.P., A.G.
7.2.87	Swing Out Sister	R.P.

The lower arete was climbed by R.P. using high,side runners. This was soloed shortly afterwards by Paul Carling. The upper arete has not been led. Pete Botterill or J.L. may have top-roped the climb (Rise And Shine?) in 1974.

Sept. '87	Indian's Revenge	G.Brown
	The Viennese Oyster	G.Brown, H. Loughran.
1987	One Hand Clapping	G.Brown (solo)
Sept 1989	Mr. Bundy's Best Friend	G.Brown

| 1991 | Mellow | P.Williams. |
| | Certainly done before. | |

LAZONBY OUTCROPS

1969	Merry Monk Variations	J.Workman, J.Simpson.
1969	Gadzowt	A.Beatty, D.Hodgson.
19.12.70	Merry Monk	R.Kenyon, J.Aldridge.
	Climbed by moving right and then back left.	
3.3.73	Direct up corner – now normal.	W.S.Lounds, S.Wilson
27.12.70	Cave Route	A.Beatty, R.Kenyon (alt.)
Adam	R.Kenyon.	
Eve	R.Kenyon.	
29.12.70	The Crack	R.Kenyon, A.Beatty.
The Mole	A.Beatty.	
	Cream Cracker Wall	R.Kenyon, A.Beatty.
	Al's Chimney	A.Beatty.
1971	Cave Corner	B.Dixon.
	Silicosis	B.Dixon, A.Beatty.
	Pneumoconiosis	B.Dixon, A.Beatty.
	The last two routes marked a new breakthrough in difficulty.	
26.9.71	The Swinger	A.Beatty, R.Kenyon.
27.12.71	Trundle Wall	P.Rigby, R.Kenyon (alt.)
	Swing Off	P.Rigby (top rope).
15.1.78	Swing Off	R.Fawcett.
27.12.71	Pseudonym	A.Beatty.
2.1.72	One Of The World's Many Problems	A.Beatty, P.Rigby, R.Kenyon, J.Workman.
16.1.72	Phred	B.Dixon, R.Kenyon.
	Bucket And Spade Job	R.Kenyon, P.Rigby.
	Compost Wall	R.Kenyon.
22.1.72	Catastrophe Corner	P.Rigby, R.Kenyon (alt.), A.Beatty.
29.1.72	Insanity Groove	R.Kenyon, P.Rigby.
5.2.72	Rat Salad	P.Rigby, R.Kenyon.
1972	Bolt Start to Rat Salad	R.Kenyon.
14.2.72	Sisyphus	A.Beatty, R.Kenyon, T.Dale.
19.2.72	Gumbo Variations	P.Rigby (unseconded).
4.3.72	Virtually Part One	P.Rigby, T.Dale, R.Kenyon.
	Teragram	R.K., P.R., T.Dale.
10.3.72	Neanderthal Man	R.K., P.R. (alt.)
27.3.72	Jamboree	R.K., T.Dale.
	Moonlight Sonata	R.K., T.D.
	Climbed by moonlight!	
30.4.72	Mij	R.K., J.Kilduff.
	Barney Left Finish	R.K., J.Kilduff.
26.12.72	Barney Right Finish	R.K., T.D., S.Laws.
1972	Dirty Old Pillar	S.Wilson, P.Hope.
	Hernia	T.D., A.B., P.R.

| | Cobweb (aid used) | P.R., T.D. |
| 10.8.74 | Cobweb (F.F.A.) | T.Proctor, A.B., B.D. |

An historic ascent, recorded as a photoclimb in Rocksport Magazine.

| 13.12.72 | Microman | T.D., P.R. (varied leads). |

Climbed on nuts and one peg for aid.

11.9.88	Machoman (F.F.A. of Microman)	K.Lunt, N.Ibberson.
30.12.72	J.J.	B.Miller, R.K.
3.3.73	The Horror	W.Lounds, T.D., S.Wilson, P.R. (top rope).
8.4.89	The Horror (First lead)	K.Lunt, A.Williamson.
13.10.73	Mandrax	R.K., S.Wilson.
22.12.73	Look To The Future Its Only Just Begun	R.K., A.Miller.
13.1.74	Inside A Cosmic Orgasm	P.R., S.Wilson.
19.1.74	Mr Woo. The Gripe.	R.K., M.Sheldon.
13.2.74	Tigerfeet	P.Botterill, J.Lamb.
Spring 1974	Gone	A.Yarrow, S.Wilson.
12.4.86	Gone Direct Start	R.K.
1975	Fingers Pitch 1	P.R. (top rope)
26.7.75	Fingers Pitch 2	P.R.
1979/80	Pitch 1 (possible First Lead?)	K.Neal.
Mid 70's	Red Chipper	J.Lamb.

Lamb enforces a sterner ethic into the valley!

1978	Ace Of Wands	P.R. (pitches 1 & 2) R.K. (pitch 3), D.Bowen.
	Variations On A Swinger (used resting point on a nut).	P.R., D.Bowen.
8.4.89	Variations On A Swinger (F.F.A.)	K.Lunt, A.Williamson.
15.3.86	Fear Is The Key	K.Lunt, C.Crowder.
	Mystery Achievement	K.Lunt, C.Crowder.
11.4.86	Lip Service	C.Crowder, K.L.
	Electric Avenue	K.L., C.C.
	Savage Rib	K.L., C.C.
12.4.86	Suspended Animation	C.C. (pitch 1), K.L. (pitch 2).
	Sahara Crossing	C.C., K.L.

An early attempt of The Fearful Void.

| 14.4.86 | Technical Ecstasy | K.L. (unseconded). |

Second attempt following a near "groundfall" from the final moves.

27.5.86	Perilous Journey	C.C. (pitch1), K.L. (pitch2).
7.9.86	Scorpion	K.L., N.Frowe, M.Carter.
3.5.87	Snowball	G.Dawson, K.L.
	Herbal Abuse	K.L., G.Dawson.
	Far Above The Splat Mat	G.Dawson, K.L.
	Cellnet	G.Dawson, K.L.

	The Neighbourhood Bully	K.L., G.D.
	The Right Stuff	K.L., G.D.
	The Cockpit	K.L., G.D.
	Red Square Dare	G.D., K.L.
30.5.87	I Can't Breakdance!	K.L., I.Makin.
	King Of The Swingers	I.Makin, K.L.
2.8.87	Stained Class	K.L., S.Williamson.
16.9.87	Gothic Horror	A.Kay, K.L.
	Nemesis Towers	K.L., A.Kay.
1.10.87	The Fearful Void	K.L., A.Kay.

An apt name, taken from the title of the book by
Geoffrey Moorhouse about his attempt to traverse
the Sahara; as much an examination of inner
feelings as a journey!

	Eye In The Sky	K.L., A.Kay.
12.5.88	Demolition Dancing	K.L., Miss S. Oliver.
11.9.88	Footfall	K.L., N.Ibberson.
	Machoman	K.L., N.Ibberson.
29.10.88	Rattle And Hum	K.L. (solo)
	Red Barchetta	K.L. (solo)
	The Toe	K.L. (solo)
	Sunflower	K.L. (solo)
31.12.88	Neptune	S.Grieve (unseconded).
4.4.89	Pavane	K.L. M.Tomlinson.
8.4.89	The Horror	K.L., A.Williamson.
	Variations On A Swinger	K.L., A.Williamson.
5.7.89	Why Flymo When You Can Napalm?	S.Grieve (unseconded).

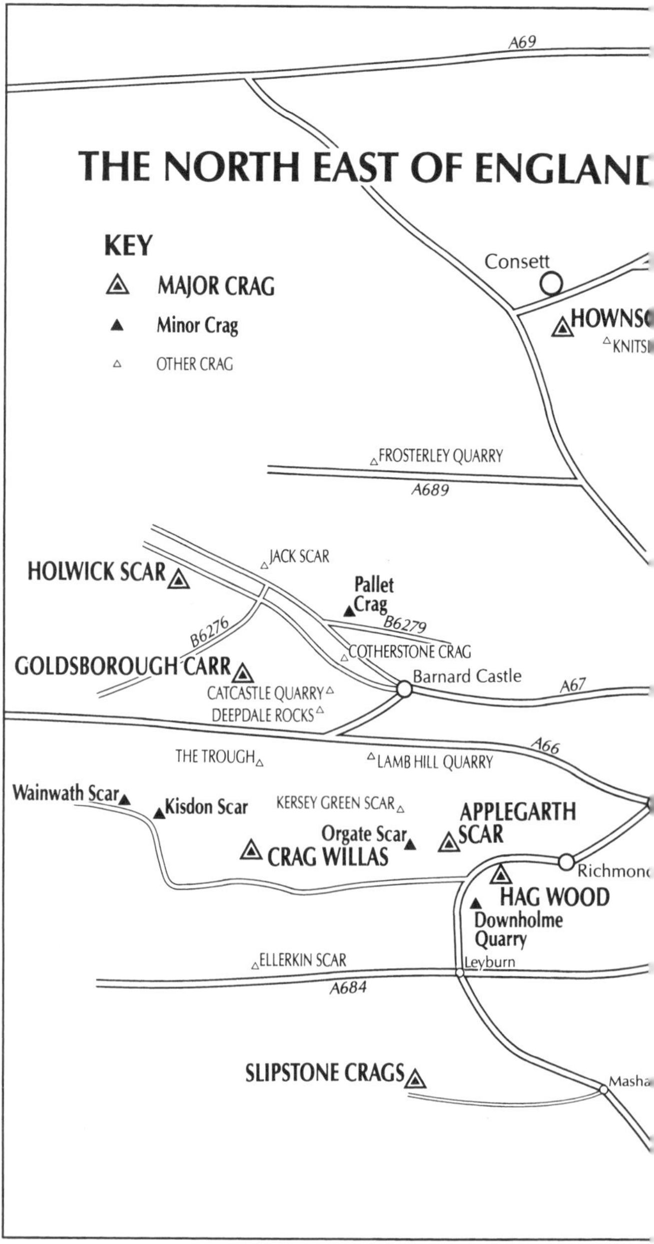

THE NORTH EAST OF ENGLAND

A69

KEY

⚠ MAJOR CRAG

▲ Minor Crag

△ OTHER CRAG

Consett

⚠ HOWNS...

△ KNITS...

△ FROSTERLEY QUARRY

A689

HOLWICK SCAR ⚠

△ JACK SCAR

Pallet Crag ▲

B6279

B6276

COTHERSTONE CRAG

GOLDSBOROUGH CARR ⚠

Barnard Castle

A67

△ CATCASTLE QUARRY

△ DEEPDALE ROCKS

THE TROUGH △

△ LAMB HILL QUARRY

A66

Wainwath Scar ▲

▲ Kisdon Scar

KERSEY GREEN SCAR △

APPLEGARTH
⚠ **SCAR**

Orgate Scar ▲

⚠ **CRAG WILLAS**

Richmond

⚠

▲ **HAG WOOD**

Downholme Quarry

Leyburn

△ ELLERKIN SCAR

A684

SLIPSTONE CRAGS ⚠

Masha...